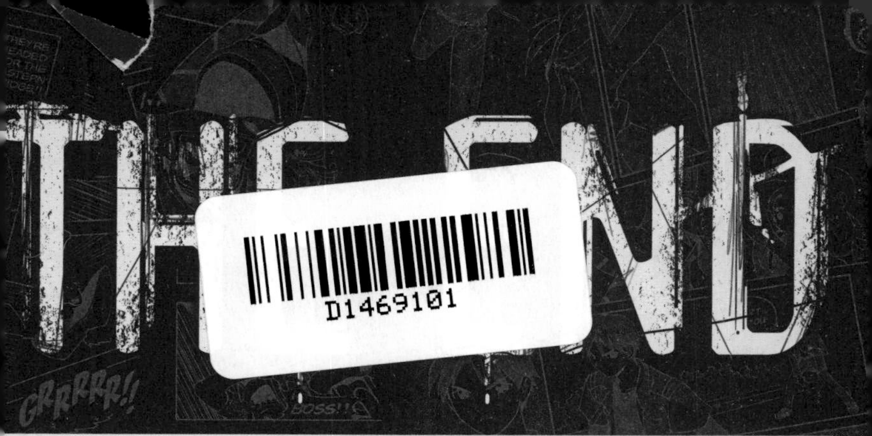
THE END
GRRRRR!!
BOSS!!

YOU'RE READING THE WRONG WAY

This is the last page of
Dance in the Vampire Bund
Volume 6

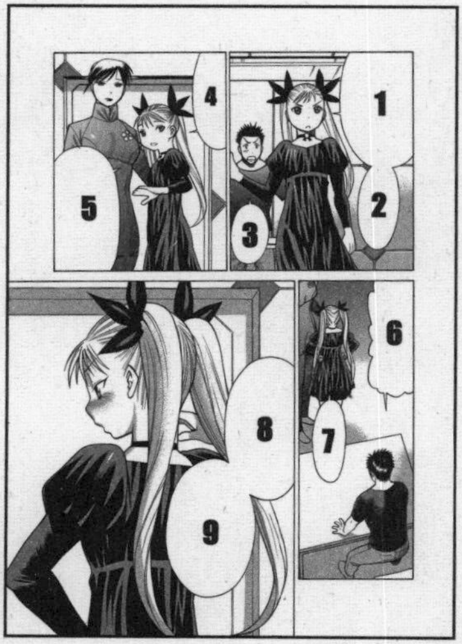
1
2
3
4
5
6
7
8
9

This book reads from right to left, Japanese style. To read from the beginning, flip the book over to the other side, start with the top right panel, and take it from there.

If this is your first time reading manga, just follow the diagram. It may seem backwards at first, but you'll get used to it! Have fun!

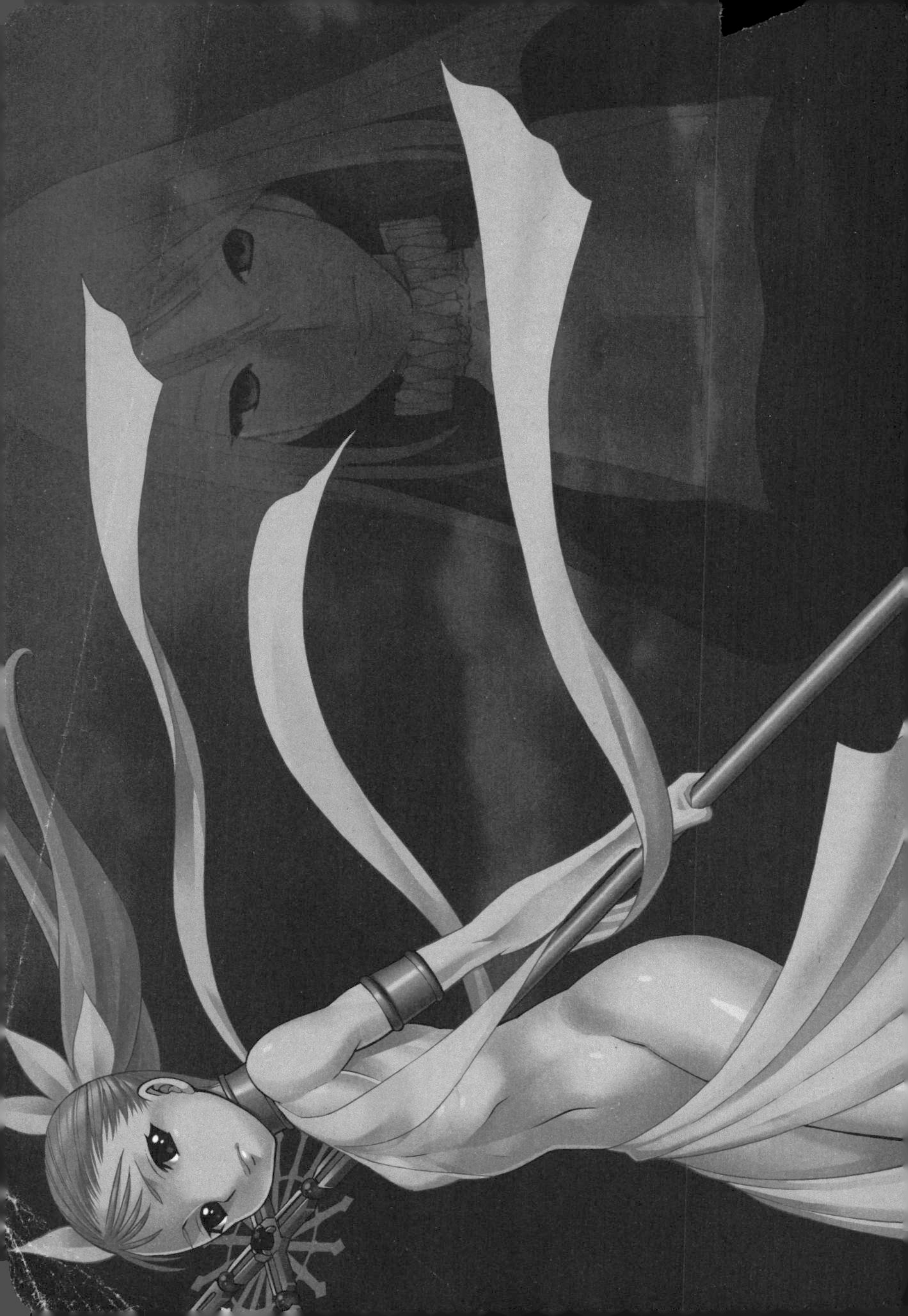

Dance in the Vampire Bund

Volume 6

story & art by Nozomu Tamaki

STAFF CREDITS

translation	Adrienne Beck
adaptation	Janet Houck
retouch & lettering	Roland Amago
cover design	Nicky Lim
layout	Bambi Eloriaga-Amago
copy editor	Shanti Whitesides
editor	Adam Arnold

publisher **Seven Seas Entertainment**

DANCE IN THE VAMPIRE BUND VOL. 6
© 2008 Nozomu Tamaki
First published in Japan in 2008 by MEDIA FACTORY, Inc.
English translation rights reserved by Seven Seas Entertainment, LLC.
Under the license from MEDIA FACTORY, Inc., Tokyo.

Visit us online at www.gomanga.com

ISBN: 978-1-934876-74-9

Printed in Canada

First printing: February 2010

10 9 8 7

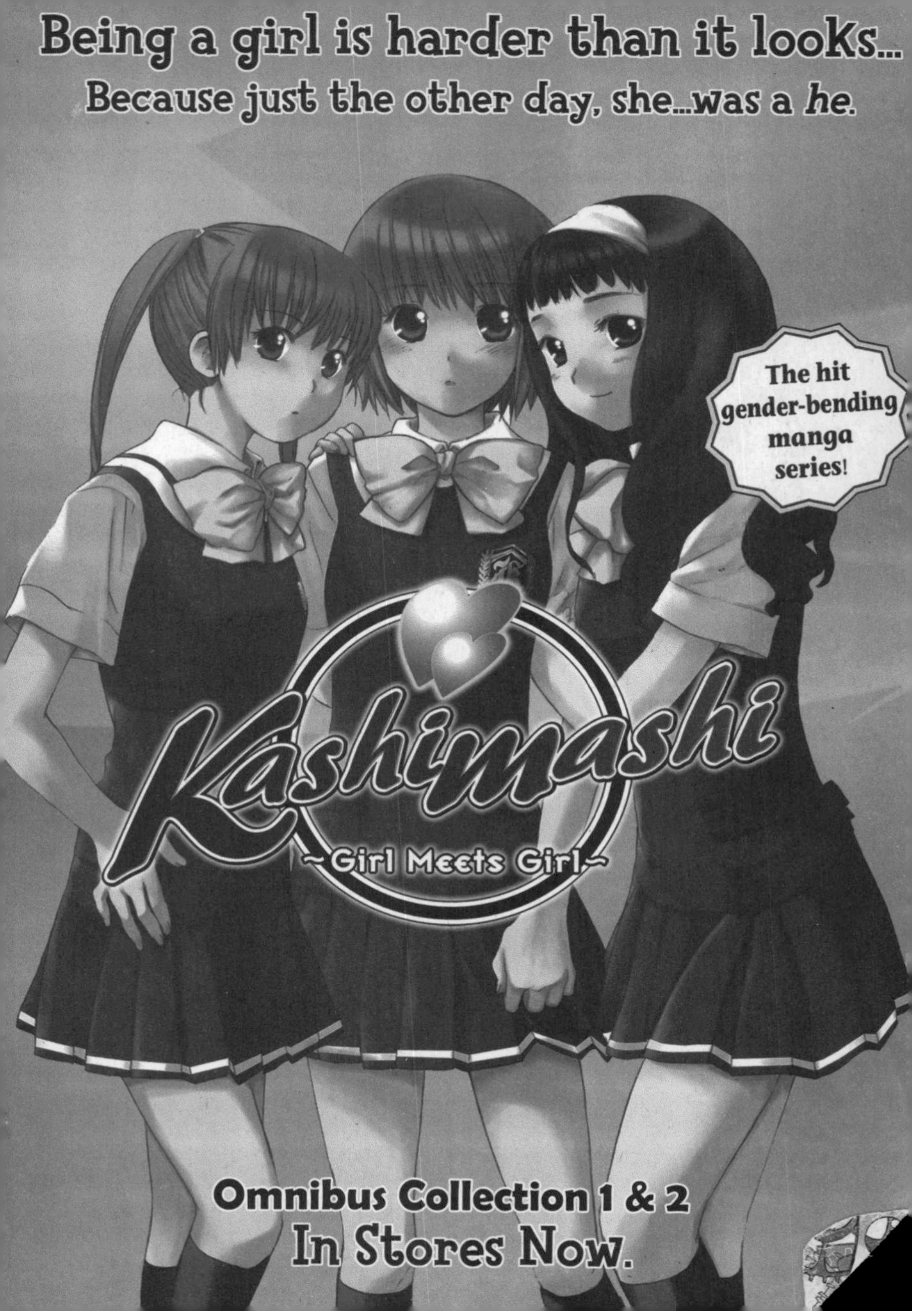
Being a girl is harder than it looks...
Because just the other day, she...was a *he*.
The hit gender-bending manga series!
Kashimashi
~Girl Meets Girl~
Omnibus Collection 1 & 2
In Stores Now.

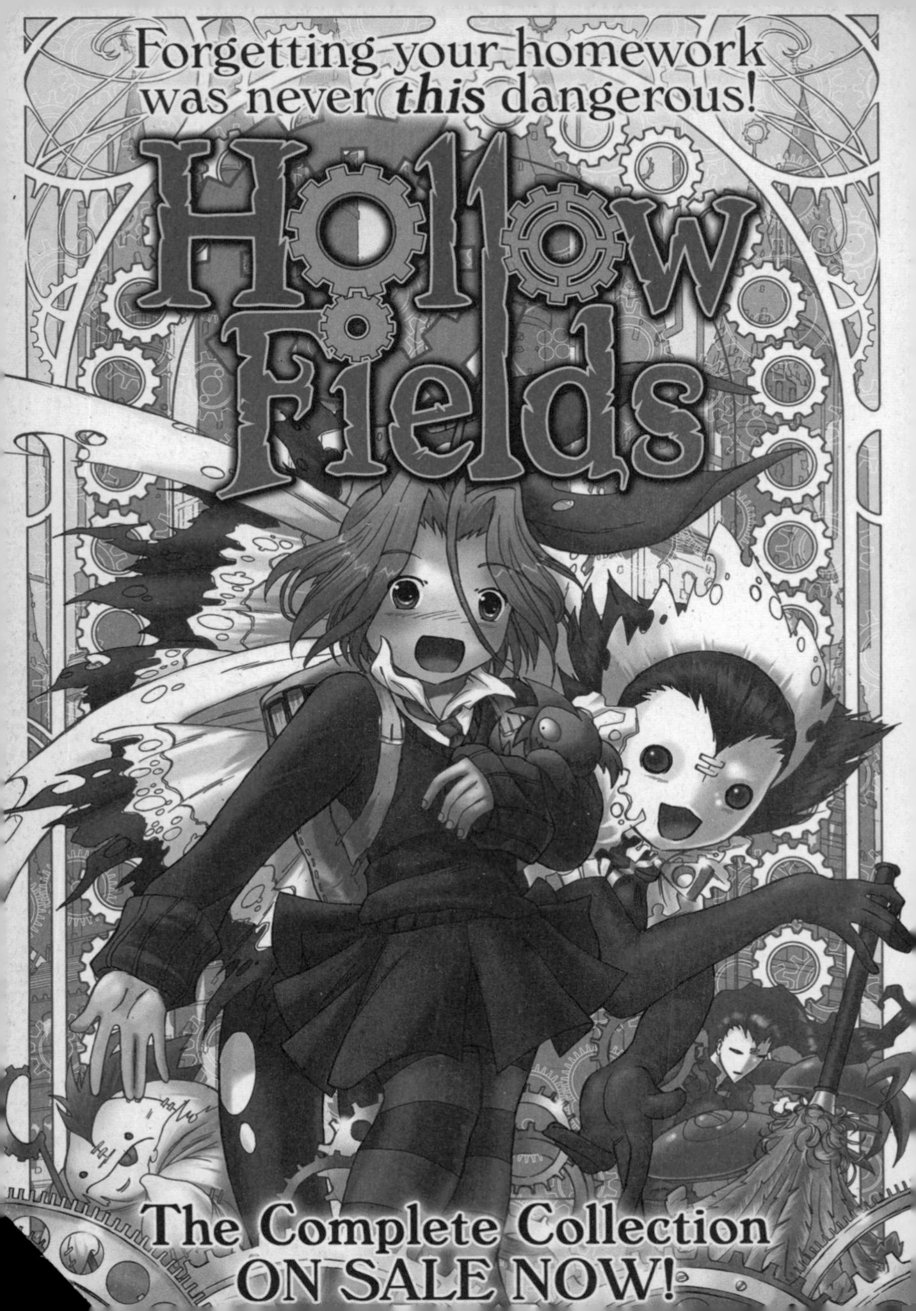
Forgetting your homework
was never *this* dangerous!
Hollow Fields
The Complete Collection
ON SALE NOW!

Destiny's HAND
INCLUDES VOLUMES 1-2 AND THE NEVER-BEFORE-RELEASED VOLUME 3!
Ultimate Pirate Collection
ON SALE NOW!

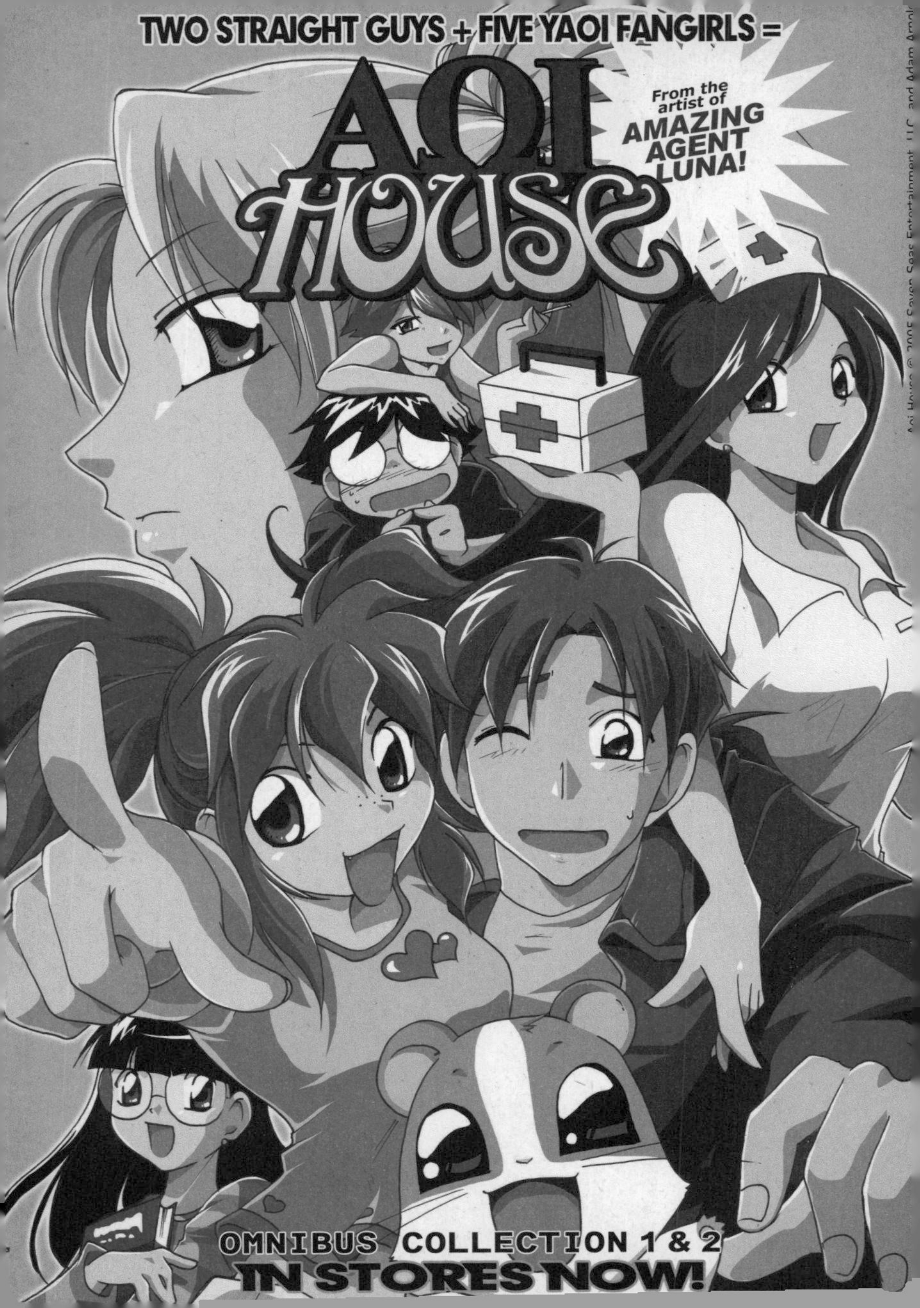
TWO STRAIGHT GUYS + FIVE YAOI FANGIRLS =
AOI HOUSE
From the artist of AMAZING AGENT LUNA!
OMNIBUS COLLECTION 1 & 2
IN STORES NOW!
Aoi House © 2005 Seven Seas Entertainment, LLC and Adam Arnold

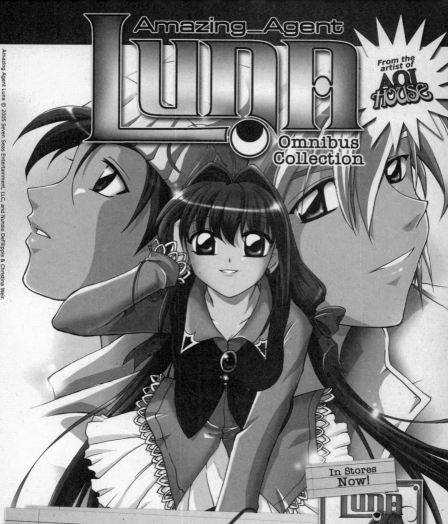

97.3.9
Matsuo Basho was a renowned Japanese poet who lived during the early Edo Period in Japan (1603-1869), and is considered one of the greatest masters of *haiku* to have ever lived.

97.2.6
Bai Juyi was a renowned Chinese poet who lived during the Tang Dynasty (772-846) and wrote almost 3,000 poems. One of his most famous is the *Changhen Ge*, or *The Song of Everlasting Sorrow*, which tells the tale of the doomed relationship between an emperor and one of his concubines. In the final lines, the concubine laments that they cannot become *renri-no-eda*, as two branches intertwined, never to part.

197.7.14
Comiket ("Comic Market") is the world's largest independent comic book fair, held twice a year in Tokyo. As space is at a premium within the convention center, any creator who has an entire cubed section (an "island") dedicated to themselves would be very, very popular.

TRANSLATION NOTES

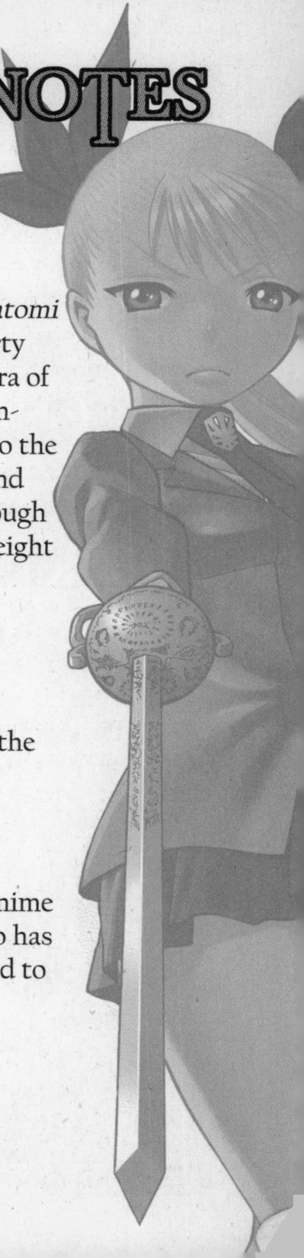

56.4.10
Kyokutei Bakin wrote his epic story "*Nansou Satomi Hakkenden*" across 106 volumes and almost thirty years from 1814 to 1842. Set in the *Muromachi* era of Japanese history (1336-1576), it tells of the adventures of eight samurai warriors in their service to the Satomi house. There have been many TV, film and manga adaptations of the story since then, although not many in English. Inuzuka Shino, one of the eight samurai, was raised as a girl, because his dying mother wished it in her will.

57.4.16-5.17
Uke and *seme* are *yaoi* terms for who gets to be the bottom and top, respectively.

57.3.10
"Lolita Complex" is a term frequently found in anime and manga to describe an adult man or teen who has a special fondness for pubescent girls, as opposed to young women.

60.4.9
BL is short for Boys Love, another term for *yaoi*.

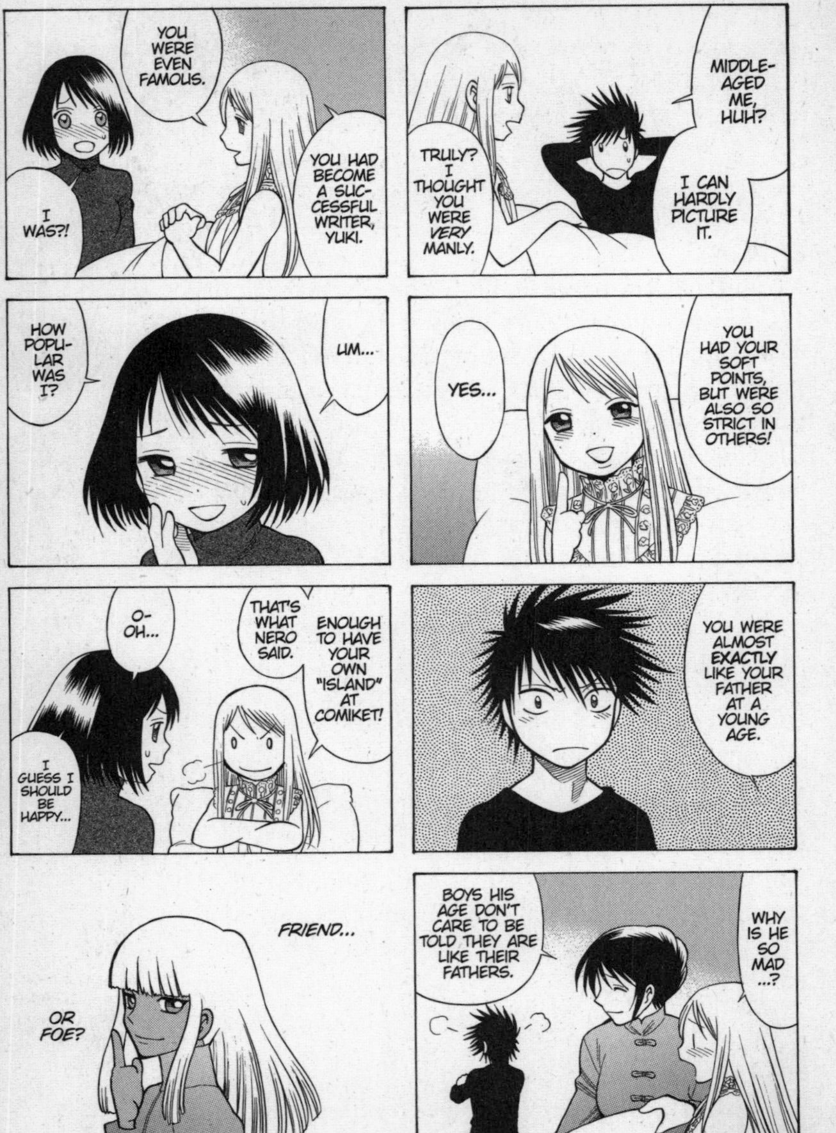
MIDDLE-AGED ME, HUH?
I CAN HARDLY PICTURE IT.
TRULY? I THOUGHT YOU WERE VERY MANLY.
YOU HAD BECOME A SUCCESSFUL WRITER, YUKI.
I WAS?!
YOU WERE EVEN FAMOUS.
YOU HAD YOUR SOFT POINTS, BUT WERE ALSO SO STRICT IN OTHERS!
YES...
UM...
HOW POPULAR WAS I?
YOU WERE ALMOST EXACTLY LIKE YOUR FATHER AT A YOUNG AGE.
ENOUGH TO HAVE YOUR OWN "ISLAND" AT COMIKET!
THAT'S WHAT NERO SAID.
O-OH...
I GUESS I SHOULD BE HAPPY...
WHY IS HE SO MAD ...?
BOYS HIS AGE DON'T CARE TO BE TOLD THEY ARE LIKE THEIR FATHERS.
FRIEND...
OR FOE?

SEE YOU IN VOLUME 7!!

Tamaki Nozomu Presents Dance In The Vampire Bund 6

ダンス イン ザ ヴァンパイアバンド
6
環望

Nenne dich nicht arm,

weil Träume nicht

in Eefüllung gegangen sind;

wirklich arm ist nur,

der nie geträumt hat.

Child, do not pity yourself
for a dream
that did not come true:

The only ones who deserve pity
are those
who have never
had dreams of their own.

Ebner-Eschenbach, Aphorismen

Dance In The Vampire Bund 6

Contents

Tamaki Nozomu Presents Dance In The Vampire Bund 6

Chapter 32: A Message to Sledgehammer

NH...

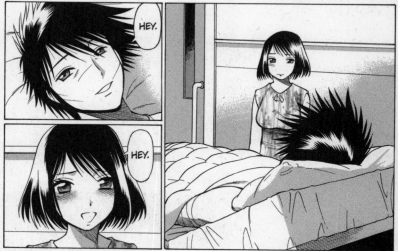

HEY.

HEY.

MADE YOU WORRY, DIDN'T I?

SORRY.

4

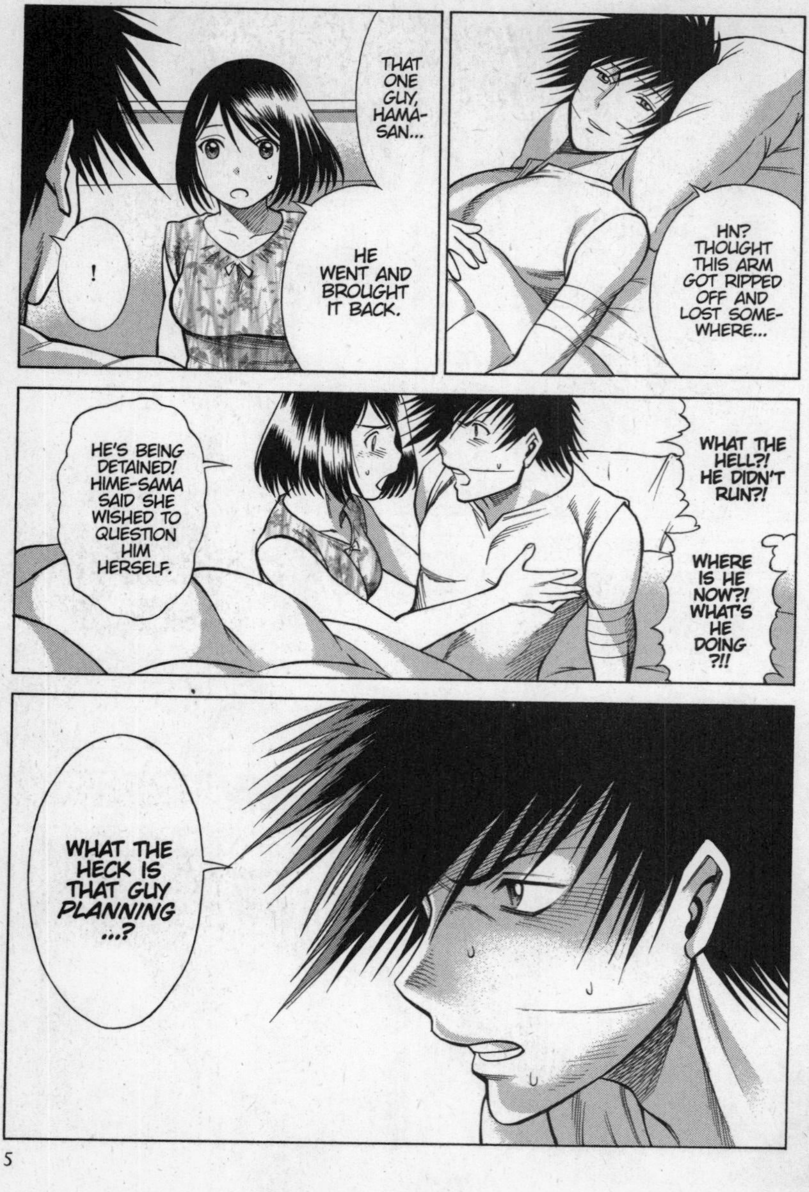
HN? THOUGHT THIS ARM GOT RIPPED OFF AND LOST SOME-WHERE...
THAT ONE GUY, HAMA-SAN...
HE WENT AND BROUGHT IT BACK.
!
WHAT THE HELL?! HE DIDN'T RUN?!
WHERE IS HE NOW?! WHAT'S HE DOING?!!
HE'S BEING DETAINED! HIME-SAMA SAID SHE WISHED TO QUESTION HIM HERSELF.
WHAT THE HECK IS THAT GUY *PLANNING* ...?

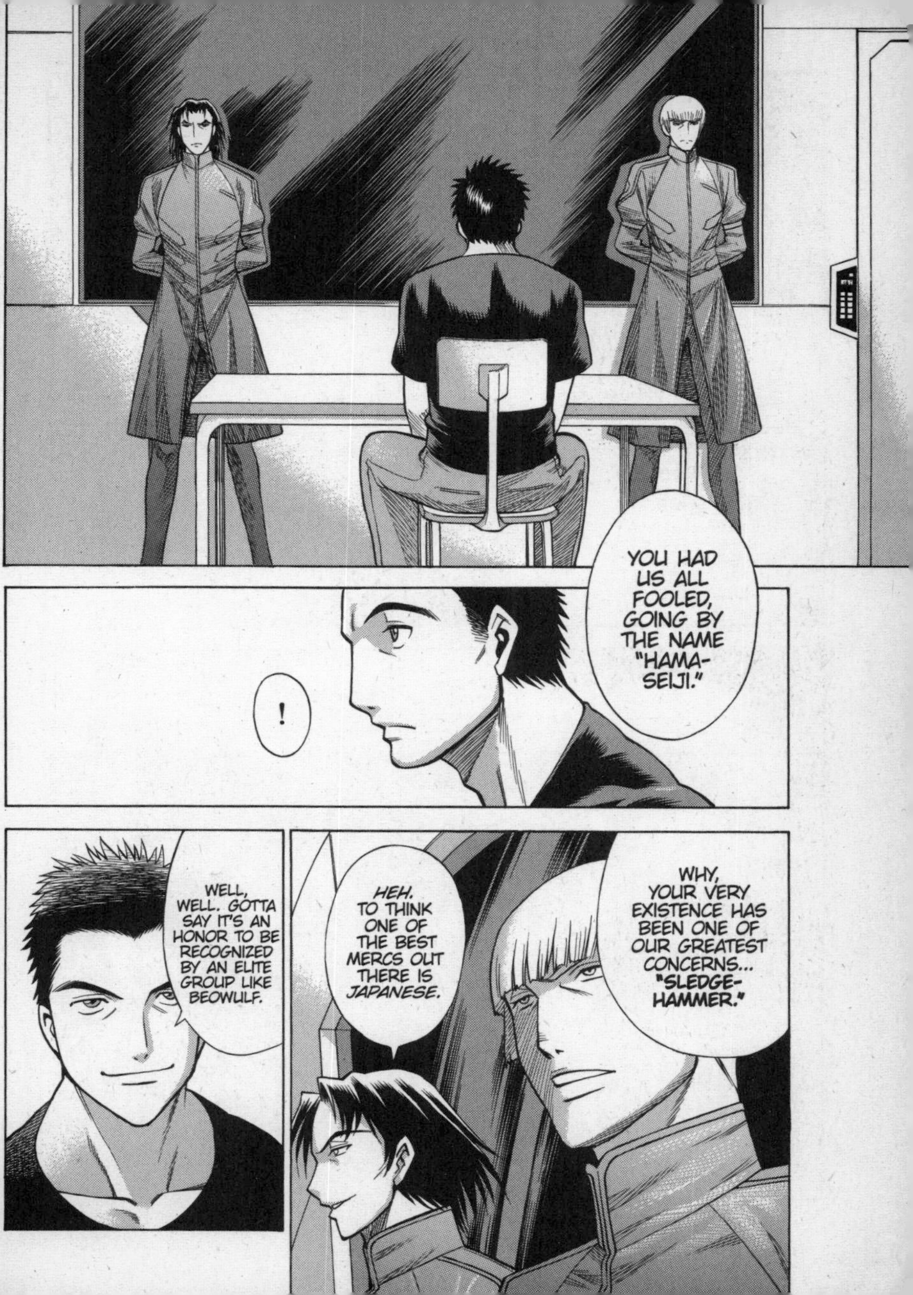

YOU HAD US ALL FOOLED, GOING BY THE NAME "HAMA-SEIJI."
!
WHY, YOUR VERY EXISTENCE HAS BEEN ONE OF OUR GREATEST CONCERNS... "SLEDGE-HAMMER."
HEH. TO THINK ONE OF THE BEST MERCS OUT THERE IS JAPANESE.
WELL, WELL.. GOTTA SAY IT'S AN HONOR TO BE RECOGNIZED BY AN ELITE GROUP LIKE BEOWULF.

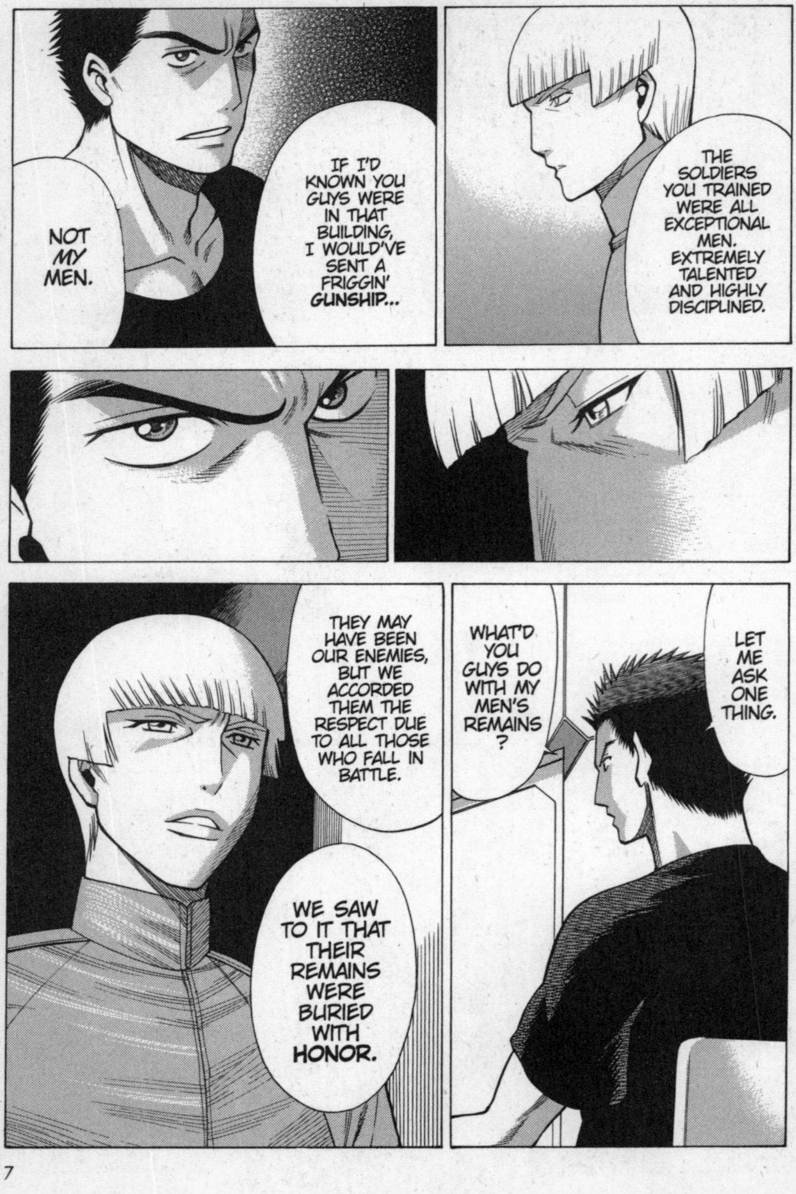
THE SOLDIERS YOU TRAINED WERE ALL EXCEPTIONAL MEN. EXTREMELY TALENTED AND HIGHLY DISCIPLINED.
IF I'D KNOWN YOU GUYS WERE IN THAT BUILDING, I WOULD'VE SENT A FRIGGIN' **GUNSHIP**...
NOT *MY* MEN.
LET ME ASK ONE THING.
WHAT'D YOU GUYS DO WITH MY MEN'S REMAINS?
THEY MAY HAVE BEEN OUR ENEMIES, BUT WE ACCORDED THEM THE RESPECT DUE TO ALL THOSE WHO FALL IN BATTLE.
WE SAW TO IT THAT THEIR REMAINS WERE BURIED WITH **HONOR**.

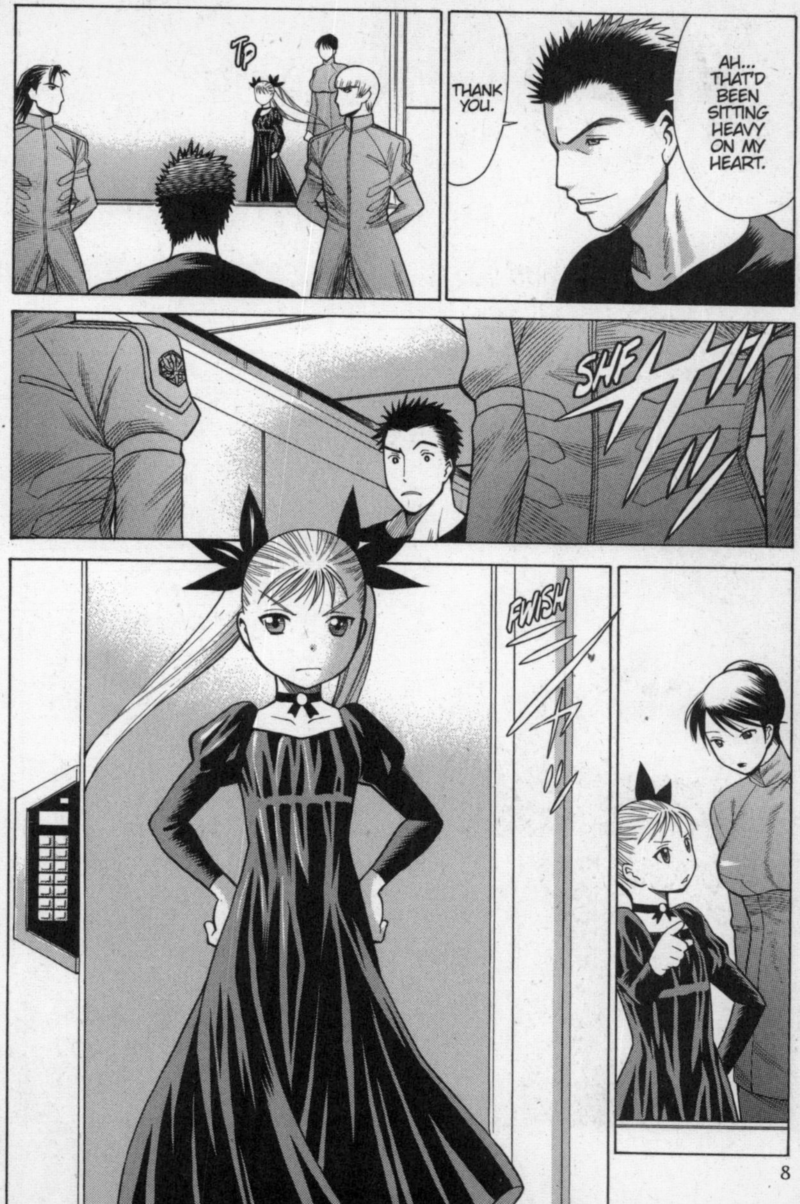
AH... THAT'D BEEN SITTING HEAVY ON MY HEART.
THANK YOU.
TP
SHF
FWISH

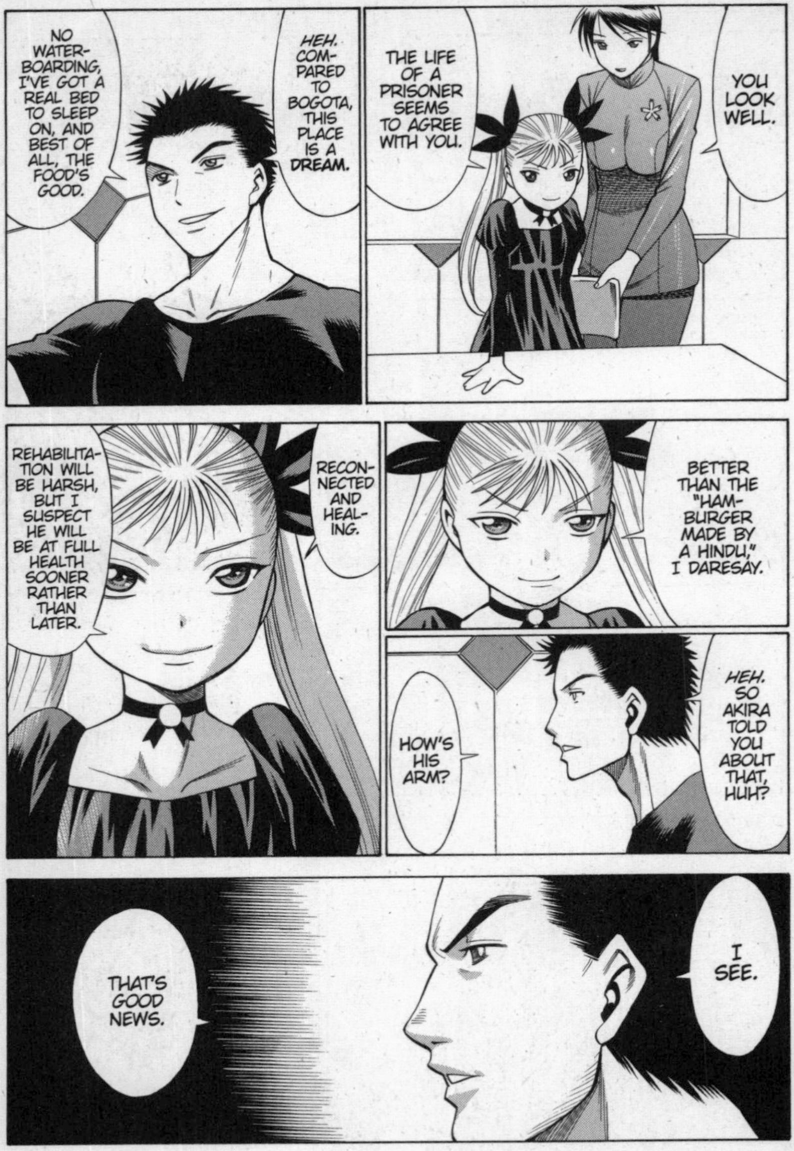
YOU LOOK WELL.
THE LIFE OF A PRISONER SEEMS TO AGREE WITH YOU.
HEH. COMPARED TO BOGOTA, THIS PLACE IS A DREAM.
NO WATER-BOARDING, I'VE GOT A REAL BED TO SLEEP ON, AND BEST OF ALL, THE FOOD'S GOOD.
BETTER THAN THE "HAMBURGER MADE BY A HINDU," I DARESAY.
HEH. SO AKIRA TOLD YOU ABOUT THAT, HUH?
HOW'S HIS ARM?
RECONNECTED AND HEALING.
REHABILITATION WILL BE HARSH, BUT I SUSPECT HE WILL BE AT FULL HEALTH SOONER RATHER THAN LATER.
I SEE.
THAT'S GOOD NEWS.

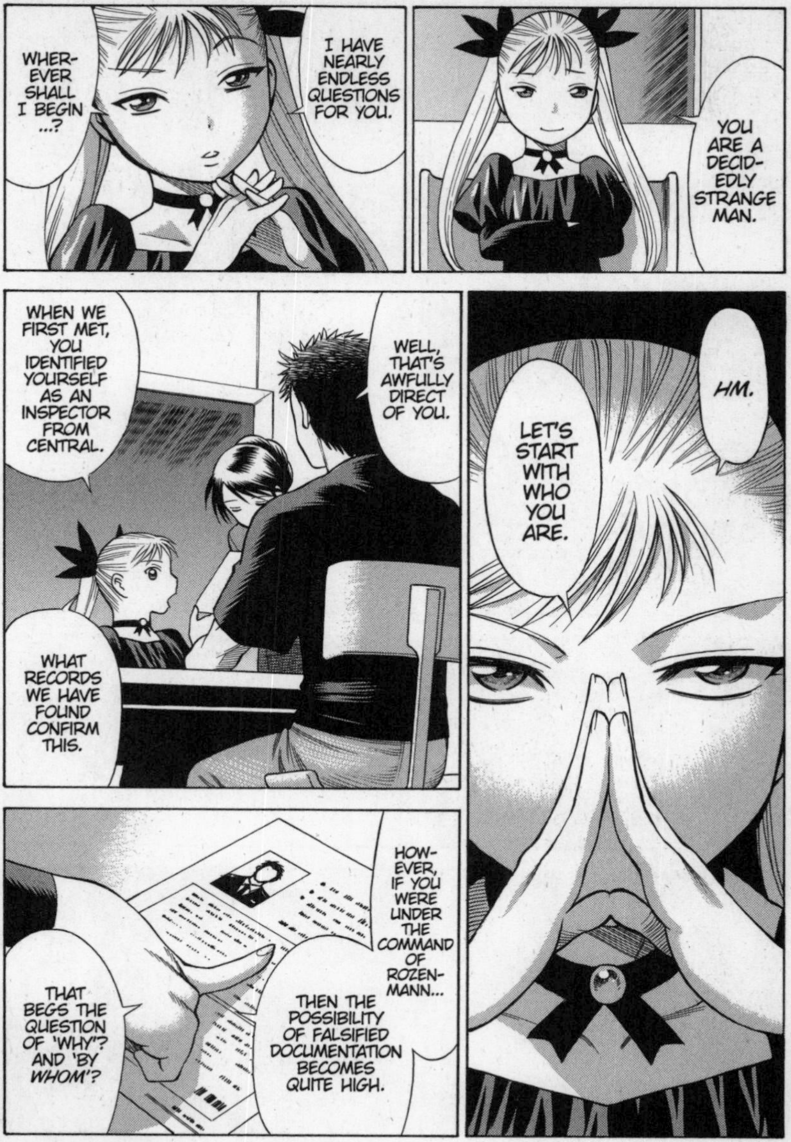
YOU ARE A DECIDEDLY STRANGE MAN.
I HAVE NEARLY ENDLESS QUESTIONS FOR YOU.
WHER-EVER SHALL I BEGIN ...?
HM.
LET'S START WITH WHO YOU ARE.
WELL, THAT'S AWFULLY DIRECT OF YOU.
WHEN WE FIRST MET, YOU IDENTIFIED YOURSELF AS AN INSPECTOR FROM CENTRAL.
WHAT RECORDS WE HAVE FOUND CONFIRM THIS.
HOW-EVER, IF YOU WERE UNDER THE COMMAND OF ROZEN-MANN...
THEN THE POSSIBILITY OF FALSIFIED DOCUMENTATION BECOMES QUITE HIGH.
THAT BEGS THE QUESTION OF 'WHY'? AND 'BY *WHOM*'?

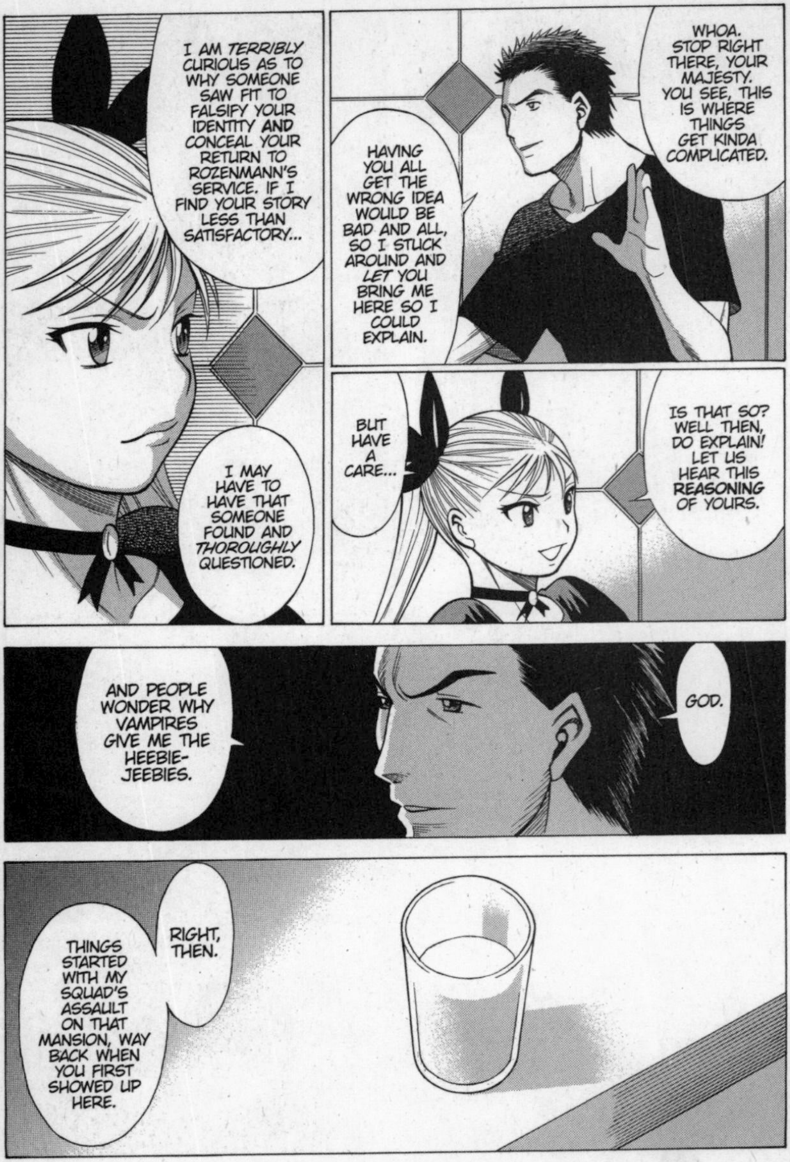
WHOA. STOP RIGHT THERE, YOUR MAJESTY. YOU SEE, THIS IS WHERE THINGS GET KINDA COMPLICATED.
HAVING YOU ALL GET THE WRONG IDEA WOULD BE BAD AND ALL, SO I STUCK AROUND AND *LET* YOU BRING ME HERE SO I COULD EXPLAIN.
IS THAT SO? WELL THEN, DO EXPLAIN! LET US HEAR THIS **REASONING** OF YOURS.
BUT HAVE A CARE...
I AM *TERRIBLY* CURIOUS AS TO WHY SOMEONE SAW FIT TO FALSIFY YOUR IDENTITY **AND** CONCEAL YOUR RETURN TO ROZENMANN'S SERVICE. IF I FIND YOUR STORY LESS THAN SATISFACTORY...
I MAY HAVE TO HAVE THAT SOMEONE FOUND AND *THOROUGHLY* QUESTIONED.
GOD.
AND PEOPLE WONDER WHY VAMPIRES GIVE ME THE HEEBIE-JEEBIES.
RIGHT, THEN.
THINGS STARTED WITH MY SQUAD'S ASSAULT ON THAT MANSION, WAY BACK WHEN YOU FIRST SHOWED UP HERE.

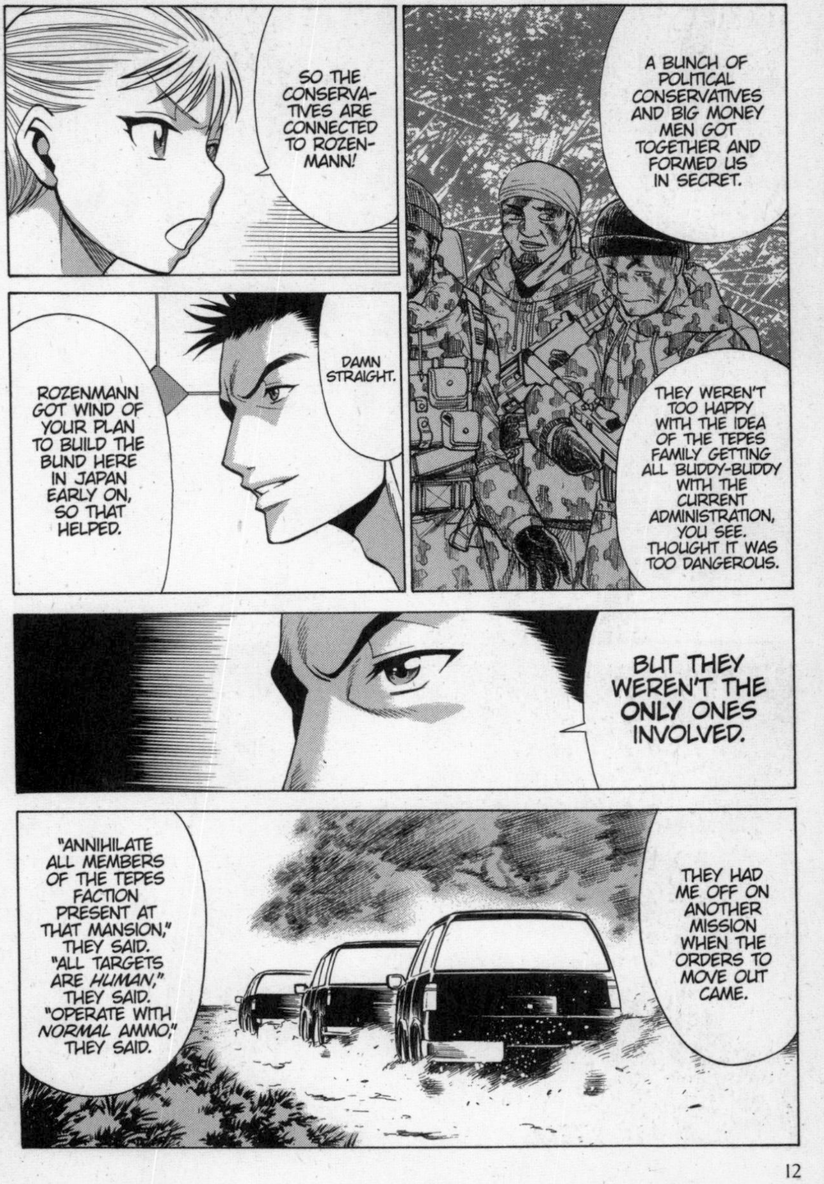
A BUNCH OF POLITICAL CONSERVATIVES AND BIG MONEY MEN GOT TOGETHER AND FORMED US IN SECRET.
THEY WEREN'T TOO HAPPY WITH THE IDEA OF THE TEPES FAMILY GETTING ALL BUDDY-BUDDY WITH THE CURRENT ADMINISTRATION, YOU SEE. THOUGHT IT WAS TOO DANGEROUS.
SO THE CONSERVA-TIVES ARE CONNECTED TO ROZEN-MANN!
DAMN STRAIGHT.
ROZENMANN GOT WIND OF YOUR PLAN TO BUILD THE BUND HERE IN JAPAN EARLY ON, SO THAT HELPED.
BUT THEY WEREN'T THE ONLY ONES INVOLVED.
THEY HAD ME OFF ON ANOTHER MISSION WHEN THE ORDERS TO MOVE OUT CAME.
"ANNIHILATE ALL MEMBERS OF THE TEPES FACTION PRESENT AT THAT MANSION," THEY SAID. "ALL TARGETS ARE *HUMAN*," THEY SAID. "OPERATE WITH *NORMAL AMMO*," THEY SAID.

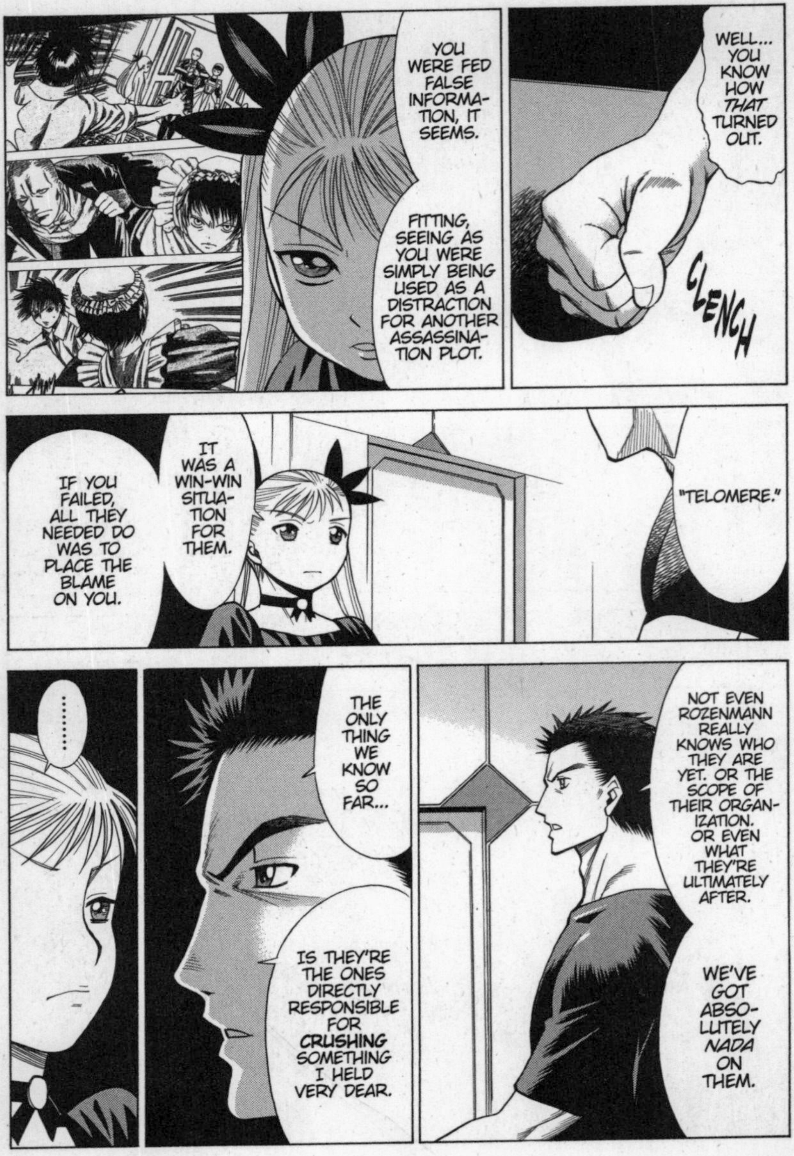
WELL... YOU KNOW HOW *THAT* TURNED OUT.
CLENCH
YOU WERE FED FALSE INFORMATION, IT SEEMS.
FITTING, SEEING AS YOU WERE SIMPLY BEING USED AS A DISTRACTION FOR ANOTHER ASSASSINATION PLOT.
"TELOMERE."
IT WAS A WIN-WIN SITUATION FOR THEM.
IF YOU FAILED, ALL THEY NEEDED DO WAS TO PLACE THE BLAME ON YOU.
NOT EVEN ROZENMANN REALLY KNOWS WHO THEY ARE YET. OR THE SCOPE OF THEIR ORGANIZATION. OR EVEN WHAT THEY'RE ULTIMATELY AFTER.
WE'VE GOT ABSOLUTELY *NADA* ON THEM.
THE ONLY THING WE KNOW SO FAR...
IS THEY'RE THE ONES DIRECTLY RESPONSIBLE FOR **CRUSHING** SOMETHING I HELD VERY DEAR.
......

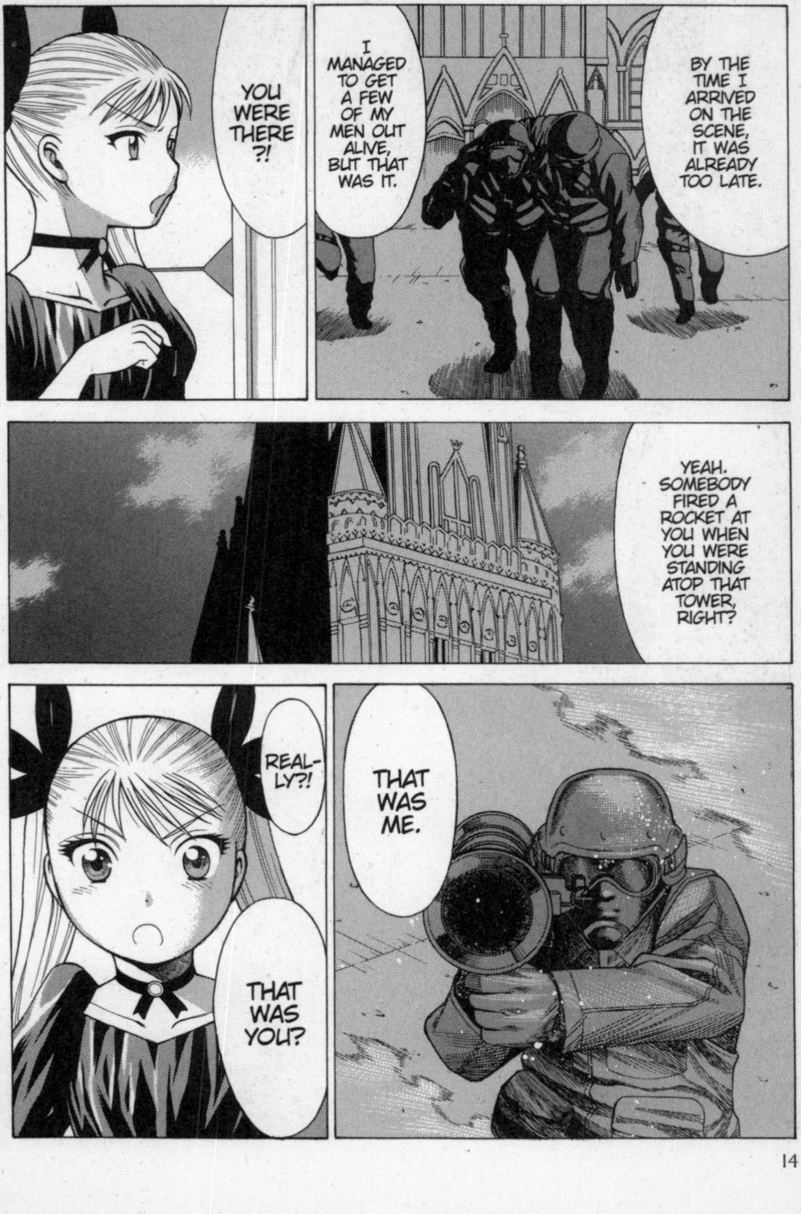
BY THE TIME I ARRIVED ON THE SCENE, IT WAS ALREADY TOO LATE.
I MANAGED TO GET A FEW OF MY MEN OUT ALIVE, BUT THAT WAS IT.
YOU WERE THERE ?!
YEAH. SOMEBODY FIRED A ROCKET AT YOU WHEN YOU WERE STANDING ATOP THAT TOWER, RIGHT?
THAT WAS ME.
REAL-LY?!
THAT WAS YOU?

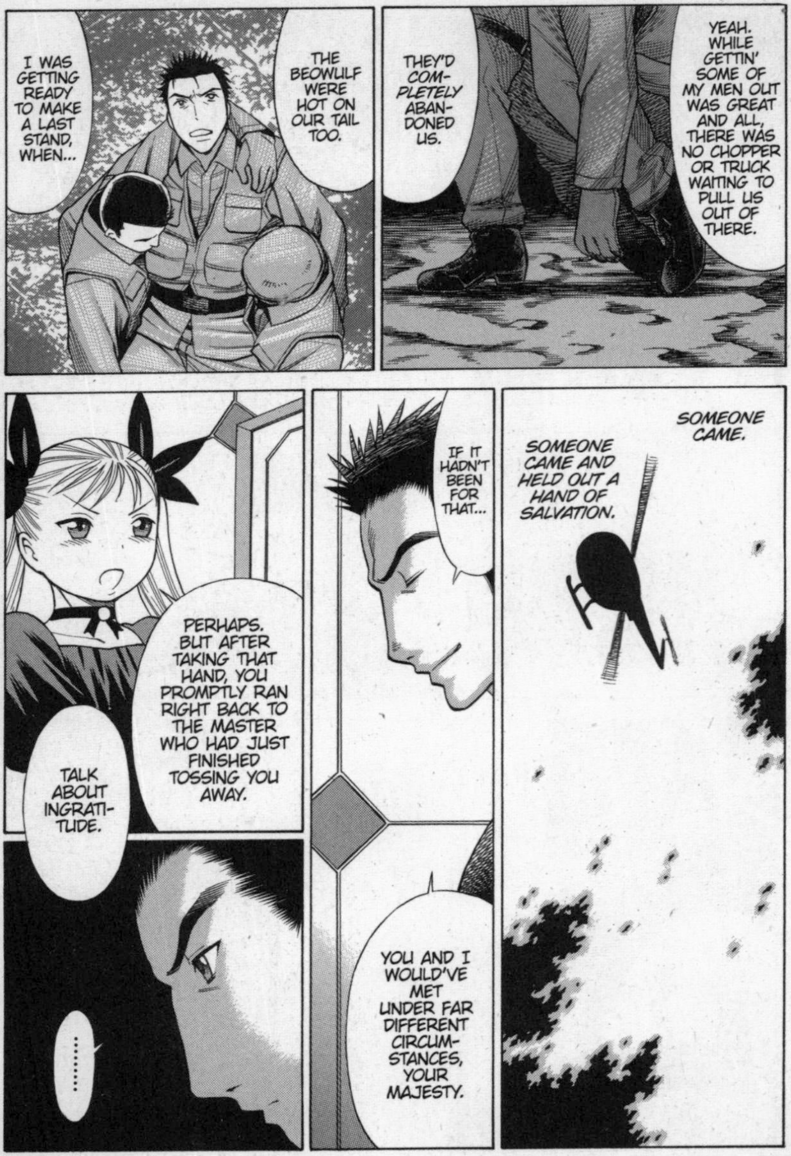
YEAH. WHILE GETTIN' SOME OF MY MEN OUT WAS GREAT AND ALL, THERE WAS NO CHOPPER OR TRUCK WAITING TO PULL US OUT OF THERE.
THEY'D COM-PLETELY ABAN-DONED US.
THE BEOWULF WERE HOT ON OUR TAIL TOO.
I WAS GETTING READY TO MAKE A LAST STAND, WHEN...
SOMEONE CAME.
SOMEONE CAME AND HELD OUT A HAND OF SALVATION.
IF IT HADN'T BEEN FOR THAT...
YOU AND I WOULD'VE MET UNDER FAR DIFFERENT CIRCUM-STANCES, YOUR MAJESTY.
PERHAPS. BUT AFTER TAKING THAT HAND, YOU PROMPTLY RAN RIGHT BACK TO THE MASTER WHO HAD JUST FINISHED TOSSING YOU AWAY.
TALK ABOUT INGRATI-TUDE.
....

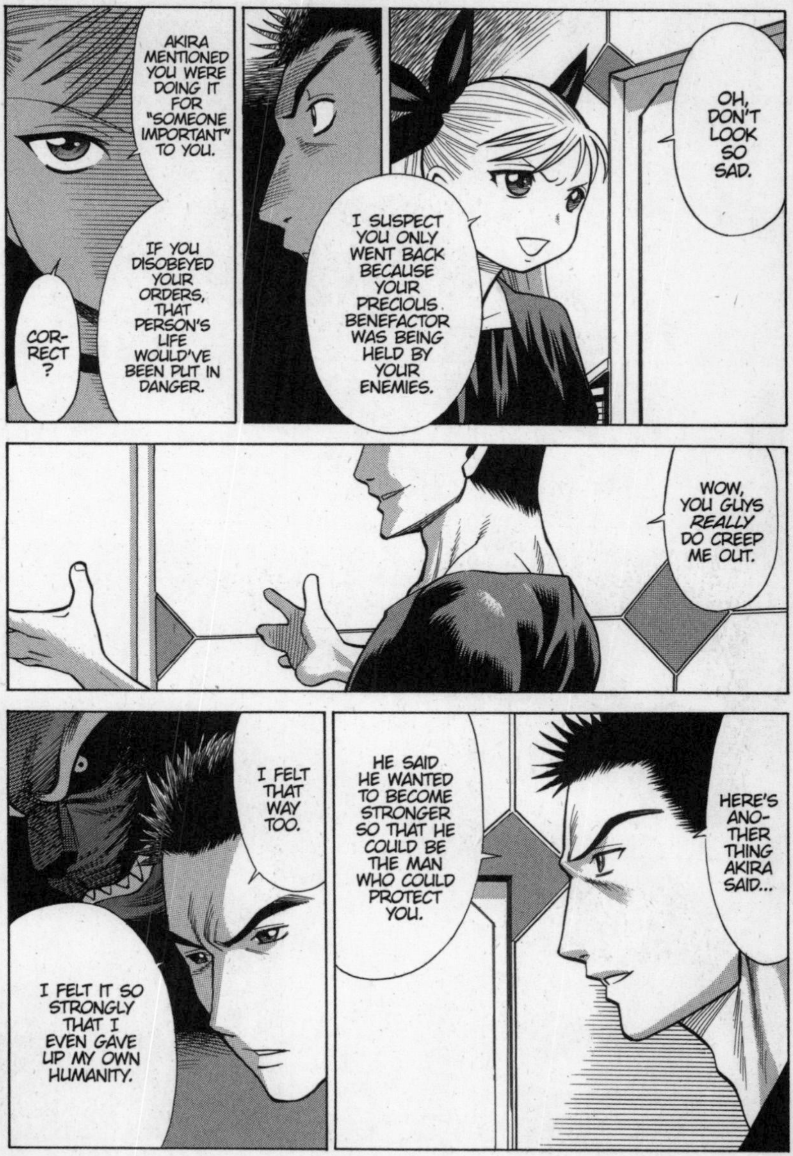
OH, DON'T LOOK SO SAD.
I SUSPECT YOU ONLY WENT BACK BECAUSE YOUR PRECIOUS BENEFACTOR WAS BEING HELD BY YOUR ENEMIES.
AKIRA MENTIONED YOU WERE DOING IT FOR "SOMEONE IMPORTANT" TO YOU.
IF YOU DISOBEYED YOUR ORDERS, THAT PERSON'S LIFE WOULD'VE BEEN PUT IN DANGER.
COR-RECT?
WOW, YOU GUYS *REALLY* DO CREEP ME OUT.
HERE'S ANO-THER THING AKIRA SAID...
HE SAID HE WANTED TO BECOME STRONGER SO THAT HE COULD BE THE MAN WHO COULD PROTECT YOU.
I FELT THAT WAY TOO.
I FELT IT SO STRONGLY THAT I EVEN GAVE UP MY OWN HUMANITY.

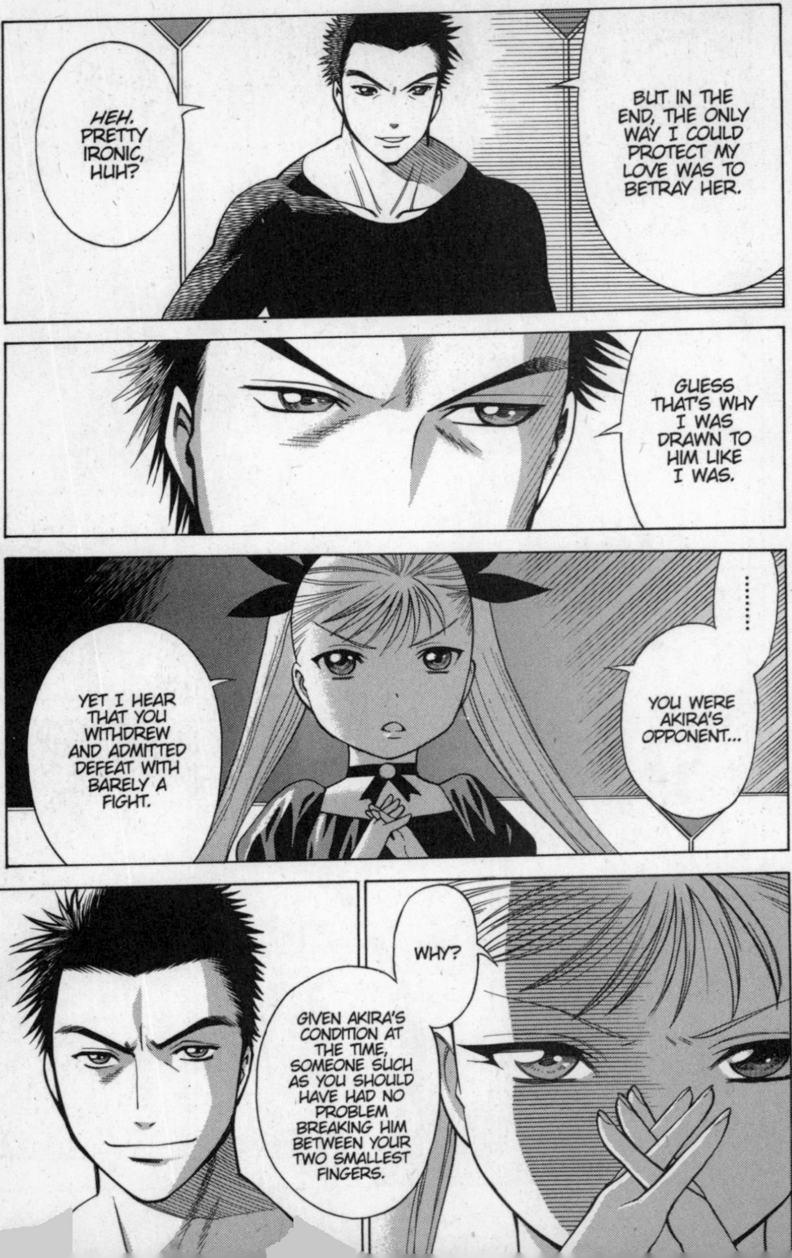
BUT IN THE END, THE ONLY WAY I COULD PROTECT MY LOVE WAS TO BETRAY HER.
HEH. PRETTY IRONIC, HUH?
GUESS THAT'S WHY I WAS DRAWN TO HIM LIKE I WAS.
......
YOU WERE AKIRA'S OPPONENT...
YET I HEAR THAT YOU WITHDREW AND ADMITTED DEFEAT WITH BARELY A FIGHT.
WHY?
GIVEN AKIRA'S CONDITION AT THE TIME, SOMEONE SUCH AS YOU SHOULD HAVE HAD NO PROBLEM BREAKING HIM BETWEEN YOUR TWO SMALLEST FINGERS.

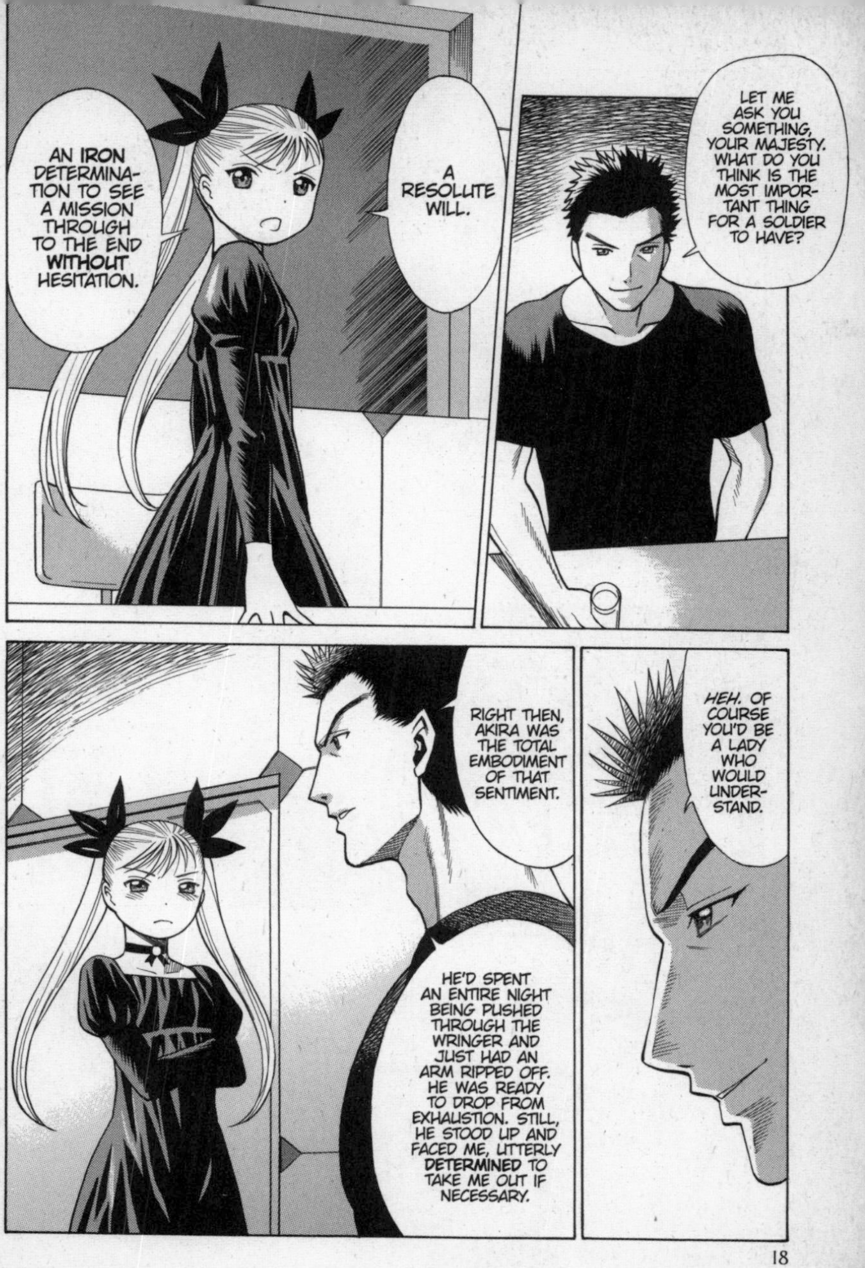
LET ME ASK YOU SOMETHING, YOUR MAJESTY. WHAT DO YOU THINK IS THE MOST IMPORTANT THING FOR A SOLDIER TO HAVE?
A RESOLUTE WILL.
AN **IRON** DETERMINATION TO SEE A MISSION THROUGH TO THE END **WITHOUT** HESITATION.
HEH. OF COURSE YOU'D BE A LADY WHO WOULD UNDERSTAND.
RIGHT THEN, AKIRA WAS THE TOTAL EMBODIMENT OF THAT SENTIMENT.
HE'D SPENT AN ENTIRE NIGHT BEING PUSHED THROUGH THE WRINGER AND JUST HAD AN ARM RIPPED OFF. HE WAS READY TO DROP FROM EXHAUSTION. STILL, HE STOOD UP AND FACED ME, UTTERLY **DETERMINED** TO TAKE ME OUT IF NECESSARY.

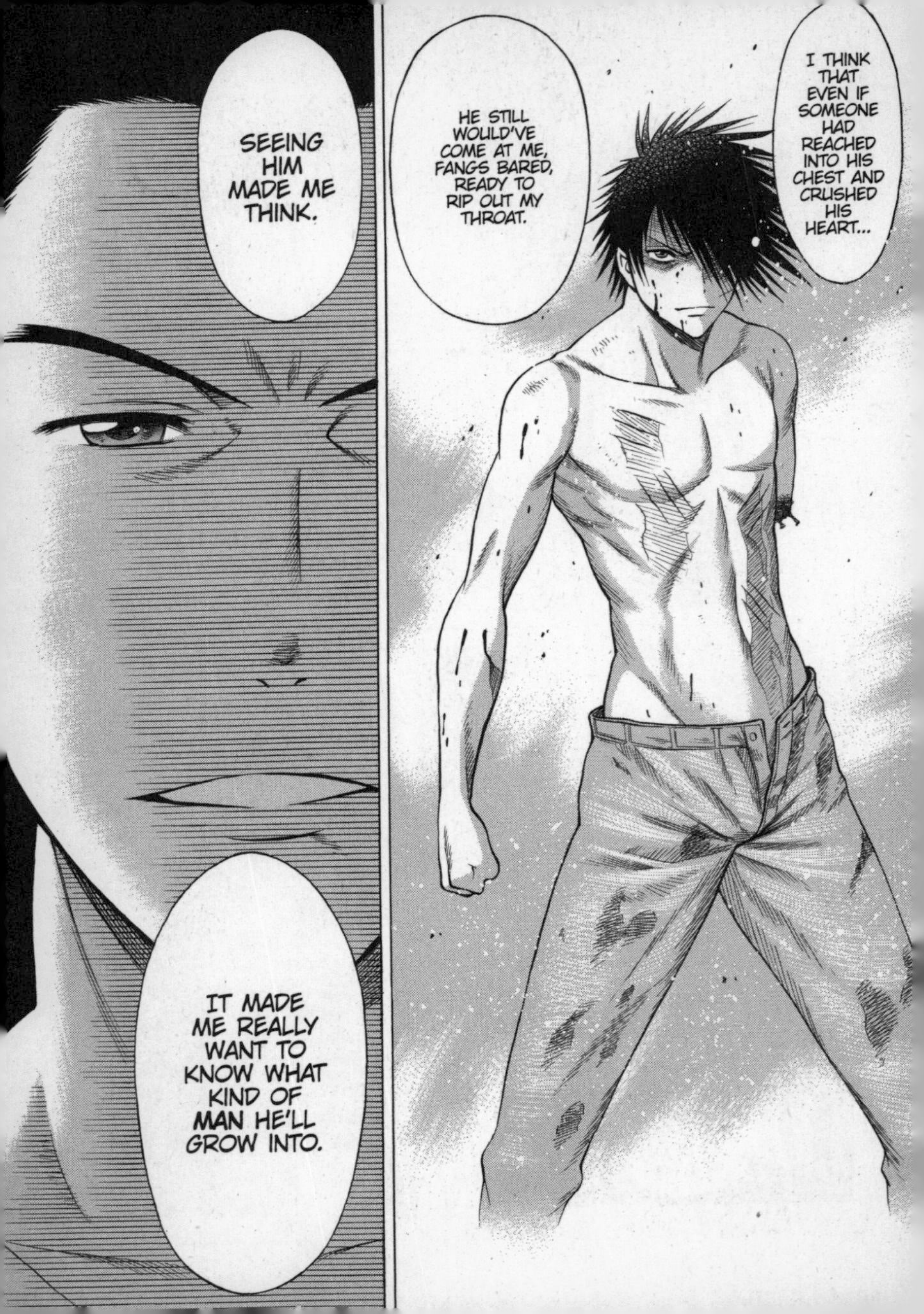
I THINK THAT EVEN IF SOMEONE HAD REACHED INTO HIS CHEST AND CRUSHED HIS HEART...
HE STILL WOULD'VE COME AT ME, FANGS BARED, READY TO RIP OUT MY THROAT.
SEEING HIM MADE ME THINK.
IT MADE ME REALLY WANT TO KNOW WHAT KIND OF MAN HE'LL GROW INTO.

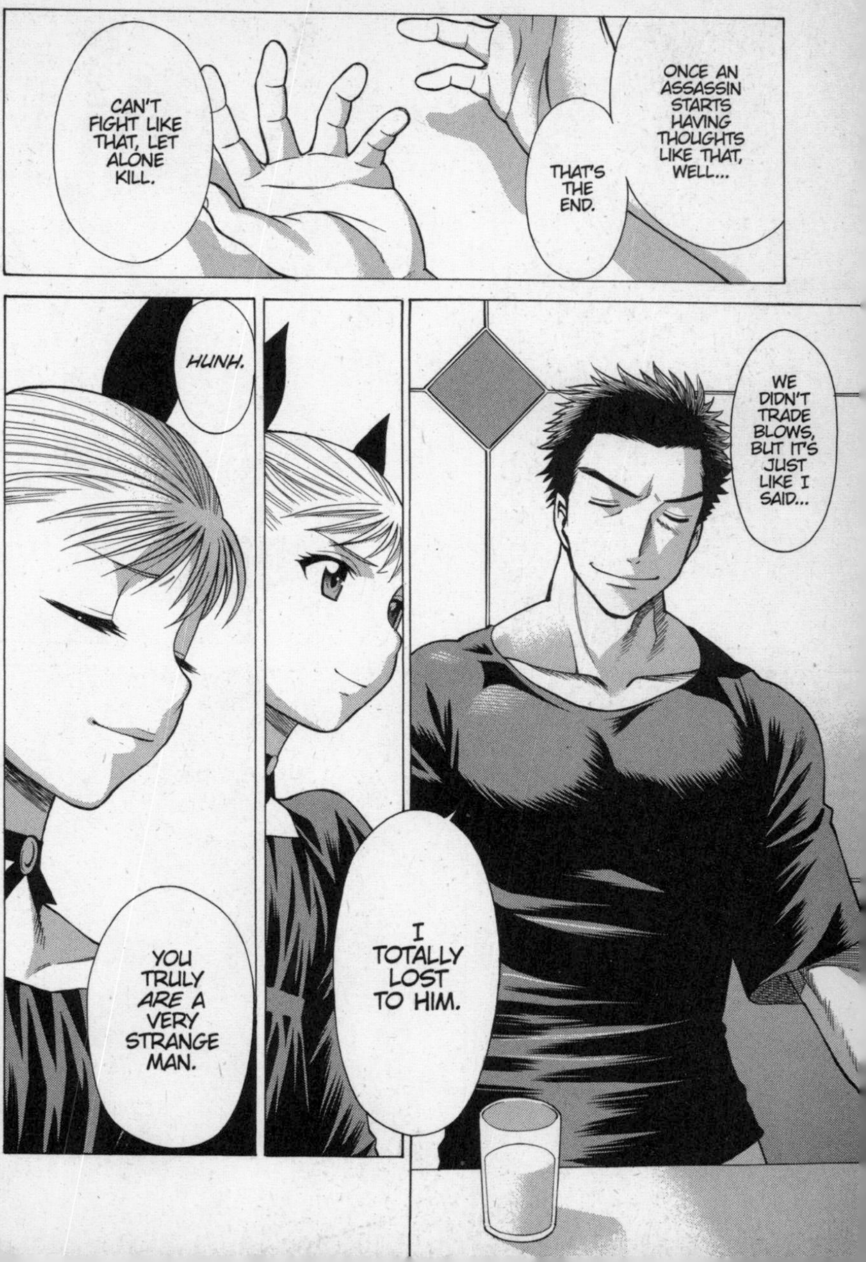

ONCE AN ASSASSIN STARTS HAVING THOUGHTS LIKE THAT, WELL...
THAT'S THE END.
CAN'T FIGHT LIKE THAT, LET ALONE KILL.
WE DIDN'T TRADE BLOWS, BUT IT'S JUST LIKE I SAID...
I TOTALLY LOST TO HIM.
HUNH.
YOU TRULY ARE A VERY STRANGE MAN.

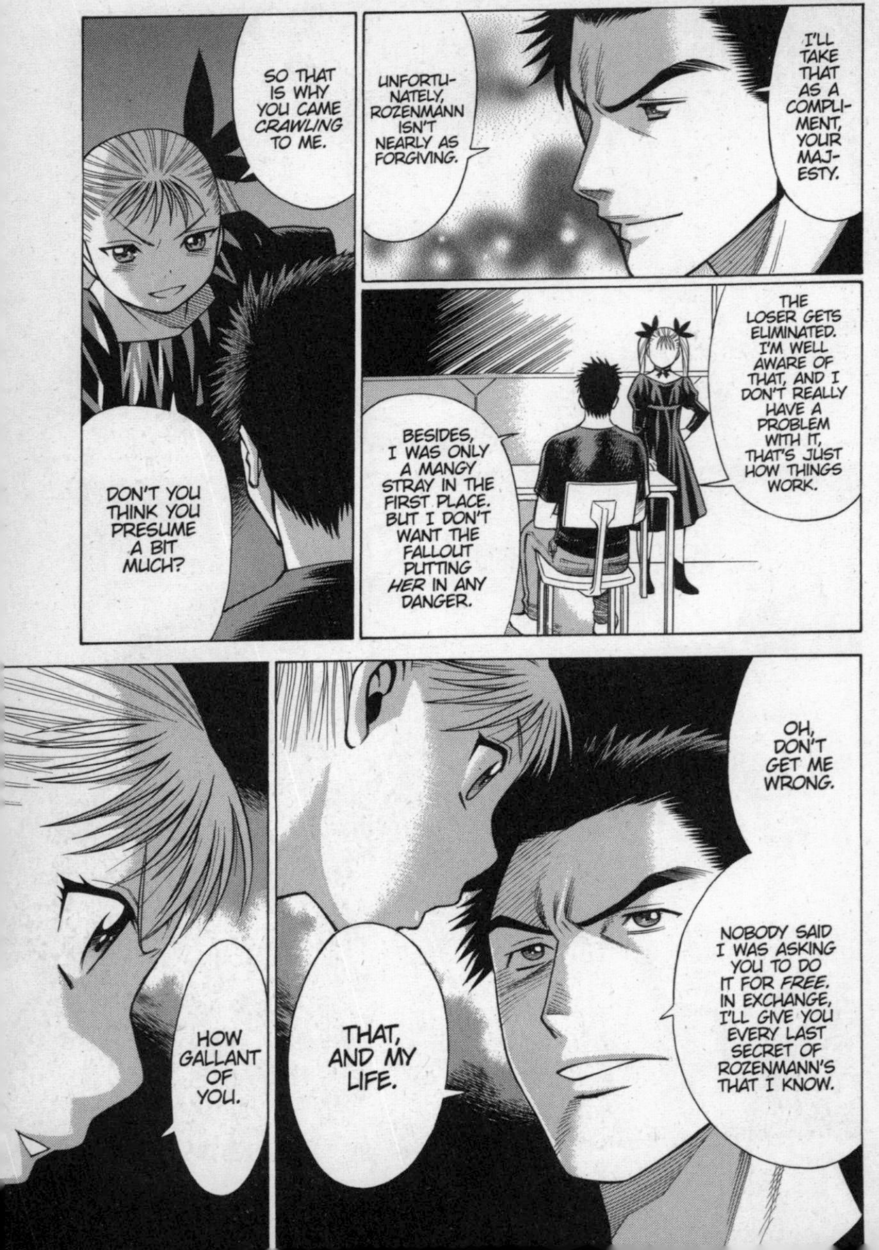
I'LL TAKE THAT AS A COMPLIMENT, YOUR MAJESTY.
UNFORTUNATELY, ROZENMANN ISN'T NEARLY AS FORGIVING.
THE LOSER GETS ELIMINATED. I'M WELL AWARE OF THAT, AND I DON'T REALLY HAVE A PROBLEM WITH IT, THAT'S JUST HOW THINGS WORK.
BESIDES, I WAS ONLY A MANGY STRAY IN THE FIRST PLACE. BUT I DON'T WANT THE FALLOUT PUTTING *HER* IN ANY DANGER.
SO THAT IS WHY YOU CAME *CRAWLING* TO ME.
DON'T YOU THINK YOU PRESUME A BIT MUCH?
OH, DON'T GET ME WRONG.
NOBODY SAID I WAS ASKING YOU TO DO IT FOR *FREE*. IN EXCHANGE, I'LL GIVE YOU EVERY LAST SECRET OF ROZENMANN'S THAT I KNOW.
THAT, AND MY LIFE.
HOW GALLANT OF YOU.

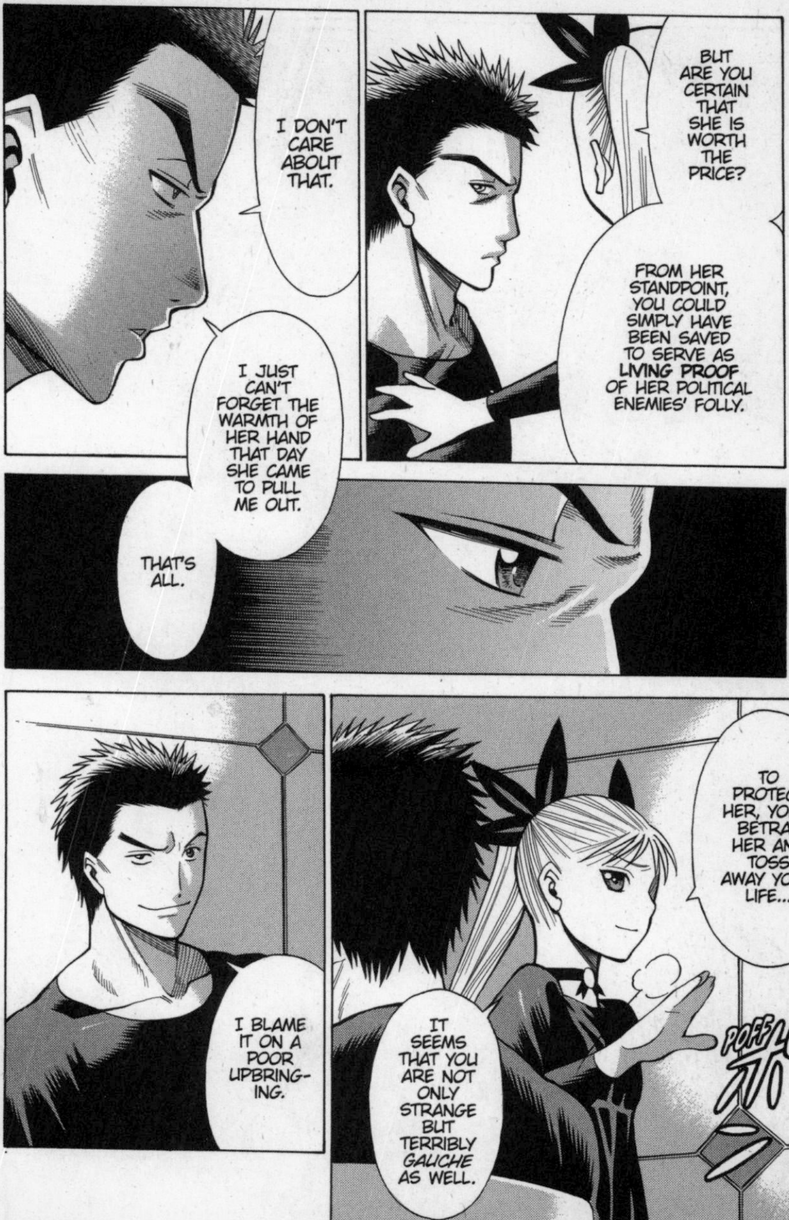
BUT ARE YOU CERTAIN THAT SHE IS WORTH THE PRICE?
FROM HER STANDPOINT, YOU COULD SIMPLY HAVE BEEN SAVED TO SERVE AS **LIVING PROOF** OF HER POLITICAL ENEMIES' FOLLY.
I DON'T CARE ABOUT THAT.
I JUST CAN'T FORGET THE WARMTH OF HER HAND THAT DAY SHE CAME TO PULL ME OUT.
THAT'S ALL.
TO PROTECT HER, YOU'D BETRAY HER AND TOSS AWAY YOUR LIFE...
IT SEEMS THAT YOU ARE NOT ONLY STRANGE BUT TERRIBLY *GAUCHE* AS WELL.
I BLAME IT ON A POOR UPBRING-ING.

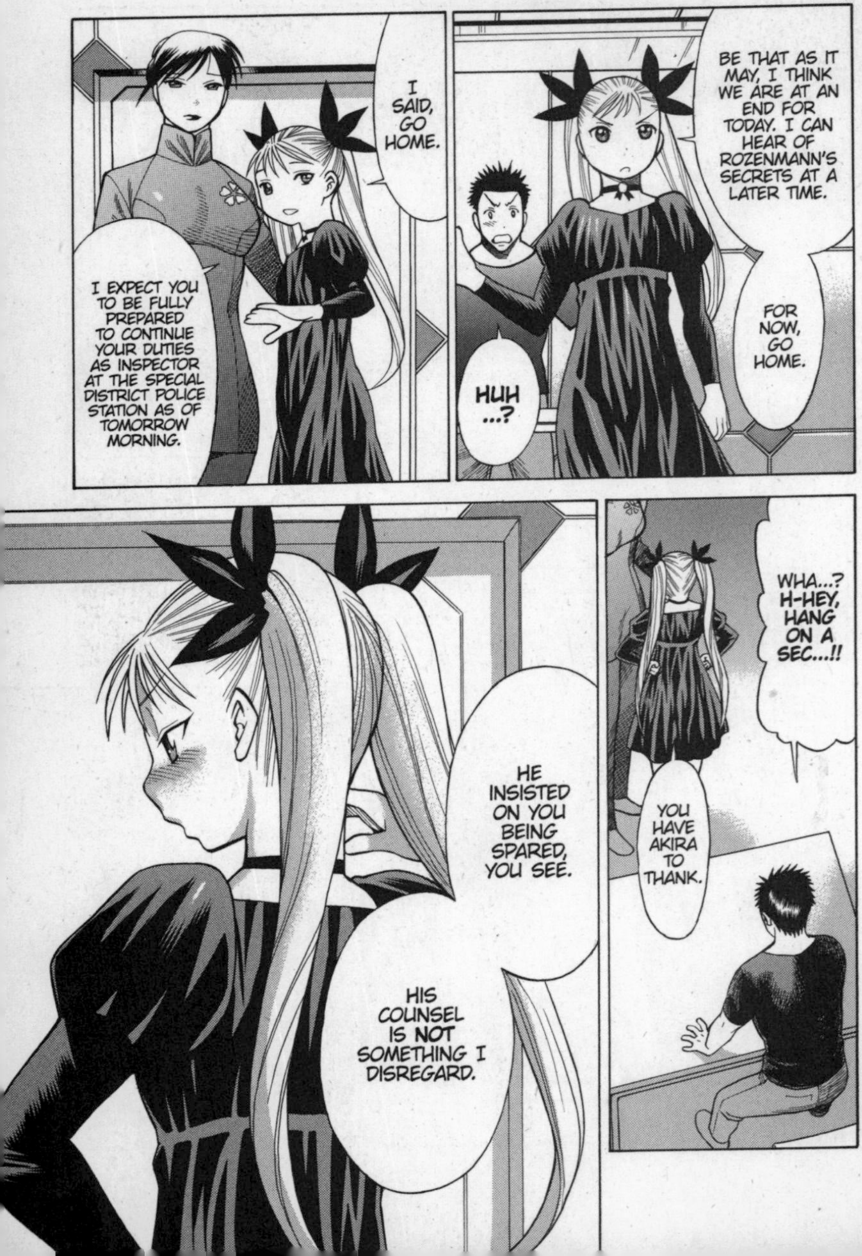
BE THAT AS IT MAY, I THINK WE ARE AT AN END FOR TODAY. I CAN HEAR OF ROZENMANN'S SECRETS AT A LATER TIME.
FOR NOW, GO HOME.
HUH ...?
I SAID, GO HOME.
I EXPECT YOU TO BE FULLY PREPARED TO CONTINUE YOUR DUTIES AS INSPECTOR AT THE SPECIAL DISTRICT POLICE STATION AS OF TOMORROW MORNING.
WHA...? H-HEY, HANG ON A SEC...!!
YOU HAVE AKIRA TO THANK.
HE INSISTED ON YOU BEING SPARED, YOU SEE.
HIS COUNSEL IS NOT SOMETHING I DISREGARD.

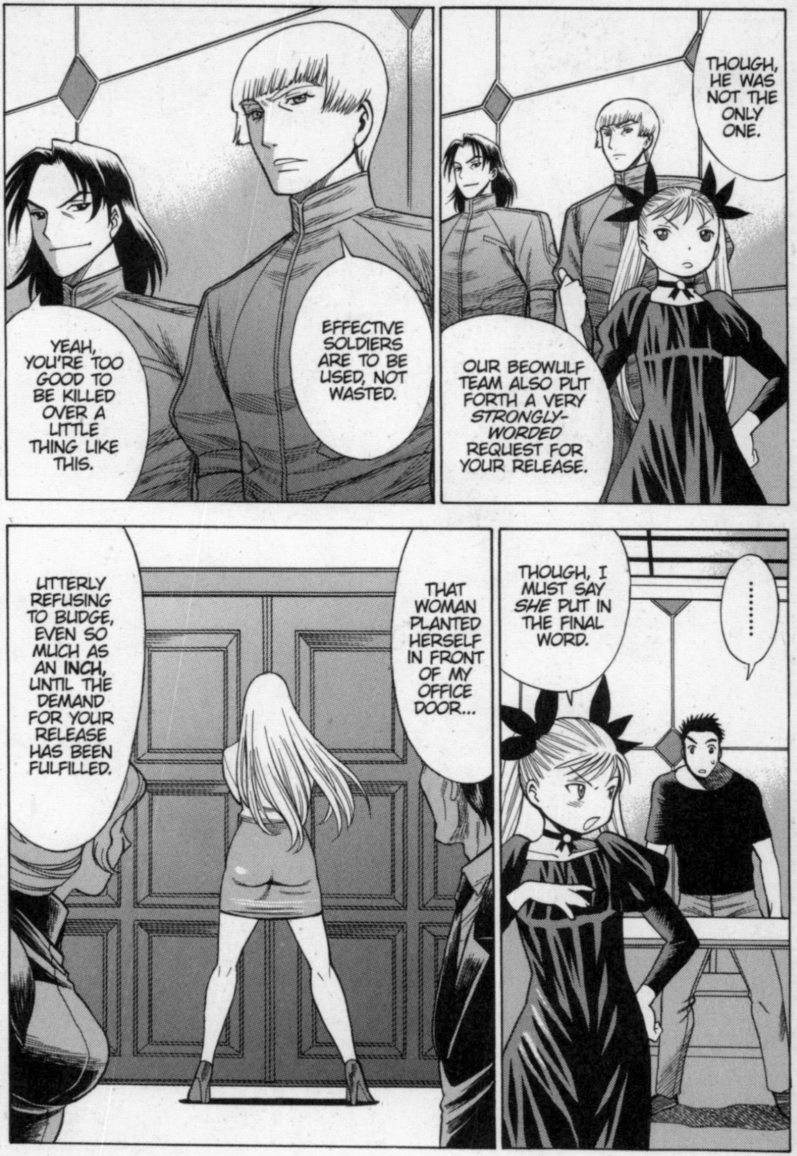
THOUGH, HE WAS NOT THE ONLY ONE.
OUR BEOWULF TEAM ALSO PUT FORTH A VERY *STRONGLY-WORDED* REQUEST FOR YOUR RELEASE.
EFFECTIVE SOLDIERS ARE TO BE USED, NOT WASTED.
YEAH, YOU'RE TOO GOOD TO BE KILLED OVER A LITTLE THING LIKE THIS.
......
THOUGH, I MUST SAY *SHE* PUT IN THE FINAL WORD.
THAT WOMAN PLANTED HERSELF IN FRONT OF MY OFFICE DOOR...
UTTERLY REFUSING TO BUDGE, EVEN SO MUCH AS AN INCH, UNTIL THE DEMAND FOR YOUR RELEASE HAS BEEN FULFILLED.

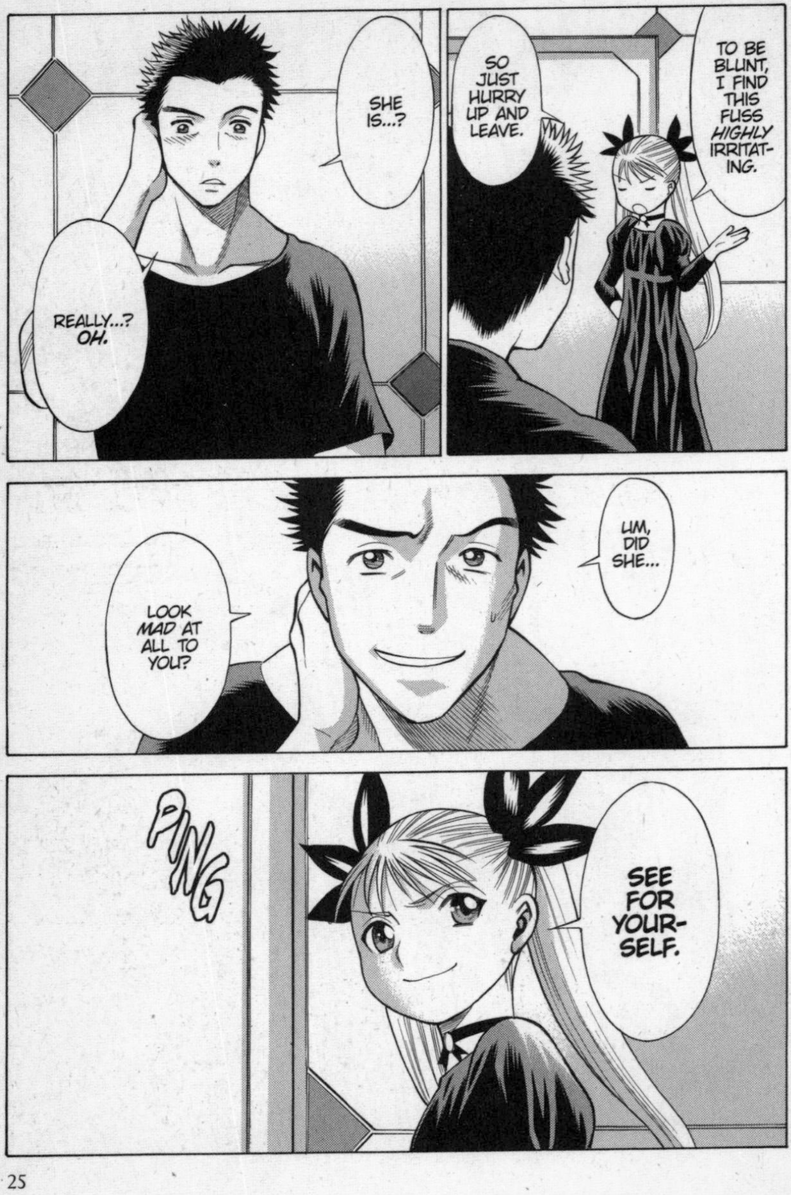
TO BE BLUNT, I FIND THIS FUSS *HIGHLY* IRRITATING.
SO JUST HURRY UP AND LEAVE.
SHE IS...?
REALLY...? *OH.*
UM, DID SHE...
LOOK *MAD* AT ALL TO YOU?
SEE FOR YOURSELF.
PING

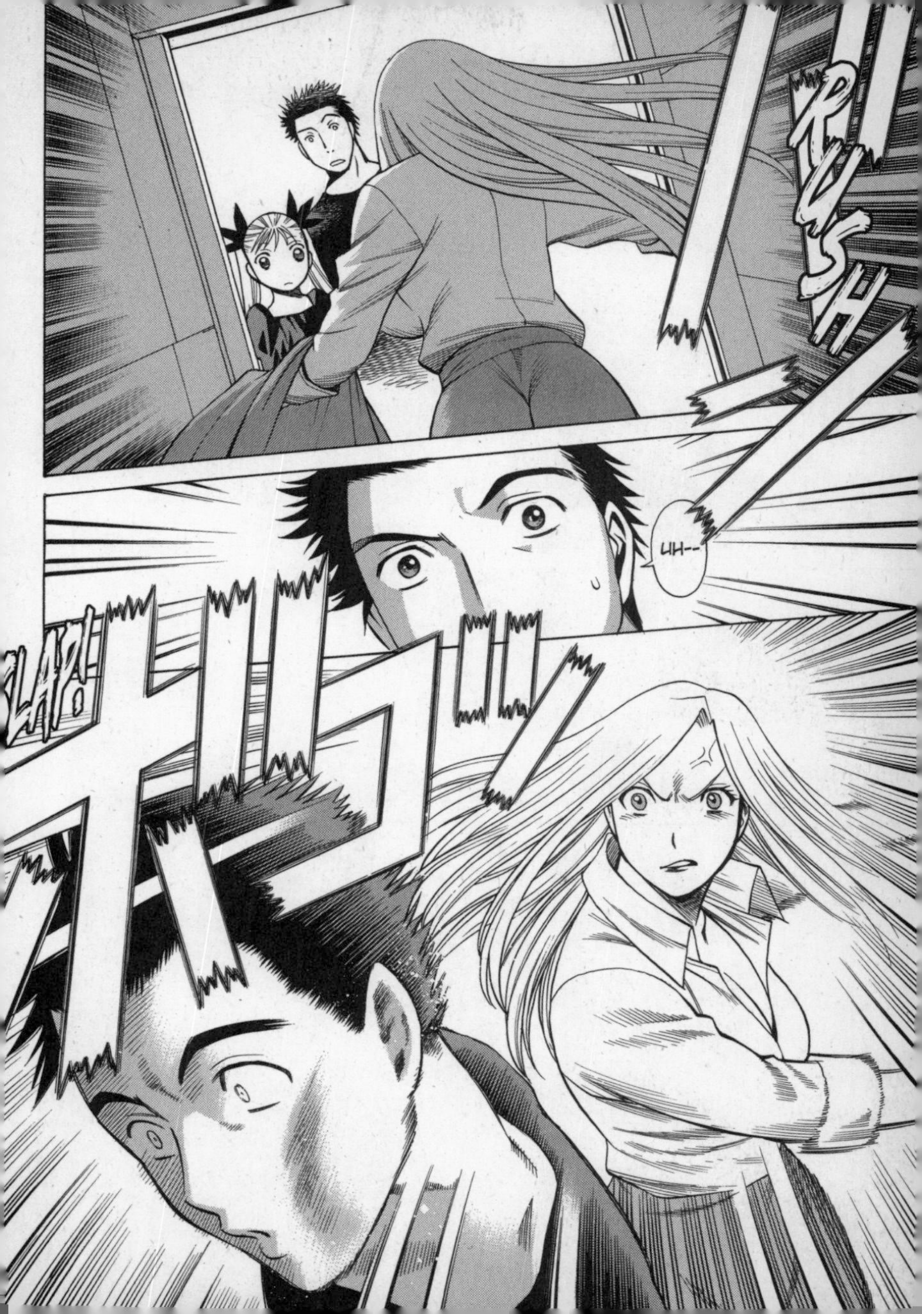
RUSH
UH--
LAP!

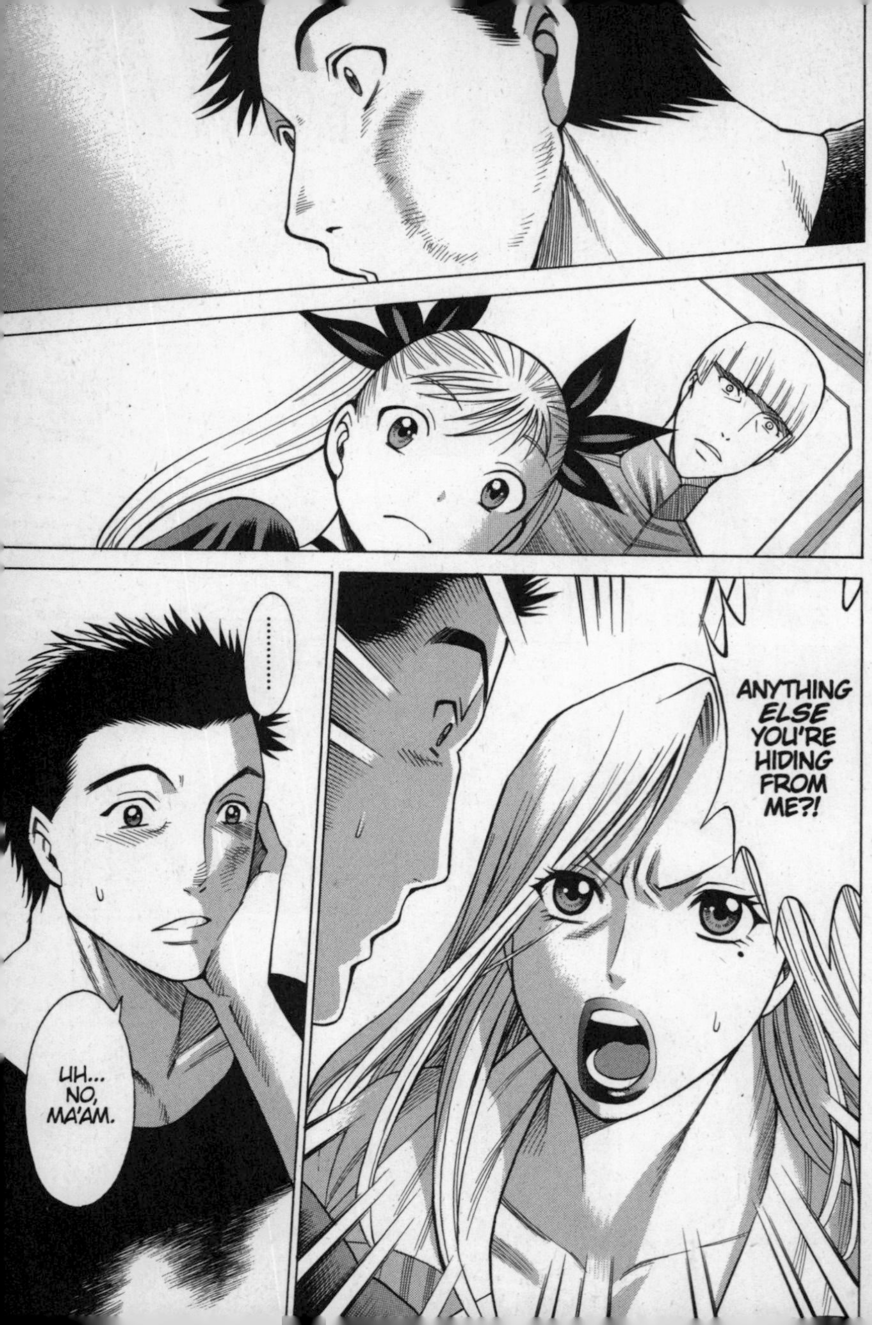
ANYTHING ELSE YOU'RE HIDING FROM ME?!
......
UH... NO, MA'AM.

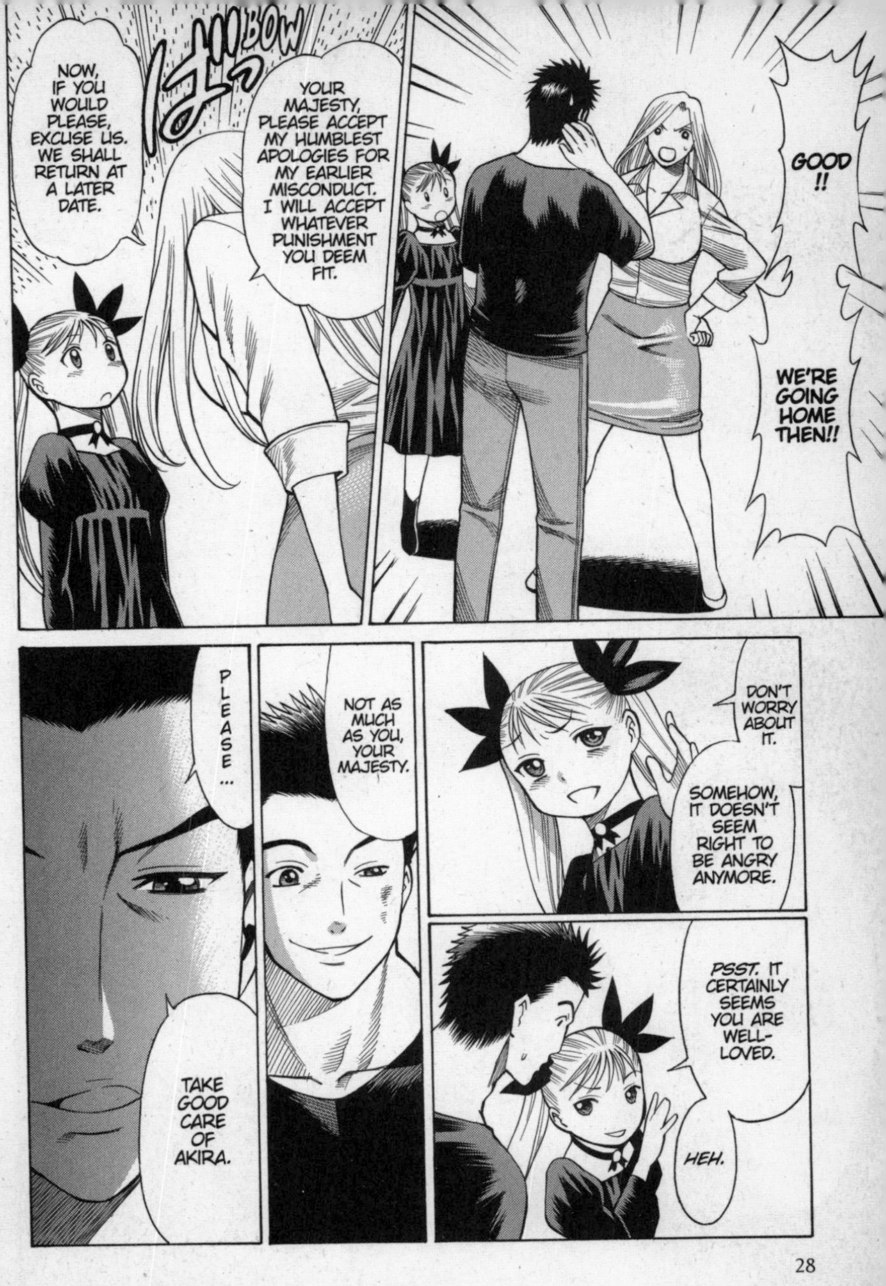
GOOD!!
WE'RE GOING HOME THEN!!
YOUR MAJESTY, PLEASE ACCEPT MY HUMBLEST APOLOGIES FOR MY EARLIER MISCONDUCT. I WILL ACCEPT WHATEVER PUNISHMENT YOU DEEM FIT.
はっ BOW
NOW, IF YOU WOULD PLEASE, EXCUSE US. WE SHALL RETURN AT A LATER DATE.
DON'T WORRY ABOUT IT.
SOMEHOW, IT DOESN'T SEEM RIGHT TO BE ANGRY ANYMORE.
PSST. IT CERTAINLY SEEMS YOU ARE WELL-LOVED.
HEH.
NOT AS MUCH AS YOU, YOUR MAJESTY.
PLEASE...
TAKE GOOD CARE OF AKIRA.

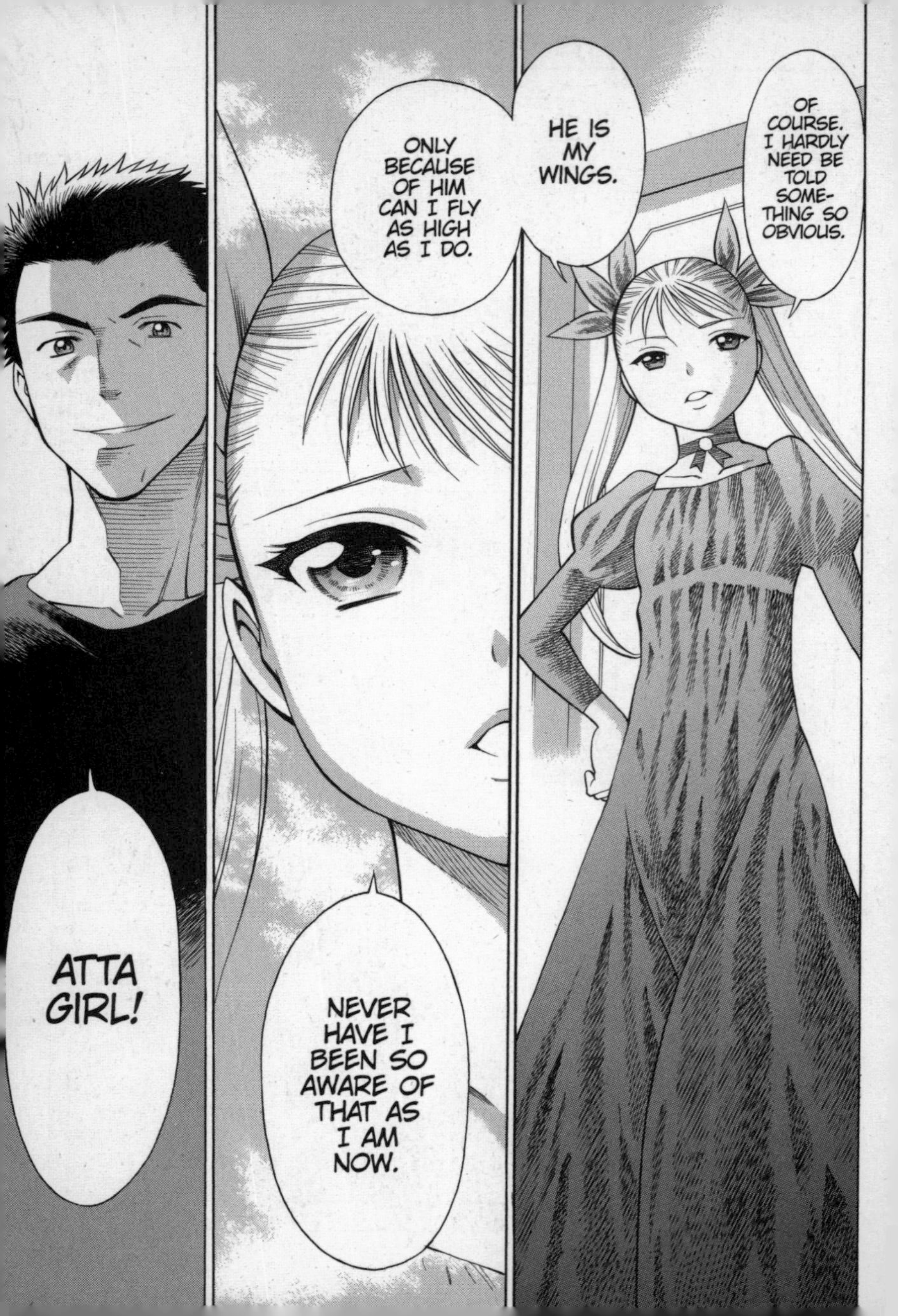

OF COURSE. I HARDLY NEED BE TOLD SOME-THING SO OBVIOUS.
HE IS MY WINGS.
ONLY BECAUSE OF HIM CAN I FLY AS HIGH AS I DO.
NEVER HAVE I BEEN SO AWARE OF THAT AS I AM NOW.
ATTA GIRL!

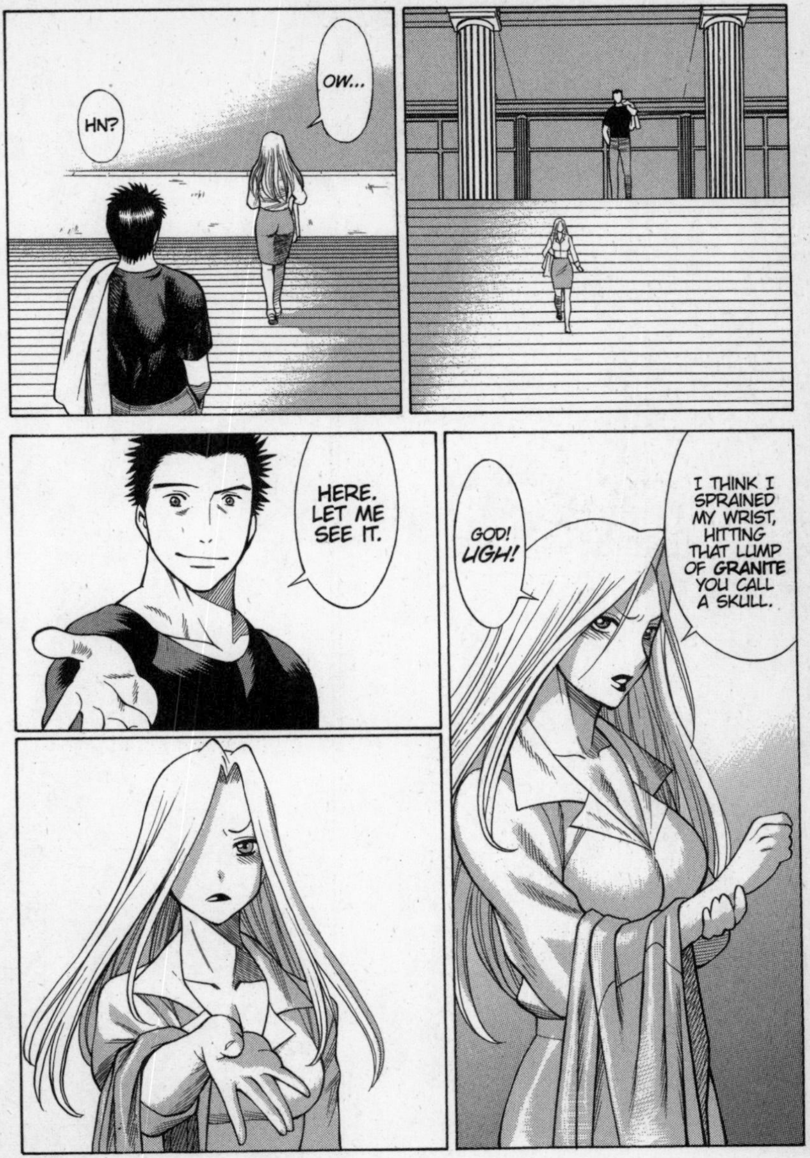
OW...
HN?
I THINK I SPRAINED MY WRIST, HITTING THAT LUMP OF GRANITE YOU CALL A SKULL.
GOD! UGH!
HERE. LET ME SEE IT.

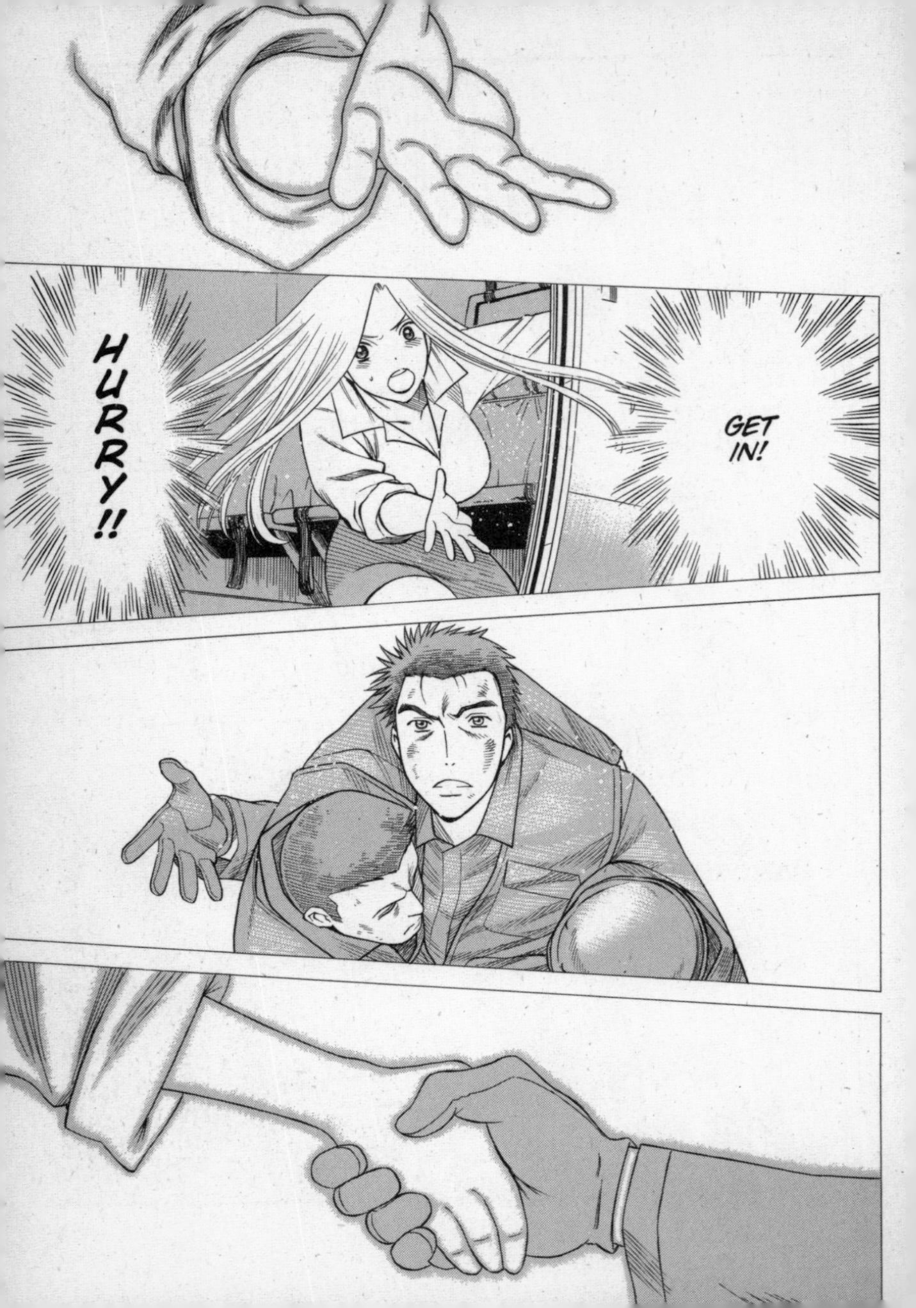
GET IN!
HURRY!!

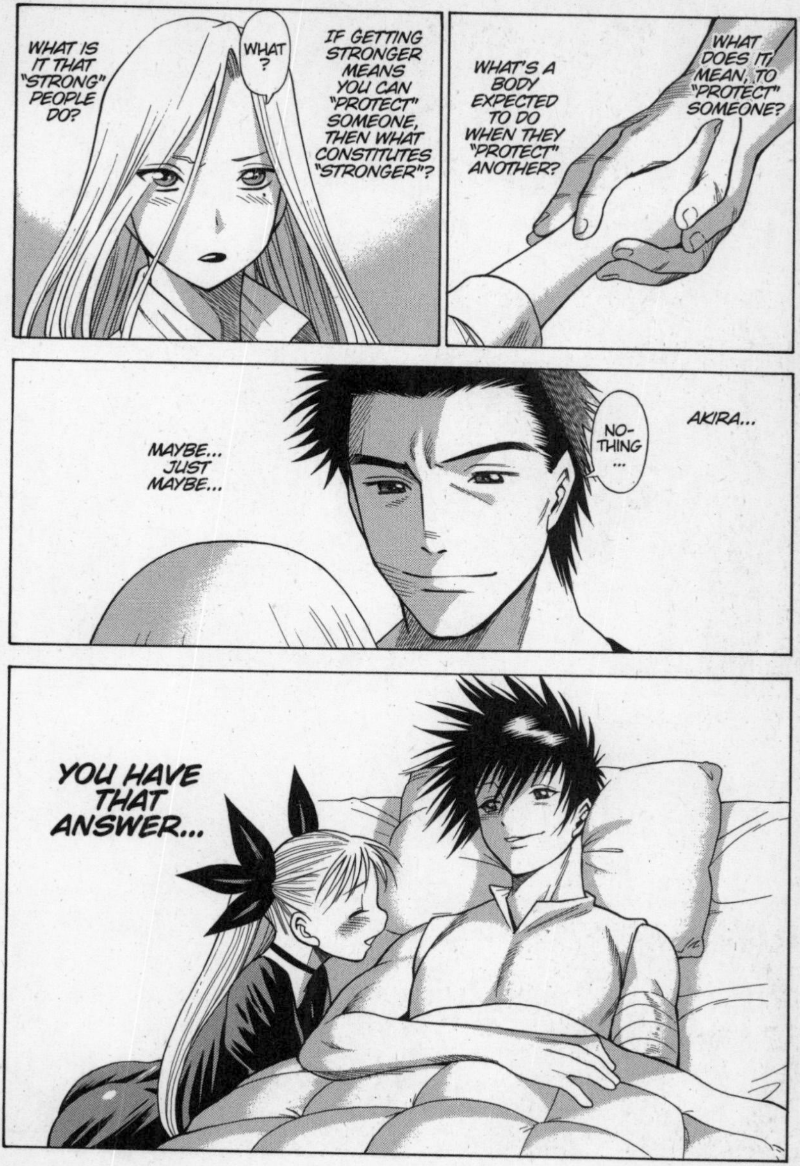
WHAT DOES IT MEAN, TO "PROTECT" SOMEONE?
WHAT'S A BODY EXPECTED TO DO WHEN THEY "PROTECT" ANOTHER?
IF GETTING STRONGER MEANS YOU CAN "PROTECT" SOMEONE, THEN WHAT CONSTITUTES "STRONGER"?
WHAT ?
WHAT IS IT THAT "STRONG" PEOPLE DO?
AKIRA...
NO-THING ...
MAYBE... JUST MAYBE...
YOU HAVE THAT ANSWER...

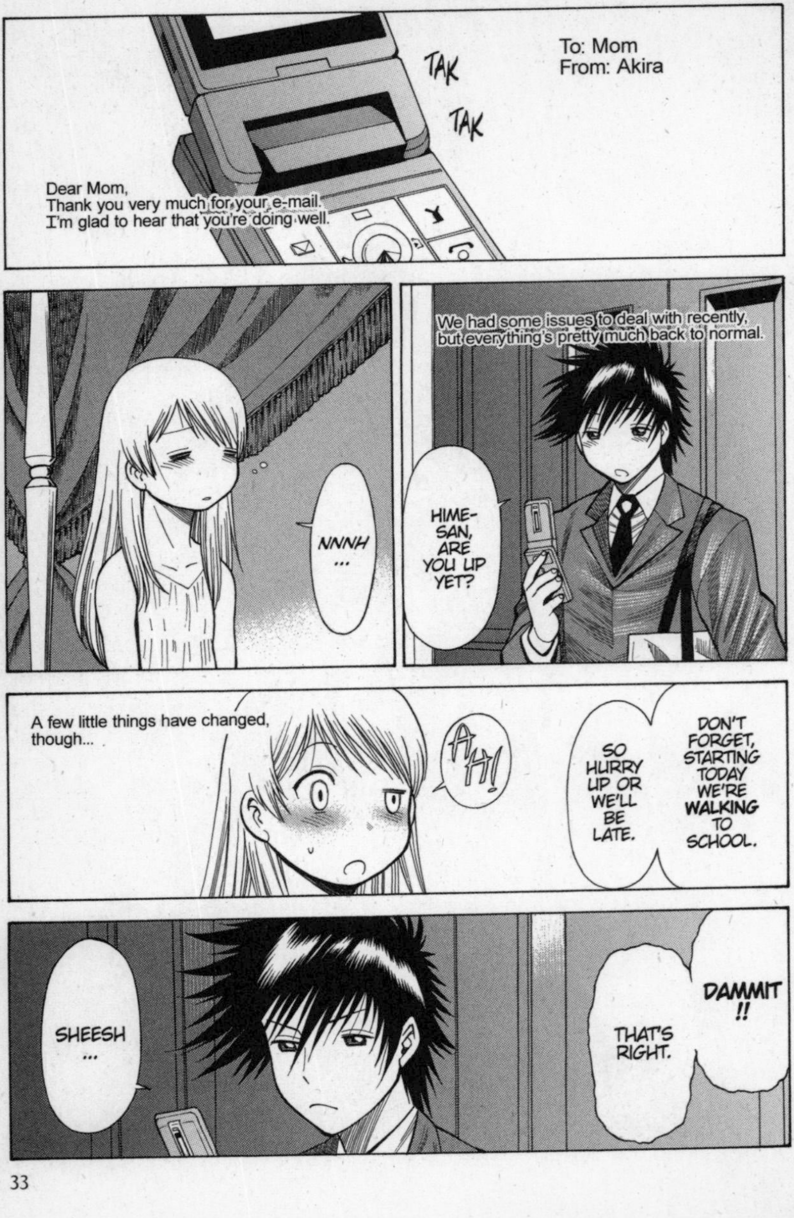

To: Mom
From: Akira
TAK
TAK
Dear Mom,
Thank you very much for your e-mail.
I'm glad to hear that you're doing well.
We had some issues to deal with recently, but everything's pretty much back to normal.
HIME-SAN, ARE YOU UP YET?
NNNH ...
DON'T FORGET, STARTING TODAY WE'RE WALKING TO SCHOOL.
SO HURRY UP OR WE'LL BE LATE.
AH!
A few little things have changed, though...
DAMMIT !!
THAT'S RIGHT.
SHEESH ...

Chapter 33: Standard Daytime

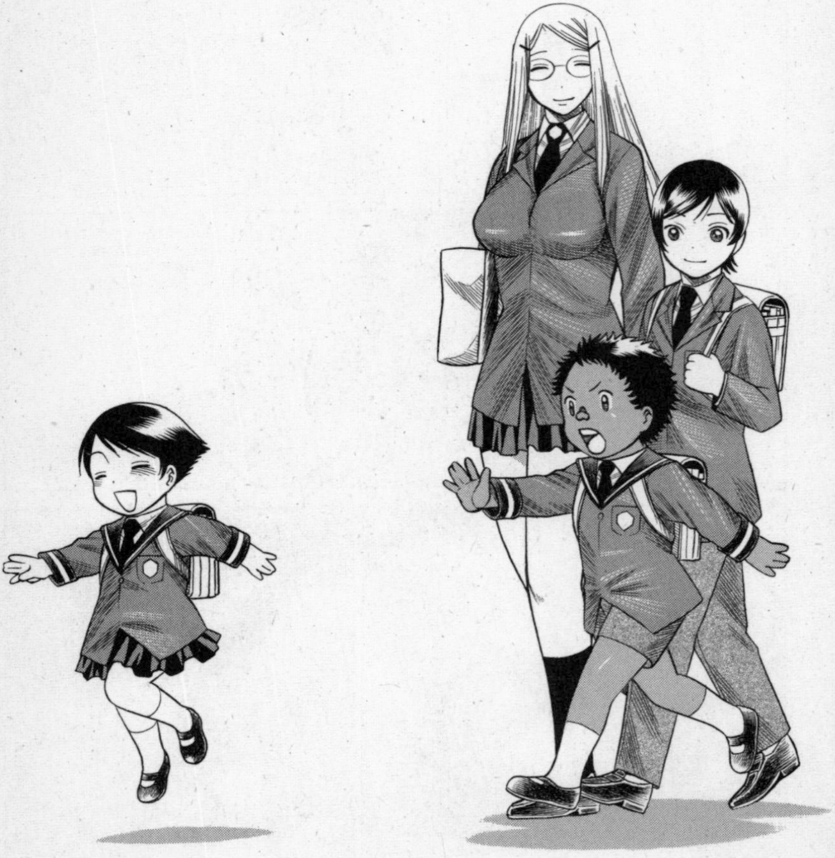

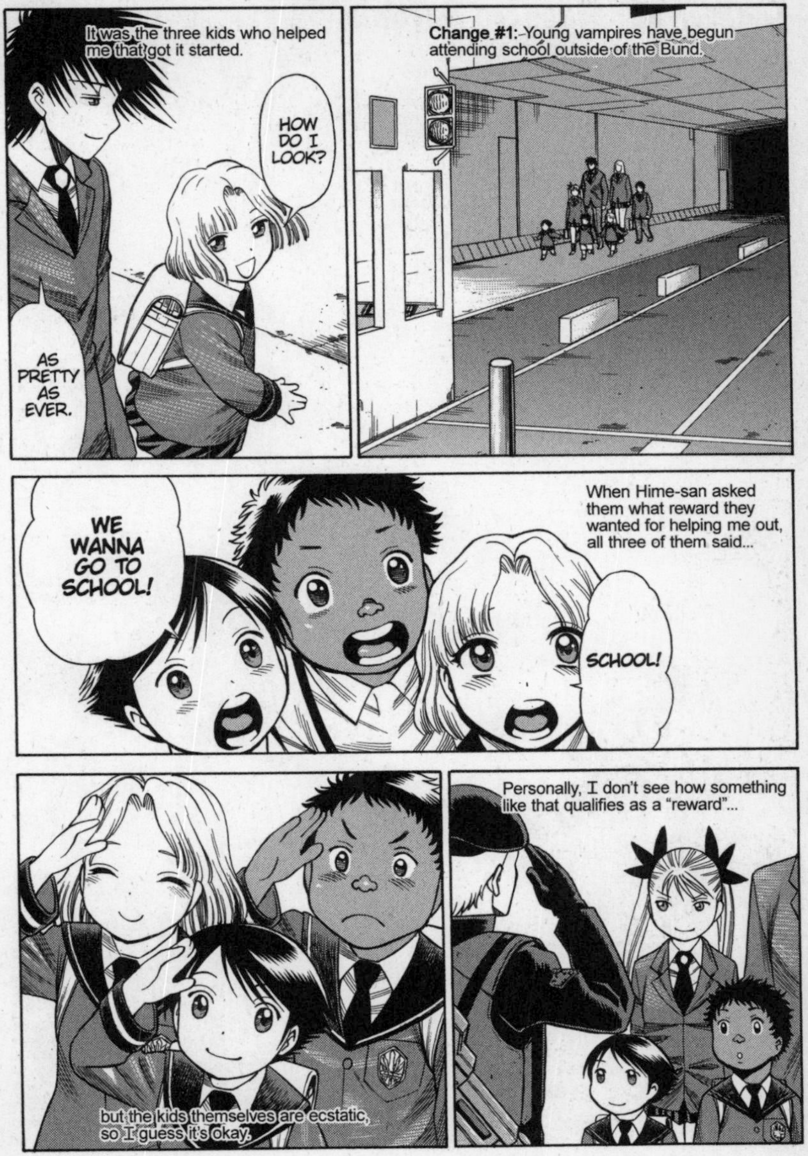
Change #1: Young vampires have begun attending school outside of the Bund.
It was the three kids who helped me that got it started.
HOW DO I LOOK?
AS PRETTY AS EVER.
When Hime-san asked them what reward they wanted for helping me out, all three of them said...
WE WANNA GO TO SCHOOL!
SCHOOL!
Personally, I don't see how something like that qualifies as a "reward"...
but the kids themselves are ecstatic, so I guess it's okay.

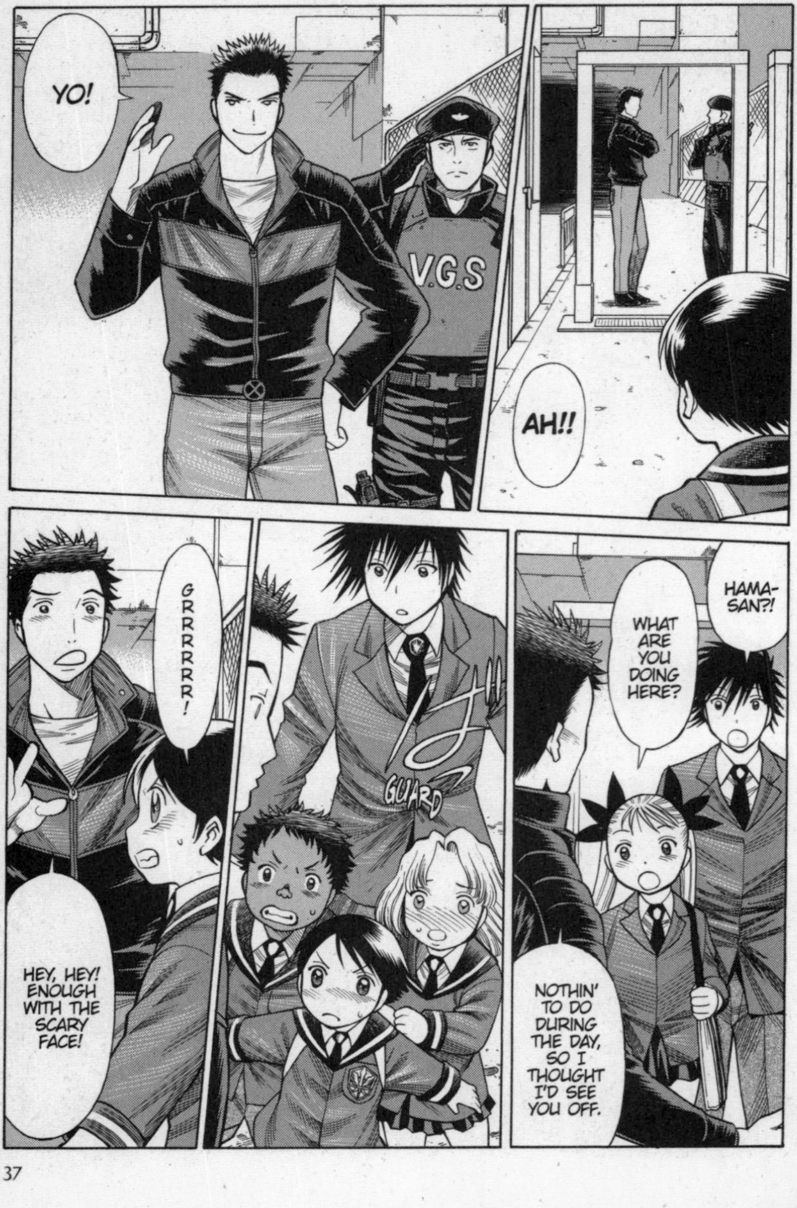
AH!!
YO!
V.G.S
HAMA-SAN?!
WHAT ARE YOU DOING HERE?
NOTHIN' TO DO DURING THE DAY, SO I THOUGHT I'D SEE YOU OFF.
GRRRRRRR!
GUARD
HEY, HEY! ENOUGH WITH THE SCARY FACE!

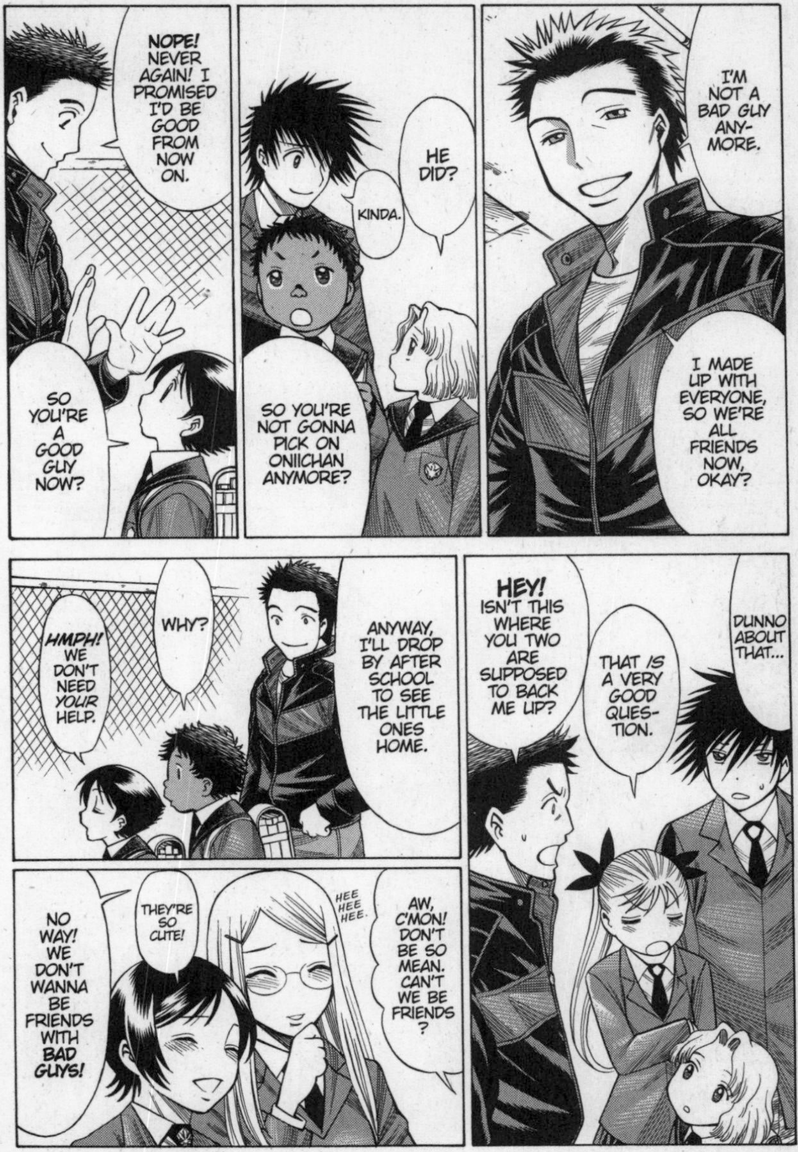
I'M NOT A BAD GUY ANY-MORE.
I MADE UP WITH EVERYONE, SO WE'RE ALL FRIENDS NOW, OKAY?
HE DID?
KINDA.
SO YOU'RE NOT GONNA PICK ON ONIICHAN ANYMORE?
NOPE! NEVER AGAIN! I PROMISED I'D BE GOOD FROM NOW ON.
SO YOU'RE A GOOD GUY NOW?
DUNNO ABOUT THAT...
THAT *IS* A VERY GOOD QUES-TION.
HEY! ISN'T THIS WHERE YOU TWO ARE SUPPOSED TO BACK ME UP?
ANYWAY, I'LL DROP BY AFTER SCHOOL TO SEE THE LITTLE ONES HOME.
WHY?
HMPH! WE DON'T NEED *YOUR* HELP.
AW, C'MON! DON'T BE SO MEAN. CAN'T WE BE FRIENDS?
HEE HEE HEE.
THEY'RE SO CUTE!
NO WAY! WE DON'T WANNA BE FRIENDS WITH **BAD GUYS!**

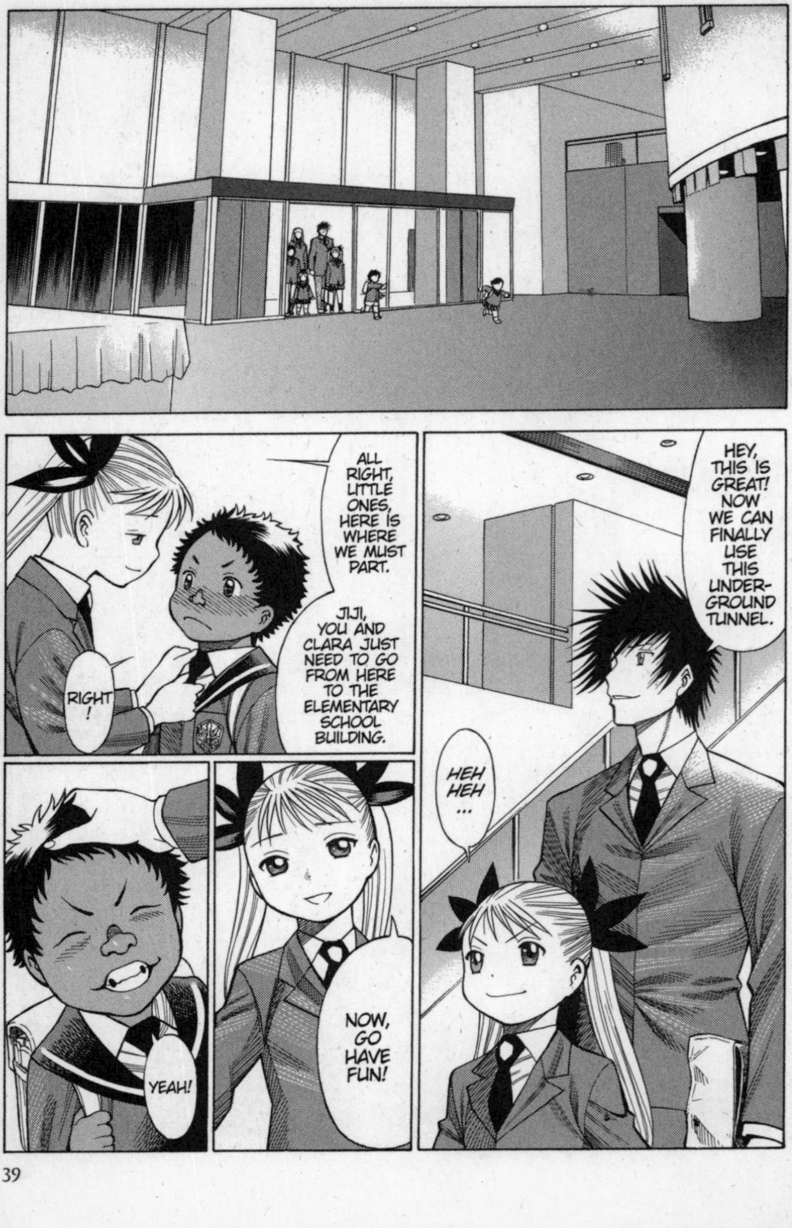
HEY, THIS IS GREAT! NOW WE CAN FINALLY USE THIS UNDER-GROUND TUNNEL.
HEH HEH ...
ALL RIGHT, LITTLE ONES, HERE IS WHERE WE MUST PART.
JIJI, YOU AND CLARA JUST NEED TO GO FROM HERE TO THE ELEMENTARY SCHOOL BUILDING.
RIGHT!
NOW, GO HAVE FUN!
YEAH!

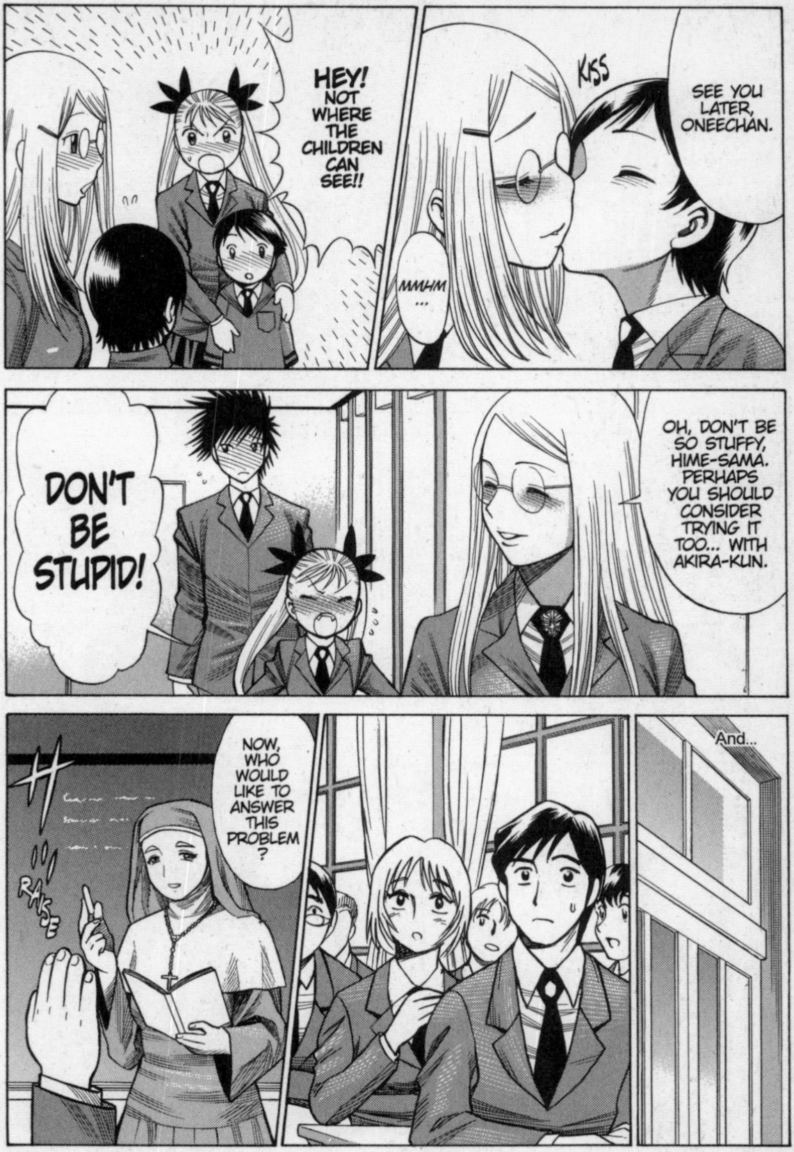
SEE YOU LATER, ONEECHAN.
KISS
MMHM...
HEY! NOT WHERE THE CHILDREN CAN SEE!!
OH, DON'T BE SO STUFFY, HIME-SAMA. PERHAPS YOU SHOULD CONSIDER TRYING IT TOO... WITH AKIRA-KUN.
DON'T BE STUPID!
And...
NOW, WHO WOULD LIKE TO ANSWER THIS PROBLEM?
RAISE

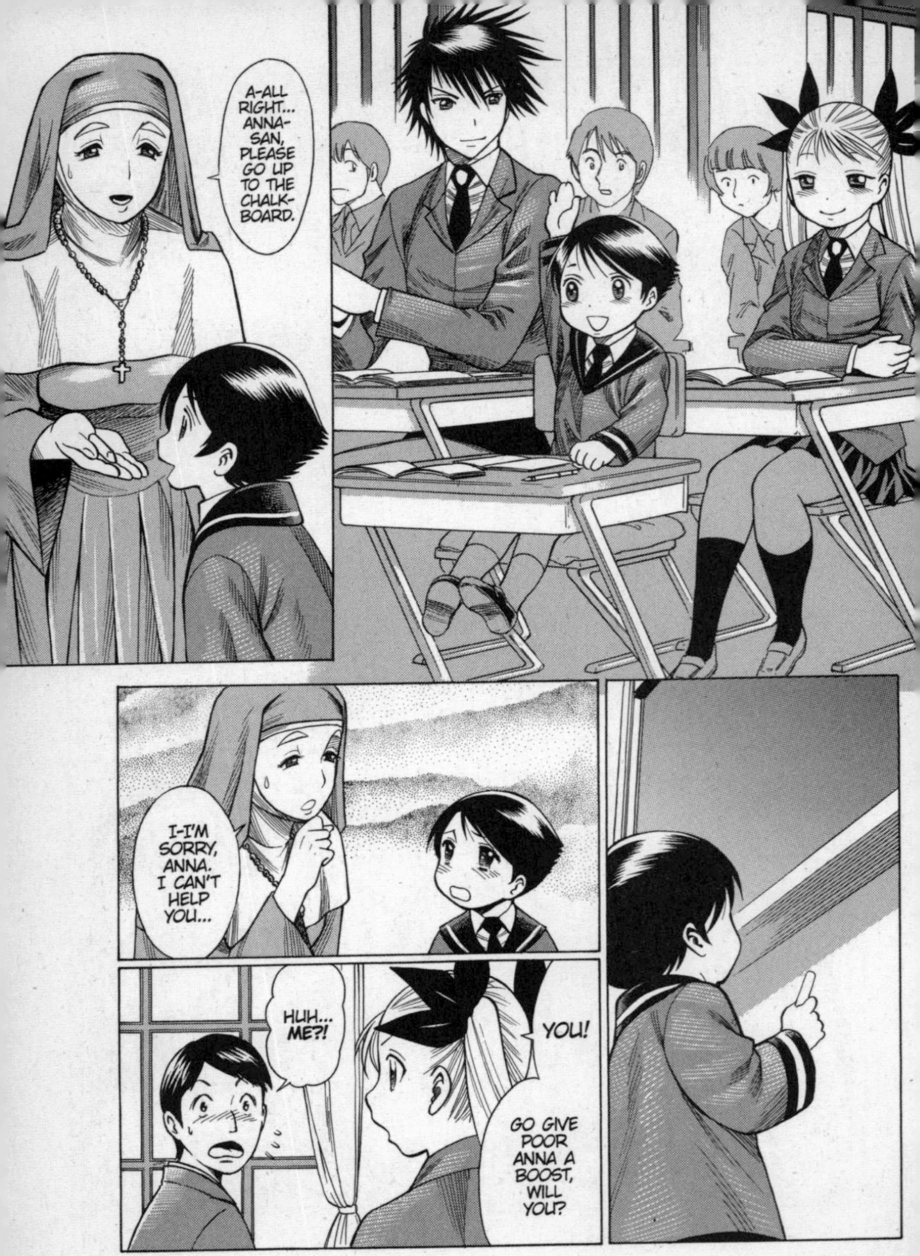
A-ALL RIGHT... ANNA-SAN, PLEASE GO UP TO THE CHALK-BOARD.
I-I'M SORRY, ANNA. I CAN'T HELP YOU...
YOU!
HUH... ME?!
GO GIVE POOR ANNA A BOOST, WILL YOU?

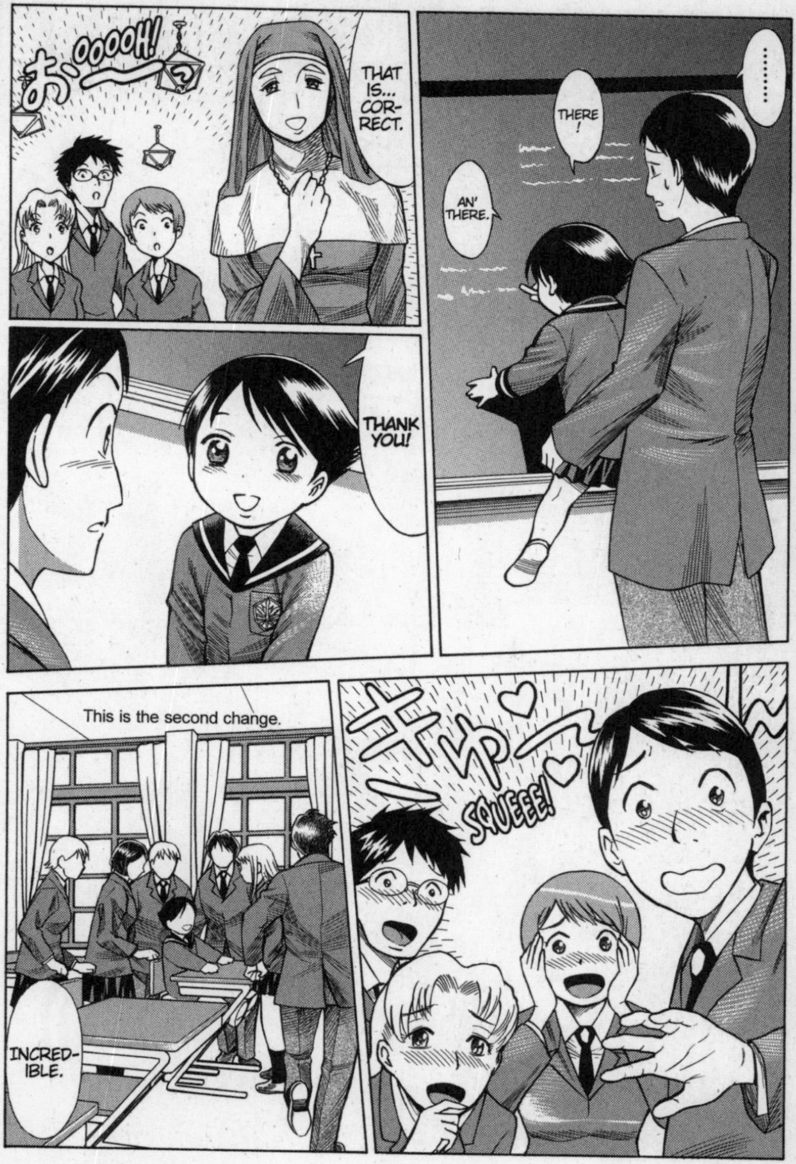
……
THERE!
AN' THERE.
お〜っ
OOOOH!
THAT IS... CORRECT.
THANK YOU!
キゅ〜
SQUEEE!
This is the second change.
INCREDIBLE.

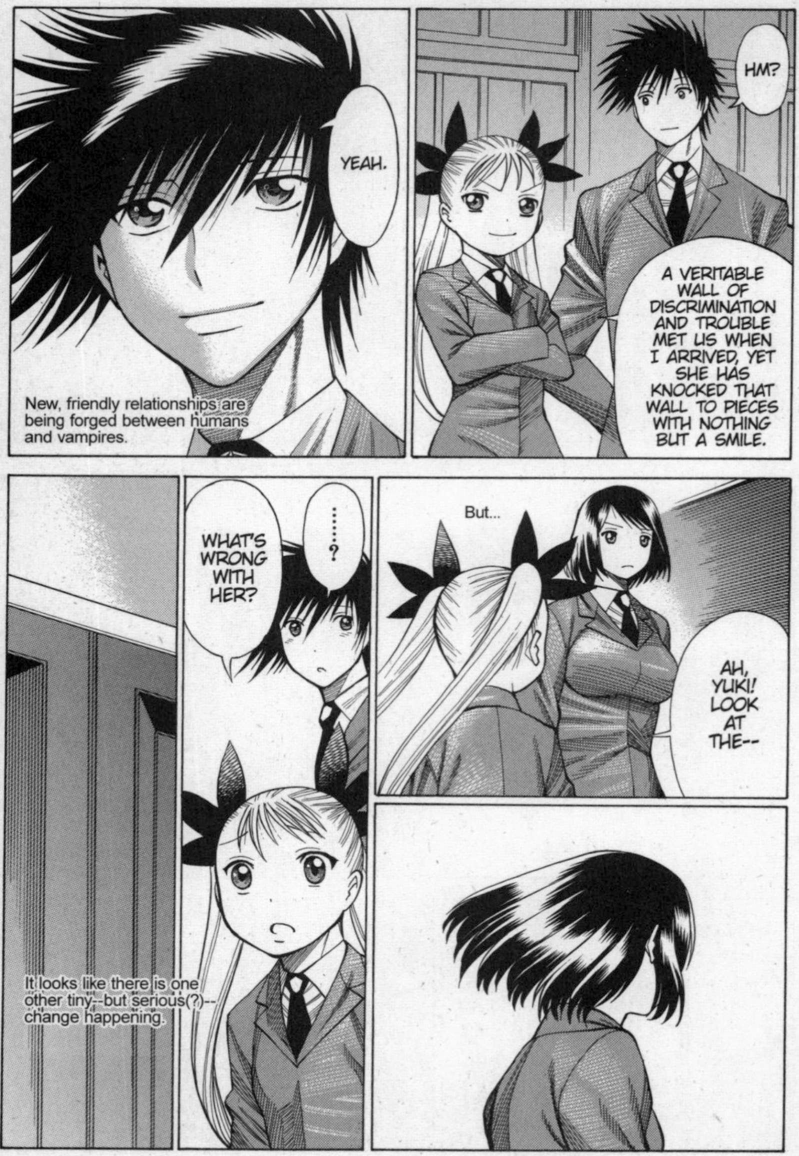
HM?
A VERITABLE WALL OF DISCRIMINATION AND TROUBLE MET US WHEN I ARRIVED, YET SHE HAS KNOCKED THAT WALL TO PIECES WITH NOTHING BUT A SMILE.
YEAH.
New, friendly relationships are being forged between humans and vampires.
But...
AH, YUKI! LOOK AT THE--
......?
WHAT'S WRONG WITH HER?
It looks like there is one other tiny--but serious(?)--change happening.

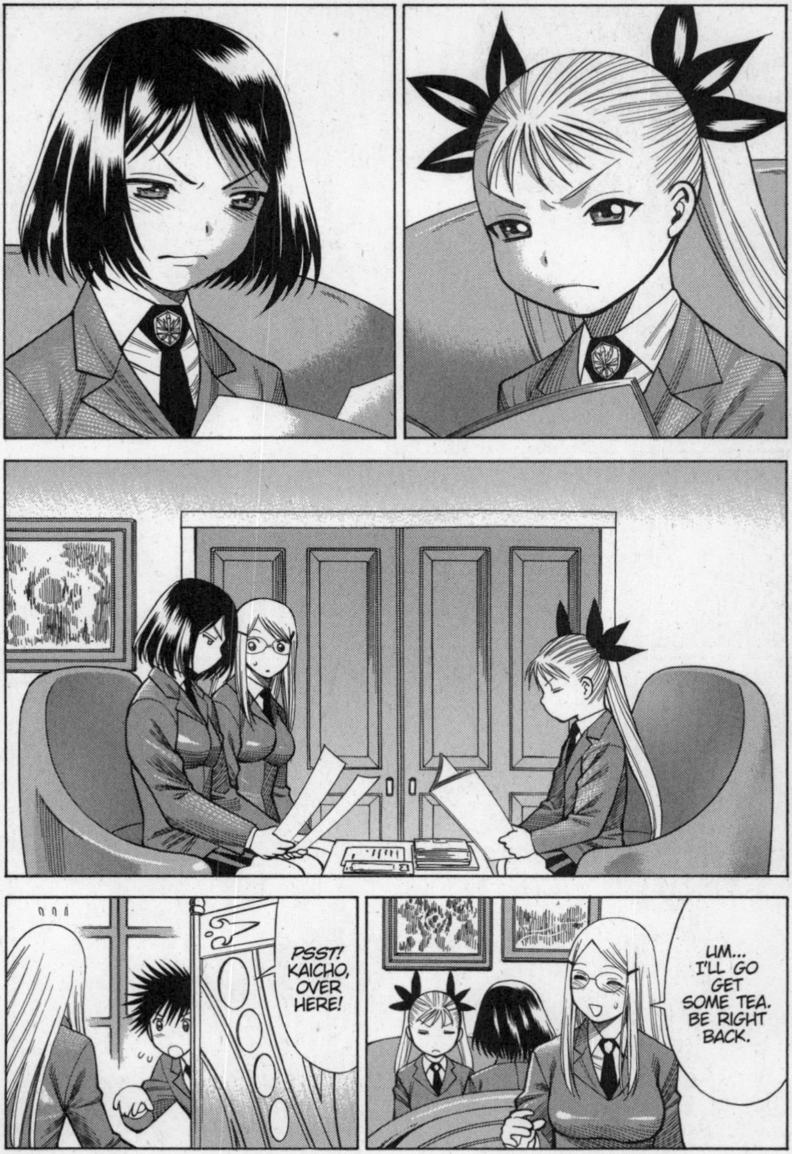
UM... I'LL GO GET SOME TEA. BE RIGHT BACK.
PSST! KAICHO, OVER HERE!

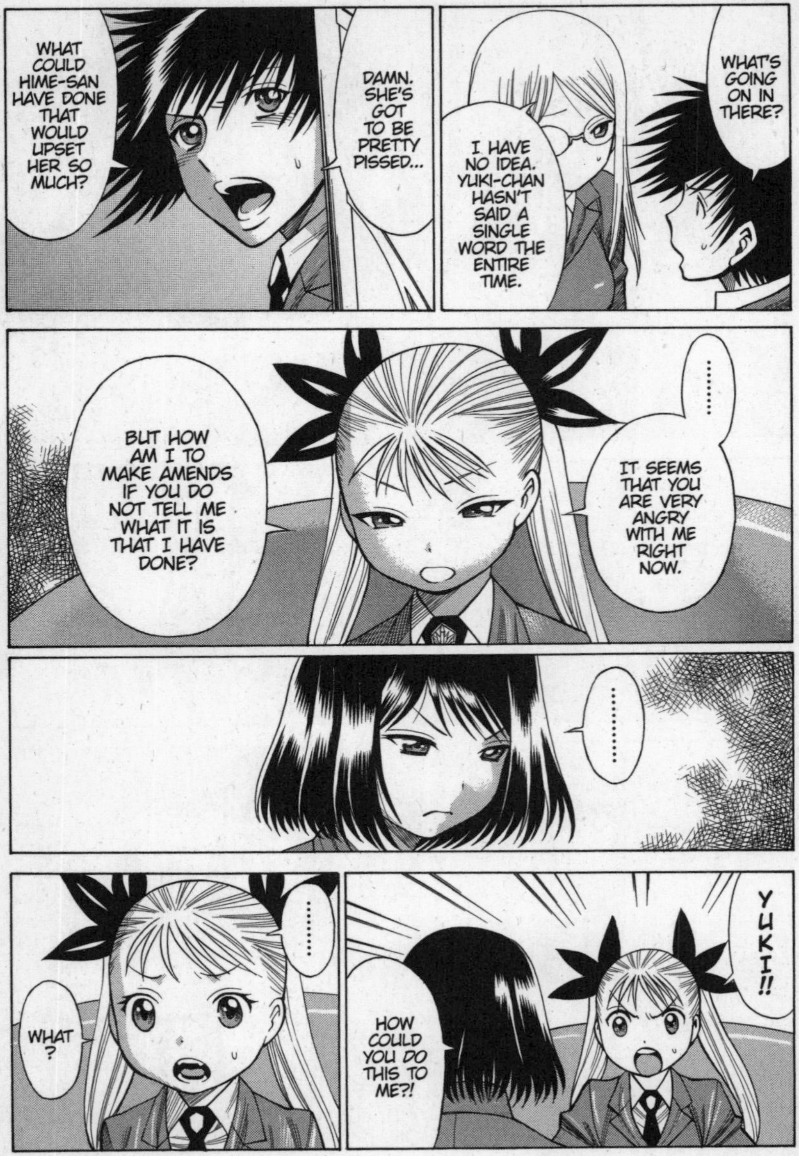
WHAT'S GOING ON IN THERE?
I HAVE NO IDEA. YUKI-CHAN HASN'T SAID A SINGLE WORD THE ENTIRE TIME.
DAMN. SHE'S GOT TO BE PRETTY PISSED...
WHAT COULD HIME-SAN HAVE DONE THAT WOULD UPSET HER SO MUCH?
......
IT SEEMS THAT YOU ARE VERY ANGRY WITH ME RIGHT NOW.
BUT HOW AM I TO MAKE AMENDS IF YOU DO NOT TELL ME WHAT IT IS THAT I HAVE DONE?
....
YUKI!!
HOW COULD YOU DO THIS TO ME?!
......
WHAT?

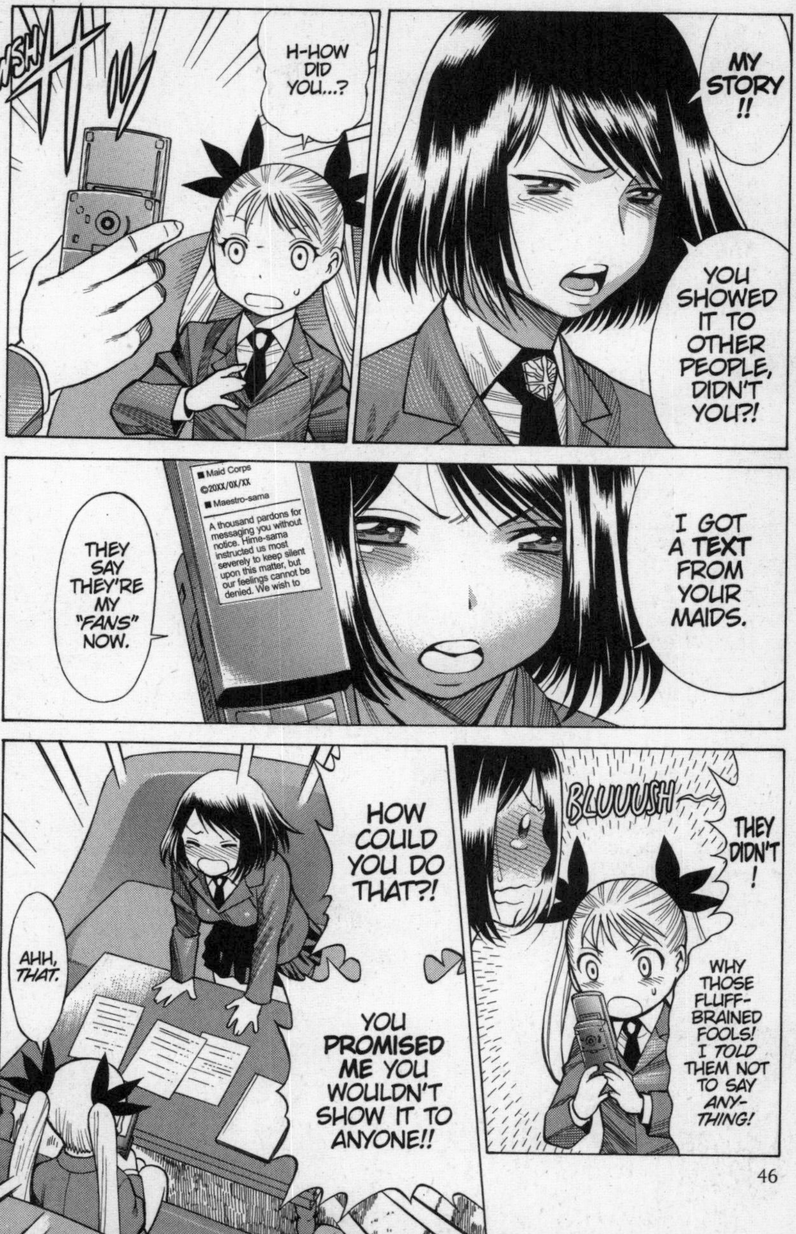
MY STORY!!
YOU SHOWED IT TO OTHER PEOPLE, DIDN'T YOU?!
WSHH
H-HOW DID YOU...?
I GOT A **TEXT** FROM YOUR MAIDS.
■ Maid Corps
©20XX/0X/XX
■ Maestro-sama
A thousand pardons for messaging you without notice. Hime-sama instructed us most severely to keep silent upon this matter, but our feelings cannot be denied. We wish to
THEY SAY THEY'RE MY *"FANS"* NOW.
BLUUUSH~
THEY DIDN'T!
WHY THOSE FLUFF-BRAINED FOOLS! I *TOLD* THEM NOT TO SAY *ANYTHING!*
HOW COULD YOU DO THAT?!
YOU **PROMISED** ME YOU WOULDN'T SHOW IT TO ANYONE!!
AHH, *THAT.*

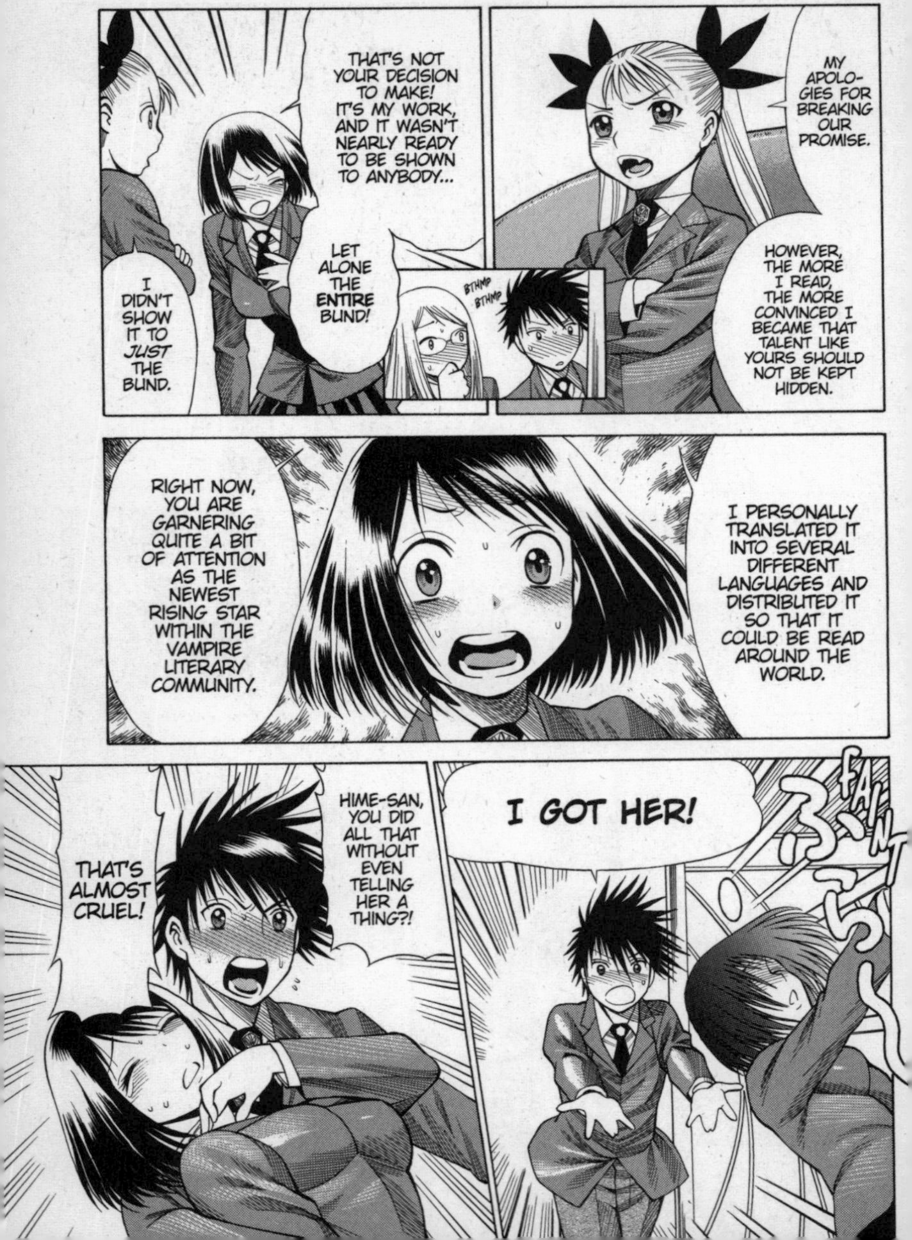
MY APOLOGIES FOR BREAKING OUR PROMISE.
HOWEVER, THE MORE I READ, THE MORE CONVINCED I BECAME THAT TALENT LIKE YOURS SHOULD NOT BE KEPT HIDDEN.
THAT'S NOT YOUR DECISION TO MAKE! IT'S MY WORK, AND IT WASN'T NEARLY READY TO BE SHOWN TO ANYBODY...
BTHMP BTHMP
LET ALONE THE **ENTIRE** BUND!
I DIDN'T SHOW IT TO *JUST* THE BUND.
I PERSONALLY TRANSLATED IT INTO SEVERAL DIFFERENT LANGUAGES AND DISTRIBUTED IT SO THAT IT COULD BE READ AROUND THE WORLD.
RIGHT NOW, YOU ARE GARNERING QUITE A BIT OF ATTENTION AS THE NEWEST RISING STAR WITHIN THE VAMPIRE LITERARY COMMUNITY.
FAINT
I GOT HER!
HIME-SAN, YOU DID ALL THAT WITHOUT EVEN TELLING HER A THING?!
THAT'S ALMOST CRUEL!

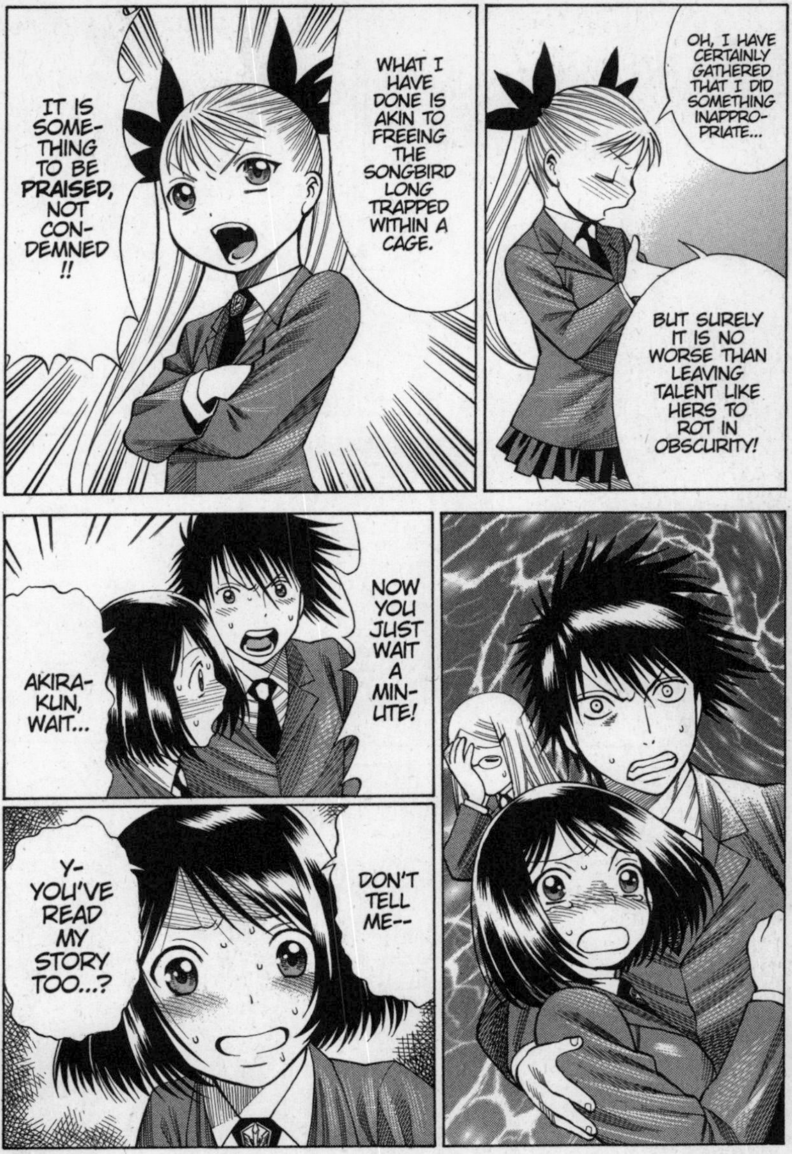
OH, I HAVE CERTAINLY GATHERED THAT I DID SOMETHING INAPPROPRIATE...
BUT SURELY IT IS NO WORSE THAN LEAVING TALENT LIKE HERS TO ROT IN OBSCURITY!
WHAT I HAVE DONE IS AKIN TO FREEING THE SONGBIRD LONG TRAPPED WITHIN A CAGE.
IT IS SOMETHING TO BE PRAISED, NOT CONDEMNED!!
NOW YOU JUST WAIT A MINUTE!
AKIRA-KUN, WAIT...
DON'T TELL ME--
Y-YOU'VE READ MY STORY TOO...?

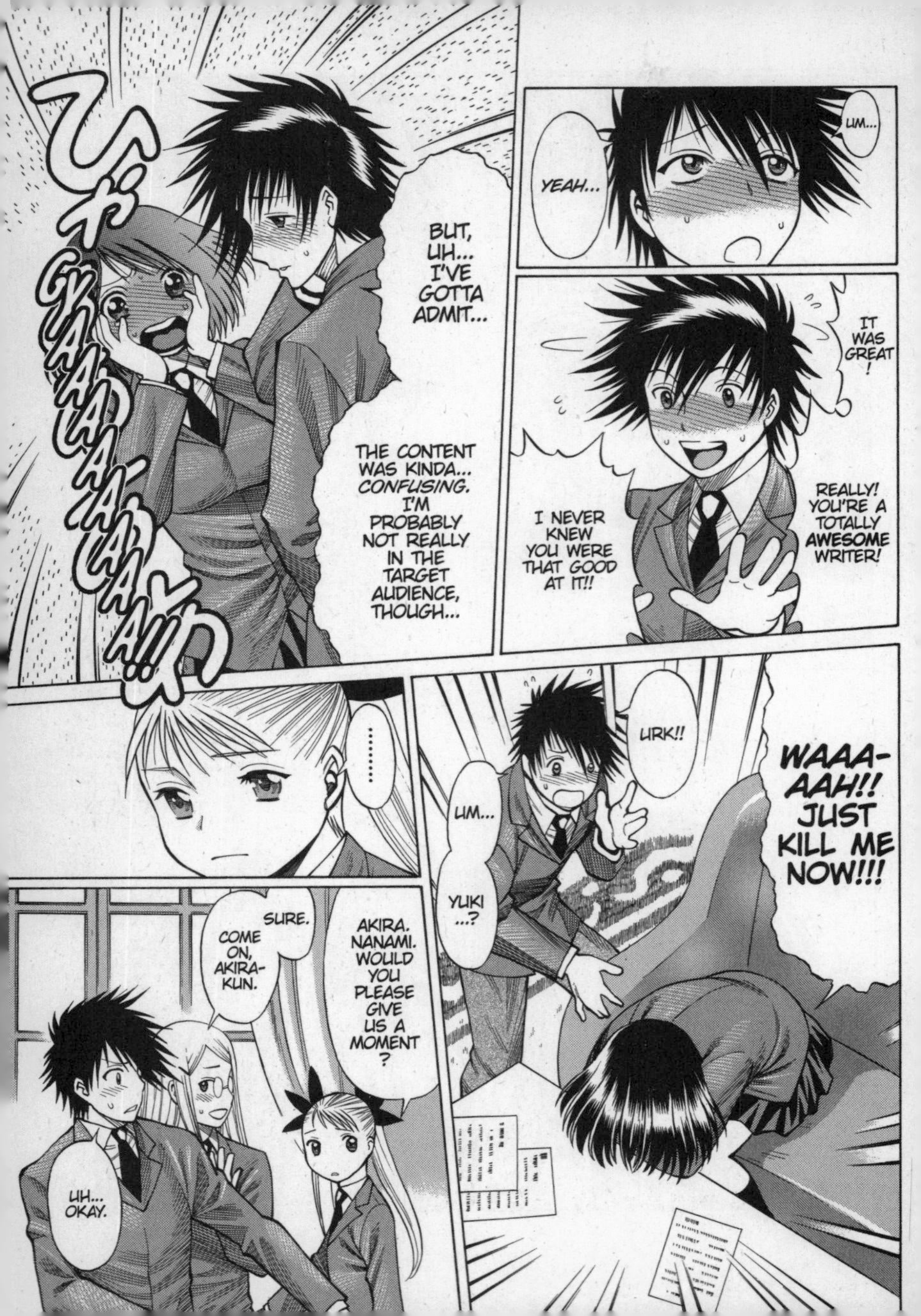
UM...
YEAH...
IT WAS GREAT!
REALLY! YOU'RE A TOTALLY AWESOME WRITER!
I NEVER KNEW YOU WERE THAT GOOD AT IT!!
BUT, UH... I'VE GOTTA ADMIT...
THE CONTENT WAS KINDA... CONFUSING. I'M PROBABLY NOT REALLY IN THE TARGET AUDIENCE, THOUGH...
ひゃ
GYAAAAAAAAA!!
WAAAA-AAH!! JUST KILL ME NOW!!!
URK!!
UM...
YUKI...?
......
AKIRA. NANAMI. WOULD YOU PLEASE GIVE US A MOMENT?
SURE. COME ON, AKIRA-KUN.
UH... OKAY.

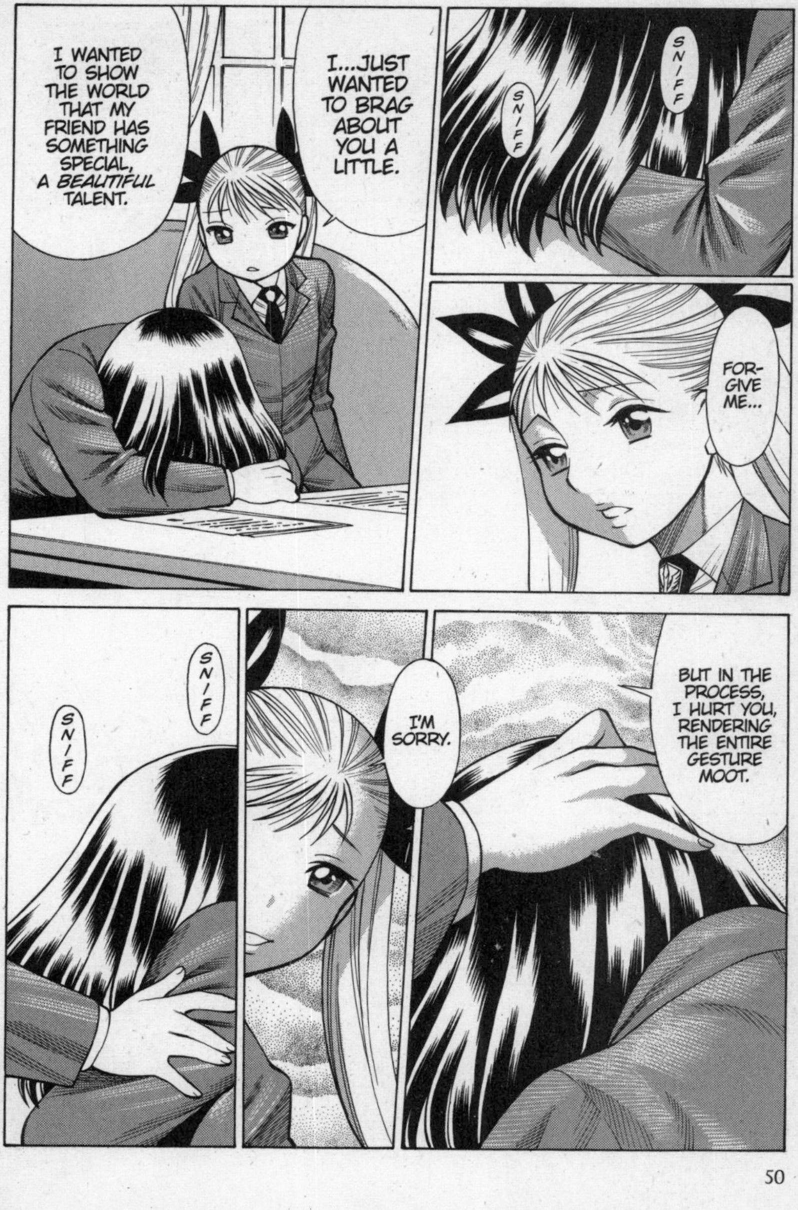
SNIFF
SNIFF
FOR-GIVE ME...
I...JUST WANTED TO BRAG ABOUT YOU A LITTLE.
I WANTED TO SHOW THE WORLD THAT MY FRIEND HAS SOMETHING SPECIAL, A *BEAUTIFUL* TALENT.
BUT IN THE PROCESS, I HURT YOU, RENDERING THE ENTIRE GESTURE MOOT.
I'M SORRY.
SNIFF
SNIFF

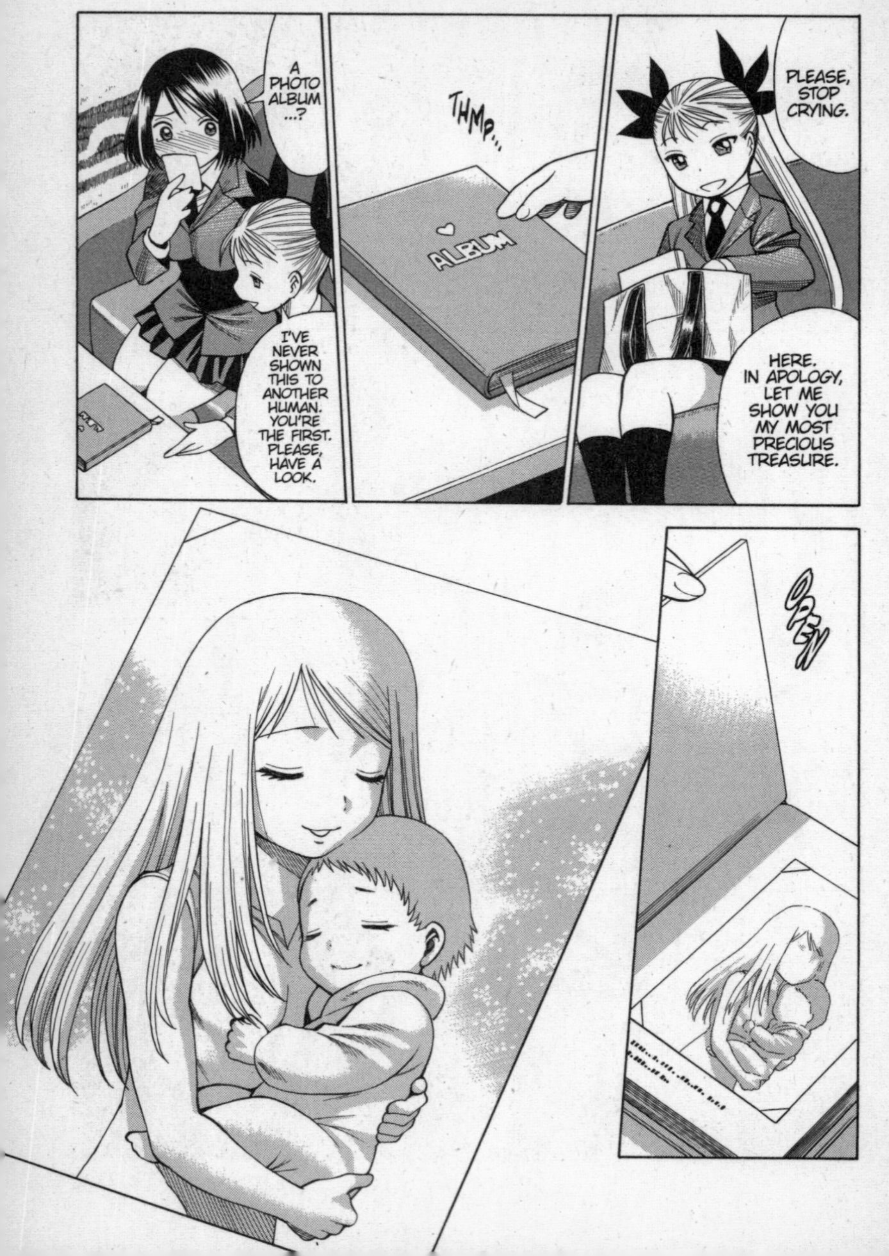
PLEASE, STOP CRYING.
HERE. IN APOLOGY, LET ME SHOW YOU MY MOST PRECIOUS TREASURE.
THMP...
ALBUM
A PHOTO ALBUM ...?
I'VE NEVER SHOWN THIS TO ANOTHER HUMAN. YOU'RE THE FIRST. PLEASE, HAVE A LOOK.
OPEN

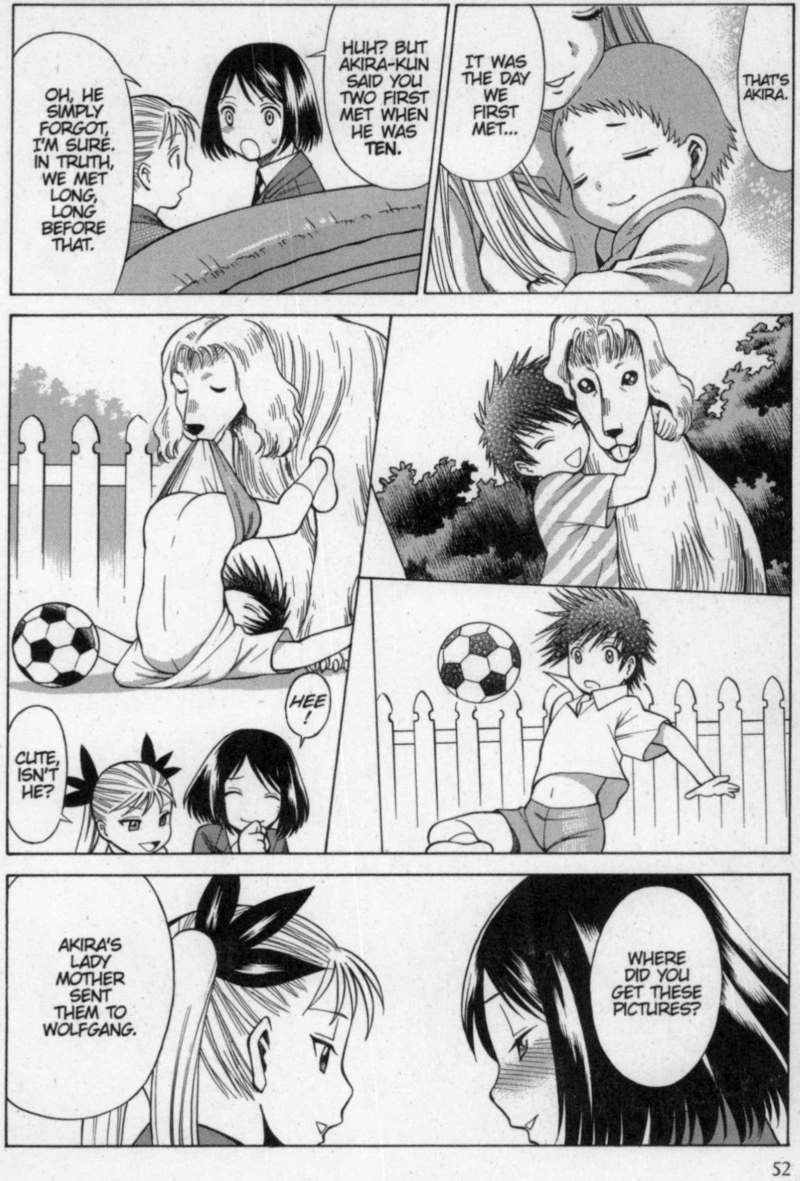
THAT'S AKIRA.
IT WAS THE DAY WE FIRST MET...
HUH? BUT AKIRA-KUN SAID YOU TWO FIRST MET WHEN HE WAS TEN.
OH, HE SIMPLY FORGOT, I'M SURE. IN TRUTH, WE MET LONG, LONG BEFORE THAT.
HEE!
CUTE, ISN'T HE?
WHERE DID YOU GET THESE PICTURES?
AKIRA'S LADY MOTHER SENT THEM TO WOLFGANG.

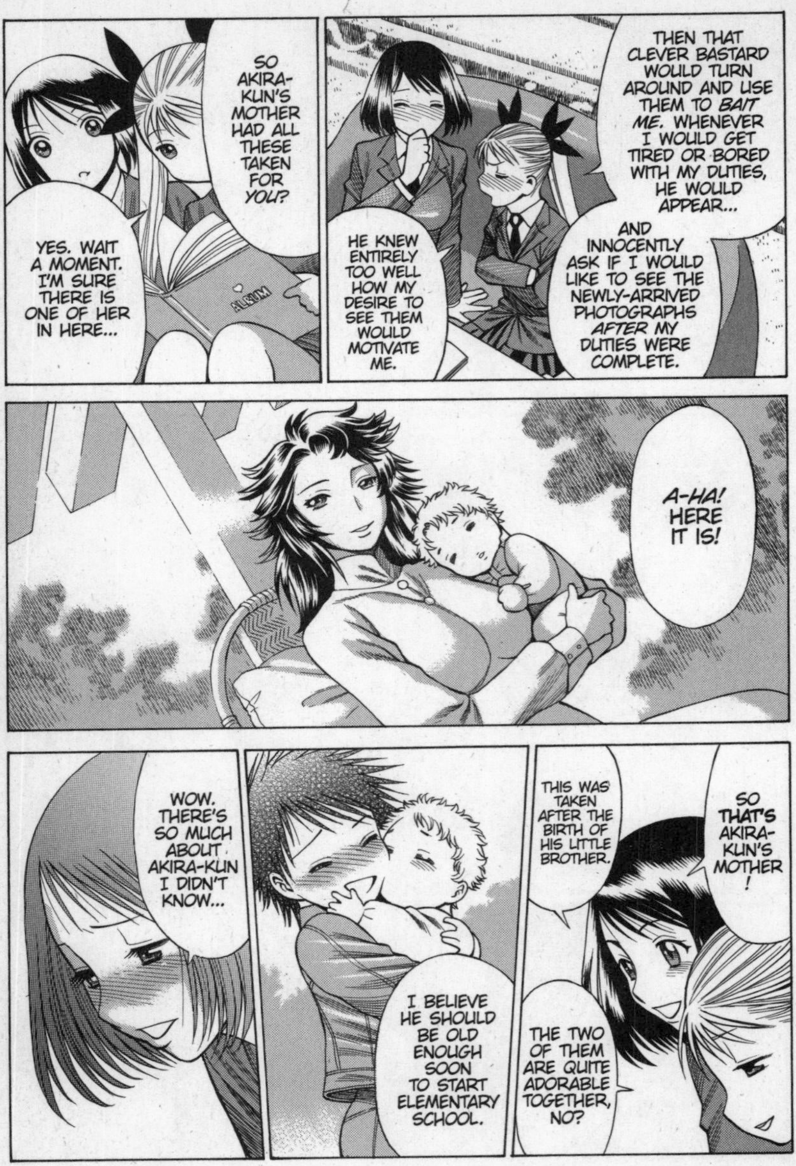
THEN THAT CLEVER BASTARD WOULD TURN AROUND AND USE THEM TO *BAIT ME*. WHENEVER I WOULD GET TIRED OR BORED WITH MY DUTIES, HE WOULD APPEAR...
AND INNOCENTLY ASK IF I WOULD LIKE TO SEE THE NEWLY-ARRIVED PHOTOGRAPHS *AFTER* MY DUTIES WERE COMPLETE.
HE KNEW ENTIRELY TOO WELL HOW MY DESIRE TO SEE THEM WOULD MOTIVATE ME.
SO AKIRA-KUN'S MOTHER HAD ALL THESE TAKEN FOR *YOU?*
YES. WAIT A MOMENT. I'M SURE THERE IS ONE OF HER IN HERE...
ALBUM
A-HA! HERE IT IS!
SO THAT'S AKIRA-KUN'S MOTHER!
THIS WAS TAKEN AFTER THE BIRTH OF HIS LITTLE BROTHER.
THE TWO OF THEM ARE QUITE ADORABLE TOGETHER, NO?
I BELIEVE HE SHOULD BE OLD ENOUGH SOON TO START ELEMENTARY SCHOOL.
WOW. THERE'S SO MUCH ABOUT AKIRA-KUN I DIDN'T KNOW...

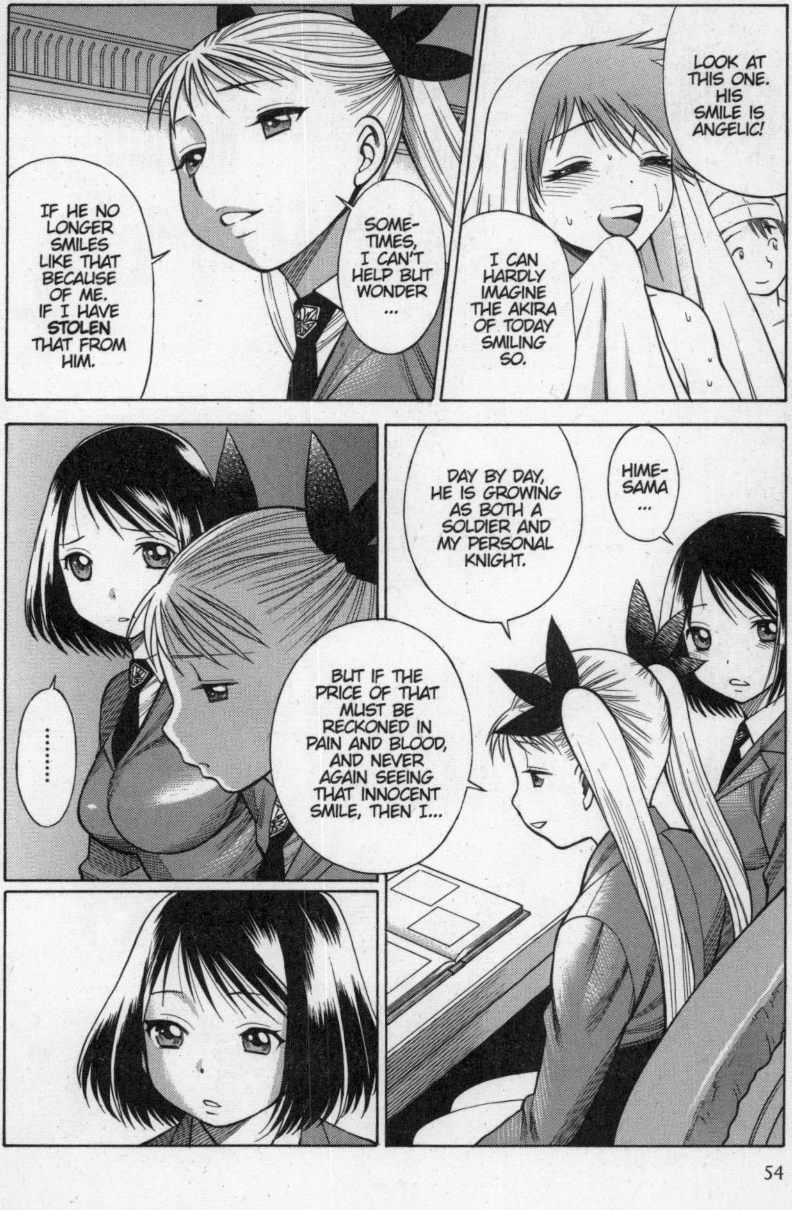
LOOK AT THIS ONE. HIS SMILE IS ANGELIC!
I CAN HARDLY IMAGINE THE AKIRA OF TODAY SMILING SO.
SOME-TIMES, I CAN'T HELP BUT WONDER ...
IF HE NO LONGER SMILES LIKE THAT BECAUSE OF ME. IF I HAVE **STOLEN** THAT FROM HIM.
HIME-SAMA ...
DAY BY DAY, HE IS GROWING AS BOTH A SOLDIER AND MY PERSONAL KNIGHT.
BUT IF THE PRICE OF THAT MUST BE RECKONED IN PAIN AND BLOOD, AND NEVER AGAIN SEEING THAT INNOCENT SMILE, THEN I...
....

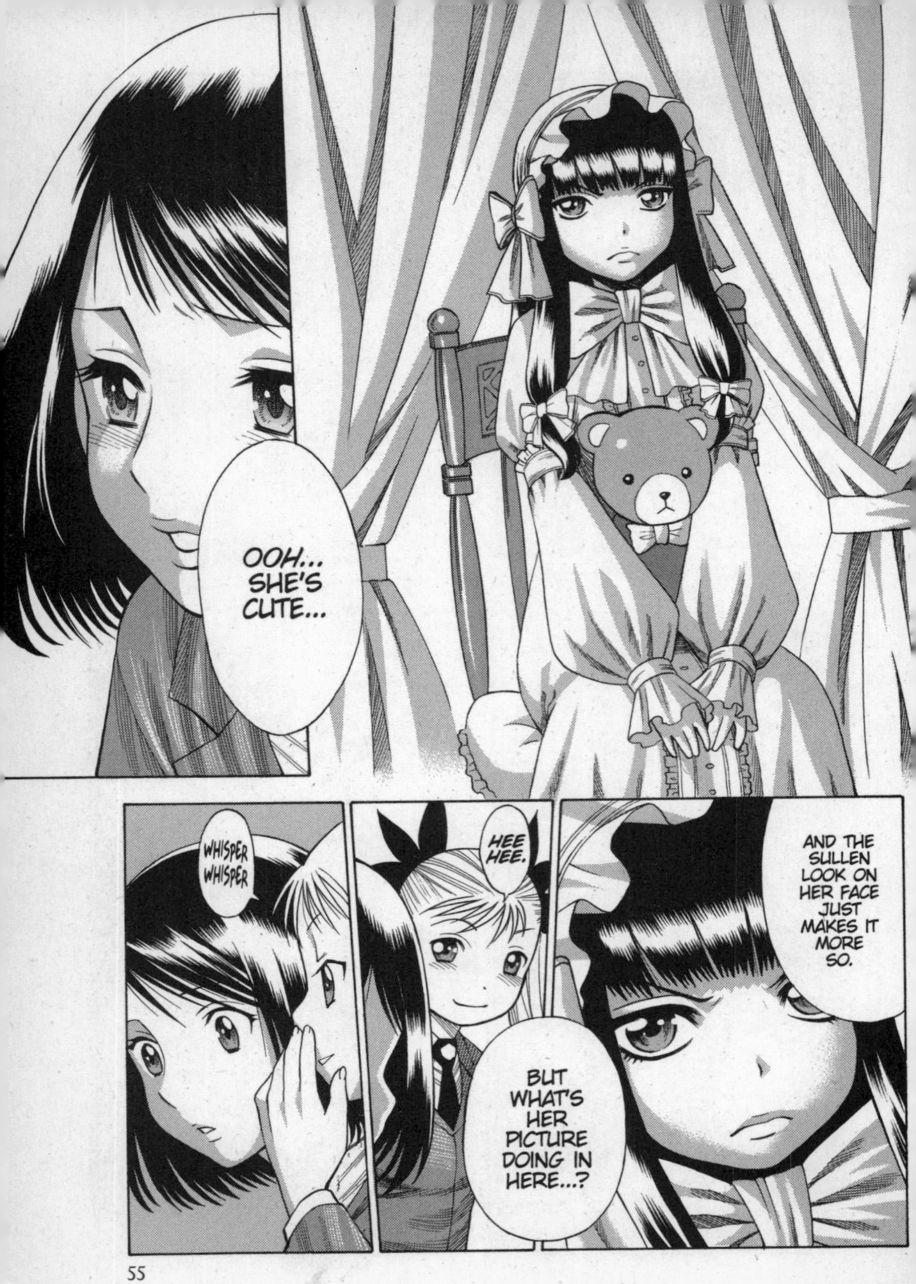
OOH... SHE'S CUTE...
AND THE SULLEN LOOK ON HER FACE JUST MAKES IT MORE SO.
HEE HEE.
BUT WHAT'S HER PICTURE DOING IN HERE...?
WHISPER WHISPER

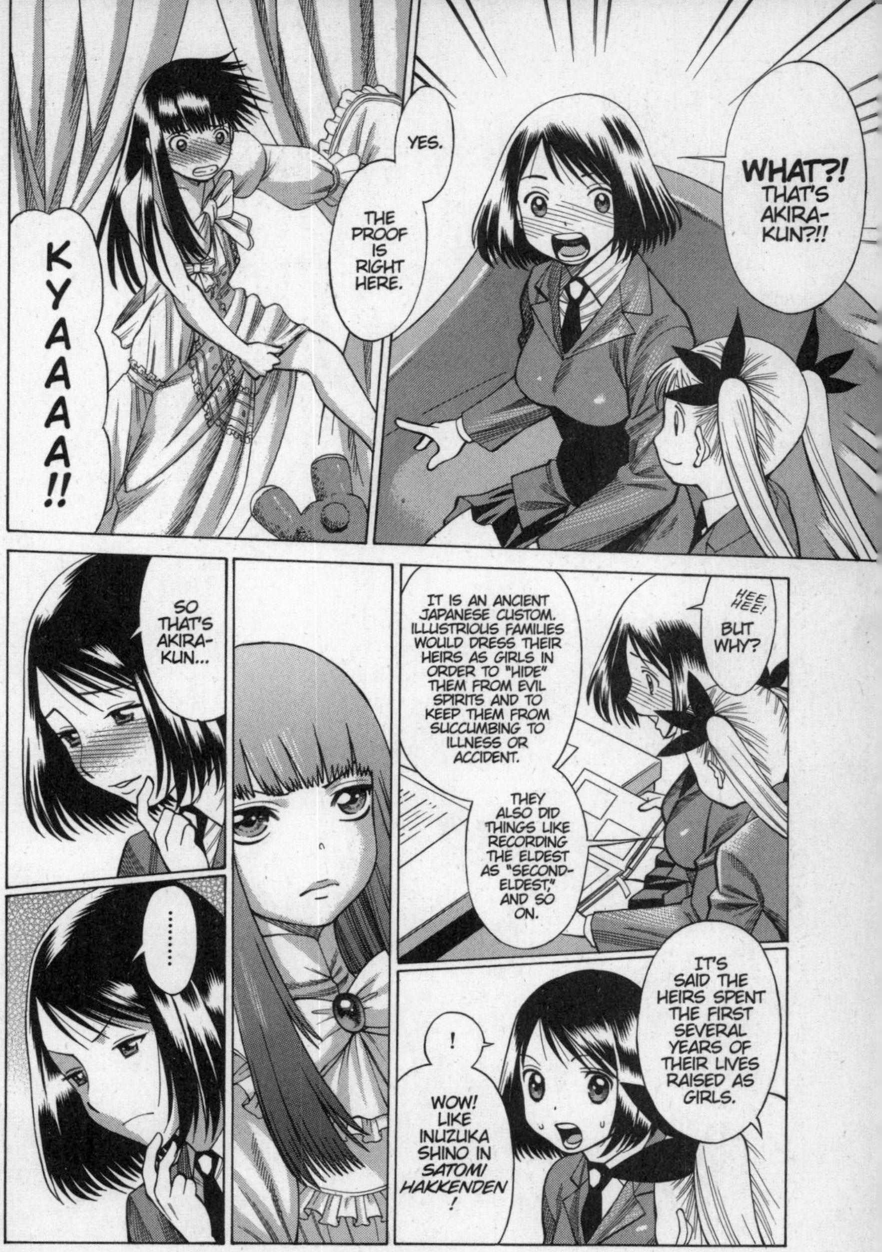
WHAT?! THAT'S AKIRA-KUN?!!
YES.
THE PROOF IS RIGHT HERE.
KYAAAAAA!!
HEE HEE!
BUT WHY?
IT IS AN ANCIENT JAPANESE CUSTOM. ILLUSTRIOUS FAMILIES WOULD DRESS THEIR HEIRS AS GIRLS IN ORDER TO "HIDE" THEM FROM EVIL SPIRITS AND TO KEEP THEM FROM SUCCUMBING TO ILLNESS OR ACCIDENT.
THEY ALSO DID THINGS LIKE RECORDING THE ELDEST AS "SECOND-ELDEST," AND SO ON.
IT'S SAID THE HEIRS SPENT THE FIRST SEVERAL YEARS OF THEIR LIVES RAISED AS GIRLS.
!
WOW! LIKE INUZUKA SHINO IN *SATOMI HAKKENDEN*!
SO THAT'S AKIRA-KUN...
......

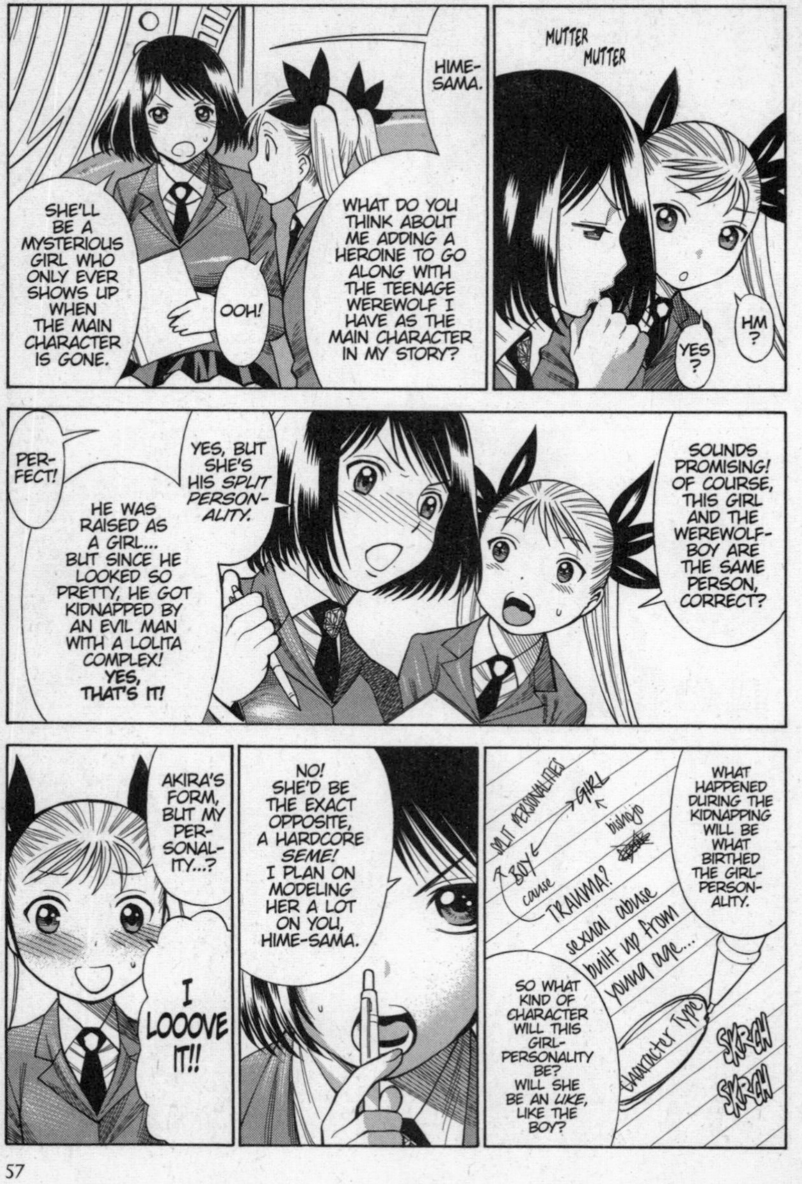
MUTTER MUTTER
HM?
YES?
HIME-SAMA.
WHAT DO YOU THINK ABOUT ME ADDING A HEROINE TO GO ALONG WITH THE TEENAGE WEREWOLF I HAVE AS THE MAIN CHARACTER IN MY STORY?
OOH!
SHE'LL BE A MYSTERIOUS GIRL WHO ONLY EVER SHOWS UP WHEN THE MAIN CHARACTER IS GONE.
SOUNDS PROMISING! OF COURSE, THIS GIRL AND THE WEREWOLF-BOY ARE THE SAME PERSON, CORRECT?
YES, BUT SHE'S HIS *SPLIT PERSONALITY*.
PERFECT!
HE WAS RAISED AS A GIRL... BUT SINCE HE LOOKED SO PRETTY, HE GOT KIDNAPPED BY AN EVIL MAN WITH A LOLITA COMPLEX! YES, THAT'S IT!
WHAT HAPPENED DURING THE KIDNAPPING WILL BE WHAT BIRTHED THE GIRL-PERSONALITY.
SPLIT PERSONALITIES
GIRL
BOY
bishojo
cause
TRAUMA?
sexual abuse
built up from
young age...
Character Type
SKRCH
SKRCH
SO WHAT KIND OF CHARACTER WILL THIS GIRL-PERSONALITY BE? WILL SHE BE AN *UKE*, LIKE THE BOY?
NO! SHE'D BE THE EXACT OPPOSITE, A HARDCORE *SEME*! I PLAN ON MODELING HER A LOT ON YOU, HIME-SAMA.
AKIRA'S FORM, BUT MY PERSONALITY...?
I LOOOVE IT!!

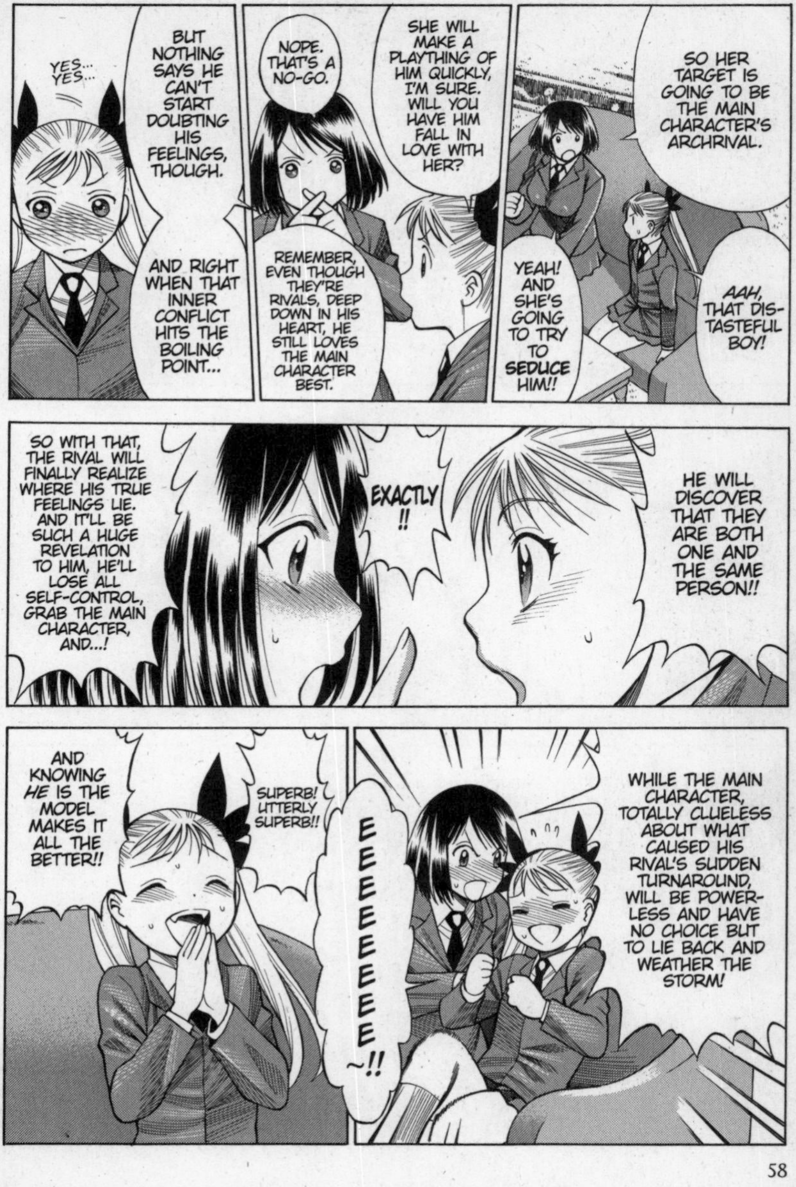
SO HER TARGET IS GOING TO BE THE MAIN CHARACTER'S ARCHRIVAL.
AAH, THAT DIS-TASTEFUL BOY!
YEAH! AND SHE'S GOING TO TRY TO **SEDUCE** HIM!!
SHE WILL MAKE A PLAYTHING OF HIM QUICKLY, I'M SURE. WILL YOU HAVE HIM FALL IN LOVE WITH HER?
NOPE. THAT'S A NO-GO.
REMEMBER, EVEN THOUGH THEY'RE RIVALS, DEEP DOWN IN HIS HEART, HE STILL LOVES THE MAIN CHARACTER BEST.
BUT NOTHING SAYS HE CAN'T START DOUBTING HIS FEELINGS, THOUGH.
YES... YES...
AND RIGHT WHEN THAT INNER CONFLICT HITS THE BOILING POINT...
HE WILL DISCOVER THAT THEY ARE BOTH ONE AND THE SAME PERSON!!
EXACTLY!!
SO WITH THAT, THE RIVAL WILL FINALLY REALIZE WHERE HIS TRUE FEELINGS LIE. AND IT'LL BE SUCH A HUGE REVELATION TO HIM, HE'LL LOSE ALL SELF-CONTROL, GRAB THE MAIN CHARACTER, AND...!
WHILE THE MAIN CHARACTER, TOTALLY CLUELESS ABOUT WHAT CAUSED HIS RIVAL'S SUDDEN TURNAROUND, WILL BE POWER-LESS AND HAVE NO CHOICE BUT TO LIE BACK AND WEATHER THE STORM!
EEEEEEEEEEE~!!
SUPERB! UTTERLY SUPERB!!
AND KNOWING *HE* IS THE MODEL MAKES IT ALL THE BETTER!!

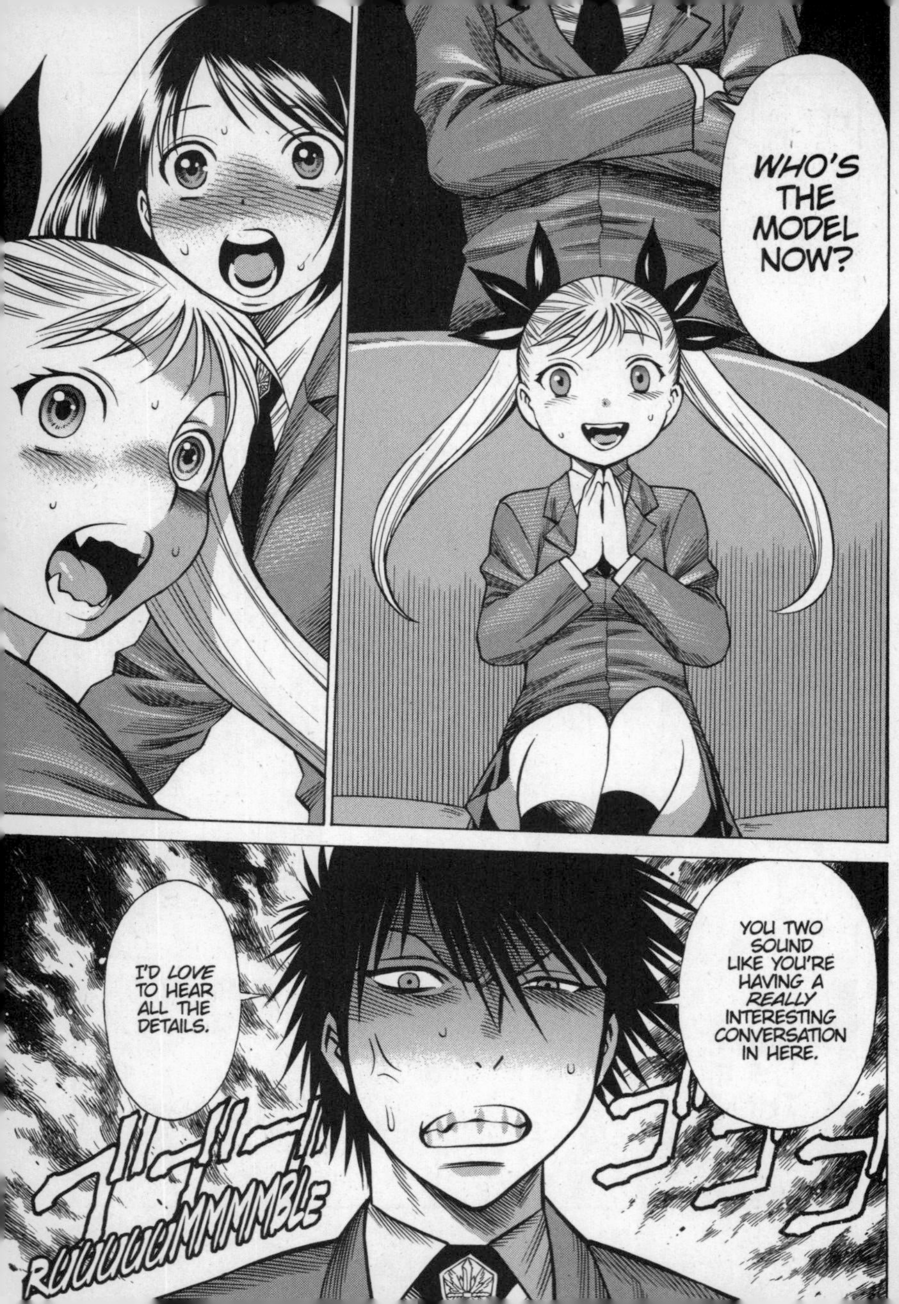
WHO'S THE MODEL NOW?
YOU TWO SOUND LIKE YOU'RE HAVING A *REALLY* INTERESTING CONVERSATION IN HERE.
I'D *LOVE* TO HEAR ALL THE DETAILS.
RUUUUUMMMMMBLE

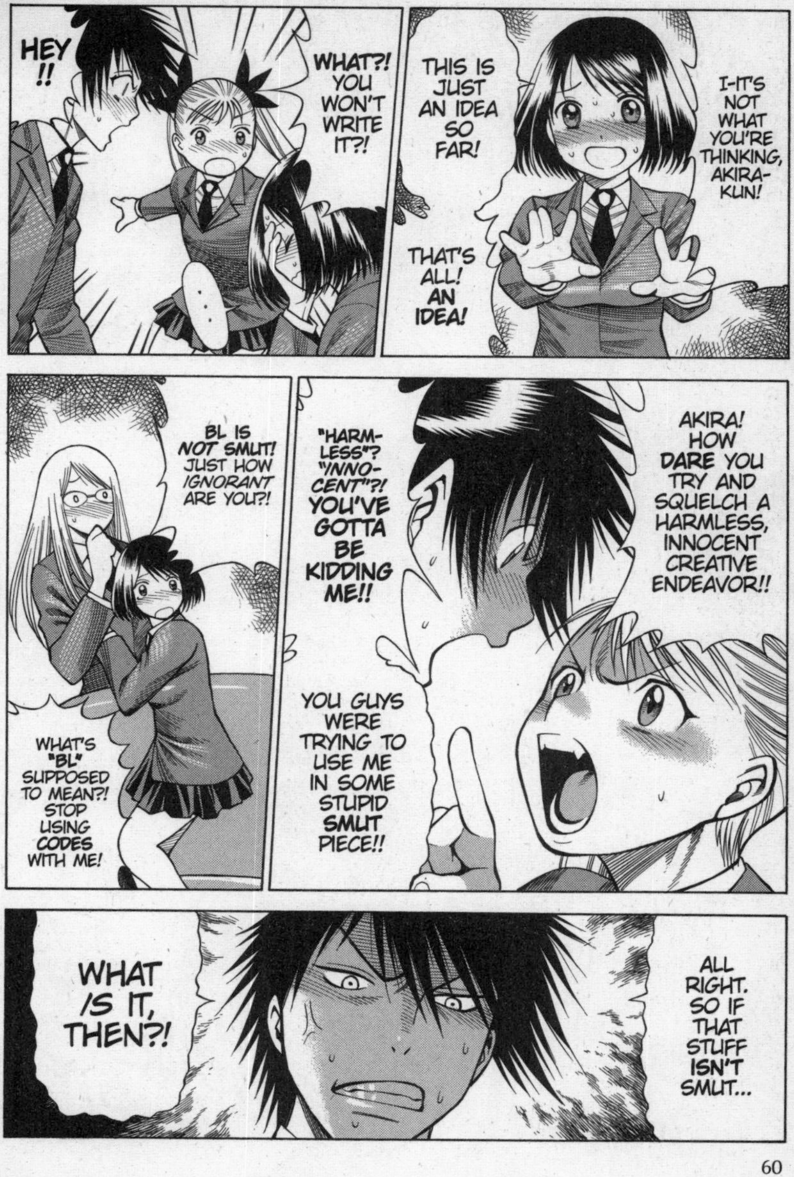
I-IT'S NOT WHAT YOU'RE THINKING, AKIRA-KUN!
THIS IS JUST AN IDEA SO FAR!
THAT'S ALL! AN IDEA!
WHAT?! YOU WON'T WRITE IT?!
HEY!!
...
AKIRA! HOW DARE YOU TRY AND SQUELCH A HARMLESS, INNOCENT CREATIVE ENDEAVOR!!
"HARMLESS"? "INNOCENT"?! YOU'VE GOTTA BE KIDDING ME!!
YOU GUYS WERE TRYING TO USE ME IN SOME STUPID SMUT PIECE!!
BL IS NOT SMUT! JUST HOW IGNORANT ARE YOU?!
WHAT'S "BL" SUPPOSED TO MEAN?! STOP USING CODES WITH ME!
ALL RIGHT. SO IF THAT STUFF ISN'T SMUT...
WHAT IS IT, THEN?!

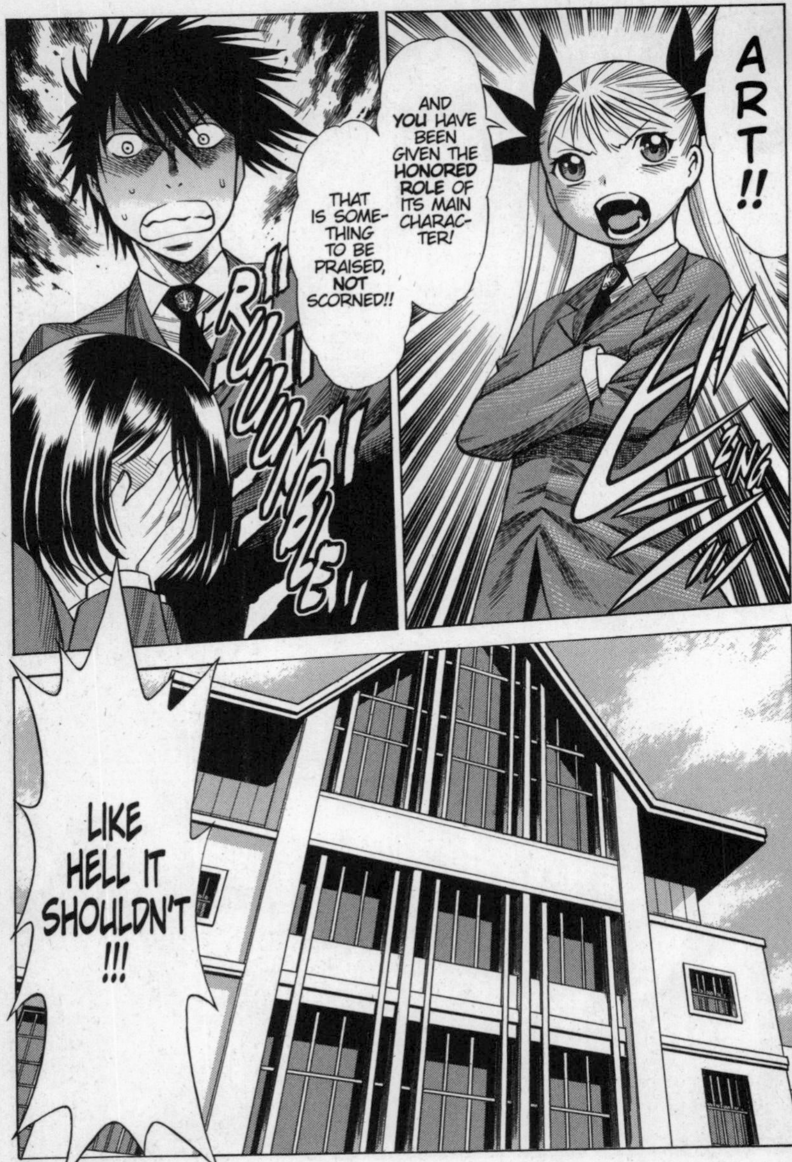
ART!!
AND YOU HAVE BEEN GIVEN THE HONORED ROLE OF ITS MAIN CHARACTER!
THAT IS SOMETHING TO BE PRAISED, NOT SCORNED!!
RUUUMBLE
LIKE HELL IT SHOULDN'T!!!

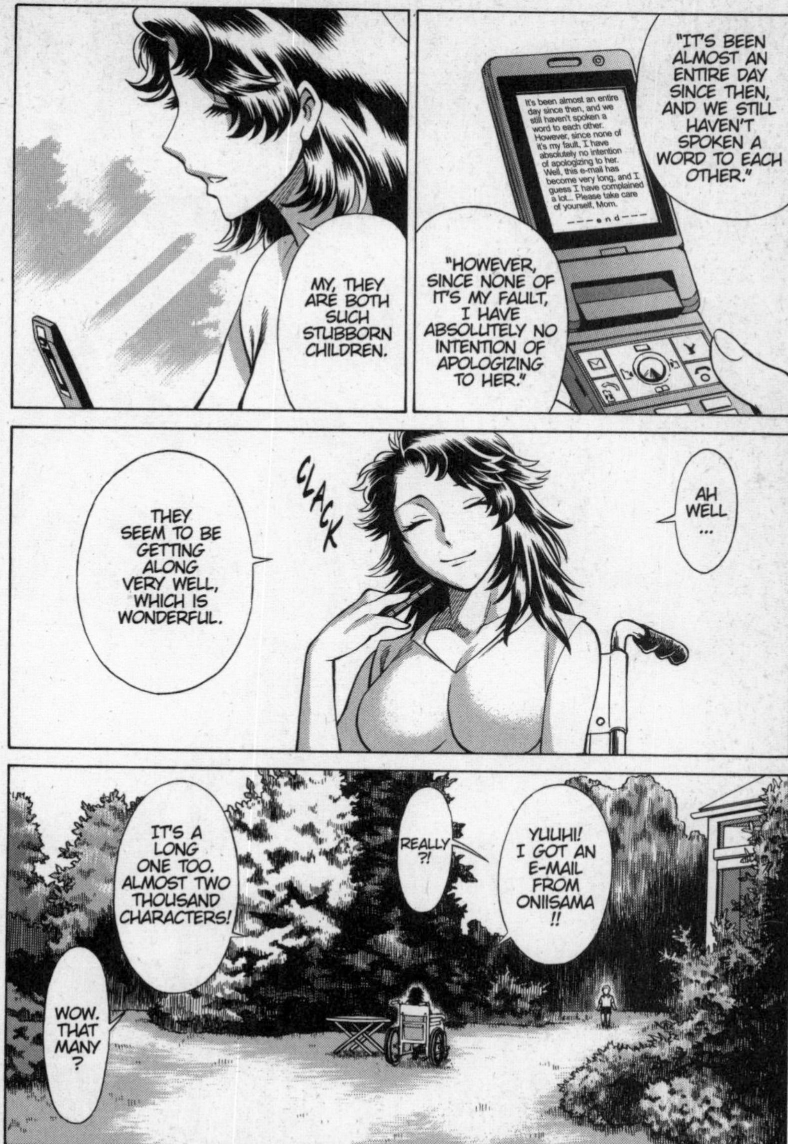
"IT'S BEEN ALMOST AN ENTIRE DAY SINCE THEN, AND WE STILL HAVEN'T SPOKEN A WORD TO EACH OTHER."
It's been almost an entire day since then, and we still haven't spoken a word to each other. However, since none of it's my fault, I have absolutely no intention of apologizing to her. Well, this e-mail has become very long, and I guess I have complained a lot... Please take care of yourself, Mom.
---end---
"HOWEVER, SINCE NONE OF IT'S MY FAULT, I HAVE ABSOLUTELY NO INTENTION OF APOLOGIZING TO HER."
MY, THEY ARE BOTH SUCH STUBBORN CHILDREN.
AH WELL ...
CLACK
THEY SEEM TO BE GETTING ALONG VERY WELL, WHICH IS WONDERFUL.
YUUHI! I GOT AN E-MAIL FROM ONIISAMA !!
REALLY ?!
IT'S A LONG ONE TOO. ALMOST TWO THOUSAND CHARACTERS!
WOW. THAT MANY ?

Chapter 34: The Queen's Wolfman

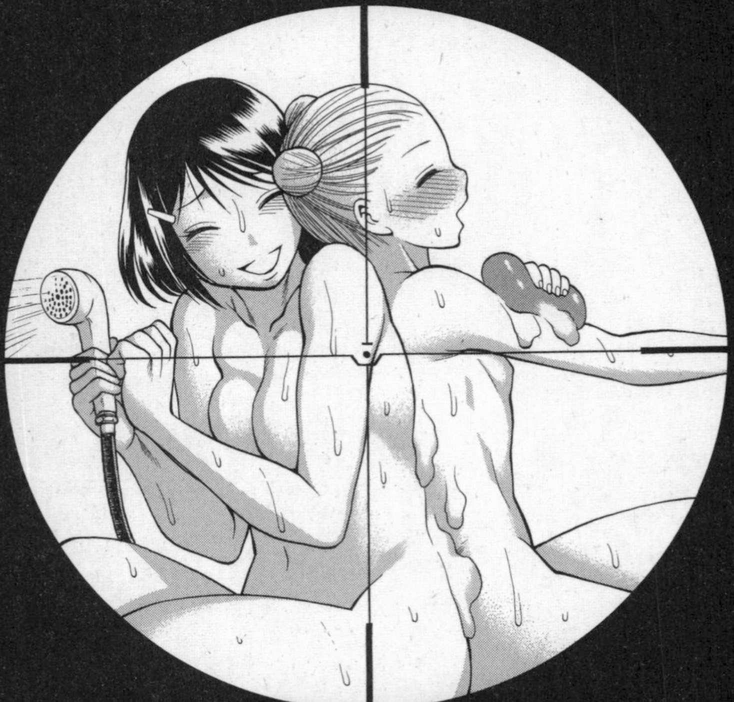

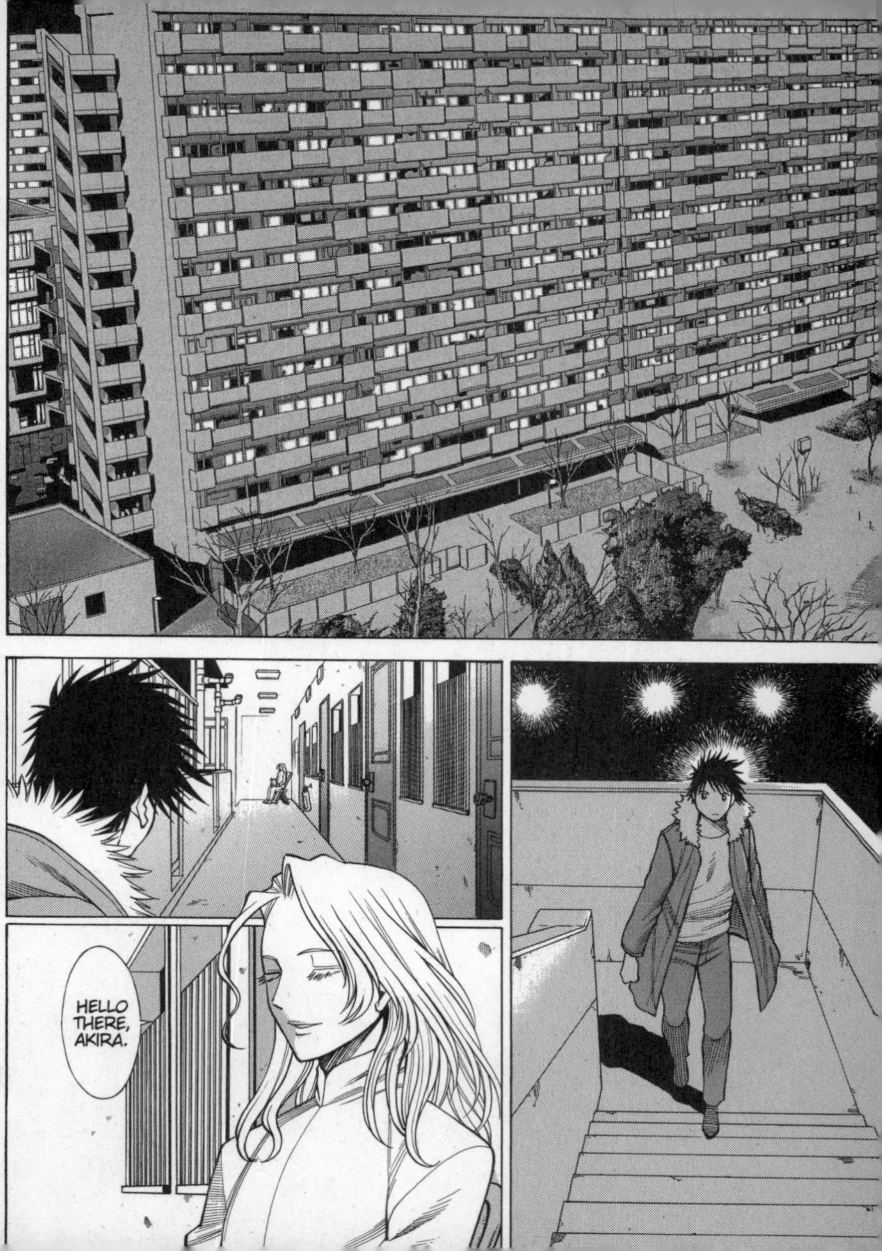
HELLO THERE, AKIRA.

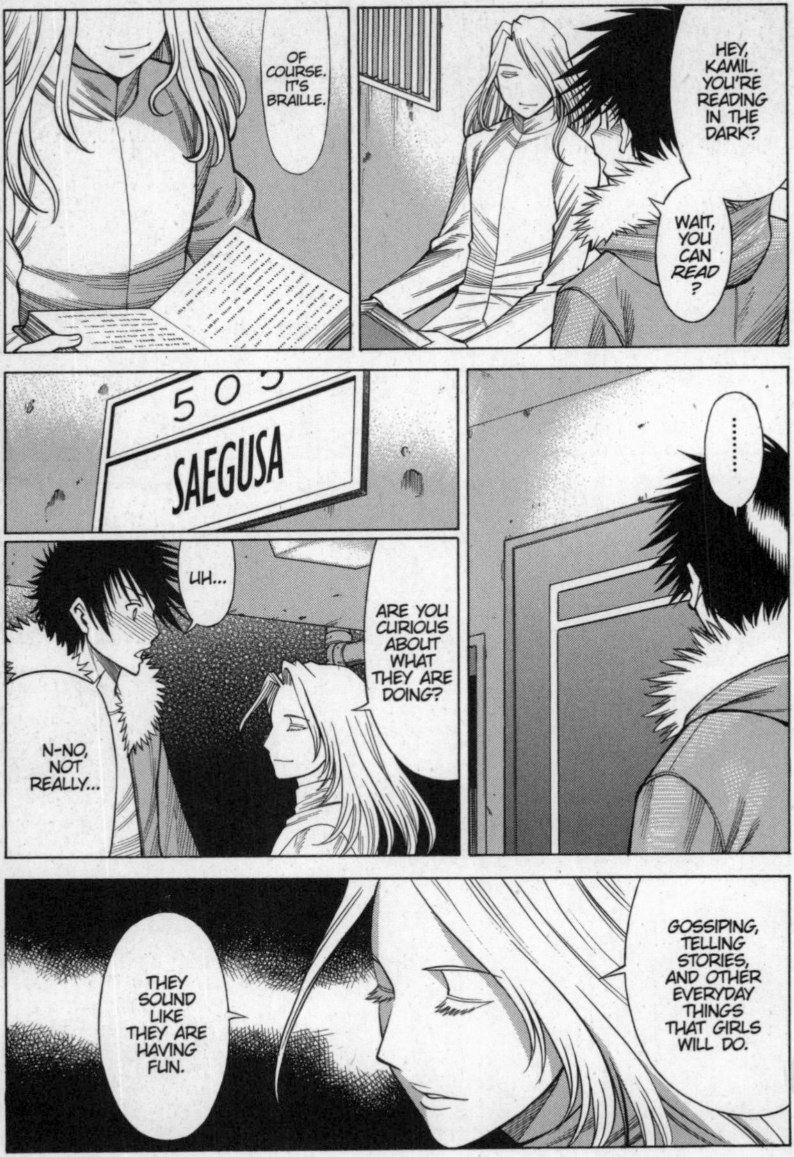
HEY, KAMIL. YOU'RE READING IN THE DARK?
WAIT, YOU CAN READ?
OF COURSE. IT'S BRAILLE.
......
505
SAEGUSA
ARE YOU CURIOUS ABOUT WHAT THEY ARE DOING?
UH...
N-NO, NOT REALLY...
GOSSIPING, TELLING STORIES, AND OTHER EVERYDAY THINGS THAT GIRLS WILL DO.
THEY SOUND LIKE THEY ARE HAVING FUN.

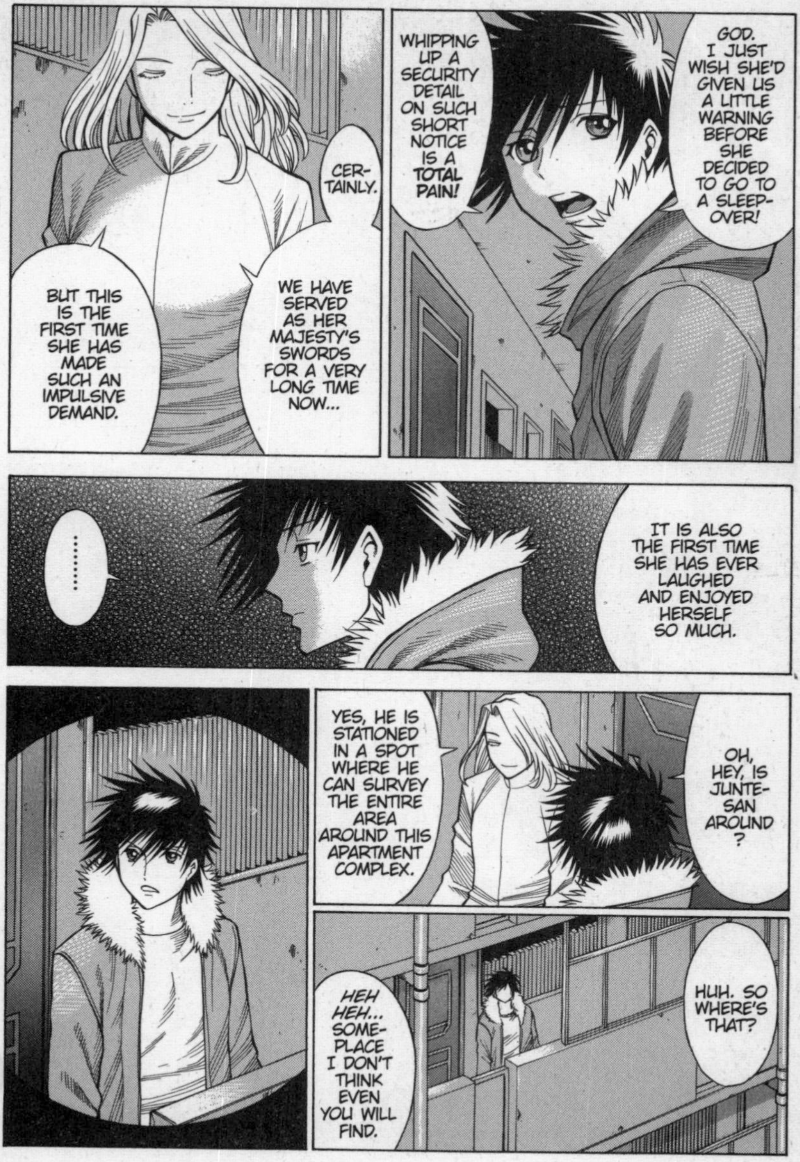
GOD. I JUST WISH SHE'D GIVEN US A LITTLE WARNING BEFORE SHE DECIDED TO GO TO A SLEEP-OVER!
WHIPPING UP A SECURITY DETAIL ON SUCH SHORT NOTICE IS A **TOTAL** PAIN!
CER-TAINLY.
WE HAVE SERVED AS HER MAJESTY'S SWORDS FOR A VERY LONG TIME NOW...
BUT THIS IS THE FIRST TIME SHE HAS MADE SUCH AN IMPULSIVE DEMAND.
IT IS ALSO THE FIRST TIME SHE HAS EVER LAUGHED AND ENJOYED HERSELF SO MUCH.
....
OH, HEY, IS JUNTE-SAN AROUND?
YES, HE IS STATIONED IN A SPOT WHERE HE CAN SURVEY THE ENTIRE AREA AROUND THIS APARTMENT COMPLEX.
HUH. SO WHERE'S THAT?
HEH HEH... SOME-PLACE I DON'T THINK EVEN YOU WILL FIND.

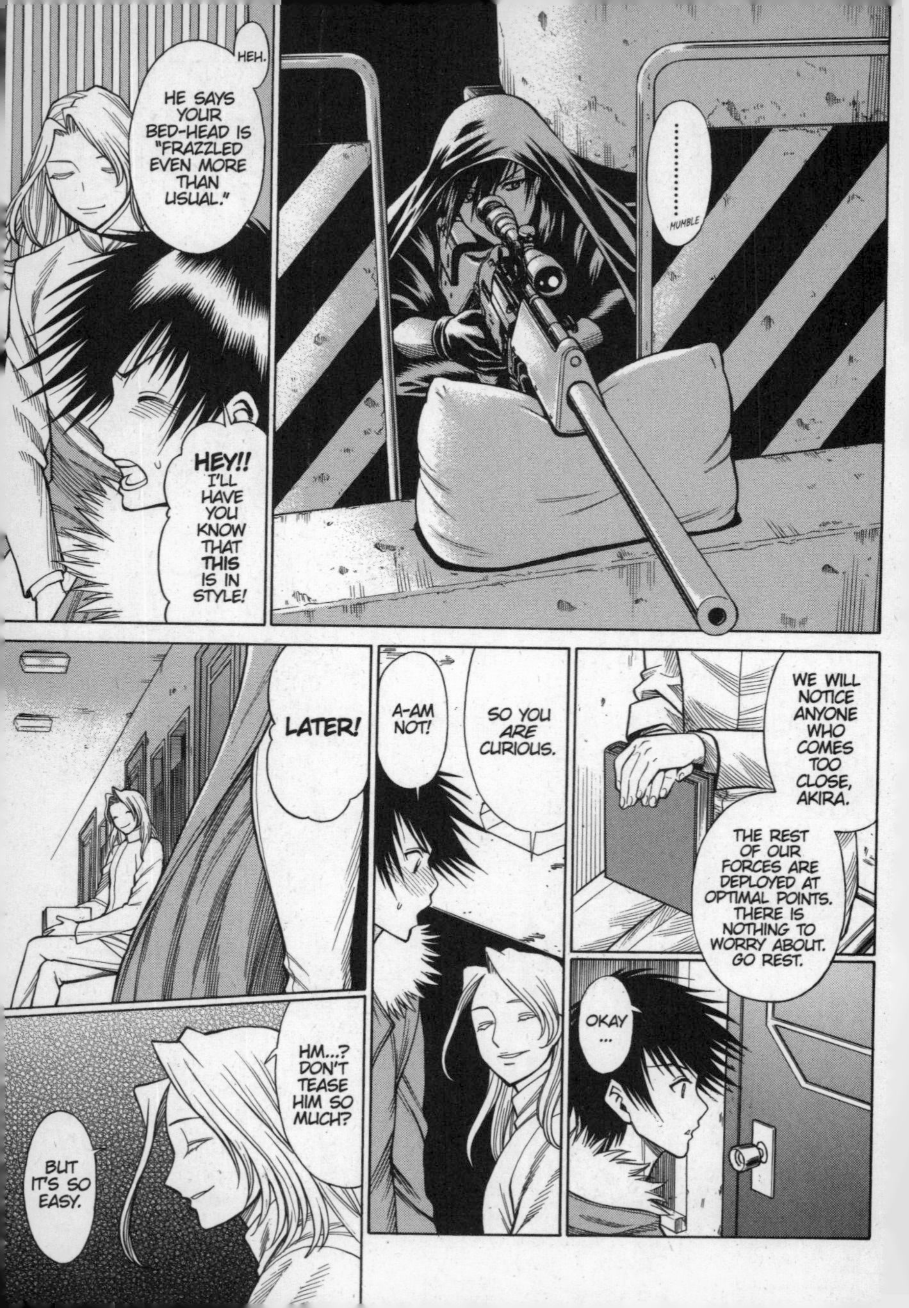
……
MUMBLE
HEH.
HE SAYS YOUR BED-HEAD IS "FRAZZLED EVEN MORE THAN USUAL."
HEY!! I'LL HAVE YOU KNOW THAT THIS IS IN STYLE!
WE WILL NOTICE ANYONE WHO COMES TOO CLOSE, AKIRA.
THE REST OF OUR FORCES ARE DEPLOYED AT OPTIMAL POINTS. THERE IS NOTHING TO WORRY ABOUT. GO REST.
OKAY ...
SO YOU ARE CURIOUS.
A-AM NOT!
LATER!
HM...? DON'T TEASE HIM SO MUCH?
BUT IT'S SO EASY.

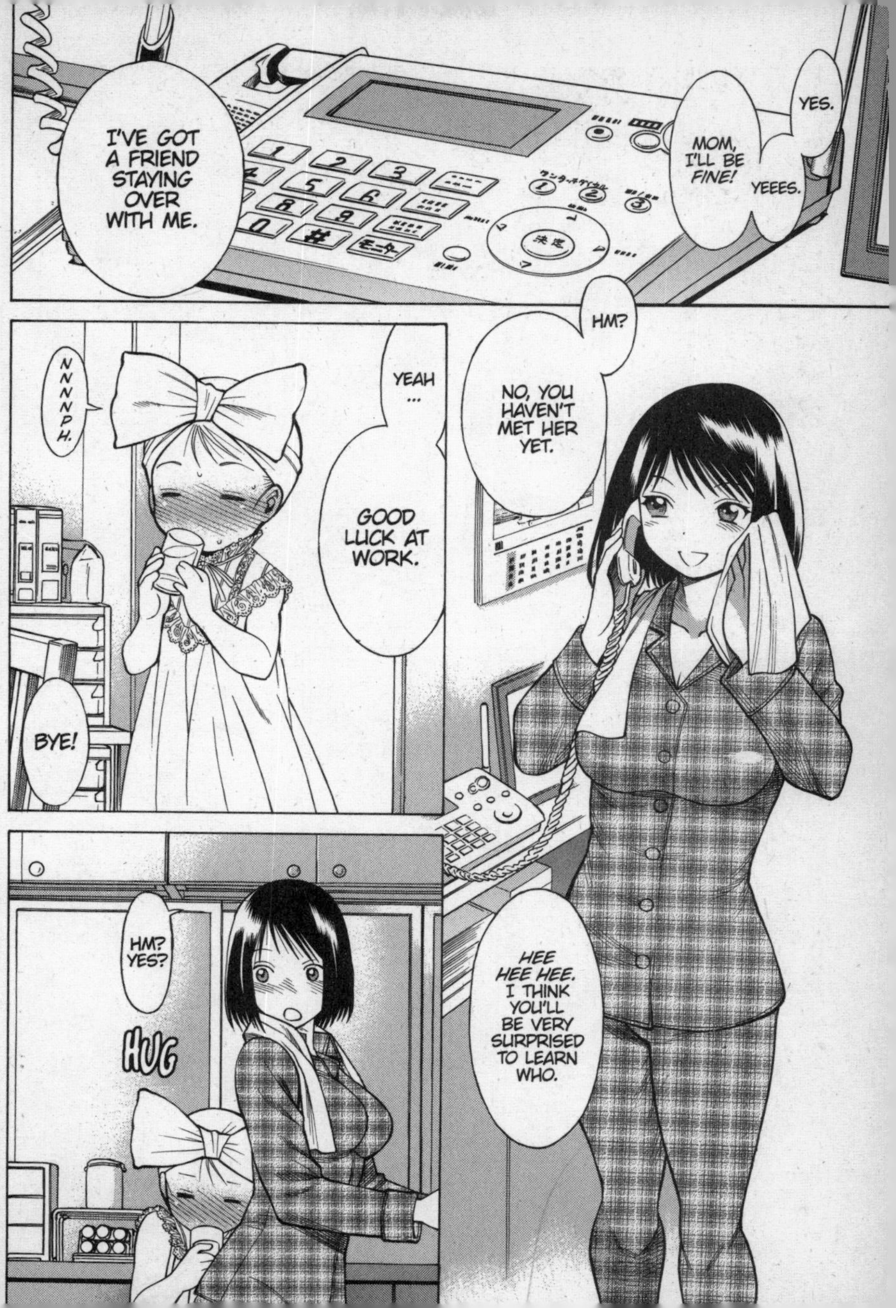
YES.
MOM, I'LL BE FINE!
YEEES.
I'VE GOT A FRIEND STAYING OVER WITH ME.
HM?
NO, YOU HAVEN'T MET HER YET.
HEE HEE HEE. I THINK YOU'LL BE VERY SURPRISED TO LEARN WHO.
YEAH ...
GOOD LUCK AT WORK.
NNNNPH.
BYE!
HM? YES?
HUG

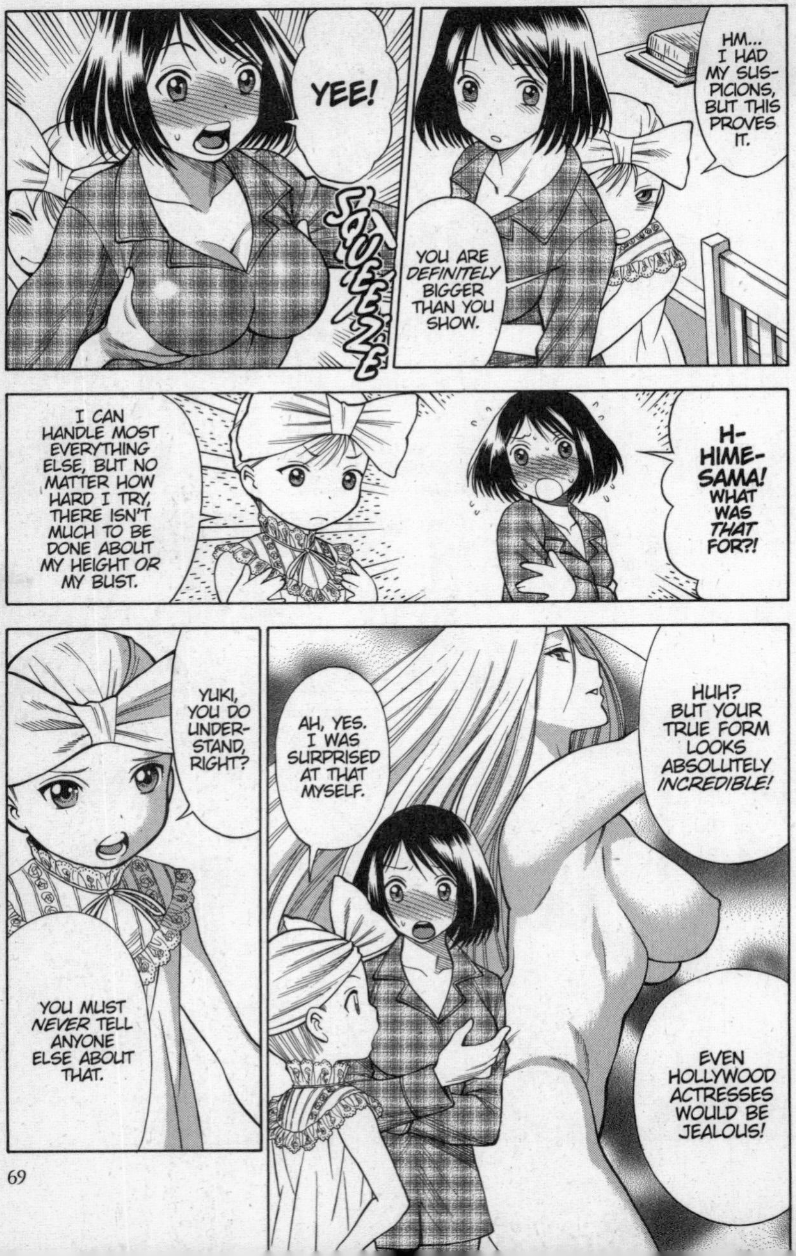
HM... I HAD MY SUSPICIONS, BUT THIS PROVES IT.
YOU ARE DEFINITELY BIGGER THAN YOU SHOW.
YEE!
SQUEEZE
H-HIME-SAMA! WHAT WAS THAT FOR?!
I CAN HANDLE MOST EVERYTHING ELSE, BUT NO MATTER HOW HARD I TRY, THERE ISN'T MUCH TO BE DONE ABOUT MY HEIGHT OR MY BUST.
HUH? BUT YOUR TRUE FORM LOOKS ABSOLUTELY INCREDIBLE!
AH, YES. I WAS SURPRISED AT THAT MYSELF.
EVEN HOLLYWOOD ACTRESSES WOULD BE JEALOUS!
YUKI, YOU DO UNDERSTAND, RIGHT?
YOU MUST NEVER TELL ANYONE ELSE ABOUT THAT.

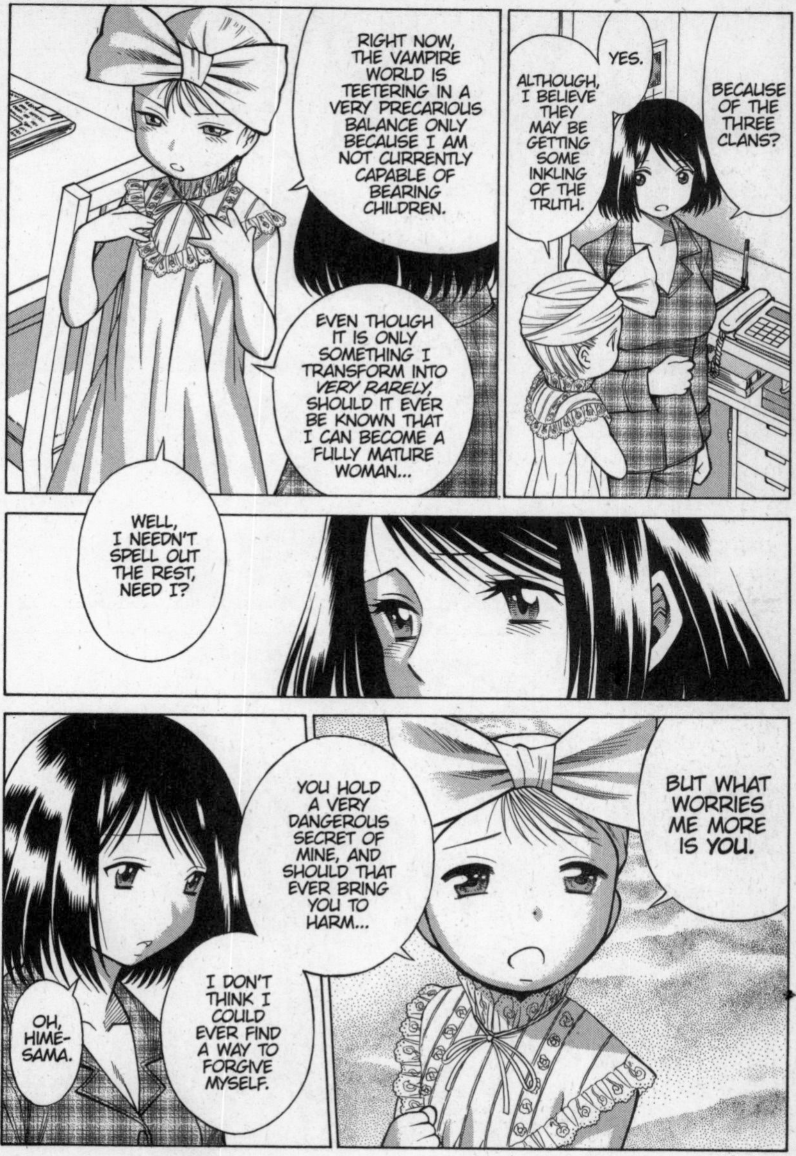
BECAUSE OF THE THREE CLANS?
YES.
ALTHOUGH, I BELIEVE THEY MAY BE GETTING SOME INKLING OF THE TRUTH.
RIGHT NOW, THE VAMPIRE WORLD IS TEETERING IN A VERY PRECARIOUS BALANCE ONLY BECAUSE I AM NOT CURRENTLY CAPABLE OF BEARING CHILDREN.
EVEN THOUGH IT IS ONLY SOMETHING I TRANSFORM INTO *VERY RARELY*, SHOULD IT EVER BE KNOWN THAT I CAN BECOME A FULLY MATURE WOMAN...
WELL, I NEEDN'T SPELL OUT THE REST, NEED I?
BUT WHAT WORRIES ME MORE IS **YOU**.
YOU HOLD A VERY DANGEROUS SECRET OF MINE, AND SHOULD THAT EVER BRING YOU TO HARM...
I DON'T THINK I COULD EVER FIND A WAY TO FORGIVE MYSELF.
OH, HIME-SAMA.

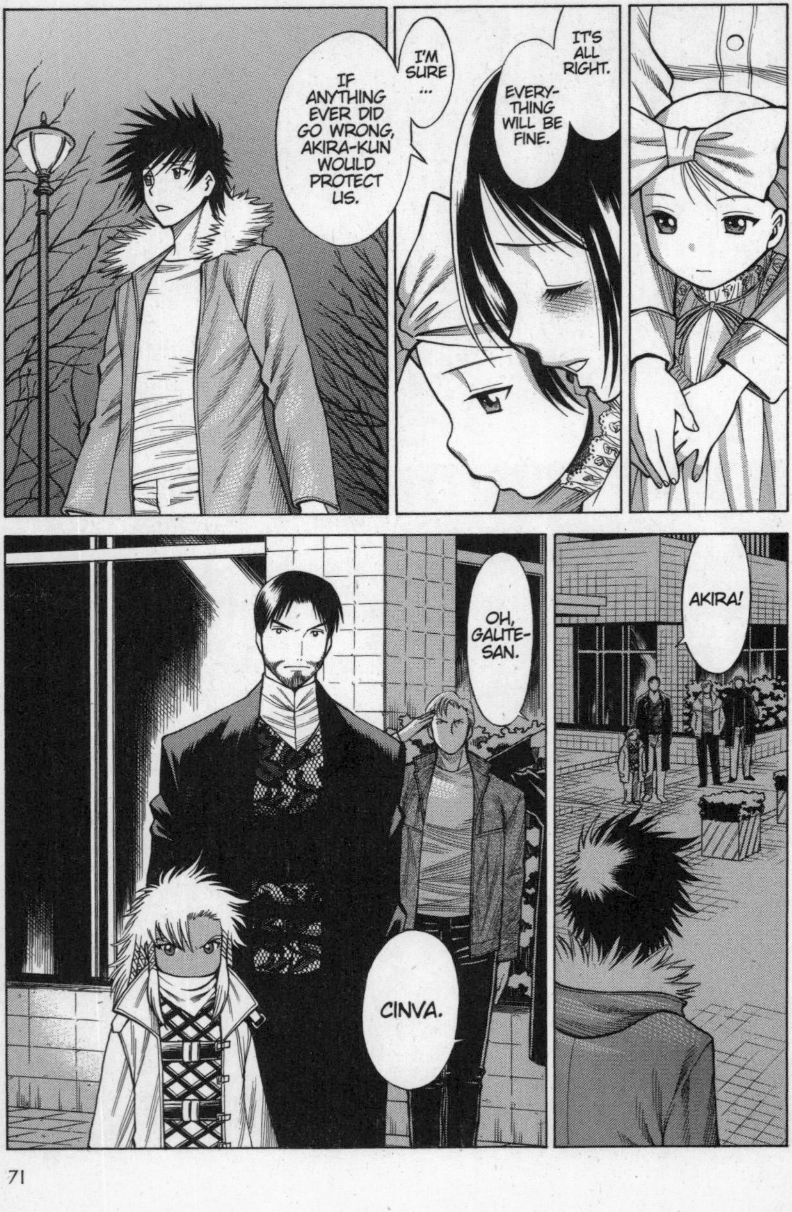
IT'S ALL RIGHT.
EVERY-THING WILL BE FINE.
I'M SURE ...
IF ANYTHING EVER DID GO WRONG, AKIRA-KUN WOULD PROTECT US.
AKIRA!
OH, GAUTE-SAN.
CINVA.

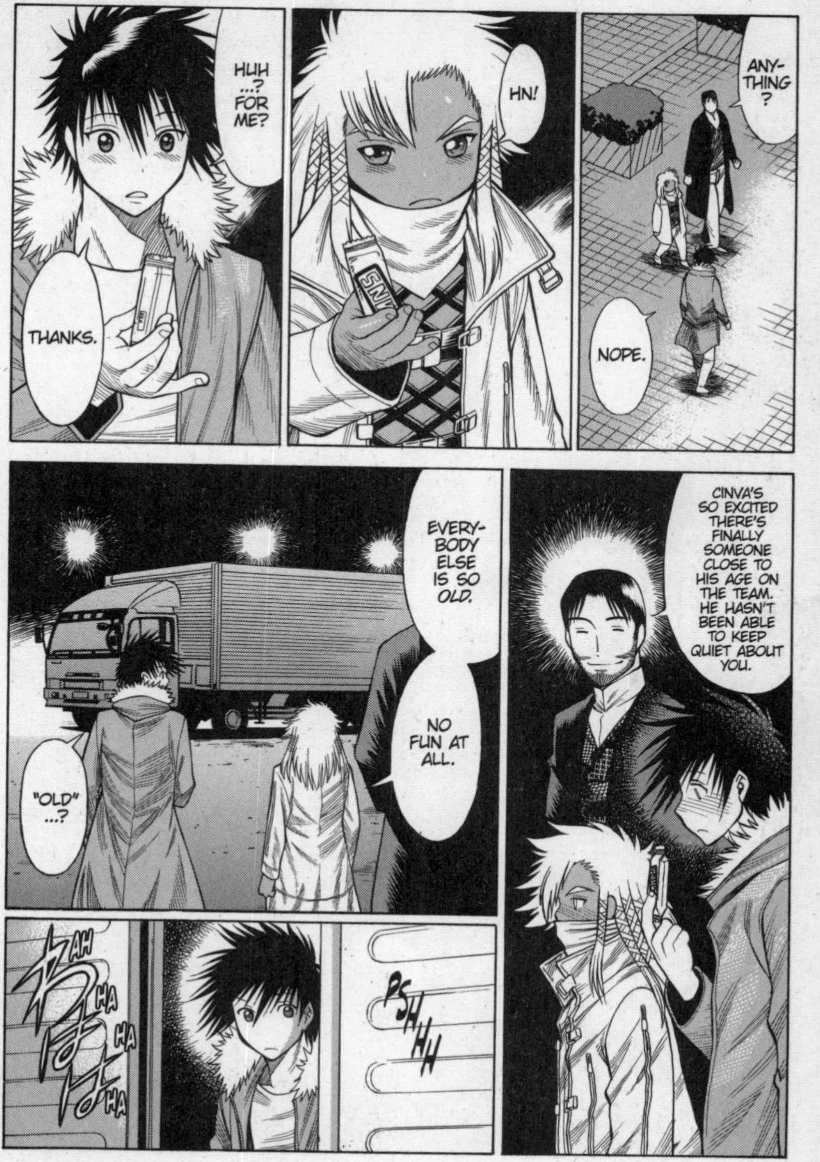
ANY-THING?
NOPE.
HN!
HUH...? FOR ME?
THANKS.
CINVA'S SO EXCITED THERE'S FINALLY SOMEONE CLOSE TO HIS AGE ON THE TEAM. HE HASN'T BEEN ABLE TO KEEP QUIET ABOUT YOU.
EVERY-BODY ELSE IS SO *OLD.*
NO FUN AT ALL.
"OLD"...?
PSHHH
AH HA HA HA

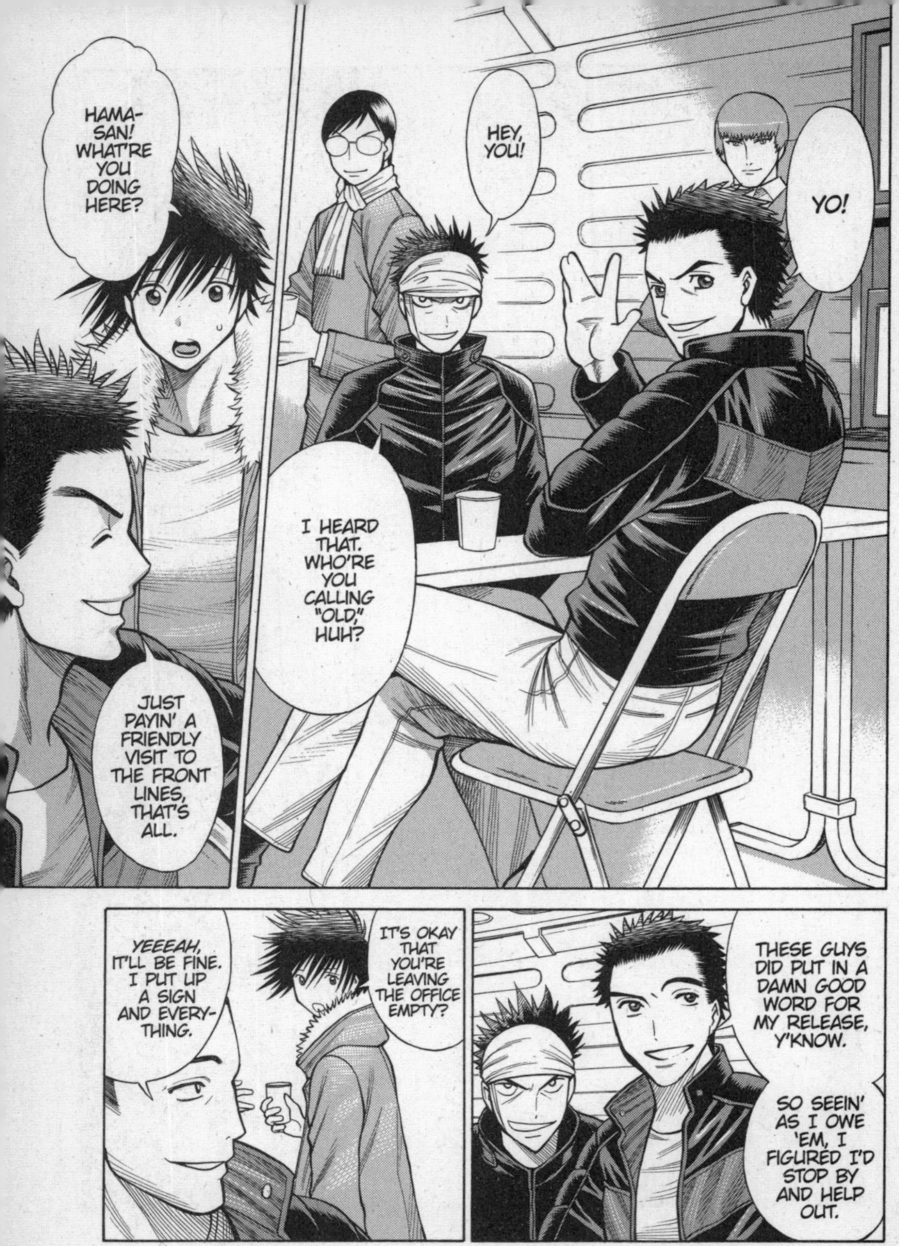
YO!
HEY, YOU!
I HEARD THAT. WHO'RE YOU CALLING "OLD," HUH?
HAMA-SAN! WHAT'RE YOU DOING HERE?
JUST PAYIN' A FRIENDLY VISIT TO THE FRONT LINES, THAT'S ALL.
THESE GUYS DID PUT IN A DAMN GOOD WORD FOR MY RELEASE, Y'KNOW.
SO SEEIN' AS I OWE 'EM, I FIGURED I'D STOP BY AND HELP OUT.
IT'S OKAY THAT YOU'RE LEAVING THE OFFICE EMPTY?
YEEEAH, IT'LL BE FINE. I PUT UP A SIGN AND EVERYTHING.

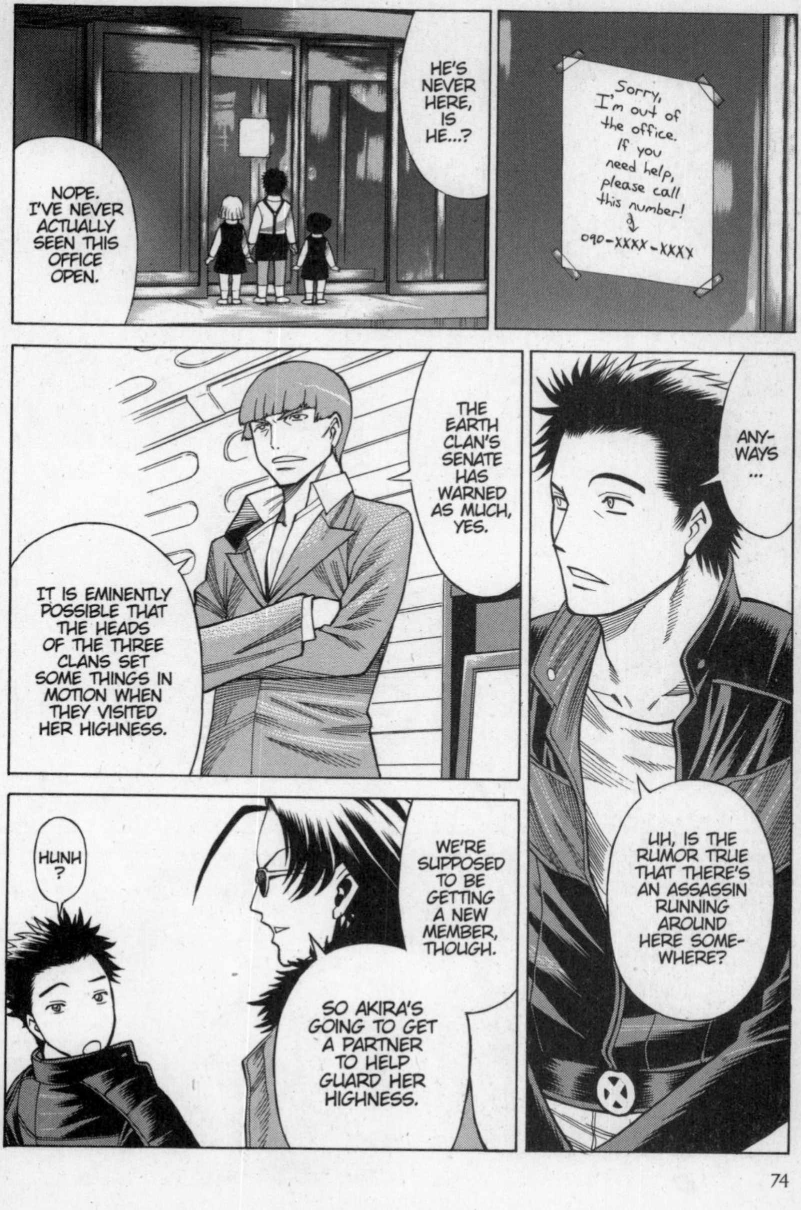
Sorry, I'm out of the office. If you need help, please call this number!
090-XXXX-XXXX
HE'S NEVER HERE, IS HE...?
NOPE. I'VE NEVER ACTUALLY SEEN THIS OFFICE OPEN.
ANYWAYS ...
UH, IS THE RUMOR TRUE THAT THERE'S AN ASSASSIN RUNNING AROUND HERE SOMEWHERE?
THE EARTH CLAN'S SENATE HAS WARNED AS MUCH, YES.
IT IS EMINENTLY POSSIBLE THAT THE HEADS OF THE THREE CLANS SET SOME THINGS IN MOTION WHEN THEY VISITED HER HIGHNESS.
WE'RE SUPPOSED TO BE GETTING A NEW MEMBER, THOUGH.
HUNH?
SO AKIRA'S GOING TO GET A PARTNER TO HELP GUARD HER HIGHNESS.

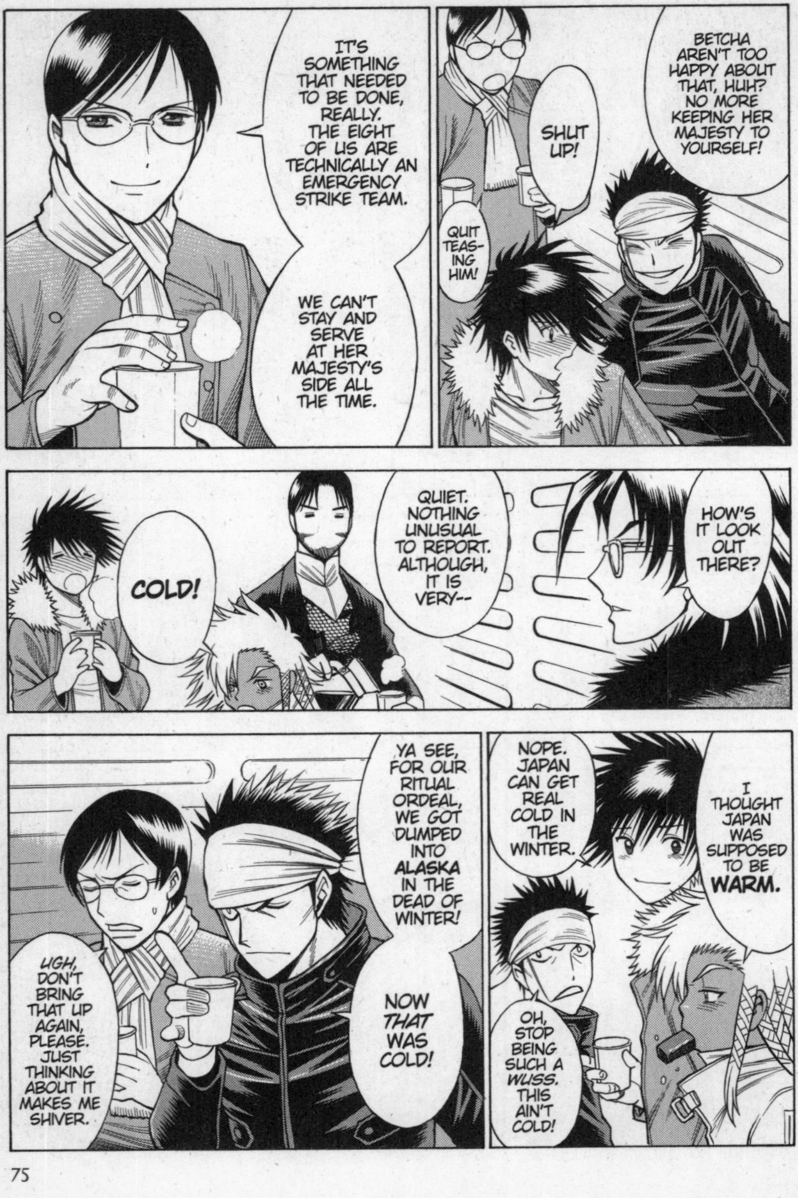
BETCHA AREN'T TOO HAPPY ABOUT THAT, HUH? NO MORE KEEPING HER MAJESTY TO YOURSELF!
SHUT UP!
QUIT TEAS-ING HIM!
IT'S SOMETHING THAT NEEDED TO BE DONE, REALLY. THE EIGHT OF US ARE TECHNICALLY AN EMERGENCY STRIKE TEAM.
WE CAN'T STAY AND SERVE AT HER MAJESTY'S SIDE ALL THE TIME.
HOW'S IT LOOK OUT THERE?
QUIET. NOTHING UNUSUAL TO REPORT. ALTHOUGH, IT IS VERY--
COLD!
I THOUGHT JAPAN WAS SUPPOSED TO BE WARM.
NOPE. JAPAN CAN GET REAL COLD IN THE WINTER.
OH, STOP BEING SUCH A WUSS. THIS AIN'T COLD!
YA SEE, FOR OUR RITUAL ORDEAL, WE GOT DUMPED INTO ALASKA IN THE DEAD OF WINTER!
NOW THAT WAS COLD!
UGH, DON'T BRING THAT UP AGAIN, PLEASE. JUST THINKING ABOUT IT MAKES ME SHIVER.

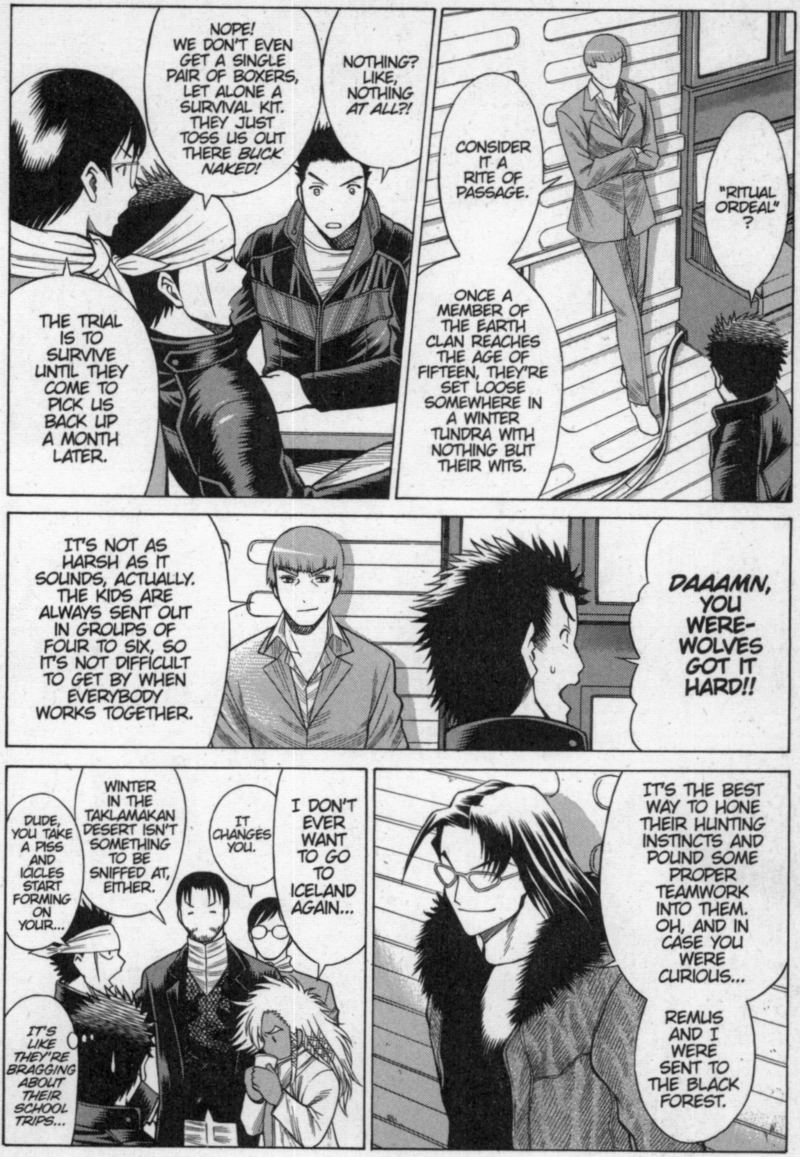
CONSIDER IT A RITE OF PASSAGE.
"RITUAL ORDEAL" ?
ONCE A MEMBER OF THE EARTH CLAN REACHES THE AGE OF FIFTEEN, THEY'RE SET LOOSE SOMEWHERE IN A WINTER TUNDRA WITH NOTHING BUT THEIR WITS.
NOTHING? LIKE, NOTHING *AT ALL*?!
NOPE! WE DON'T EVEN GET A SINGLE PAIR OF BOXERS, LET ALONE A SURVIVAL KIT. THEY JUST TOSS US OUT THERE *BUCK NAKED!*
THE TRIAL IS TO SURVIVE UNTIL THEY COME TO PICK US BACK UP A MONTH LATER.
DAAAMN, YOU WERE-WOLVES GOT IT HARD!!
IT'S NOT AS HARSH AS IT SOUNDS, ACTUALLY. THE KIDS ARE ALWAYS SENT OUT IN GROUPS OF FOUR TO SIX, SO IT'S NOT DIFFICULT TO GET BY WHEN EVERYBODY WORKS TOGETHER.
IT'S THE BEST WAY TO HONE THEIR HUNTING INSTINCTS AND POUND SOME PROPER TEAMWORK INTO THEM. OH, AND IN CASE YOU WERE CURIOUS...
REMUS AND I WERE SENT TO THE BLACK FOREST.
I DON'T EVER WANT TO GO TO ICELAND AGAIN...
IT CHANGES YOU.
WINTER IN THE TAKLAMAKAN DESERT ISN'T SOMETHING TO BE SNIFFED AT, EITHER.
DUDE, YOU TAKE A PISS AND ICICLES START FORMING ON YOUR...
IT'S LIKE THEY'RE BRAGGING ABOUT THEIR SCHOOL TRIPS...

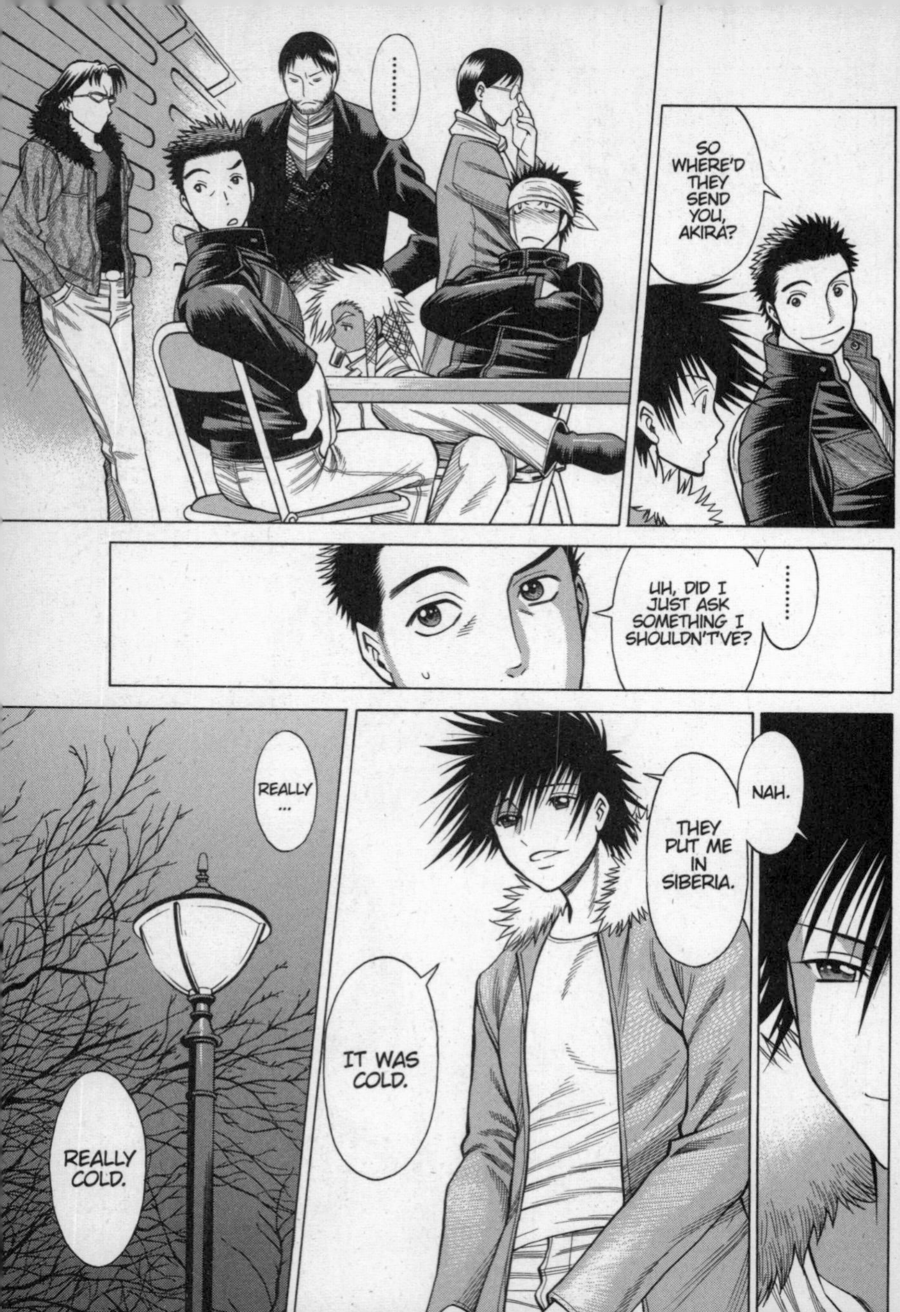
SO WHERE'D THEY SEND YOU, AKIRA?
......
......
UH, DID I JUST ASK SOMETHING I SHOULDN'T'VE?
NAH.
THEY PUT ME IN SIBERIA.
IT WAS COLD.
REALLY ...
REALLY COLD.

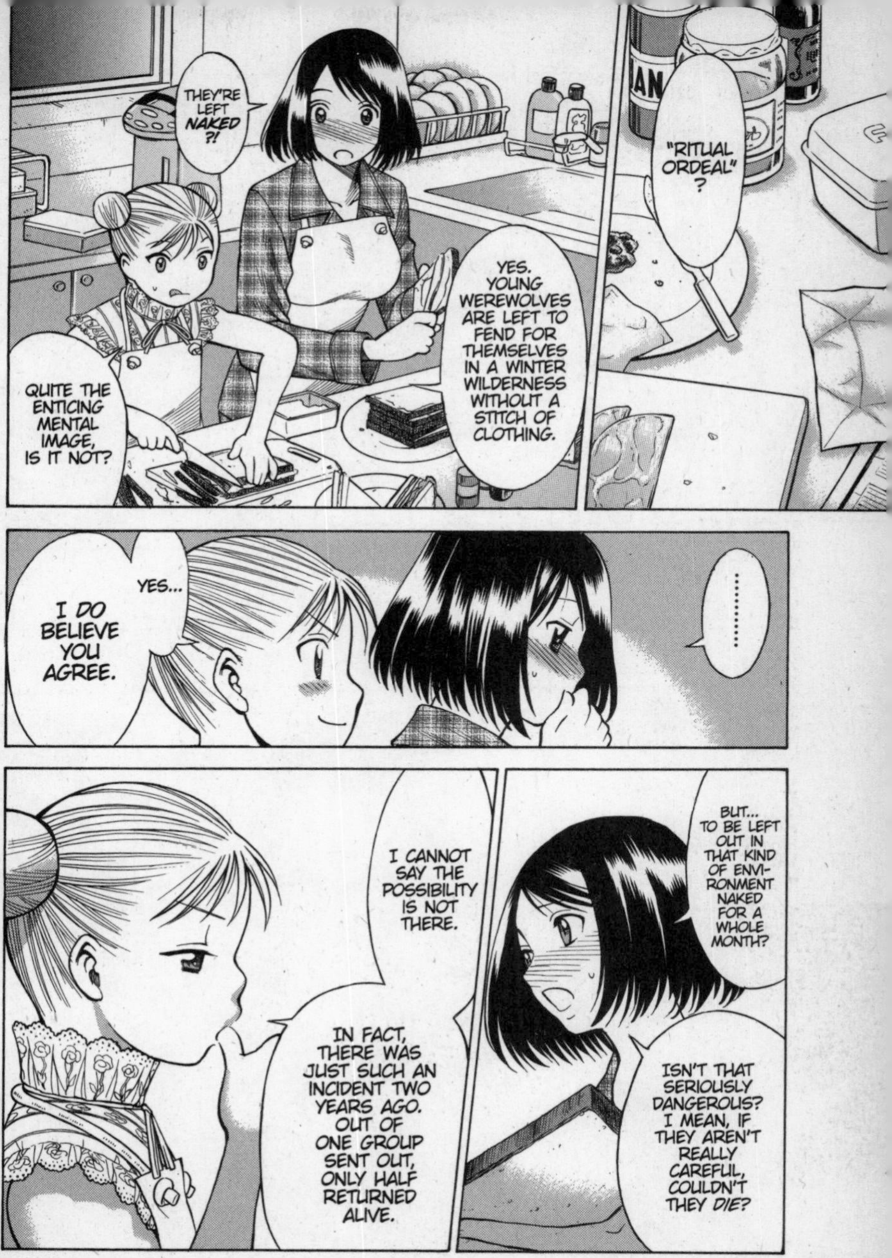
"RITUAL ORDEAL"?
YES. YOUNG WEREWOLVES ARE LEFT TO FEND FOR THEMSELVES IN A WINTER WILDERNESS WITHOUT A STITCH OF CLOTHING.
THEY'RE LEFT *NAKED*?!
QUITE THE ENTICING MENTAL IMAGE, IS IT NOT?
....
YES...
I *DO* BELIEVE YOU AGREE.
BUT... TO BE LEFT OUT IN THAT KIND OF ENVIRONMENT NAKED FOR A WHOLE MONTH?
ISN'T THAT SERIOUSLY DANGEROUS? I MEAN, IF THEY AREN'T REALLY CAREFUL, COULDN'T THEY *DIE*?
I CANNOT SAY THE POSSIBILITY IS NOT THERE.
IN FACT, THERE WAS JUST SUCH AN INCIDENT TWO YEARS AGO. OUT OF ONE GROUP SENT OUT, ONLY HALF RETURNED ALIVE.

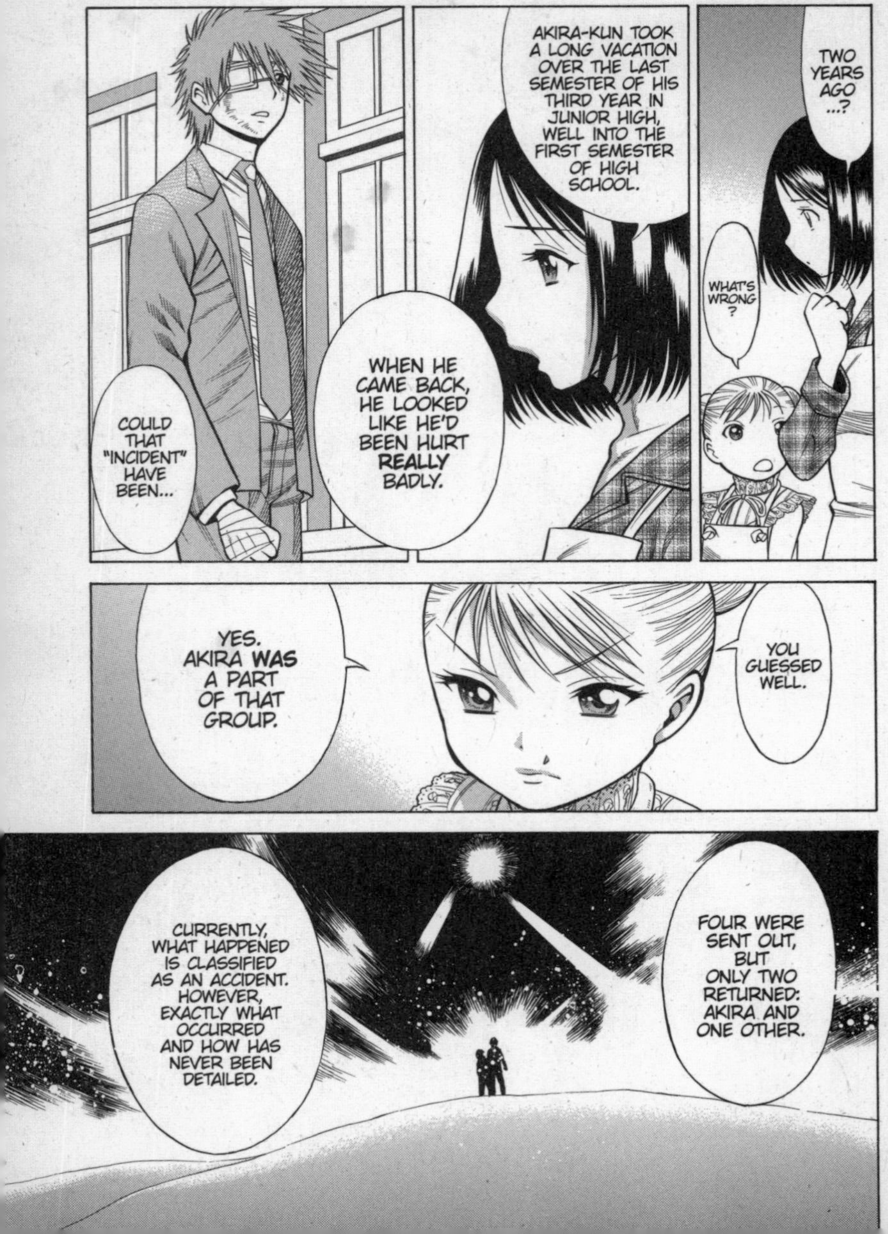
TWO YEARS AGO ...?
WHAT'S WRONG ?
AKIRA-KUN TOOK A LONG VACATION OVER THE LAST SEMESTER OF HIS THIRD YEAR IN JUNIOR HIGH, WELL INTO THE FIRST SEMESTER OF HIGH SCHOOL.
WHEN HE CAME BACK, HE LOOKED LIKE HE'D BEEN HURT **REALLY** BADLY.
COULD THAT "INCIDENT" HAVE BEEN...
YOU GUESSED WELL.
YES. AKIRA **WAS** A PART OF THAT GROUP.
FOUR WERE SENT OUT, BUT ONLY TWO RETURNED: AKIRA AND ONE OTHER.
CURRENTLY, WHAT HAPPENED IS CLASSIFIED AS AN ACCIDENT. HOWEVER, EXACTLY WHAT OCCURRED AND HOW HAS NEVER BEEN DETAILED.

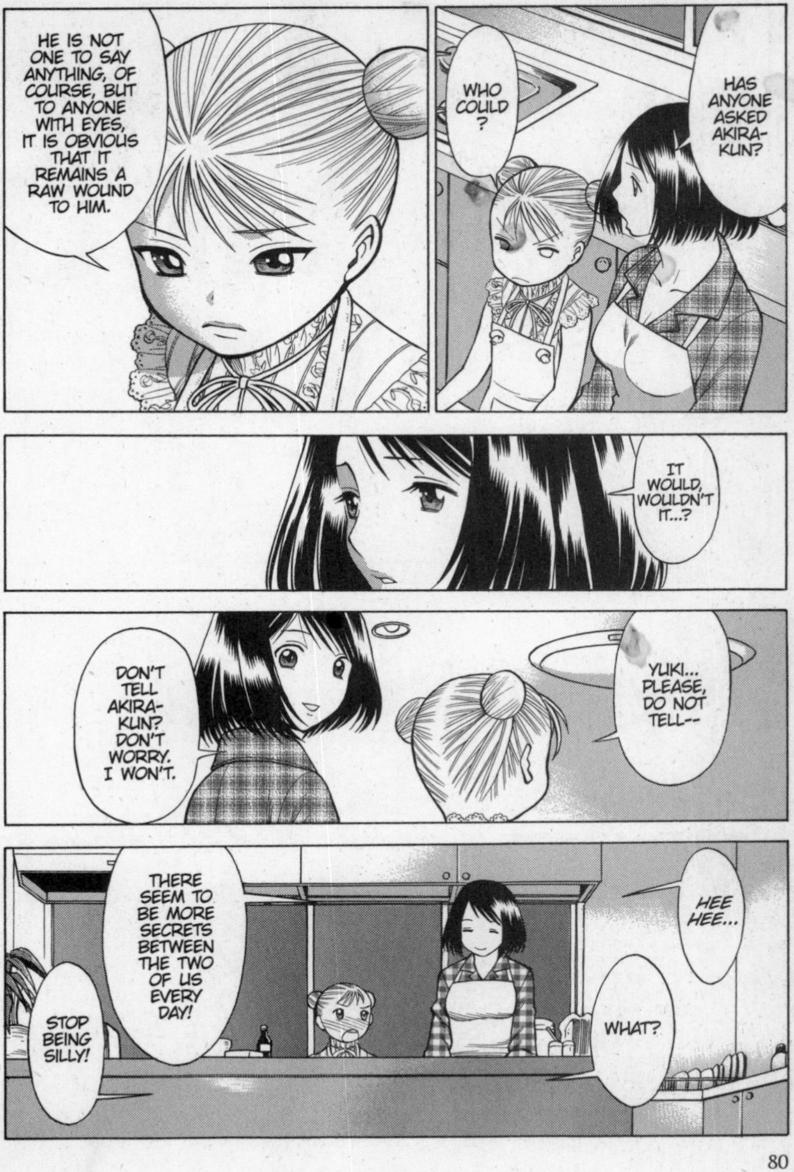
HAS ANYONE ASKED AKIRA-KUN?
WHO COULD?
HE IS NOT ONE TO SAY ANYTHING, OF COURSE, BUT TO ANYONE WITH EYES, IT IS OBVIOUS THAT IT REMAINS A RAW WOUND TO HIM.
IT WOULD, WOULDN'T IT...?
YUKI... PLEASE, DO NOT TELL--
DON'T TELL AKIRA-KUN? DON'T WORRY. I WON'T.
HEE HEE...
THERE SEEM TO BE MORE SECRETS BETWEEN THE TWO OF US EVERY DAY!
WHAT?
STOP BEING SILLY!

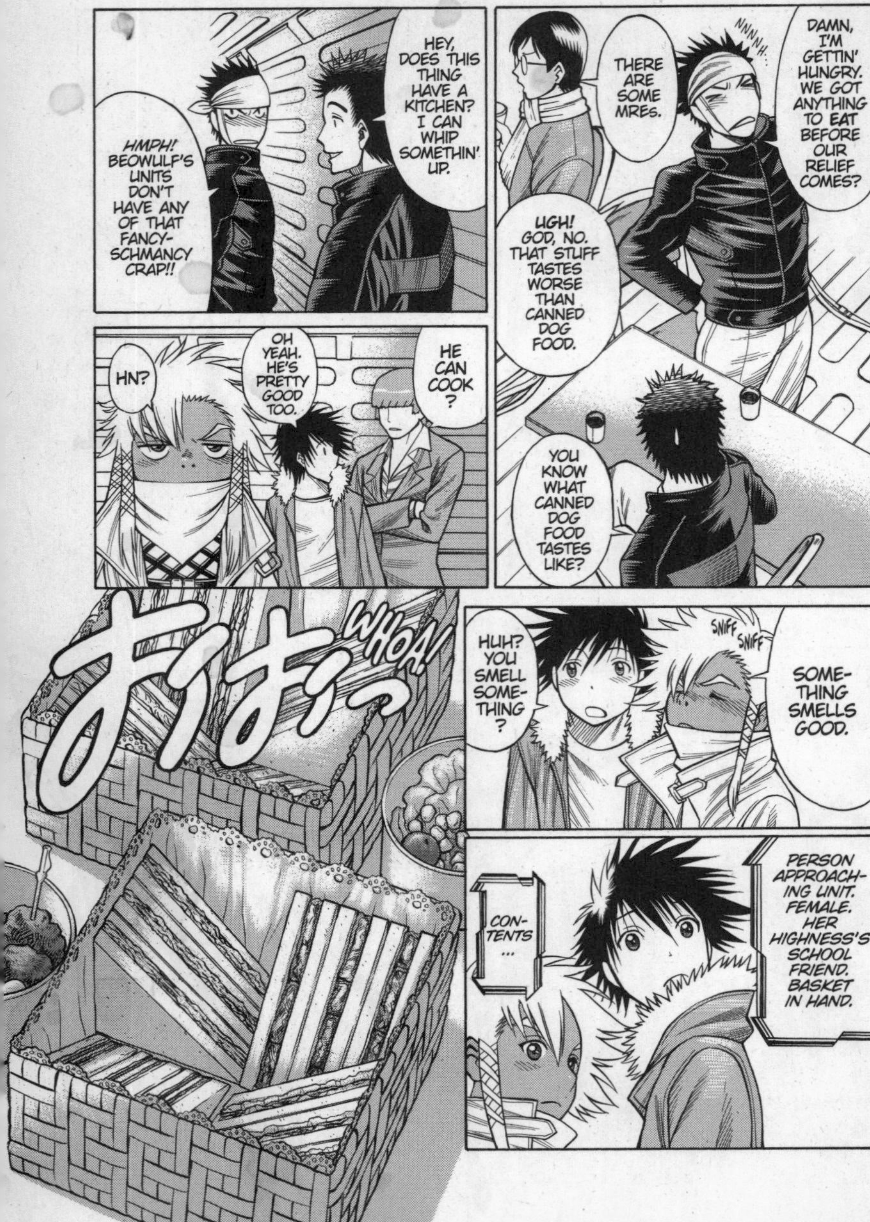
NNNNH...
DAMN, I'M GETTIN' HUNGRY. WE GOT ANYTHING TO EAT BEFORE OUR RELIEF COMES?
THERE ARE SOME MRES.
UGH! GOD, NO. THAT STUFF TASTES WORSE THAN CANNED DOG FOOD.
YOU KNOW WHAT CANNED DOG FOOD TASTES LIKE?
HEY, DOES THIS THING HAVE A KITCHEN? I CAN WHIP SOMETHIN' UP.
HMPH! BEOWULF'S UNITS DON'T HAVE ANY OF THAT FANCY-SCHMANCY CRAP!!
HE CAN COOK?
OH YEAH. HE'S PRETTY GOOD TOO.
HN?
SNIFF SNIFF
SOME-THING SMELLS GOOD.
HUH? YOU SMELL SOME-THING?
PERSON APPROACHING UNIT. FEMALE. HER HIGHNESS'S SCHOOL FRIEND. BASKET IN HAND.
CON-TENTS...
WHOA!

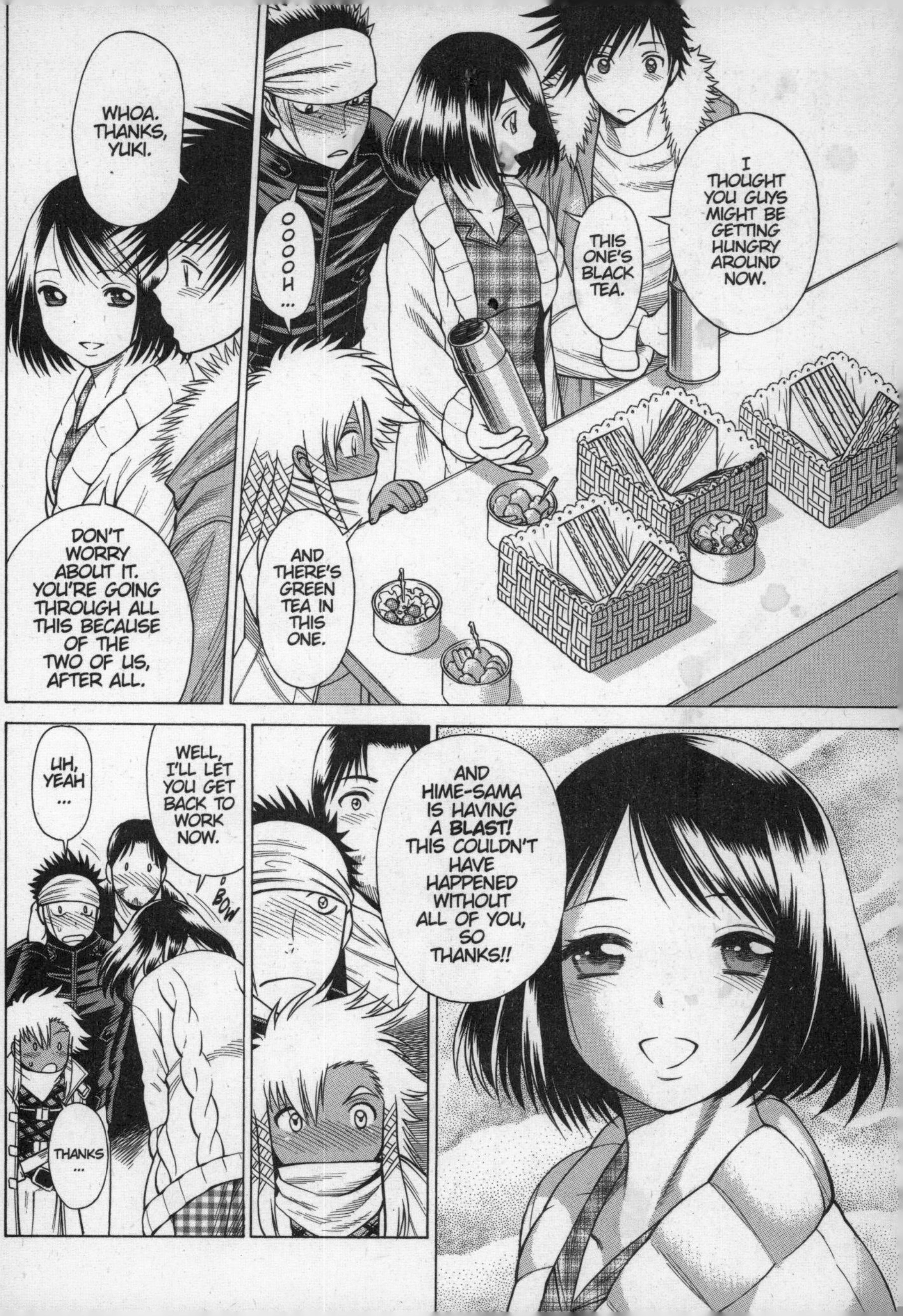
I THOUGHT YOU GUYS MIGHT BE GETTING HUNGRY AROUND NOW.
THIS ONE'S BLACK TEA.
OOOOH ...
AND THERE'S GREEN TEA IN THIS ONE.
WHOA. THANKS, YUKI.
DON'T WORRY ABOUT IT. YOU'RE GOING THROUGH ALL THIS BECAUSE OF THE TWO OF US, AFTER ALL.
AND HIME-SAMA IS HAVING A **BLAST**! THIS COULDN'T HAVE HAPPENED WITHOUT ALL OF YOU, SO THANKS!!
WELL, I'LL LET YOU GET BACK TO WORK NOW.
BOW
UH, YEAH ...
THANKS ...

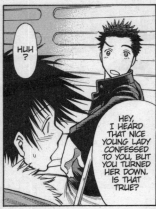

PSHHHH
YEAH ...
PAJAMAS...
SHE'S A SWEET GIRL.
HEY, I HEARD THAT NICE YOUNG LADY CONFESSED TO YOU, BUT YOU TURNED HER DOWN. IS THAT TRUE?
HUH ?
UH... WELL... IN THE END, *YEAH*, IT WOUND UP THAT WAY...
I GUESS... SORTA.
ARE YOU STUPID ?!!
HEY!!
UM...

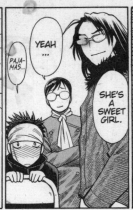

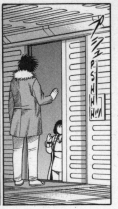

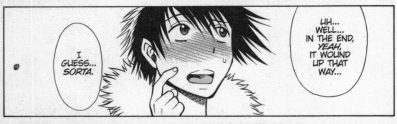

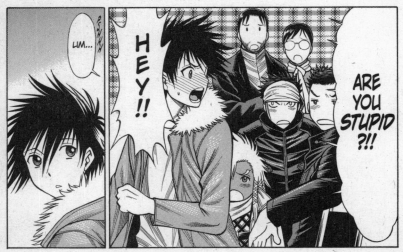

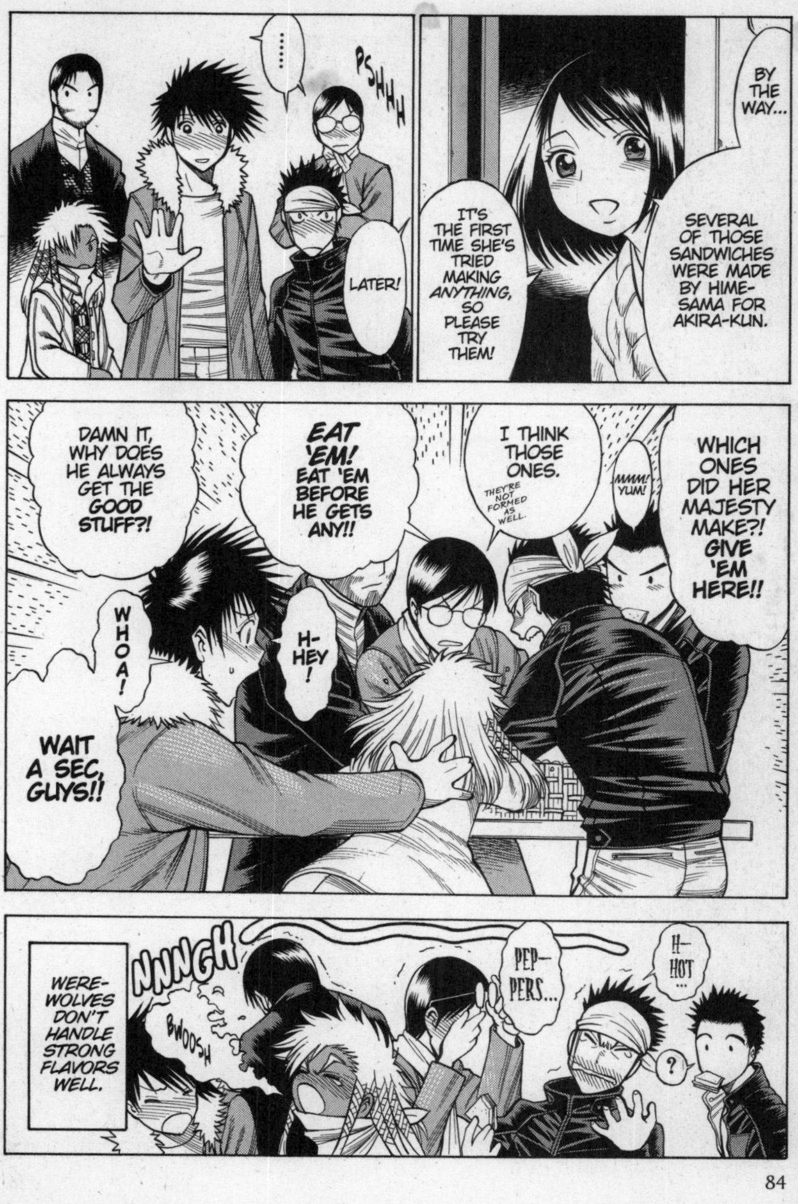
BY THE WAY...
SEVERAL OF THOSE SANDWICHES WERE MADE BY HIME-SAMA FOR AKIRA-KUN.
IT'S THE FIRST TIME SHE'S TRIED MAKING *ANYTHING*, SO PLEASE TRY THEM!
PSHHHH
......
LATER!
WHICH ONES DID HER MAJESTY MAKE?! GIVE 'EM HERE!!
MMM! YUM!
I THINK THOSE ONES.
THEY'RE NOT FORMED AS WELL.
EAT 'EM! EAT 'EM BEFORE HE GETS ANY!!
DAMN IT, WHY DOES HE ALWAYS GET THE GOOD STUFF?!
H-HEY!
WHOA!
WAIT A SEC, GUYS!!
H-HOT...
?
PEP-PERS...
NNNGH
BWOOSH
WERE-WOLVES DON'T HANDLE STRONG FLAVORS WELL.

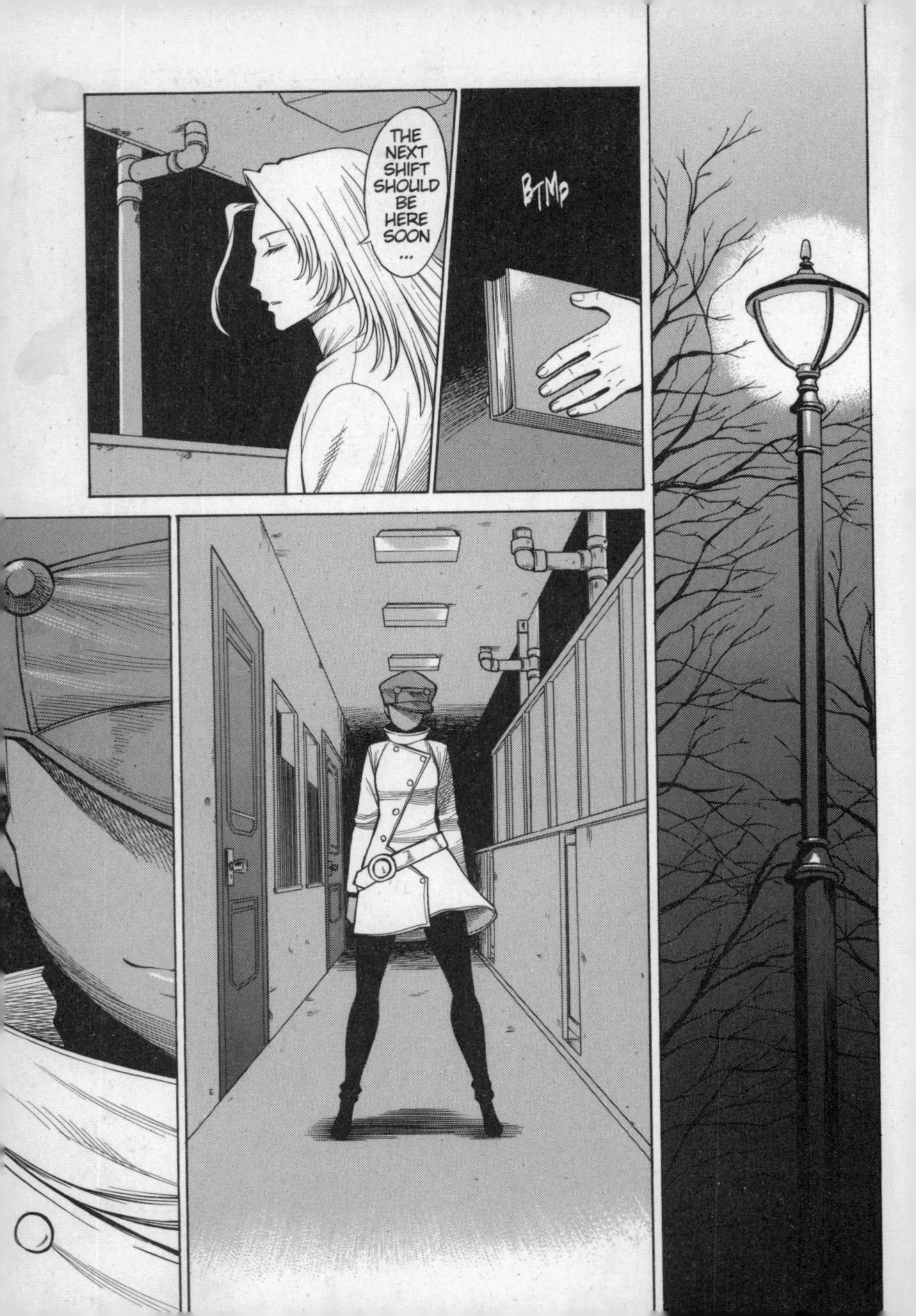
BTMP
THE NEXT SHIFT SHOULD BE HERE SOON ...

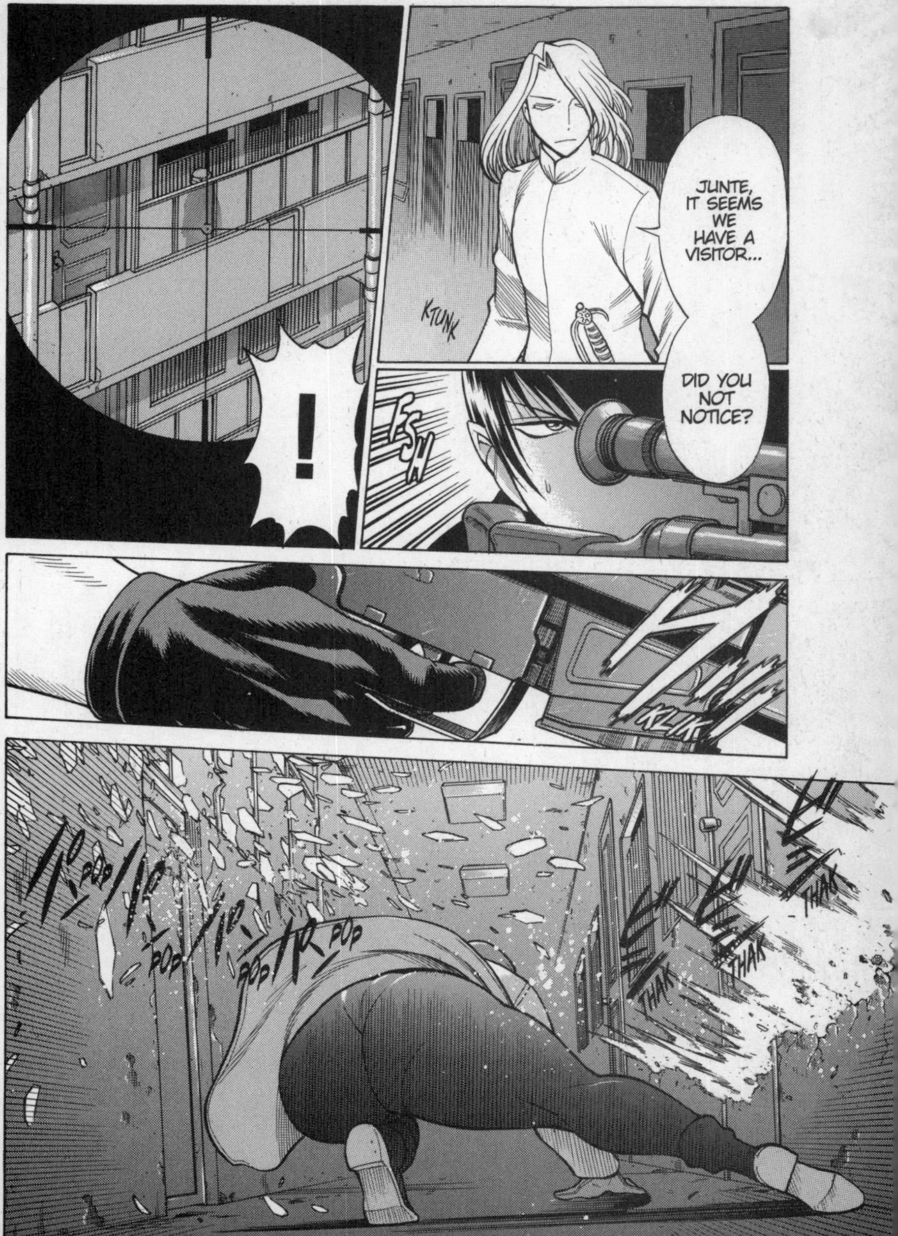
JUNTE, IT SEEMS WE HAVE A VISITOR...
KTUNK
DID YOU NOT NOTICE?
FSH
!
KLIK
THAK
THAK
THAK
POP
POP
POP
POP

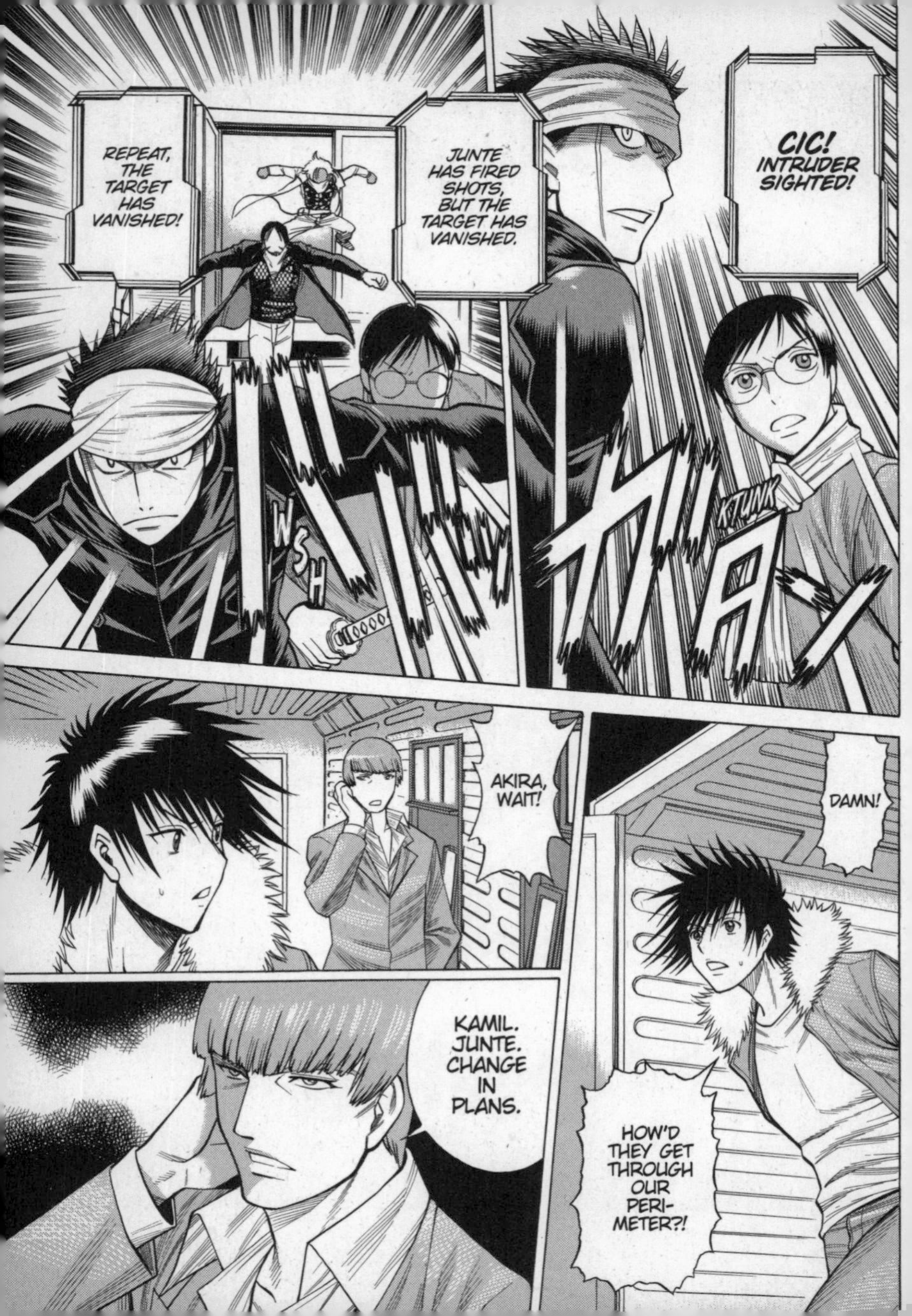
CIC! INTRUDER SIGHTED!
JUNTE HAS FIRED SHOTS, BUT THE TARGET HAS VANISHED.
REPEAT, THE TARGET HAS VANISHED!
KTUNK
WSH
DAMN!
HOW'D THEY GET THROUGH OUR PERI-METER?!
AKIRA, WAIT!
KAMIL. JUNTE. CHANGE IN PLANS.

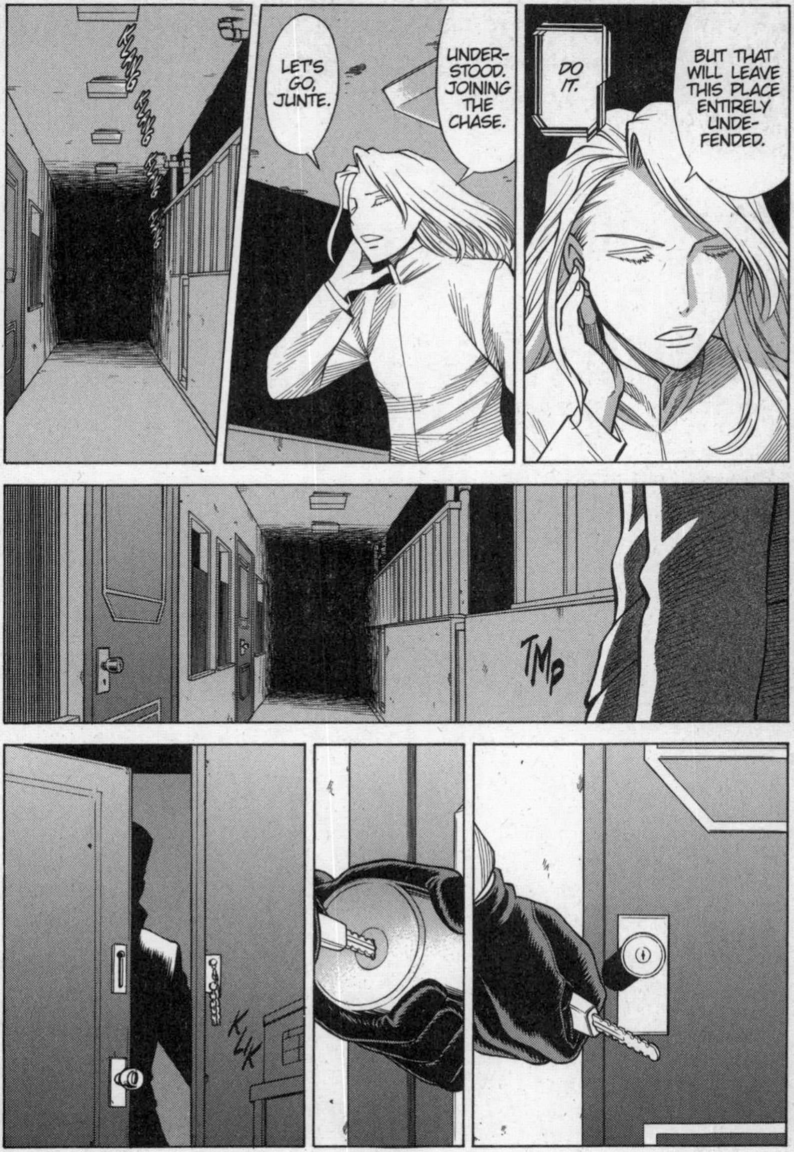
BUT THAT WILL LEAVE THIS PLACE ENTIRELY UNDE-FENDED.
DO IT.
UNDER-STOOD. JOINING THE CHASE.
LET'S GO, JUNTE.
TMP
KLIK

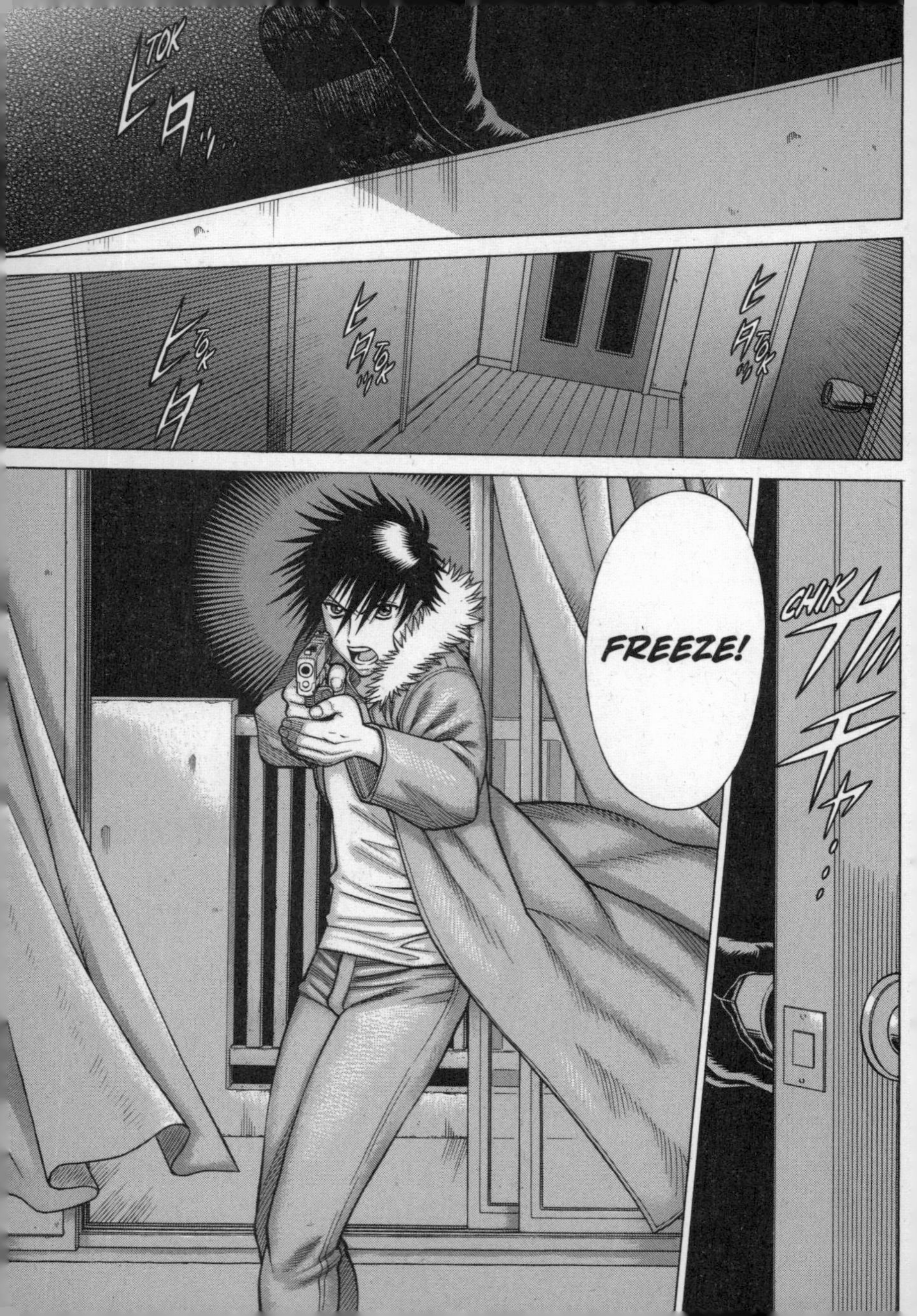
TOK
TOK
TOK
TOK
CHIK
FREEZE!

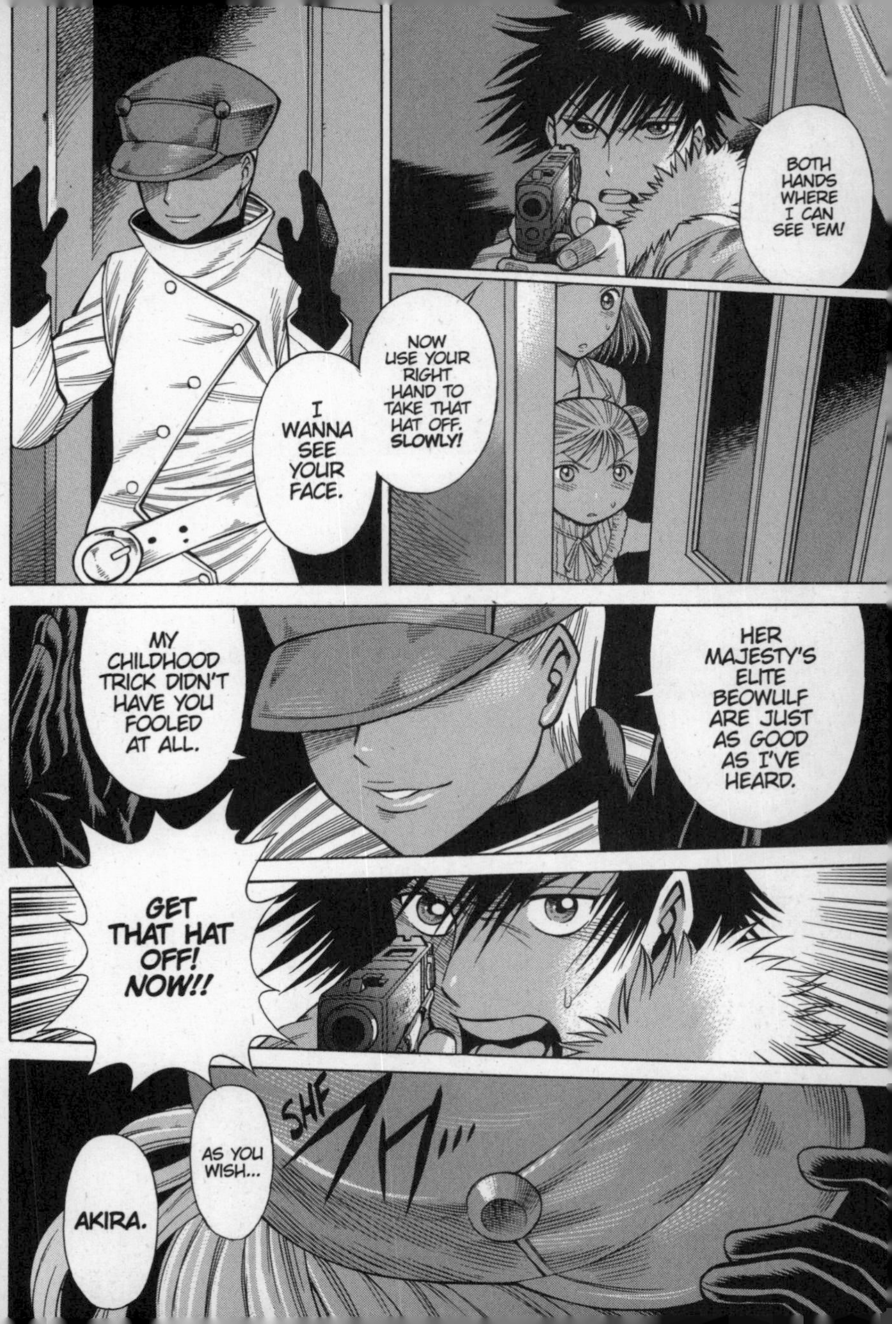
BOTH HANDS WHERE I CAN SEE 'EM!
NOW USE YOUR RIGHT HAND TO TAKE THAT HAT OFF. SLOWLY!
I WANNA SEE YOUR FACE.
HER MAJESTY'S ELITE BEOWULF ARE JUST AS GOOD AS I'VE HEARD.
MY CHILDHOOD TRICK DIDN'T HAVE YOU FOOLED AT ALL.
GET THAT HAT OFF! NOW!!
SHF
AS YOU WISH...
AKIRA.

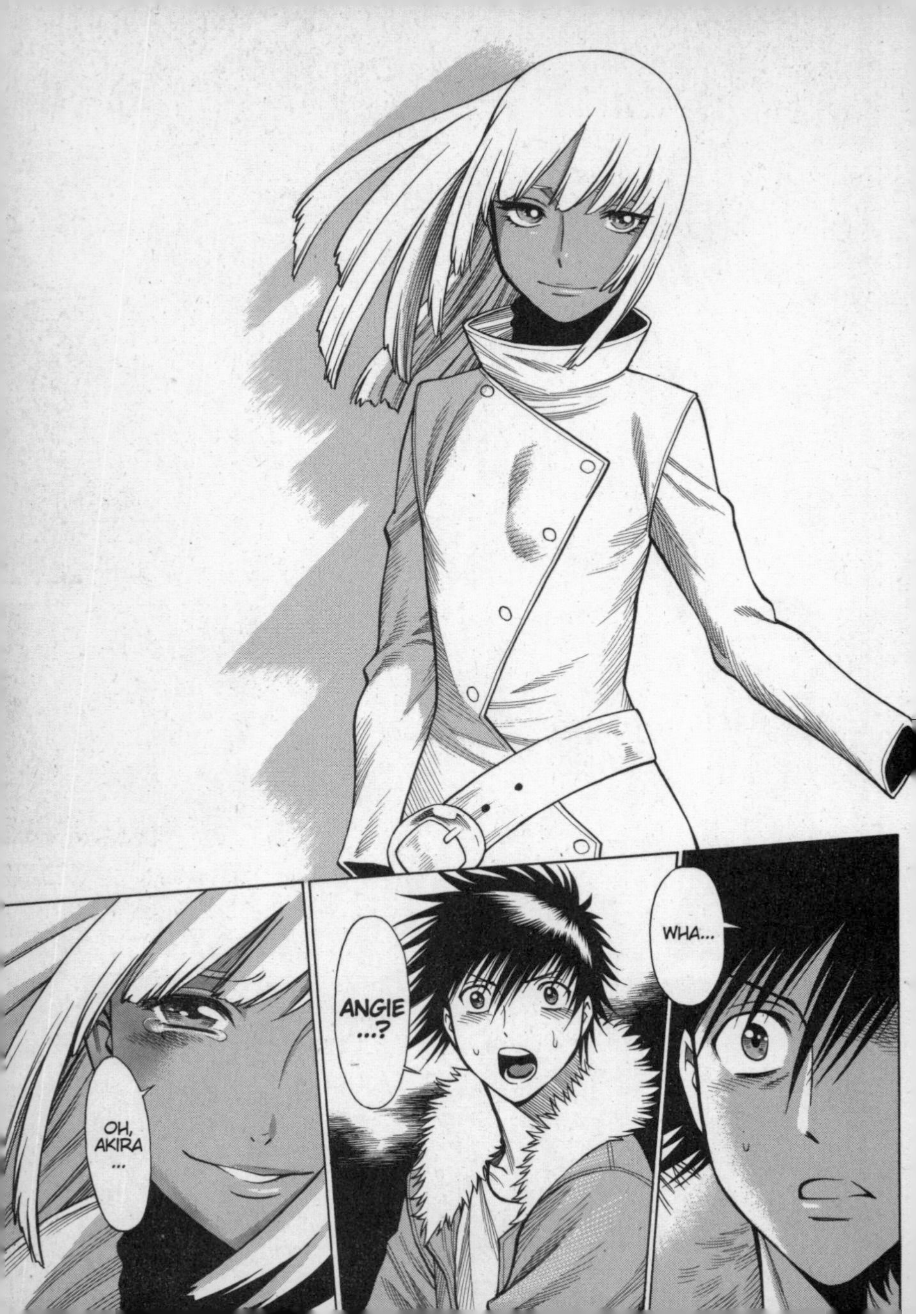
WHA...
ANGIE ...?
OH, AKIRA ...

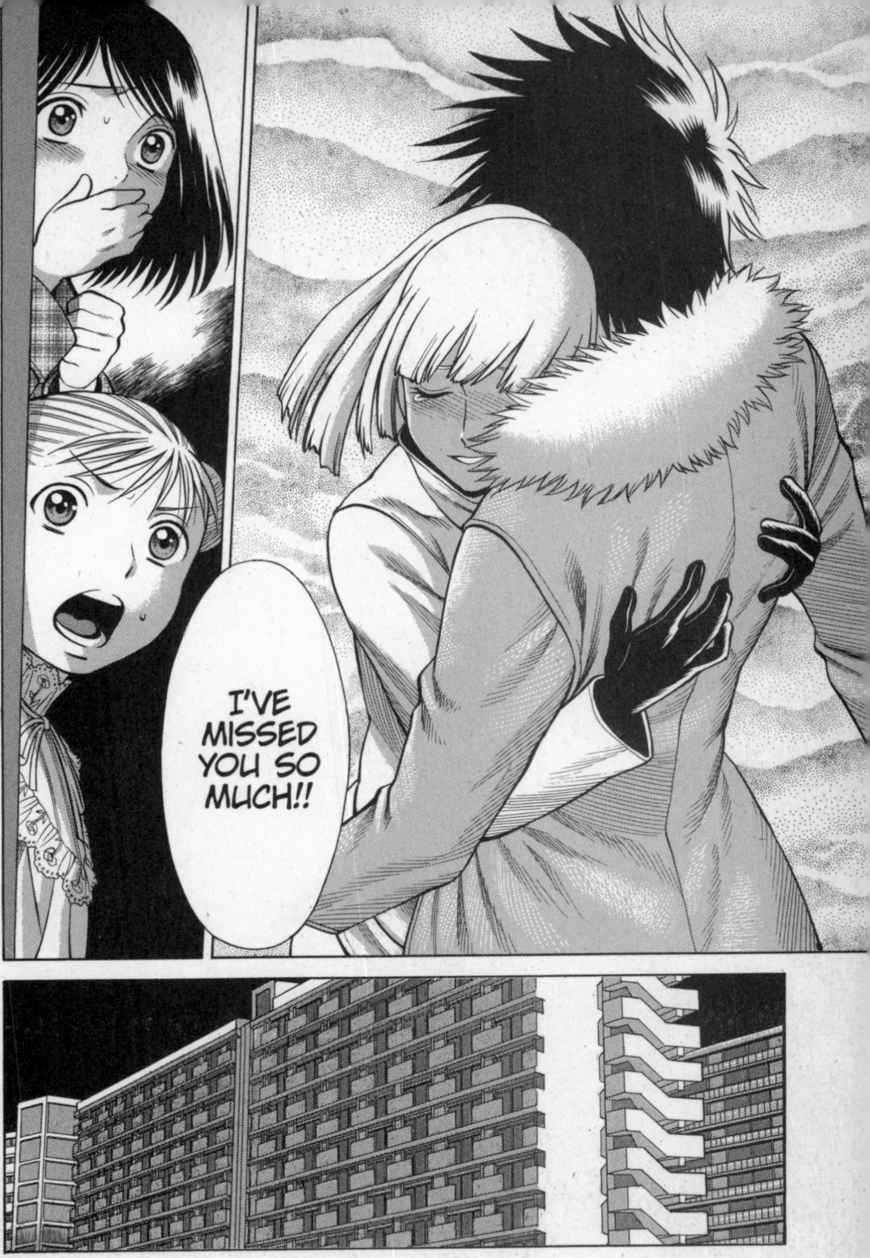
I'VE MISSED YOU SO MUCH!!

Chapter 35: Marital Vows

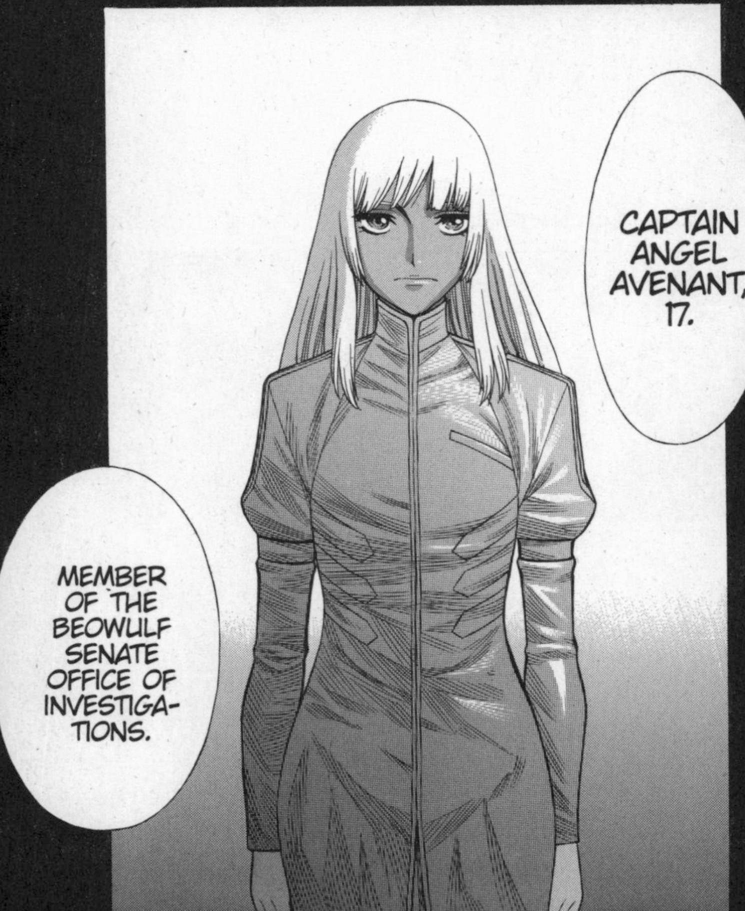
CAPTAIN ANGEL AVENANT, 17.
MEMBER OF THE BEOWULF SENATE OFFICE OF INVESTIGA-TIONS.

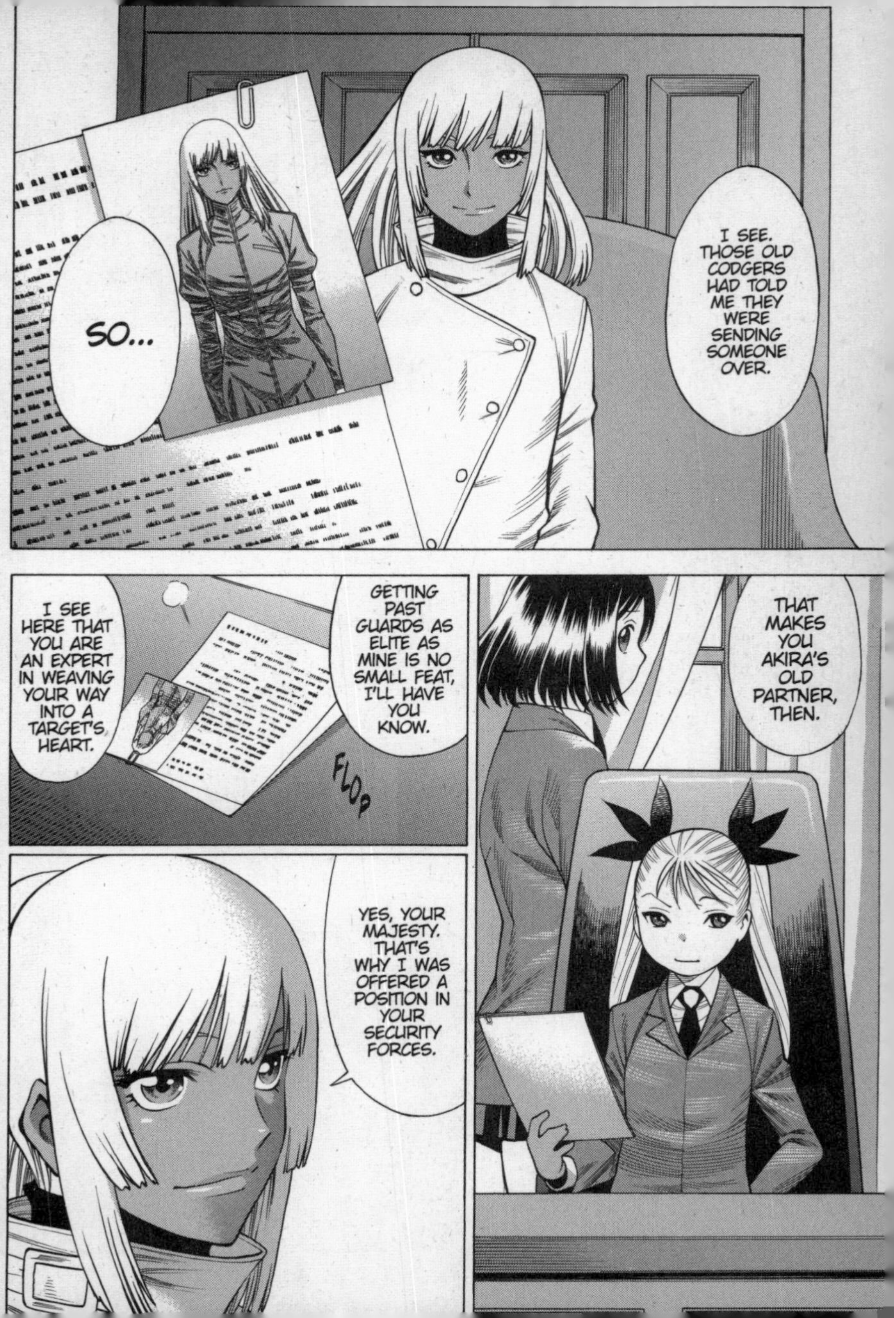
I SEE. THOSE OLD CODGERS HAD TOLD ME THEY WERE SENDING SOMEONE OVER.
SO...
THAT MAKES YOU AKIRA'S OLD PARTNER, THEN.
GETTING PAST GUARDS AS ELITE AS MINE IS NO SMALL FEAT, I'LL HAVE YOU KNOW.
I SEE HERE THAT YOU ARE AN EXPERT IN WEAVING YOUR WAY INTO A TARGET'S HEART.
FLOP
YES, YOUR MAJESTY. THAT'S WHY I WAS OFFERED A POSITION IN YOUR SECURITY FORCES.

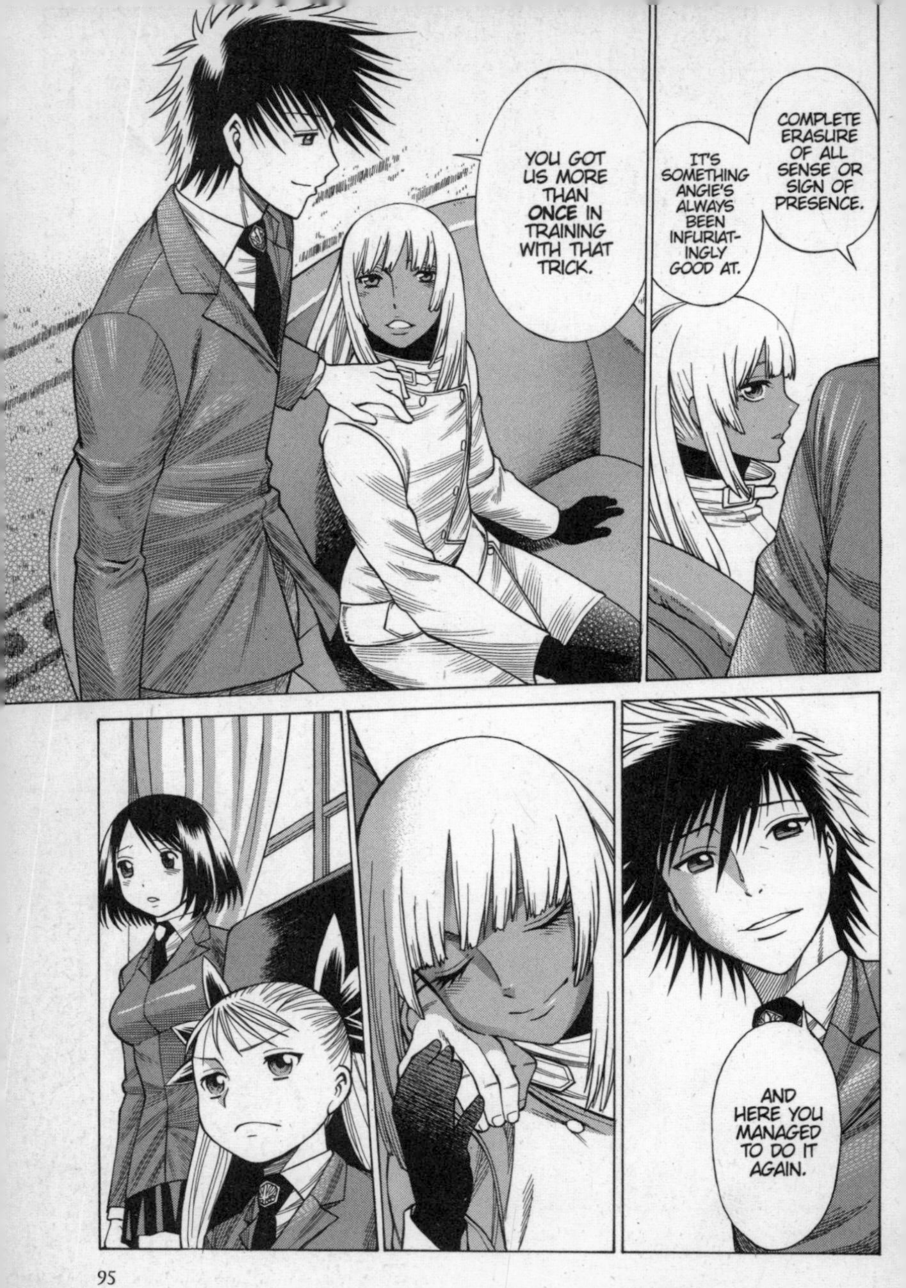
COMPLETE ERASURE OF ALL SENSE OR SIGN OF PRESENCE.
IT'S SOMETHING ANGIE'S ALWAYS BEEN INFURIAT-INGLY GOOD AT.
YOU GOT US MORE THAN ONCE IN TRAINING WITH THAT TRICK.
AND HERE YOU MANAGED TO DO IT AGAIN.

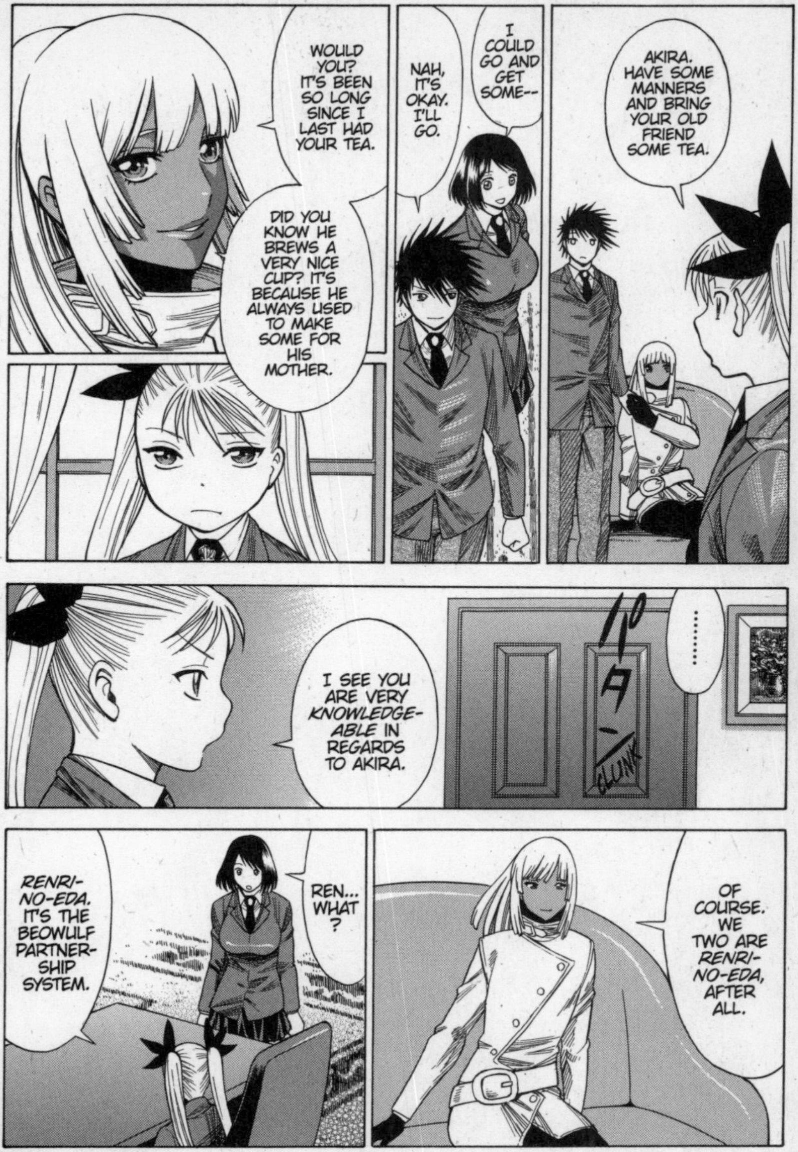
AKIRA. HAVE SOME MANNERS AND BRING YOUR OLD FRIEND SOME TEA.
I COULD GO AND GET SOME--
NAH, IT'S OKAY. I'LL GO.
WOULD YOU? IT'S BEEN SO LONG SINCE I LAST HAD YOUR TEA.
DID YOU KNOW HE BREWS A VERY NICE CUP? IT'S BECAUSE HE ALWAYS USED TO MAKE SOME FOR HIS MOTHER.
......
パタン
CLUNK
I SEE YOU ARE VERY *KNOWLEDGEABLE* IN REGARDS TO AKIRA.
OF COURSE. WE TWO ARE *RENRI-NO-EDA*, AFTER ALL.
REN... WHAT?
RENRI-NO-EDA. IT'S THE BEOWULF PARTNERSHIP SYSTEM.

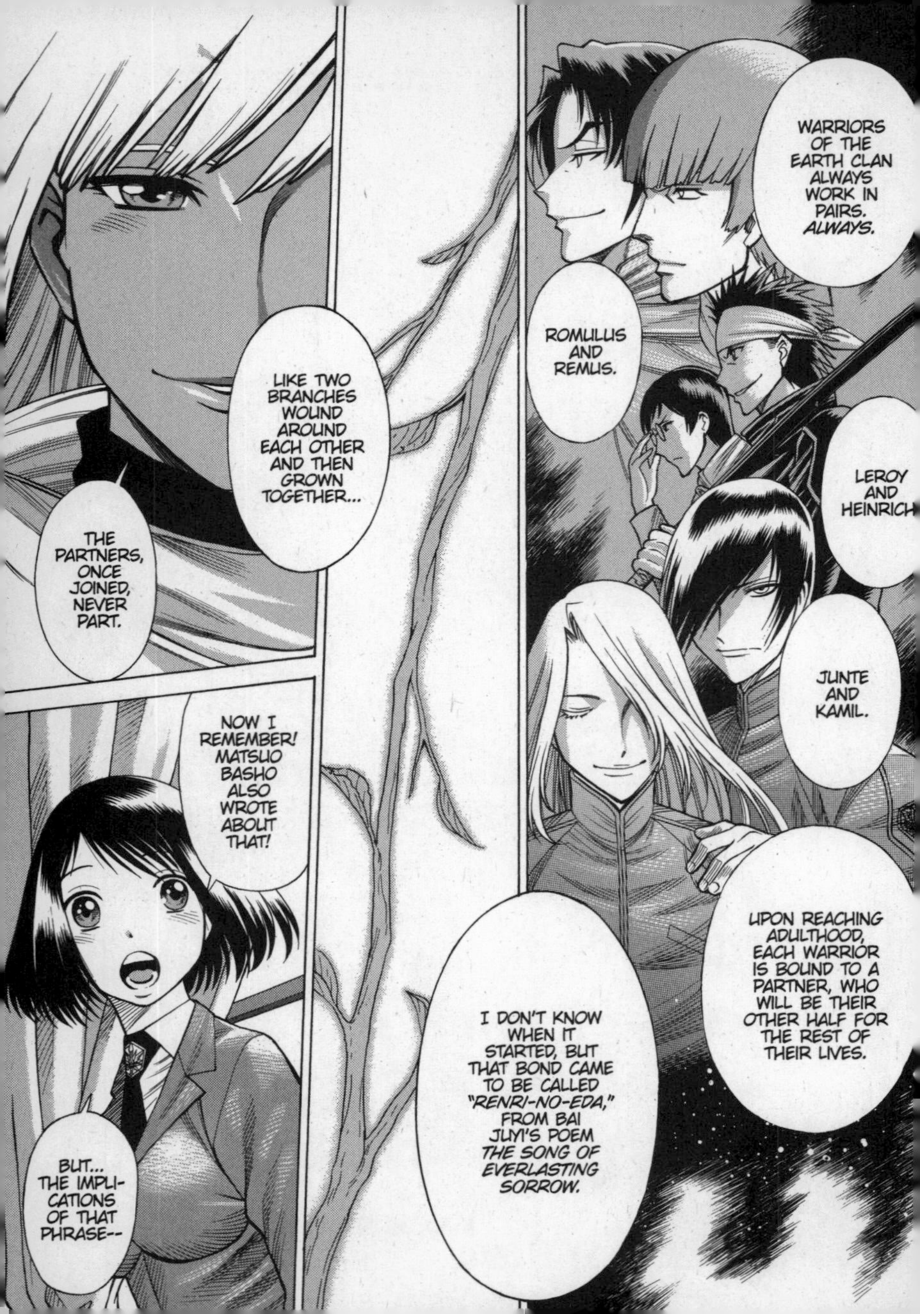
WARRIORS OF THE EARTH CLAN ALWAYS WORK IN PAIRS. *ALWAYS.*
ROMULUS AND REMUS.
LEROY AND HEINRICH
JUNTE AND KAMIL.
UPON REACHING ADULTHOOD, EACH WARRIOR IS BOUND TO A PARTNER, WHO WILL BE THEIR OTHER HALF FOR THE REST OF THEIR LIVES.
I DON'T KNOW WHEN IT STARTED, BUT THAT BOND CAME TO BE CALLED *"RENRI-NO-EDA,"* FROM BAI JUYI'S POEM *THE SONG OF EVERLASTING SORROW.*
LIKE TWO BRANCHES WOUND AROUND EACH OTHER AND THEN GROWN TOGETHER...
THE PARTNERS, ONCE JOINED, NEVER PART.
NOW I REMEMBER! MATSUO BASHO ALSO WROTE ABOUT THAT!
BUT... THE IMPLI- CATIONS OF THAT PHRASE--

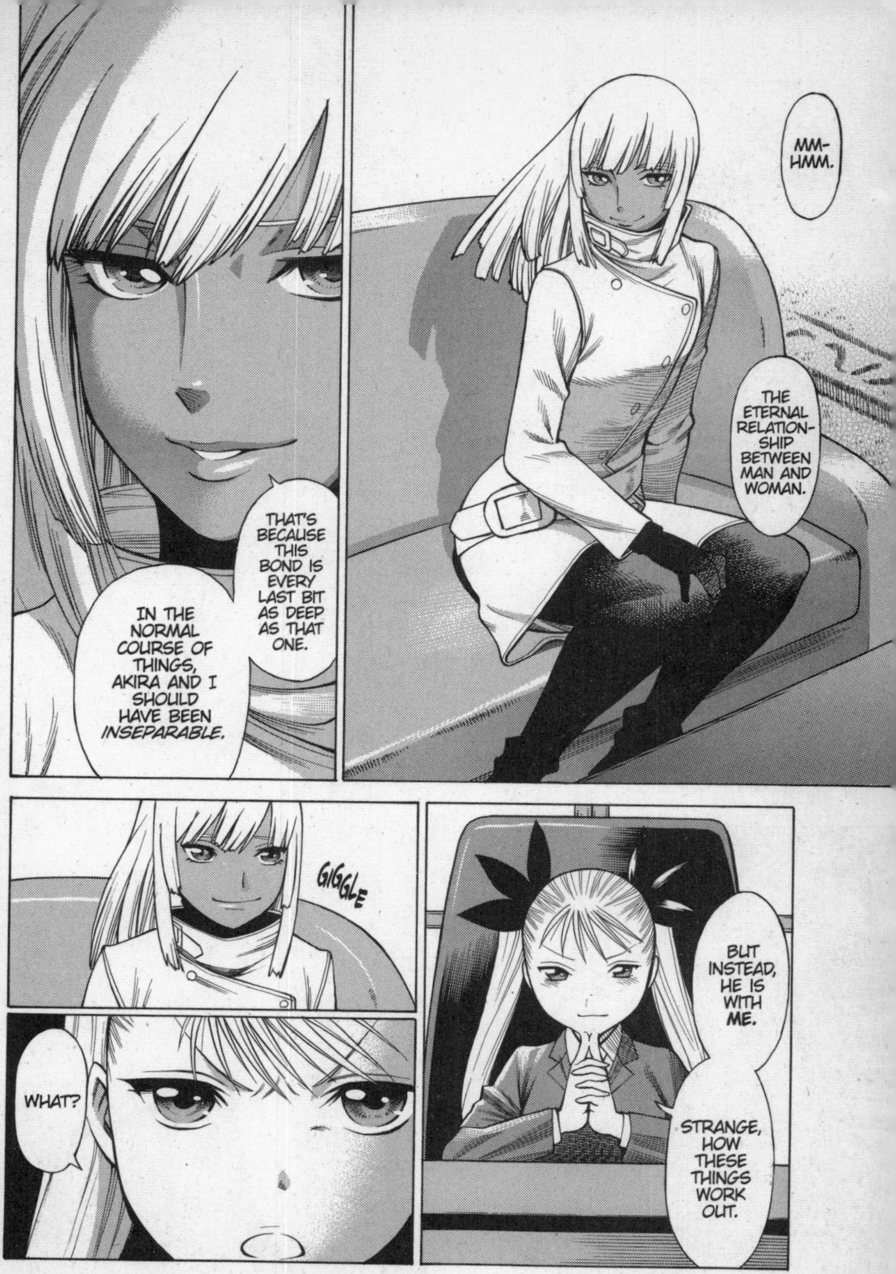
MM-HMM.
THE ETERNAL RELATION-SHIP BETWEEN MAN AND WOMAN.
THAT'S BECAUSE THIS BOND IS EVERY LAST BIT AS DEEP AS THAT ONE.
IN THE NORMAL COURSE OF THINGS, AKIRA AND I SHOULD HAVE BEEN *INSEPARABLE.*
BUT INSTEAD, HE IS WITH ME.
STRANGE, HOW THESE THINGS WORK OUT.
GIGGLE
WHAT?

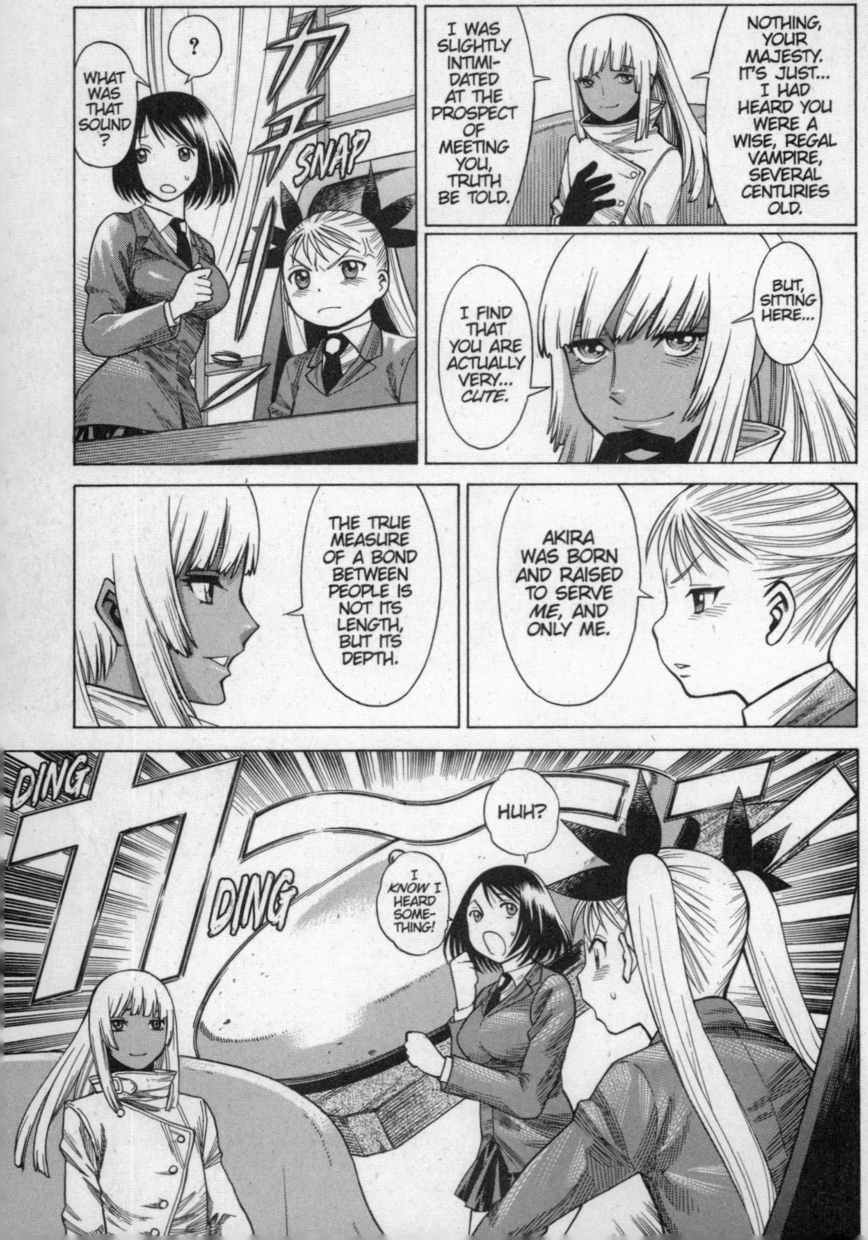
NOTHING, YOUR MAJESTY. IT'S JUST... I HAD HEARD YOU WERE A WISE, REGAL VAMPIRE, SEVERAL CENTURIES OLD.
I WAS SLIGHTLY INTIMI-DATED AT THE PROSPECT OF MEETING YOU, TRUTH BE TOLD.
BUT, SITTING HERE...
I FIND THAT YOU ARE ACTUALLY VERY... *CUTE.*
?
WHAT WAS THAT SOUND?
SNAP
AKIRA WAS BORN AND RAISED TO SERVE *ME*, AND ONLY ME.
THE TRUE MEASURE OF A BOND BETWEEN PEOPLE IS NOT ITS LENGTH, BUT ITS DEPTH.
DING
HUH?
DING
I *KNOW* I HEARD SOME-THING!

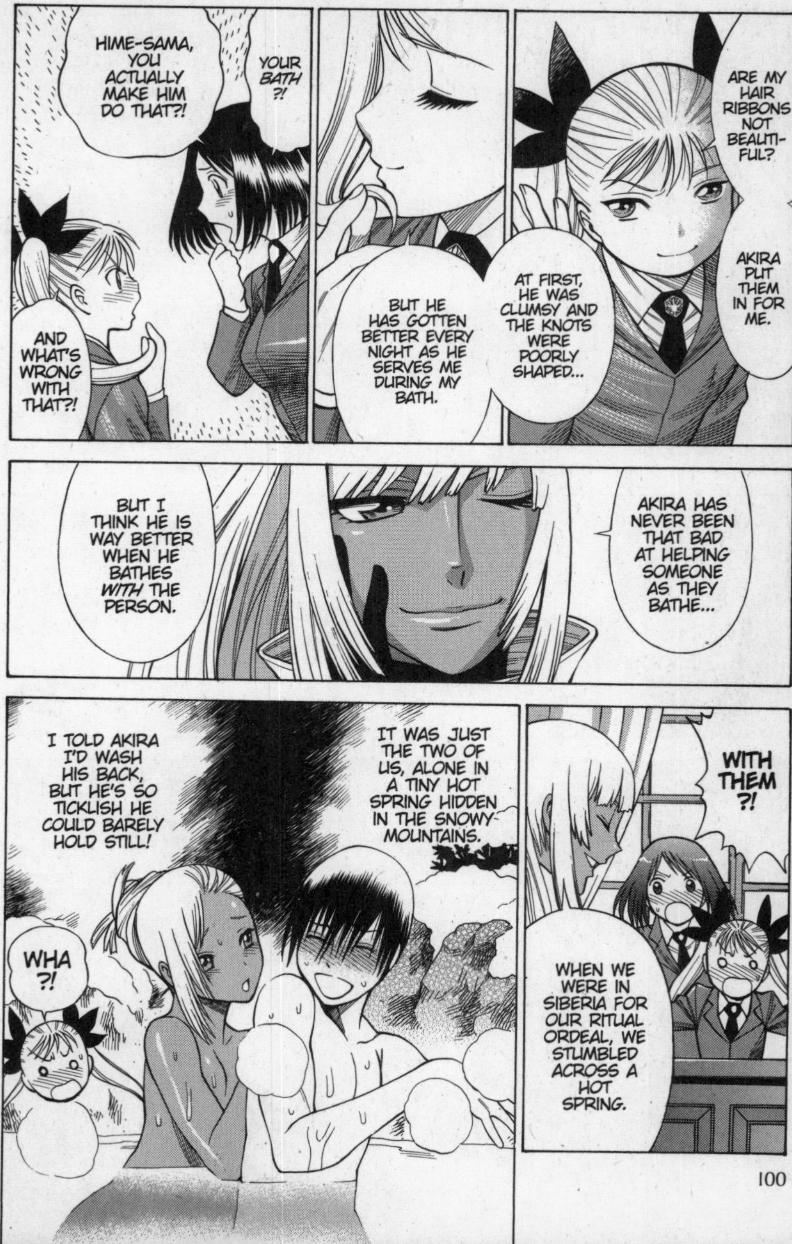
ARE MY HAIR RIBBONS NOT BEAUTIFUL?
AKIRA PUT THEM IN FOR ME.
AT FIRST, HE WAS CLUMSY AND THE KNOTS WERE POORLY SHAPED...
BUT HE HAS GOTTEN BETTER EVERY NIGHT AS HE SERVES ME DURING MY BATH.
YOUR BATH ?!
HIME-SAMA, YOU ACTUALLY MAKE HIM DO THAT?!
AND WHAT'S WRONG WITH THAT?!
AKIRA HAS NEVER BEEN THAT BAD AT HELPING SOMEONE AS THEY BATHE...
BUT I THINK HE IS WAY BETTER WHEN HE BATHES *WITH* THE PERSON.
WITH THEM ?!
WHEN WE WERE IN SIBERIA FOR OUR RITUAL ORDEAL, WE STUMBLED ACROSS A HOT SPRING.
IT WAS JUST THE TWO OF US, ALONE IN A TINY HOT SPRING HIDDEN IN THE SNOWY MOUNTAINS.
I TOLD AKIRA I'D WASH HIS BACK, BUT HE'S SO TICKLISH HE COULD BARELY HOLD STILL!
WHA ?!

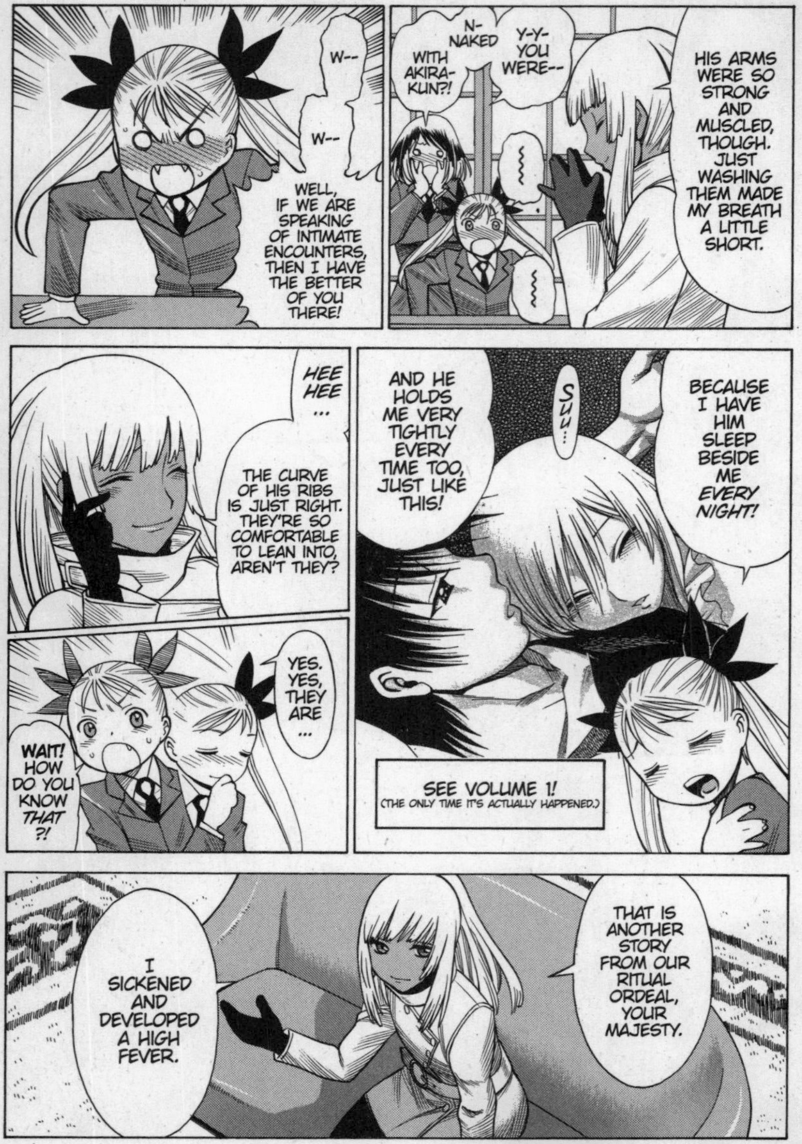
HIS ARMS WERE SO STRONG AND MUSCLED, THOUGH. JUST WASHING THEM MADE MY BREATH A LITTLE SHORT.
Y-Y-YOU WERE--
N-NAKED WITH AKIRA-KUN?!
W--
W--
WELL, IF WE ARE SPEAKING OF INTIMATE ENCOUNTERS, THEN I HAVE THE BETTER OF YOU THERE!
BECAUSE I HAVE HIM SLEEP BESIDE ME *EVERY NIGHT!*
Suu...
AND HE HOLDS ME VERY TIGHTLY EVERY TIME TOO, JUST LIKE THIS!
SEE VOLUME 1!
(THE ONLY TIME IT'S ACTUALLY HAPPENED.)
HEE HEE ...
THE CURVE OF HIS RIBS IS JUST RIGHT. THEY'RE SO COMFORTABLE TO LEAN INTO, AREN'T THEY?
YES. YES, THEY ARE ...
WAIT! HOW DO YOU KNOW *THAT*?!
THAT IS ANOTHER STORY FROM OUR RITUAL ORDEAL, YOUR MAJESTY.
I SICKENED AND DEVELOPED A HIGH FEVER.

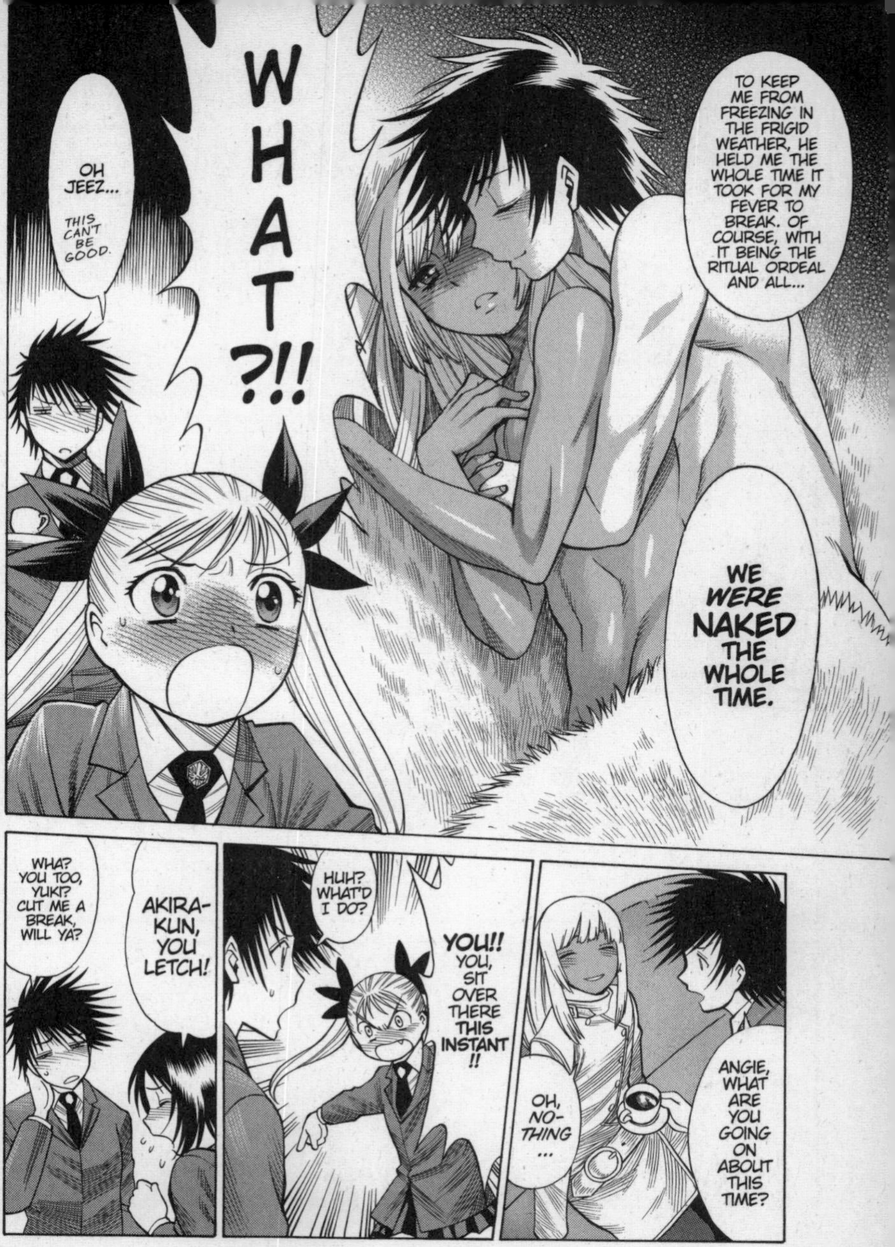
TO KEEP ME FROM FREEZING IN THE FRIGID WEATHER, HE HELD ME THE WHOLE TIME IT TOOK FOR MY FEVER TO BREAK. OF COURSE, WITH IT BEING THE RITUAL ORDEAL AND ALL...
WE *WERE* NAKED THE WHOLE TIME.
WHAT?!!
OH JEEZ...
THIS CAN'T BE GOOD.
ANGIE, WHAT ARE YOU GOING ON ABOUT THIS TIME?
OH, NO-THING...
YOU!! YOU, SIT OVER THERE THIS INSTANT!!
HUH? WHAT'D I DO?
AKIRA-KUN, YOU LETCH!
WHA? YOU TOO, YUKI? CUT ME A BREAK, WILL YA?

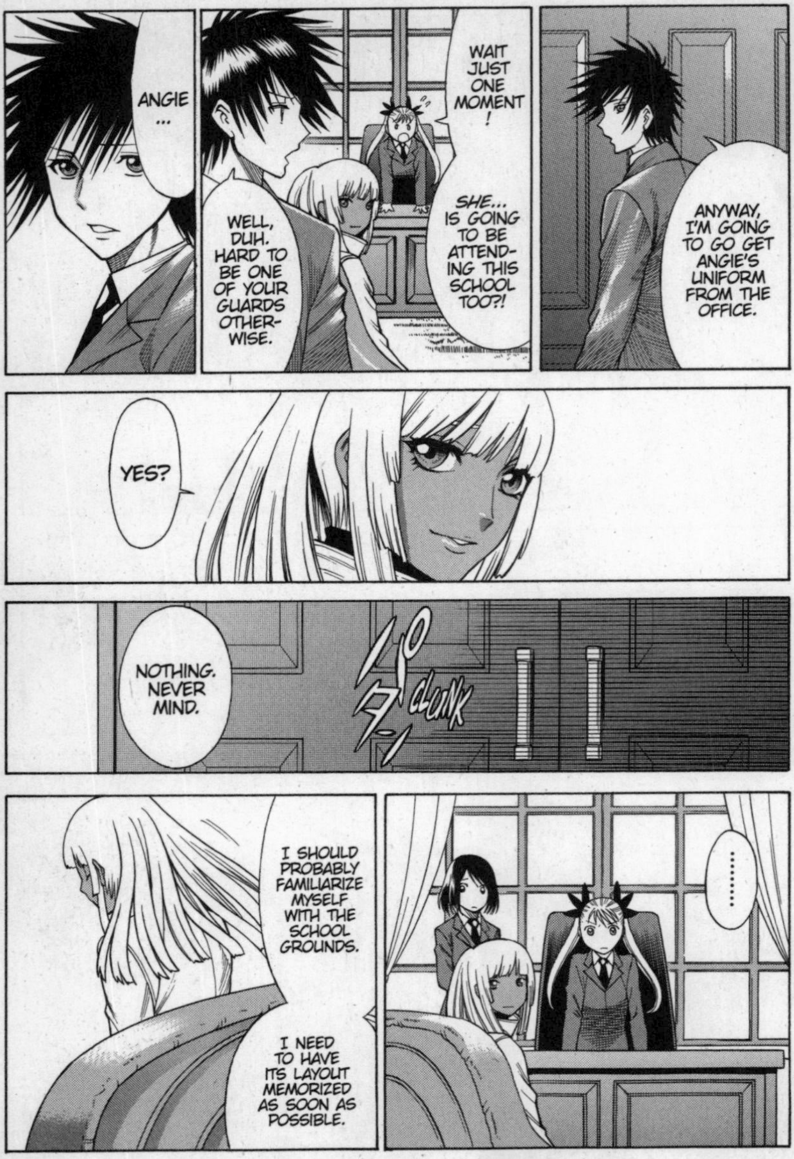
ANYWAY, I'M GOING TO GO GET ANGIE'S UNIFORM FROM THE OFFICE.
WAIT JUST ONE MOMENT!
SHE... IS GOING TO BE ATTENDING THIS SCHOOL TOO?!
WELL, DUH. HARD TO BE ONE OF YOUR GUARDS OTHERWISE.
ANGIE ...
YES?
NOTHING. NEVER MIND.
CLUNK
......
I SHOULD PROBABLY FAMILIARIZE MYSELF WITH THE SCHOOL GROUNDS.
I NEED TO HAVE ITS LAYOUT MEMORIZED AS SOON AS POSSIBLE.

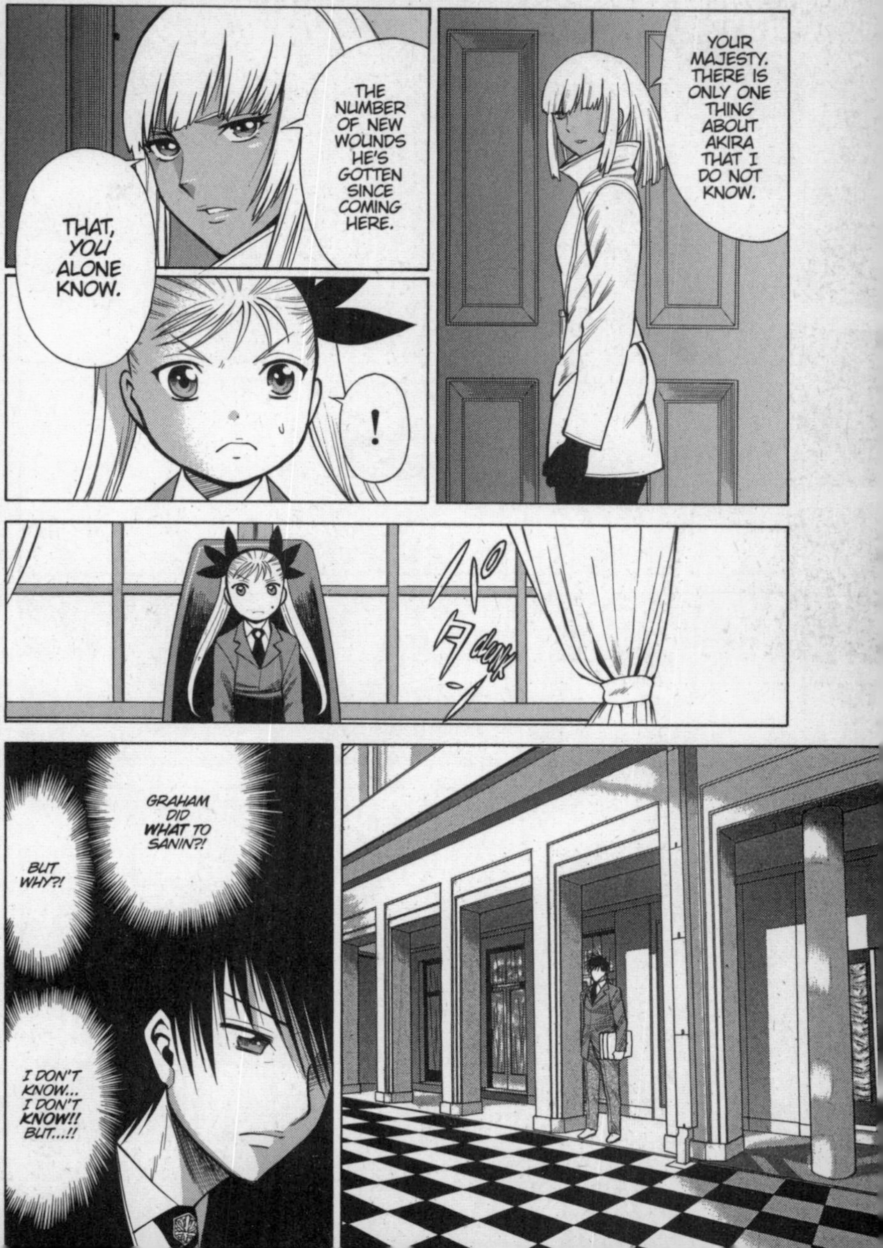
YOUR MAJESTY. THERE IS ONLY ONE THING ABOUT AKIRA THAT I DO NOT KNOW.
THE NUMBER OF NEW WOUNDS HE'S GOTTEN SINCE COMING HERE.
THAT, YOU ALONE KNOW.
!
パタ
clack
GRAHAM DID WHAT TO SANIN?!
BUT WHY?!
I DON'T KNOW... I DON'T KNOW!! BUT...!!

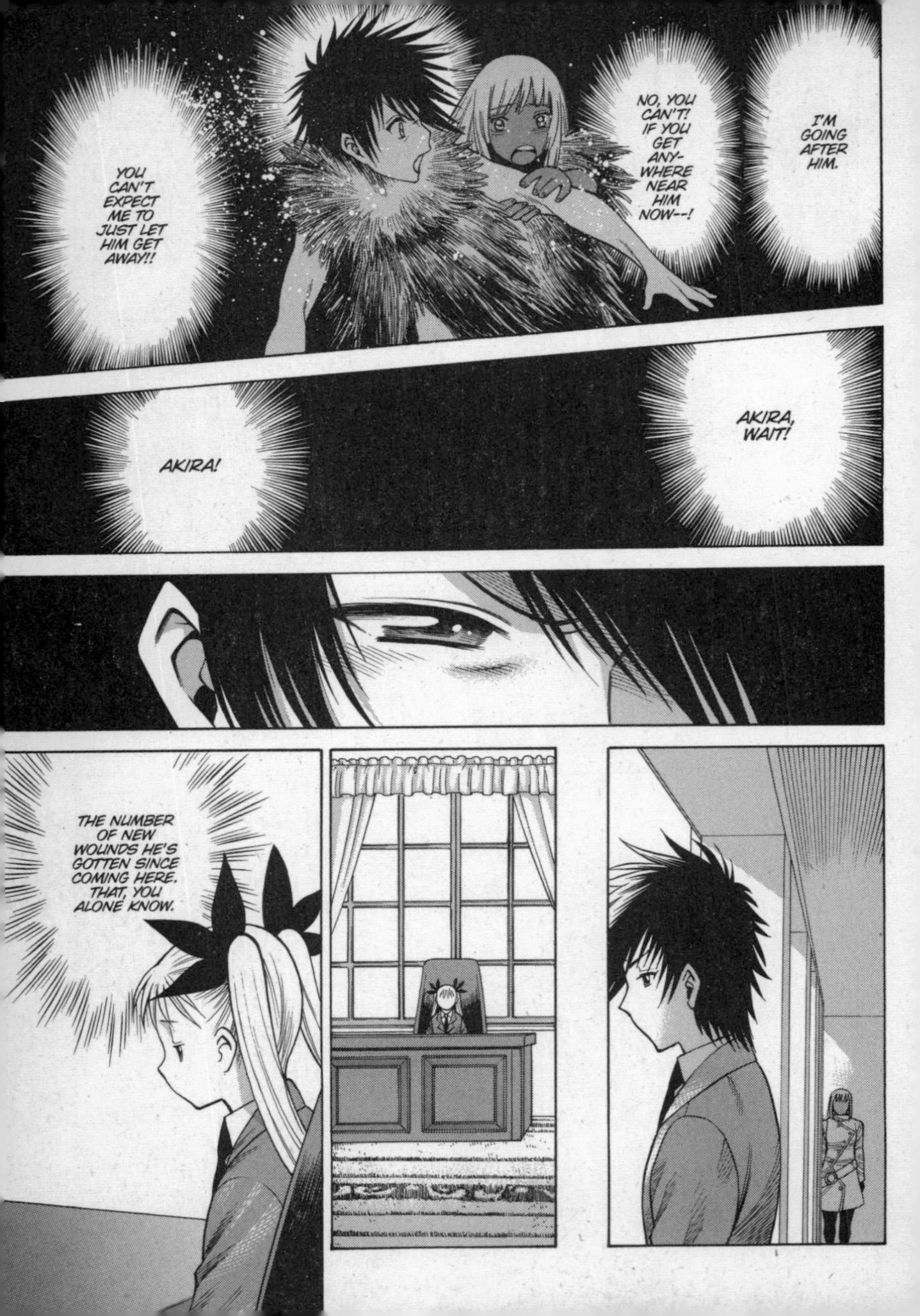
I'M GOING AFTER HIM.
NO, YOU CAN'T! IF YOU GET ANY-WHERE NEAR HIM NOW--!
YOU CAN'T EXPECT ME TO JUST LET HIM GET AWAY!!
AKIRA, WAIT!
AKIRA!
THE NUMBER OF NEW WOUNDS HE'S GOTTEN SINCE COMING HERE. THAT, YOU ALONE KNOW.

YUKI, I HAVE DECIDED TO TAKE MY MEAL A LITTLE EARLY TODAY.

THERE IS SOME STIGMA IN THE CABINET. WOULD YOU MIND BRINGING SOME FOR ME?

SURE! I'LL BE BACK IN A MINLITE.

K-CHAK

PLIP

!

CLUNK

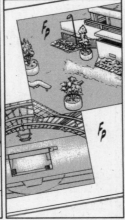

ENABLE VERBAL COMMAND.

SEARCH FACILITY SECURITY CAMERAS FOR VIDEO IMAGES FOR KABURAGI AKIRA.

TAK
TAK

TAK

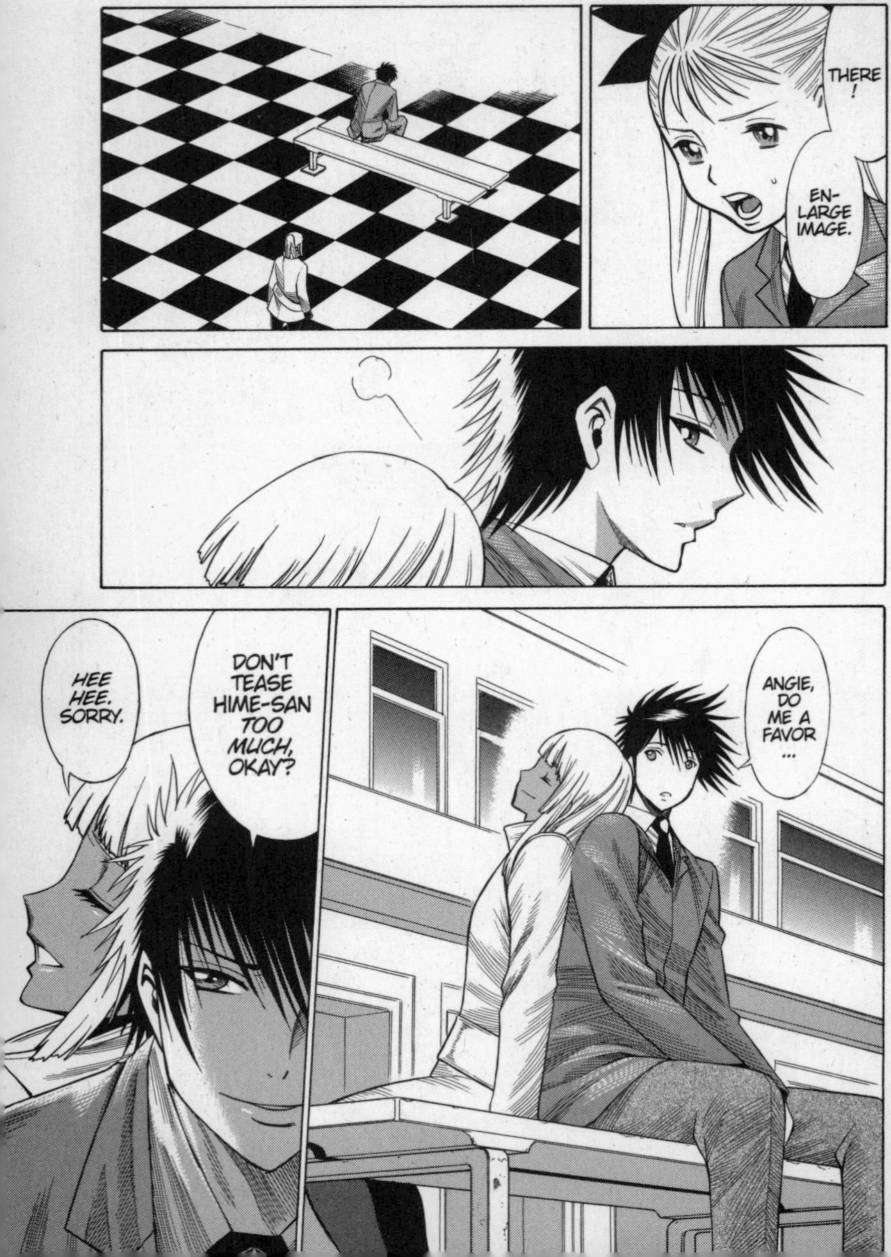
THERE!
EN-LARGE IMAGE.
ANGIE, DO ME A FAVOR...
DON'T TEASE HIME-SAN TOO MUCH, OKAY?
HEE HEE. SORRY.

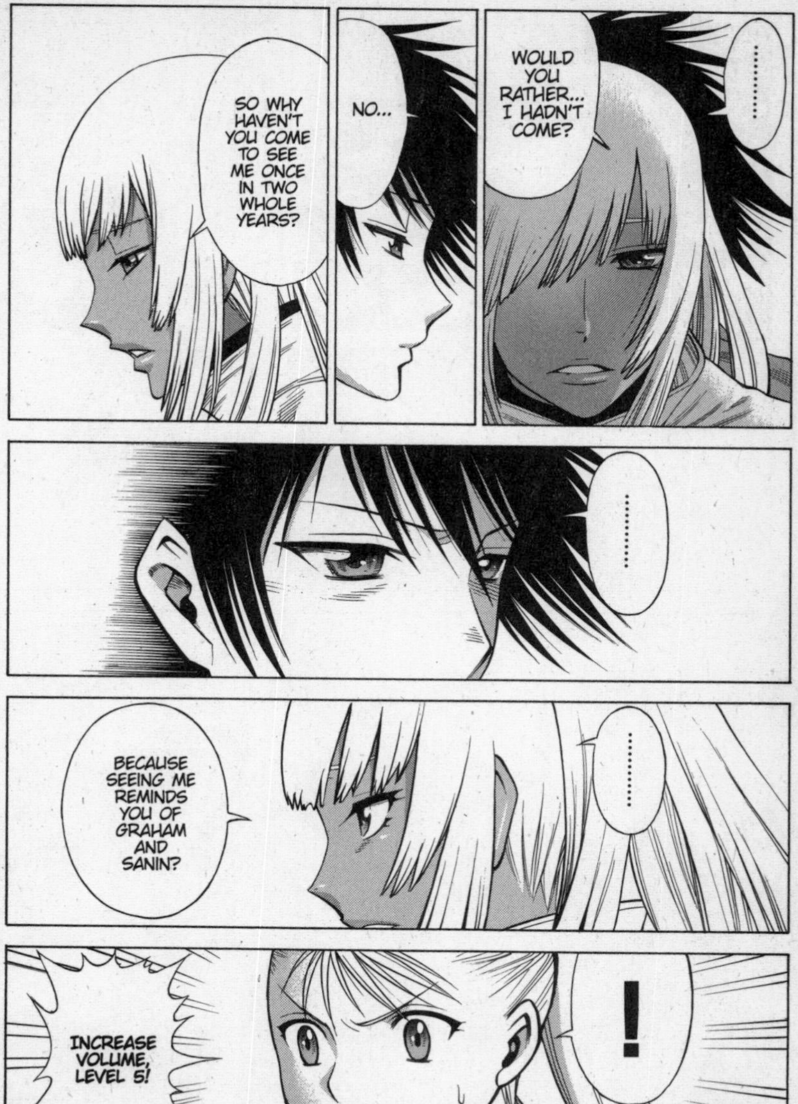
......
WOULD YOU RATHER... I HADN'T COME?
NO...
SO WHY HAVEN'T YOU COME TO SEE ME ONCE IN TWO WHOLE YEARS?
......
......
BECAUSE SEEING ME REMINDS YOU OF GRAHAM AND SANIN?
!
INCREASE VOLUME, LEVEL 5!

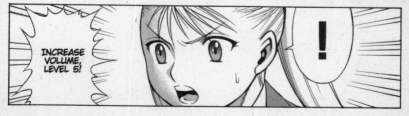

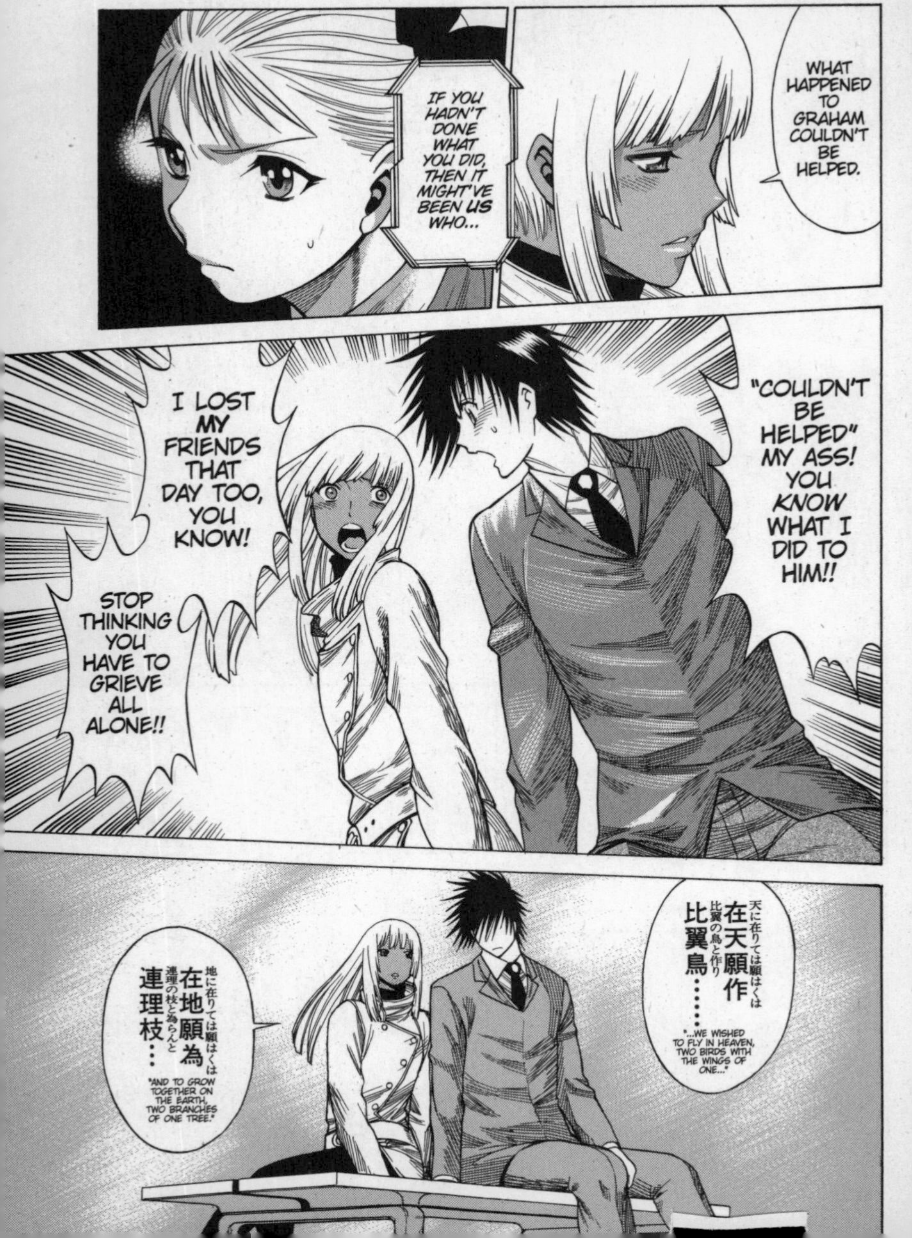
WHAT HAPPENED TO GRAHAM COULDN'T BE HELPED.
IF YOU HADN'T DONE WHAT YOU DID, THEN IT MIGHT'VE BEEN US WHO...
"COULDN'T BE HELPED" MY ASS! YOU KNOW WHAT I DID TO HIM!!
I LOST MY FRIENDS THAT DAY TOO, YOU KNOW!
STOP THINKING YOU HAVE TO GRIEVE ALL ALONE!!
天に在りては願はくは
在天願作
比翼の鳥と作り
比翼鳥……
"...WE WISHED TO FLY IN HEAVEN, TWO BIRDS WITH THE WINGS OF ONE..."
地に在りては願はくは
在地願為
連理の枝と為らんと
連理枝…
"AND TO GROW TOGETHER ON THE EARTH, TWO BRANCHES OF ONE TREE."

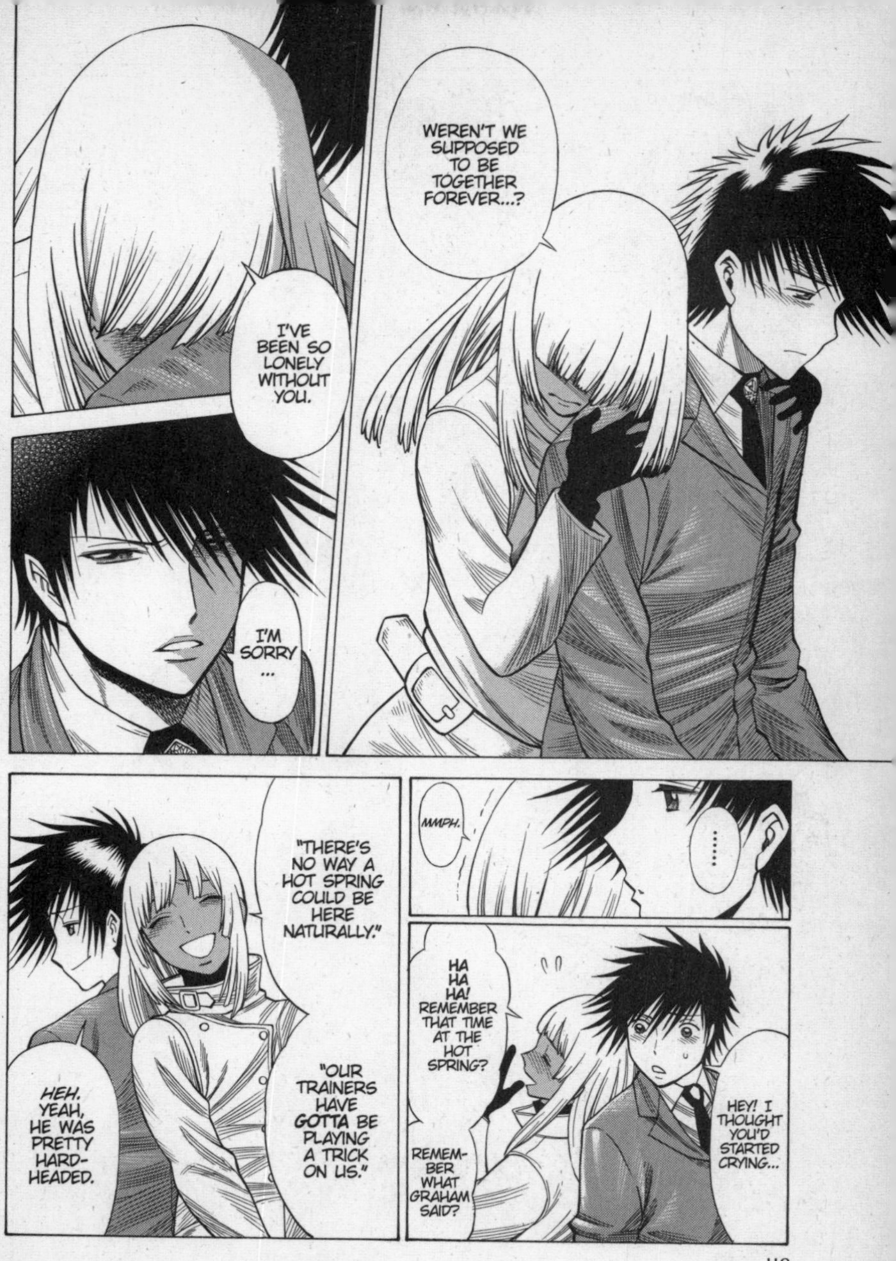
WEREN'T WE SUPPOSED TO BE TOGETHER FOREVER...?
I'VE BEEN SO LONELY WITHOUT YOU.
I'M SORRY ...
......
MMPH.
HEY! I THOUGHT YOU'D STARTED CRYING...
HA HA HA! REMEMBER THAT TIME AT THE HOT SPRING?
REMEMBER WHAT GRAHAM SAID?
"THERE'S NO WAY A HOT SPRING COULD BE HERE NATURALLY."
"OUR TRAINERS HAVE GOTTA BE PLAYING A TRICK ON US."
HEH. YEAH, HE WAS PRETTY HARD-HEADED.

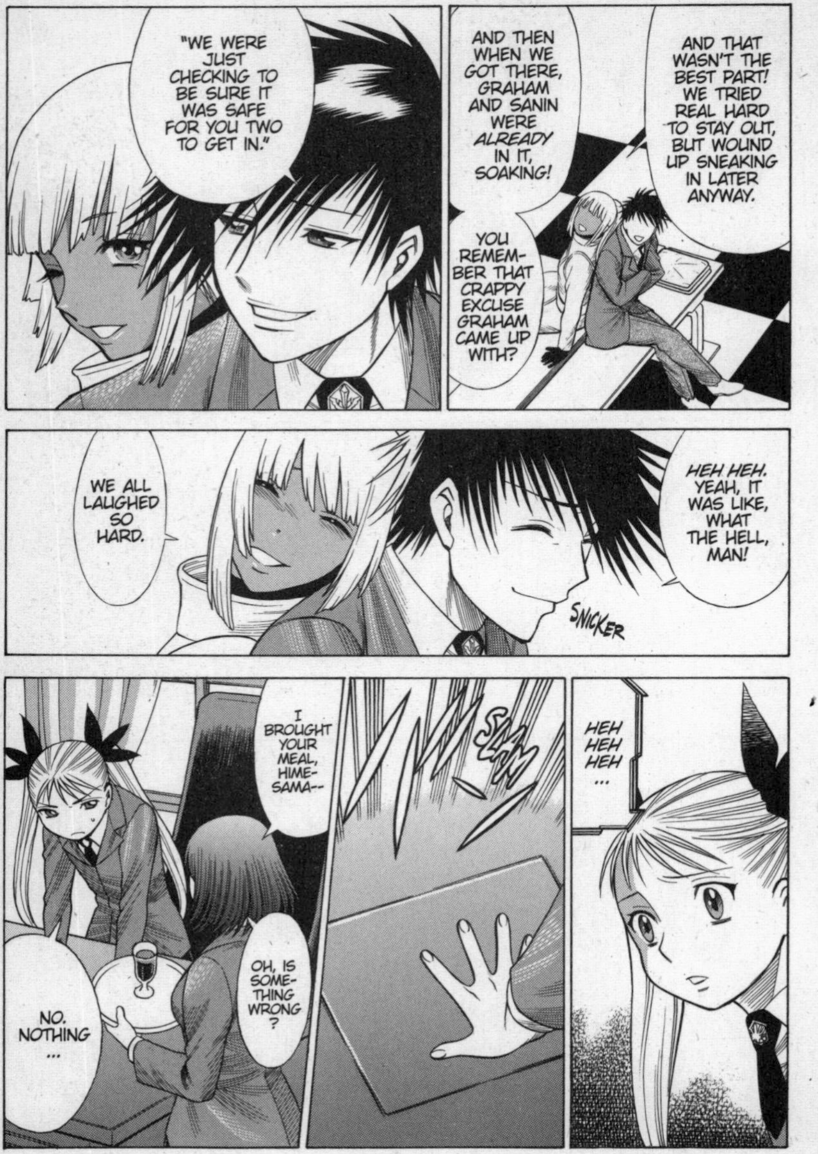
AND THAT WASN'T THE BEST PART! WE TRIED REAL HARD TO STAY OUT, BUT WOUND UP SNEAKING IN LATER ANYWAY.
AND THEN WHEN WE GOT THERE, GRAHAM AND SANIN WERE *ALREADY* IN IT, SOAKING!
YOU REMEMBER THAT CRAPPY EXCUSE GRAHAM CAME UP WITH?
"WE WERE JUST CHECKING TO BE SURE IT WAS SAFE FOR YOU TWO TO GET IN."
HEH HEH. YEAH, IT WAS LIKE, WHAT THE HELL, MAN!
SNICKER
WE ALL LAUGHED SO HARD.
HEH HEH HEH ...
SLAM
I BROUGHT YOUR MEAL, HIME-SAMA--
OH, IS SOMETHING WRONG?
NO. NOTHING ...

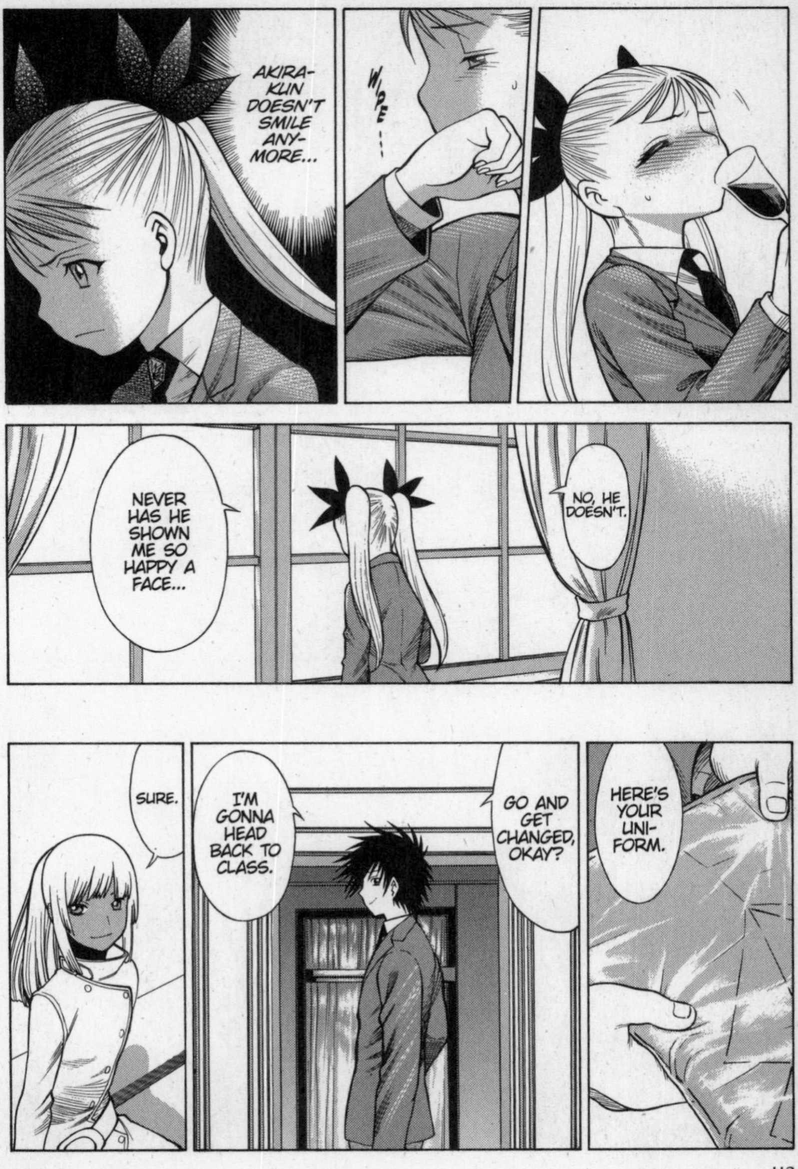
WIPE...
AKIRA-KUN DOESN'T SMILE ANYMORE...
NO, HE DOESN'T.
NEVER HAS HE SHOWN ME SO HAPPY A FACE...
HERE'S YOUR UNIFORM.
GO AND GET CHANGED, OKAY?
I'M GONNA HEAD BACK TO CLASS.
SURE.

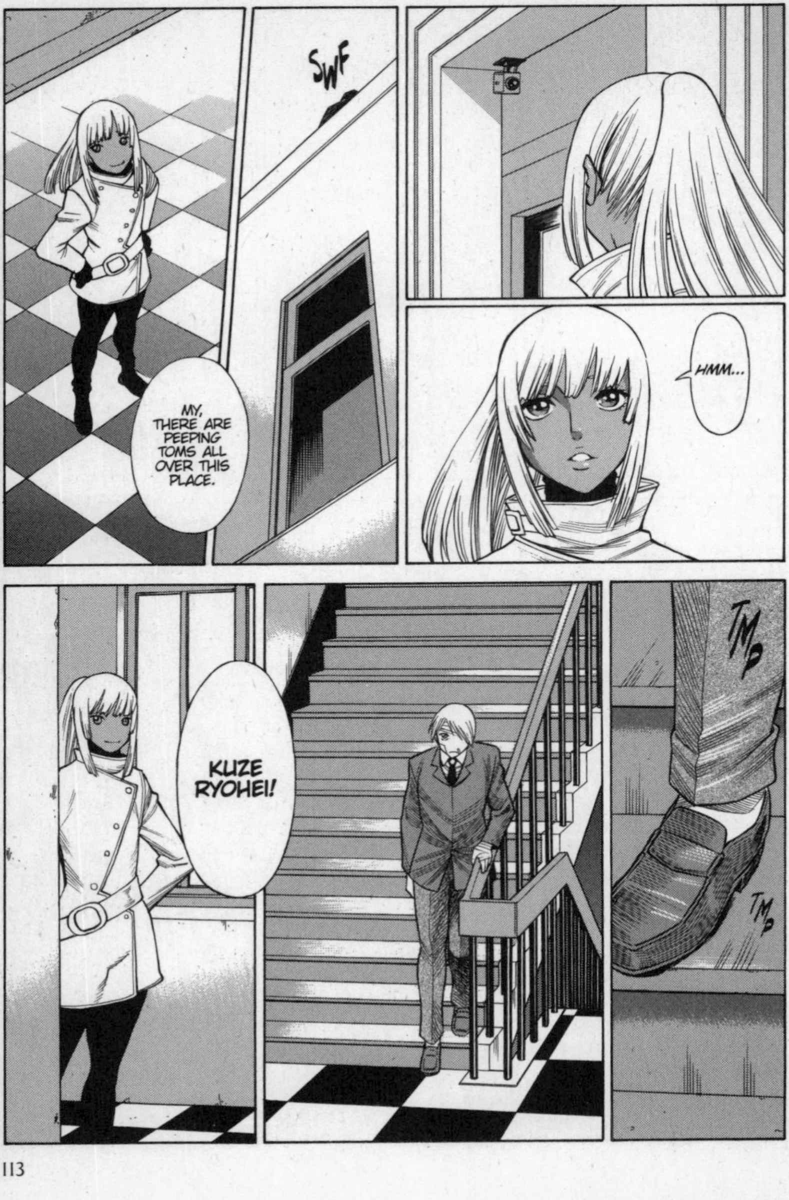
HMM...
SWF
MY, THERE ARE PEEPING TOMS ALL OVER THIS PLACE.
TMP
TMP
KUZE RYOHEI!

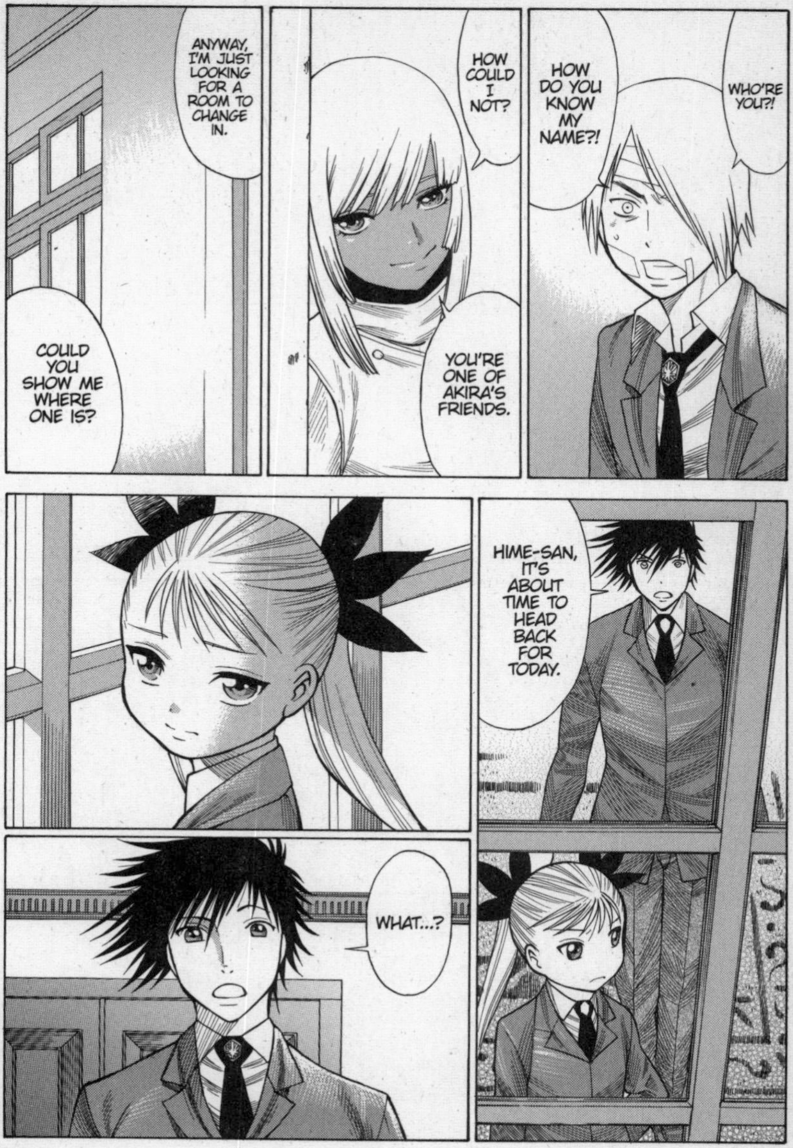
WHO'RE YOU?!
HOW DO YOU KNOW MY NAME?!
HOW COULD I NOT?
YOU'RE ONE OF AKIRA'S FRIENDS.
ANYWAY, I'M JUST LOOKING FOR A ROOM TO CHANGE IN.
COULD YOU SHOW ME WHERE ONE IS?
HIME-SAN, IT'S ABOUT TIME TO HEAD BACK FOR TODAY.
WHAT...?

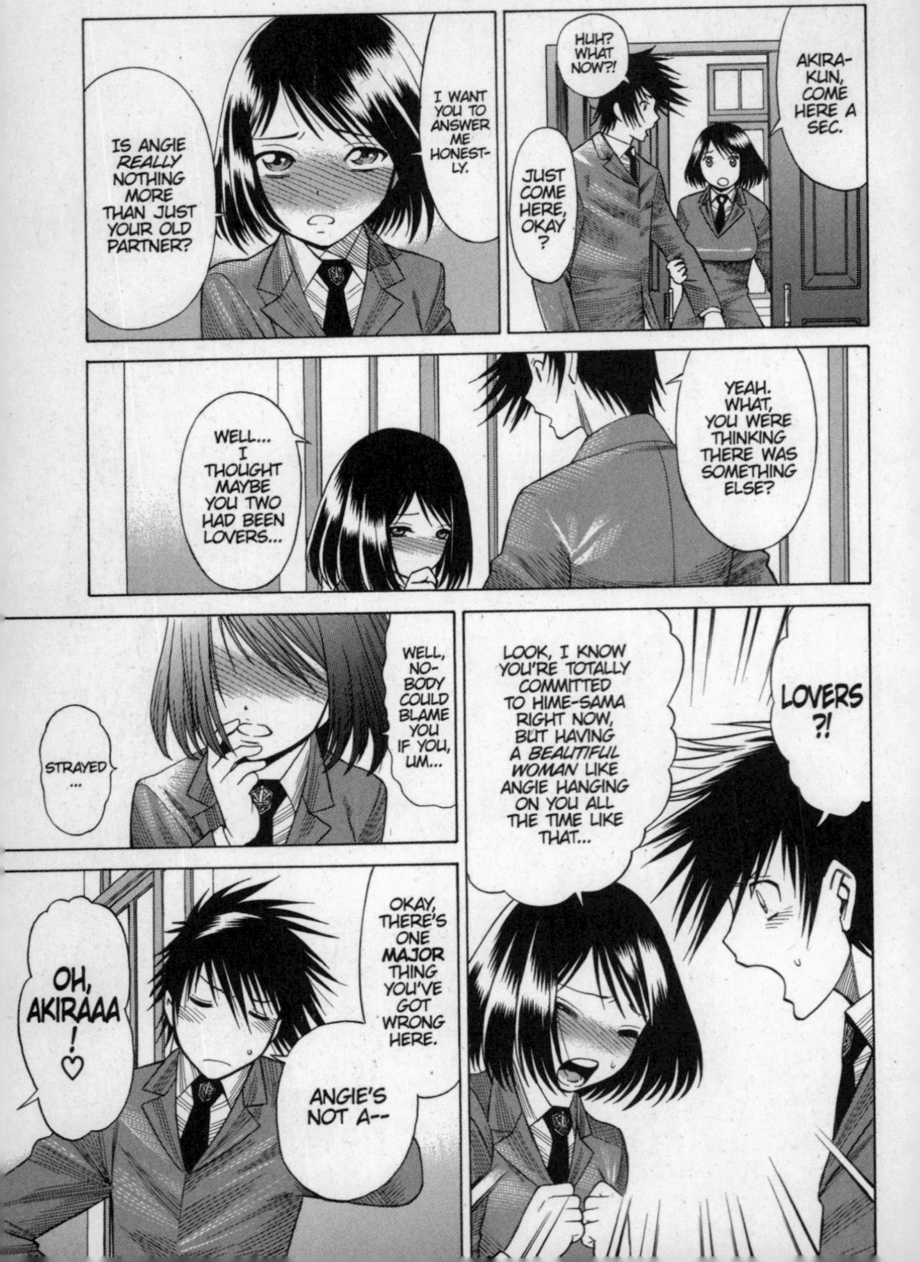
AKIRA-KUN, COME HERE A SEC.
HUH? WHAT NOW?!
JUST COME HERE, OKAY?
I WANT YOU TO ANSWER ME HONEST-LY.
IS ANGIE *REALLY* NOTHING MORE THAN JUST YOUR OLD PARTNER?
YEAH. WHAT, YOU WERE THINKING THERE WAS SOMETHING ELSE?
WELL... I THOUGHT MAYBE YOU TWO HAD BEEN LOVERS...
LOVERS?!
LOOK, I KNOW YOU'RE TOTALLY COMMITTED TO HIME-SAMA RIGHT NOW, BUT HAVING A *BEAUTIFUL WOMAN* LIKE ANGIE HANGING ON YOU ALL THE TIME LIKE THAT...
WELL, NO-BODY COULD BLAME YOU IF YOU, UM...
STRAYED...
OKAY, THERE'S ONE **MAJOR** THING YOU'VE GOT WRONG HERE.
ANGIE'S NOT A--
OH, AKIRAAA! ♡

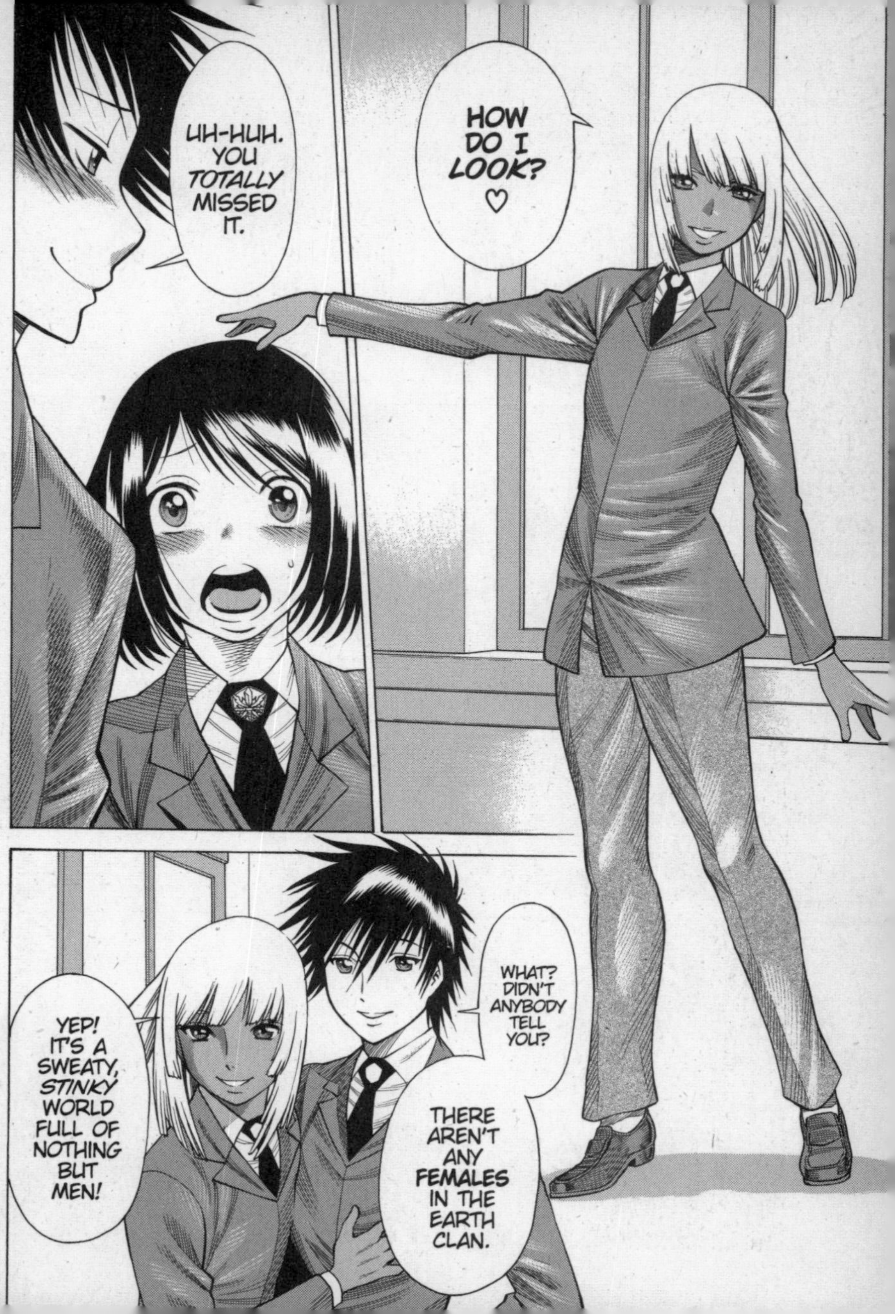
HOW DO I LOOK? ♡
UH-HUH. YOU TOTALLY MISSED IT.
WHAT? DIDN'T ANYBODY TELL YOU?
THERE AREN'T ANY FEMALES IN THE EARTH CLAN.
YEP! IT'S A SWEATY, STINKY WORLD FULL OF NOTHING BUT MEN!

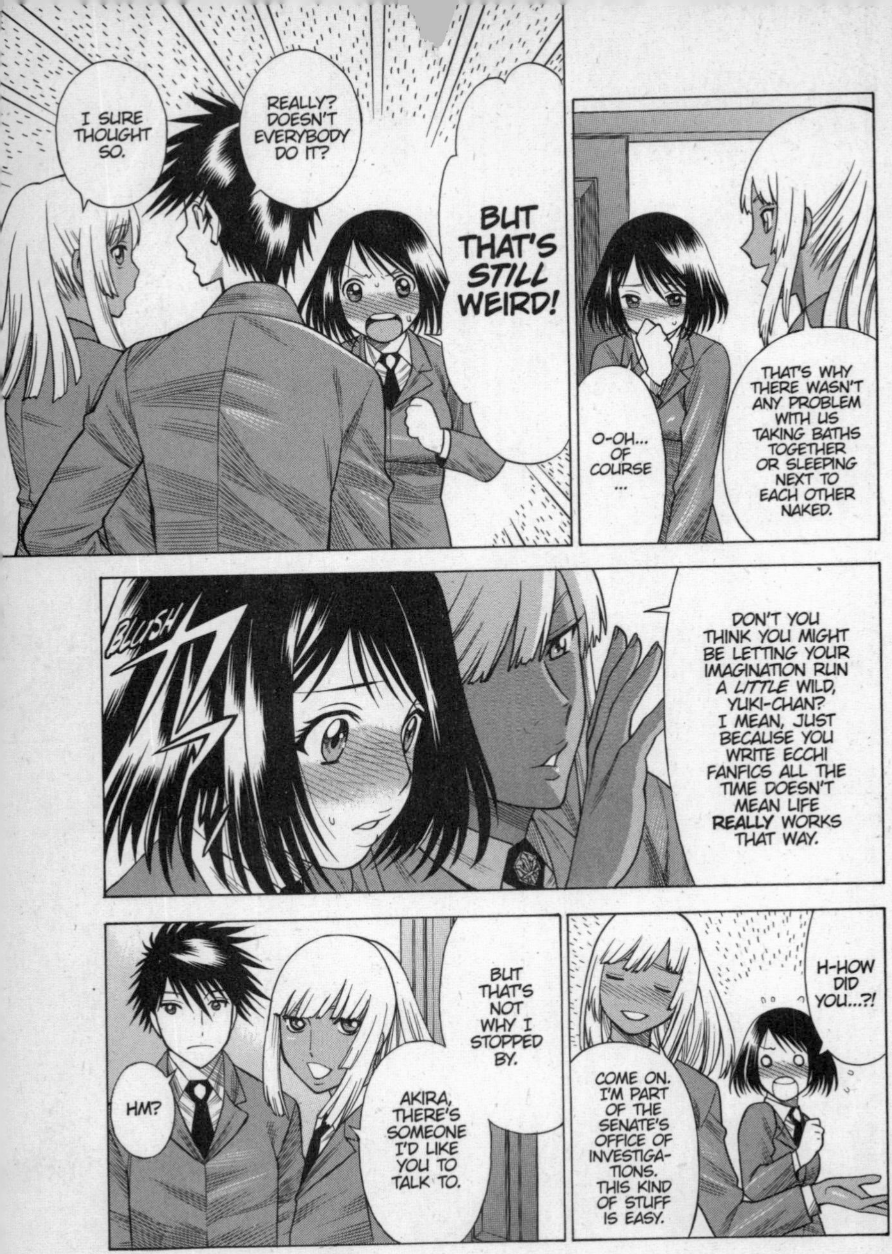
THAT'S WHY THERE WASN'T ANY PROBLEM WITH US TAKING BATHS TOGETHER OR SLEEPING NEXT TO EACH OTHER NAKED.
O-OH... OF COURSE...
BUT THAT'S STILL WEIRD!
REALLY? DOESN'T EVERYBODY DO IT?
I SURE THOUGHT SO.
DON'T YOU THINK YOU MIGHT BE LETTING YOUR IMAGINATION RUN A LITTLE WILD, YUKI-CHAN? I MEAN, JUST BECAUSE YOU WRITE ECCHI FANFICS ALL THE TIME DOESN'T MEAN LIFE REALLY WORKS THAT WAY.
BLUSH
H-HOW DID YOU...?!
COME ON. I'M PART OF THE SENATE'S OFFICE OF INVESTIGATIONS. THIS KIND OF STUFF IS EASY.
BUT THAT'S NOT WHY I STOPPED BY.
AKIRA, THERE'S SOMEONE I'D LIKE YOU TO TALK TO.
HM?

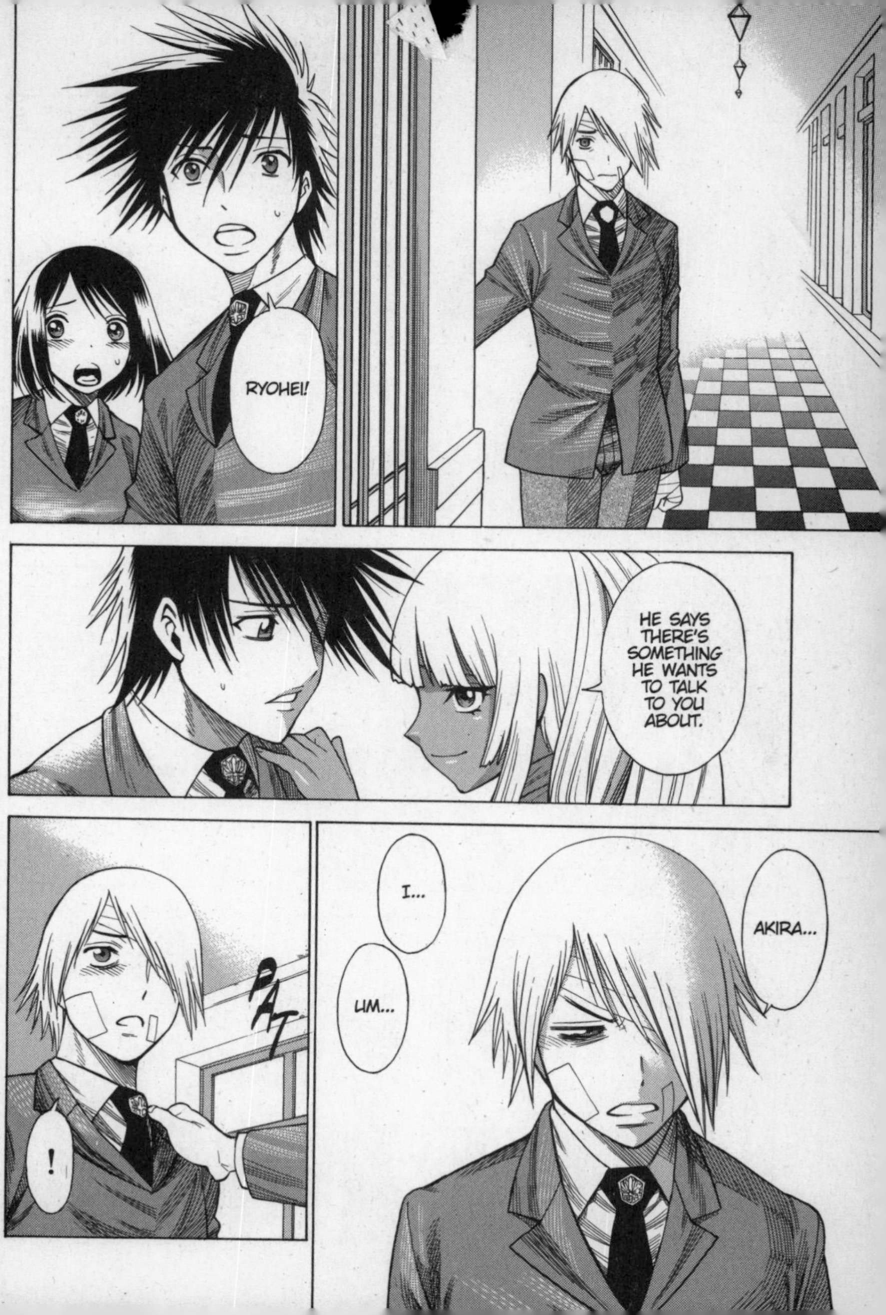
RYOHEI!
HE SAYS THERE'S SOMETHING HE WANTS TO TALK TO YOU ABOUT.
AKIRA...
I...
UM...
PAT
!

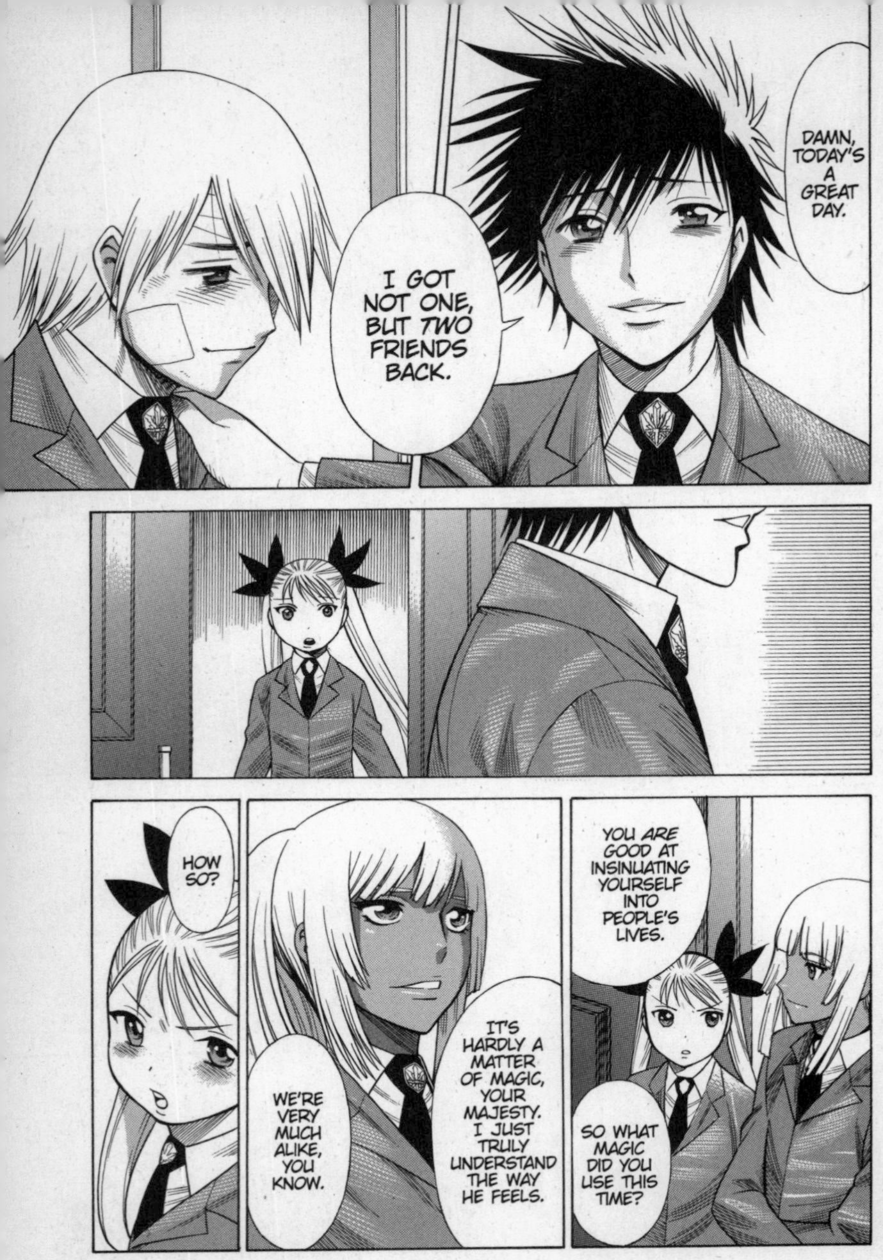
DAMN, TODAY'S A GREAT DAY.
I GOT NOT ONE, BUT TWO FRIENDS BACK.
YOU ARE GOOD AT INSINUATING YOURSELF INTO PEOPLE'S LIVES.
SO WHAT MAGIC DID YOU USE THIS TIME?
IT'S HARDLY A MATTER OF MAGIC, YOUR MAJESTY. I JUST TRULY UNDERSTAND THE WAY HE FEELS.
WE'RE VERY MUCH ALIKE, YOU KNOW.
HOW SO?

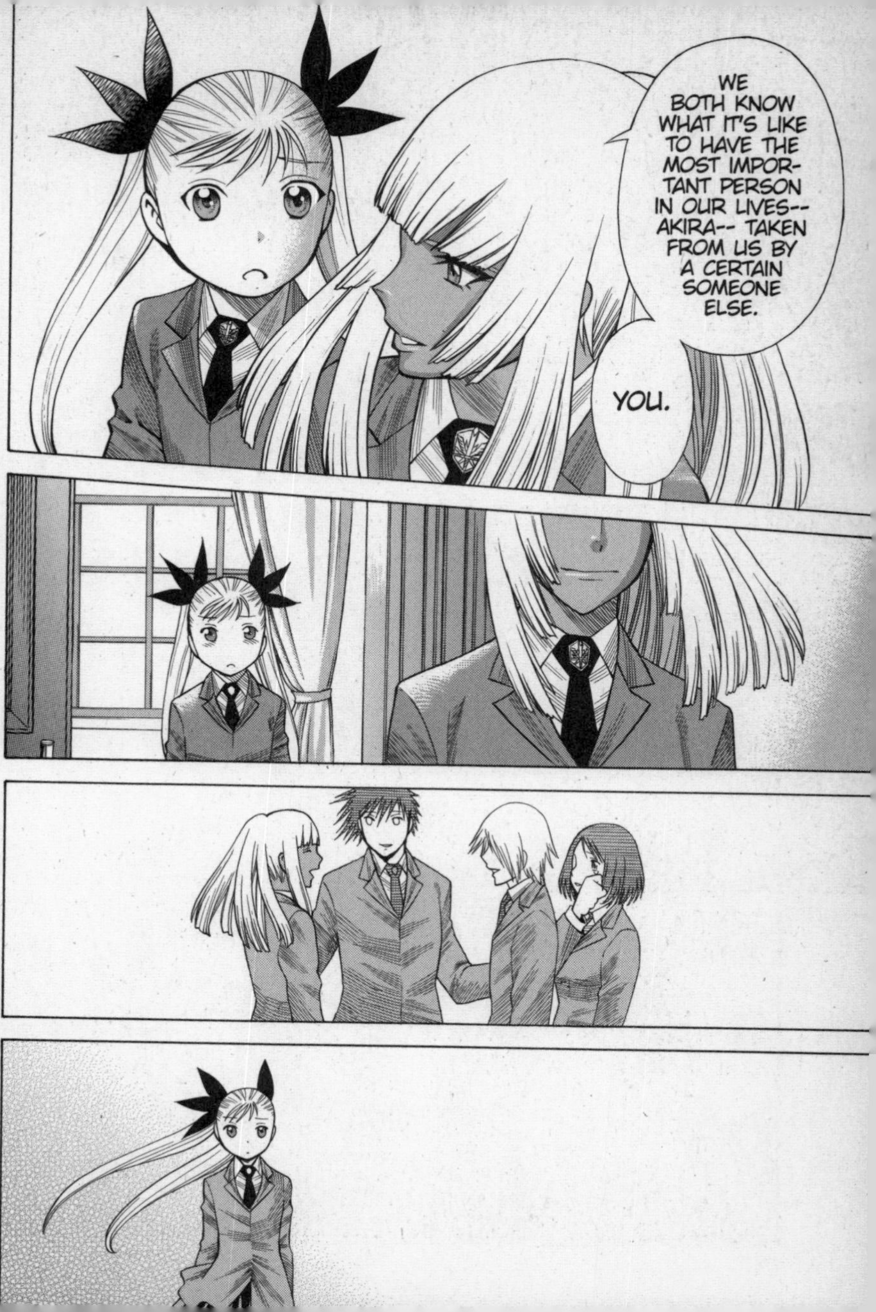
WE BOTH KNOW WHAT IT'S LIKE TO HAVE THE MOST IMPOR-TANT PERSON IN OUR LIVES-- AKIRA-- TAKEN FROM US BY A CERTAIN SOMEONE ELSE.
YOU.

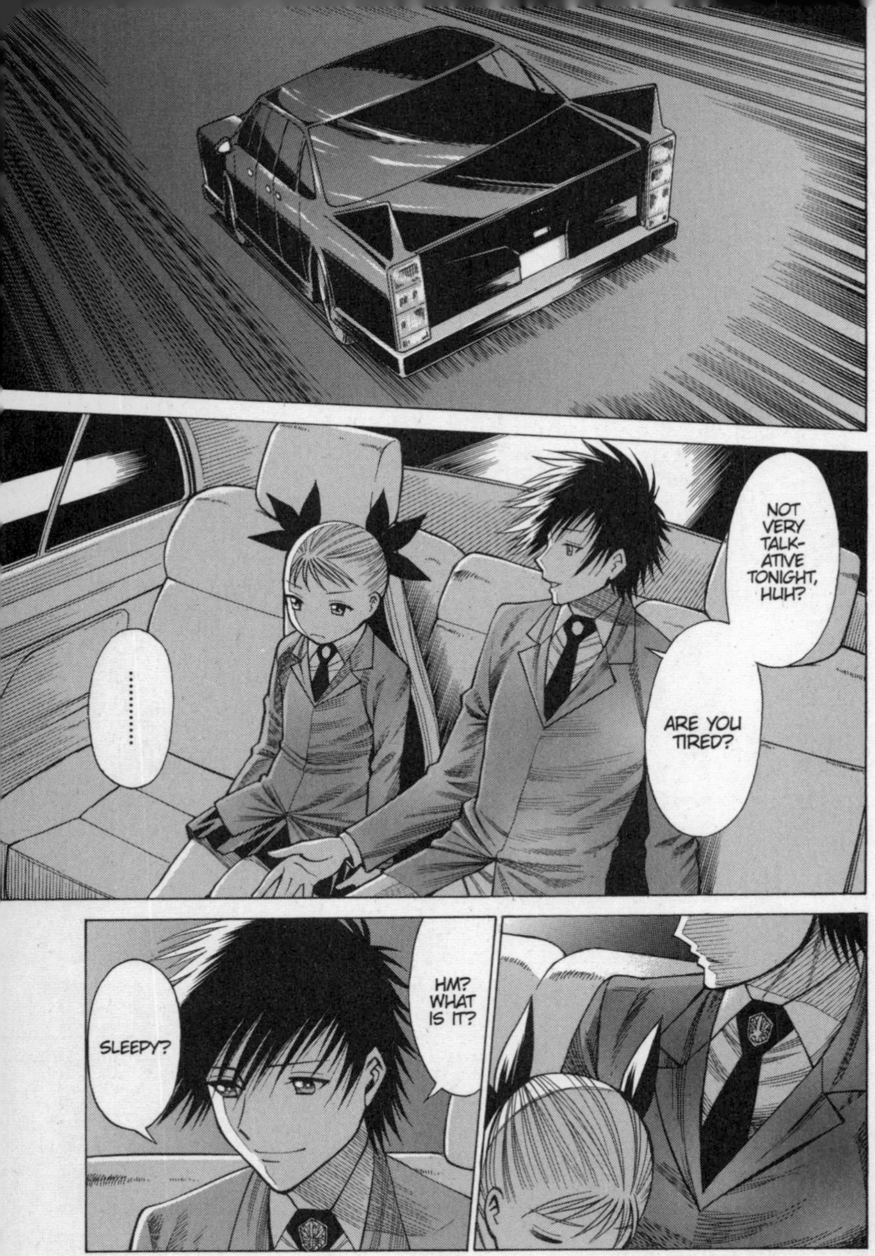
NOT VERY TALK-ATIVE TONIGHT, HUH?
ARE YOU TIRED?
......
HM? WHAT IS IT?
SLEEPY?

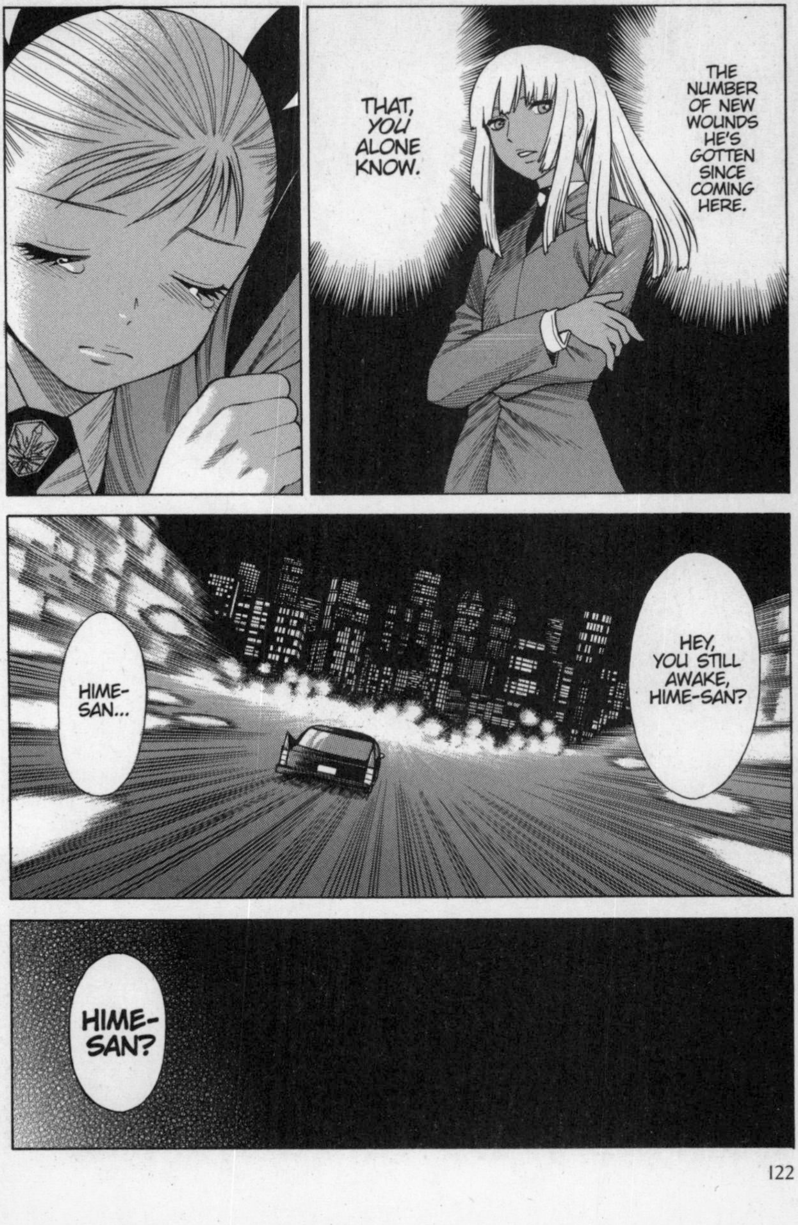
THE NUMBER OF NEW WOUNDS HE'S GOTTEN SINCE COMING HERE.
THAT, YOU ALONE KNOW.
HEY, YOU STILL AWAKE, HIME-SAN?
HIME-SAN...
HIME-SAN?

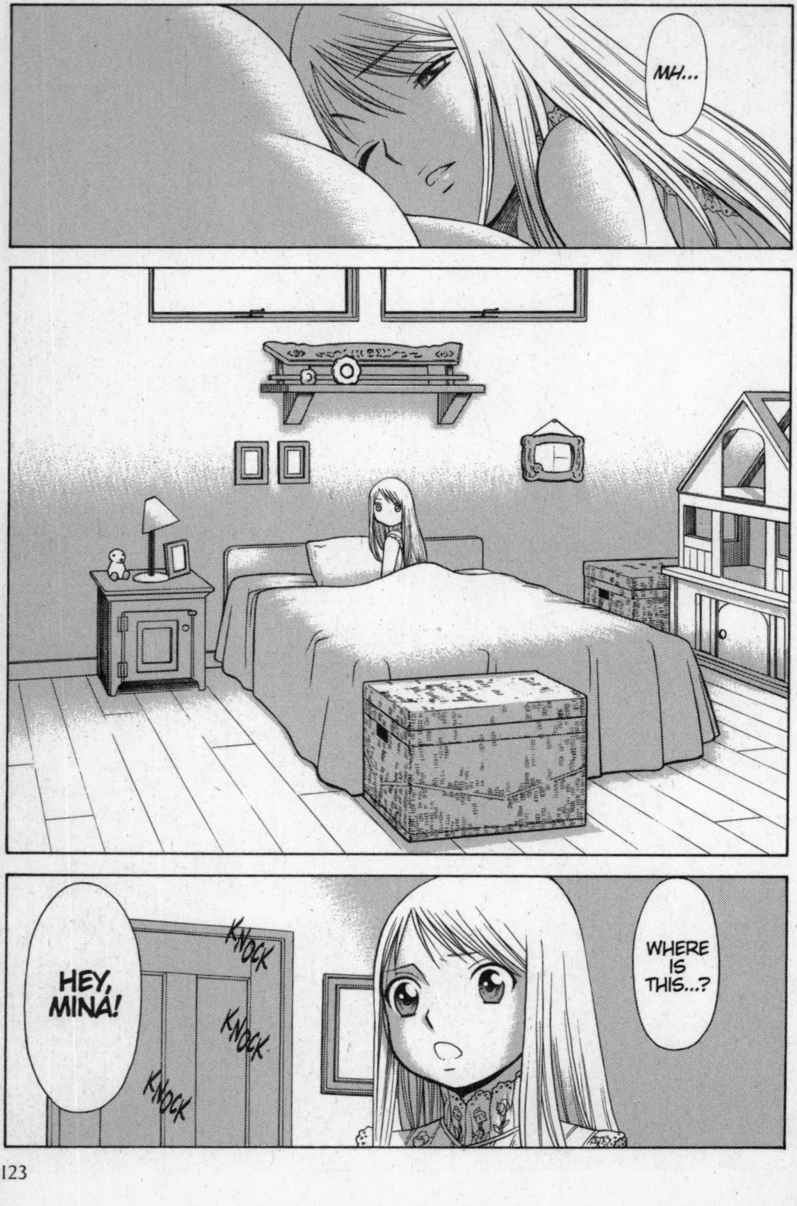
MH...
WHERE IS THIS...?
KNOCK
KNOCK
KNOCK
HEY, MINA!

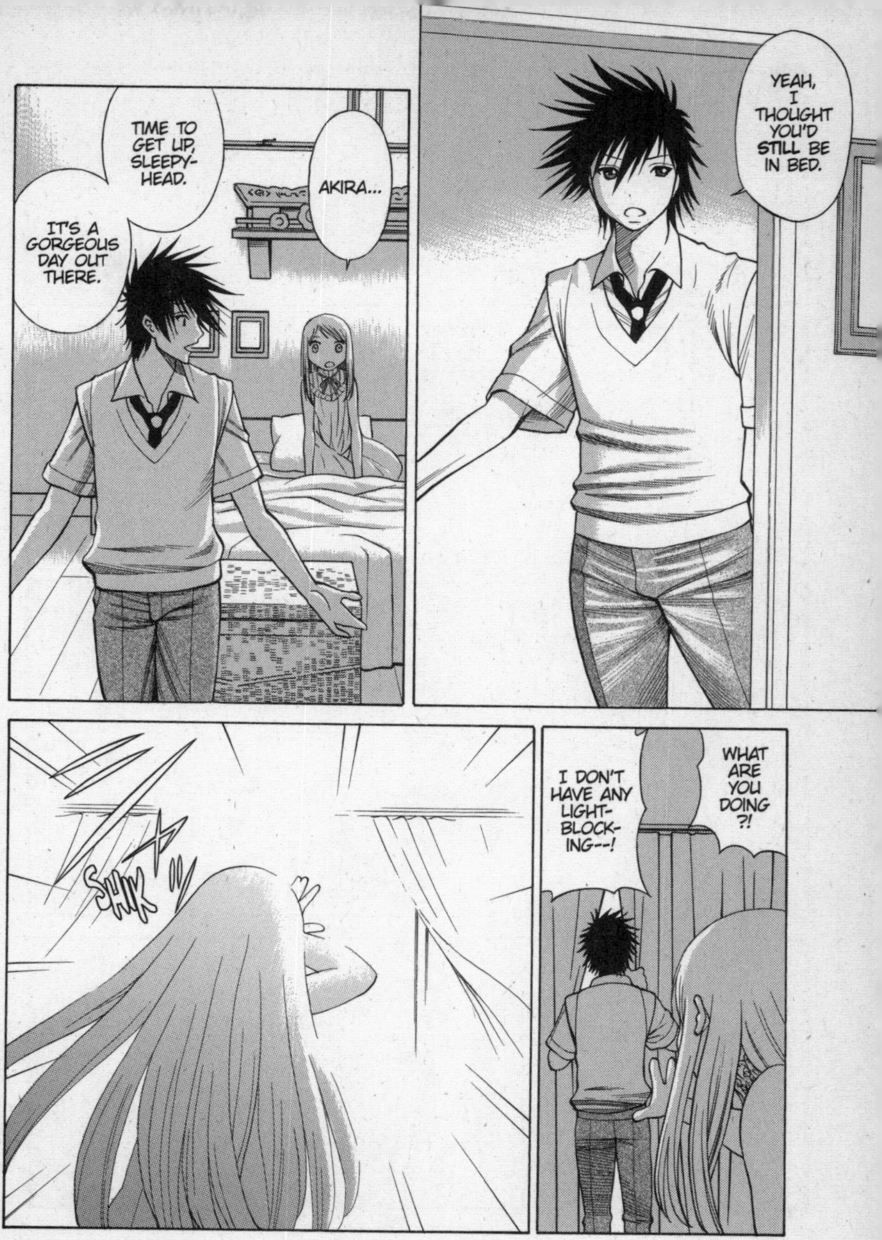
YEAH, I THOUGHT YOU'D STILL BE IN BED.
AKIRA...
TIME TO GET UP, SLEEPY-HEAD.
IT'S A GORGEOUS DAY OUT THERE.
WHAT ARE YOU DOING ?!
I DON'T HAVE ANY LIGHT-BLOCKING--!
SHIK

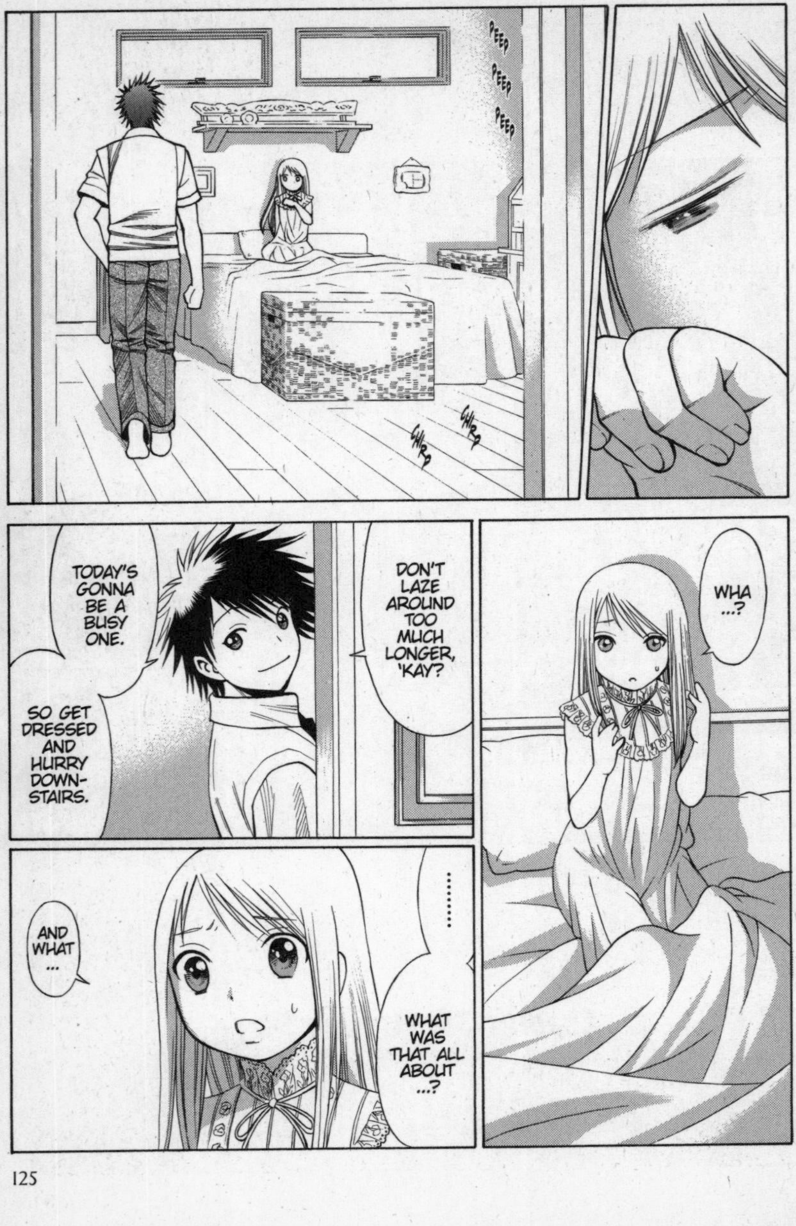
PEEP
PEEP
PEEP
CHIRP
CHIRP
WHA ...?
DON'T LAZE AROUND TOO MUCH LONGER, 'KAY?
TODAY'S GONNA BE A BUSY ONE.
SO GET DRESSED AND HURRY DOWN-STAIRS.
....
AND WHAT ...
WHAT WAS THAT ALL ABOUT ...?

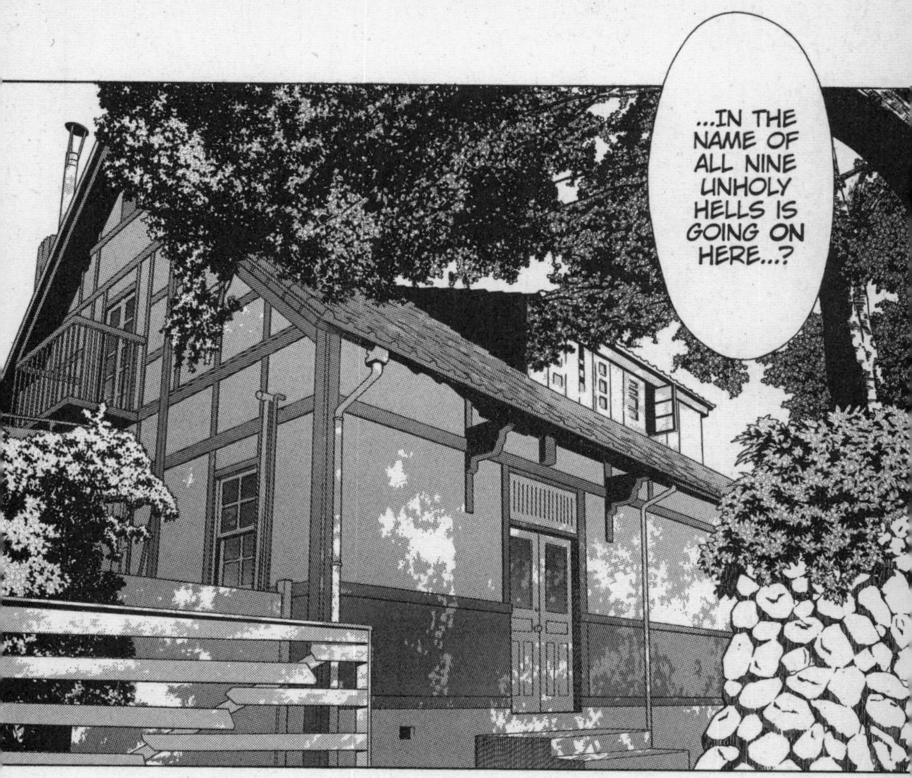
...IN THE NAME OF ALL NINE UNHOLY HELLS IS GOING ON HERE...?

Chapter 36: Passion Play

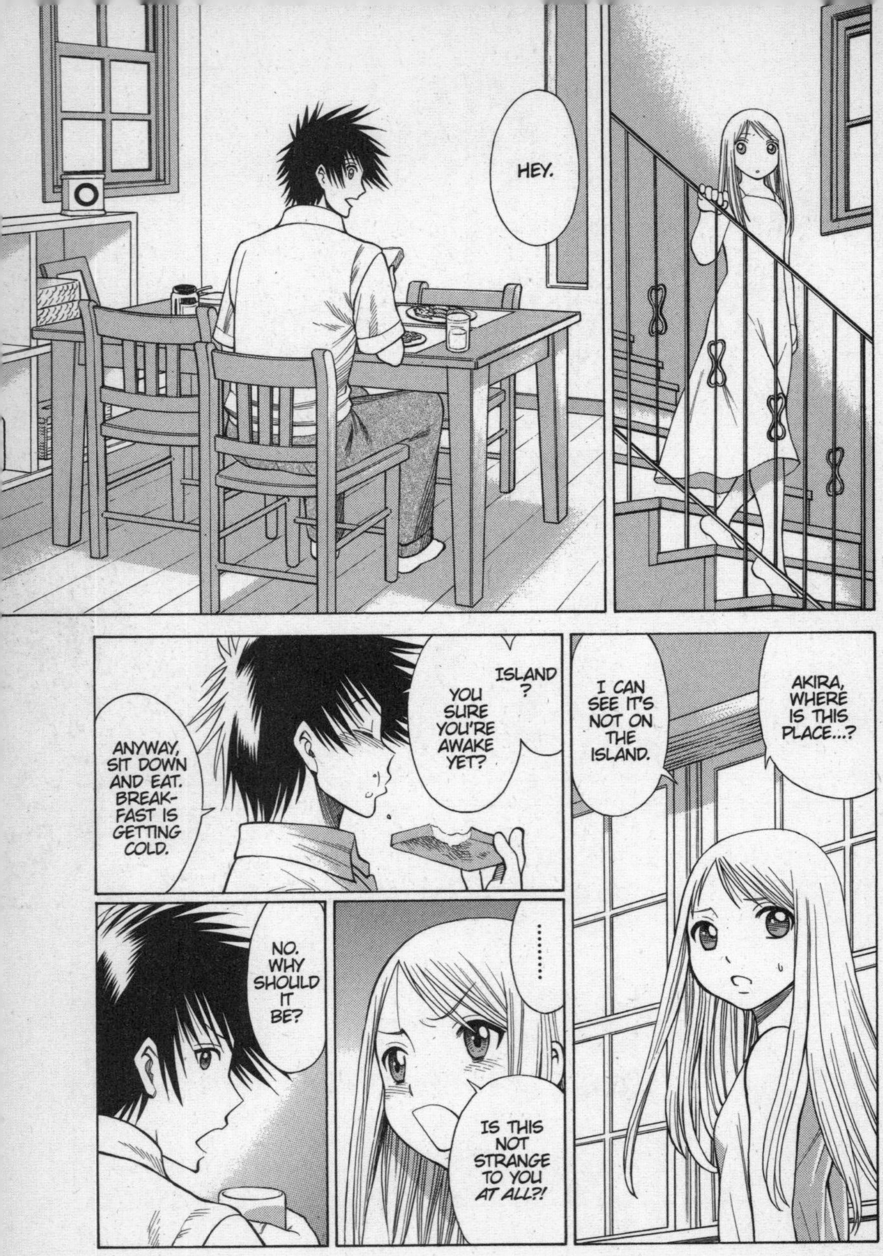
HEY.
AKIRA, WHERE IS THIS PLACE...?
I CAN SEE IT'S NOT ON THE ISLAND.
ISLAND? YOU SURE YOU'RE AWAKE YET?
ANYWAY, SIT DOWN AND EAT. BREAK-FAST IS GETTING COLD.
......
IS THIS NOT STRANGE TO YOU *AT ALL*?!
NO. WHY SHOULD IT BE?

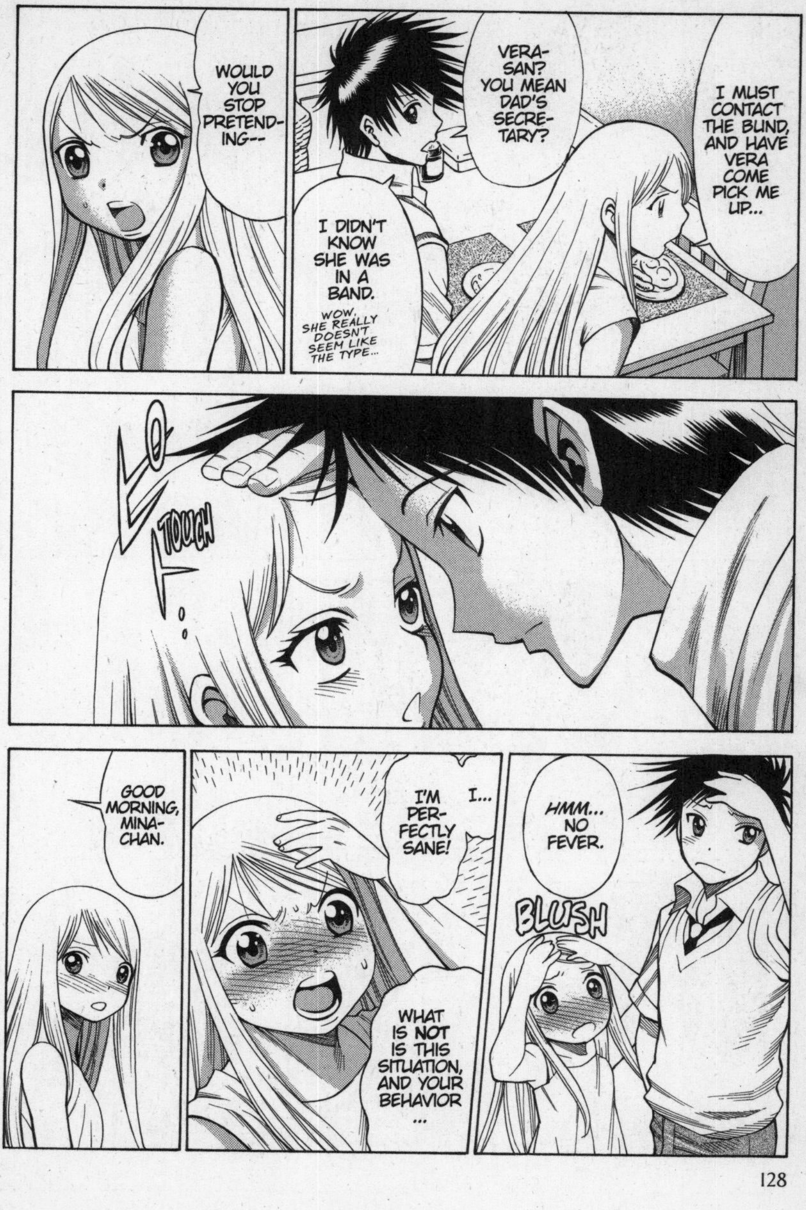
I MUST CONTACT THE BUND, AND HAVE VERA COME PICK ME UP...
VERA-SAN? YOU MEAN DAD'S SECRE-TARY?
I DIDN'T KNOW SHE WAS IN A BAND.
WOW, SHE REALLY DOESN'T SEEM LIKE THE TYPE...
WOULD YOU STOP PRETEND-ING--
TOUCH
HMM... NO FEVER.
BLUSH
I...
I'M PER-FECTLY SANE!
WHAT IS NOT IS THIS SITUATION, AND YOUR BEHAVIOR ...
GOOD MORNING, MINA-CHAN.

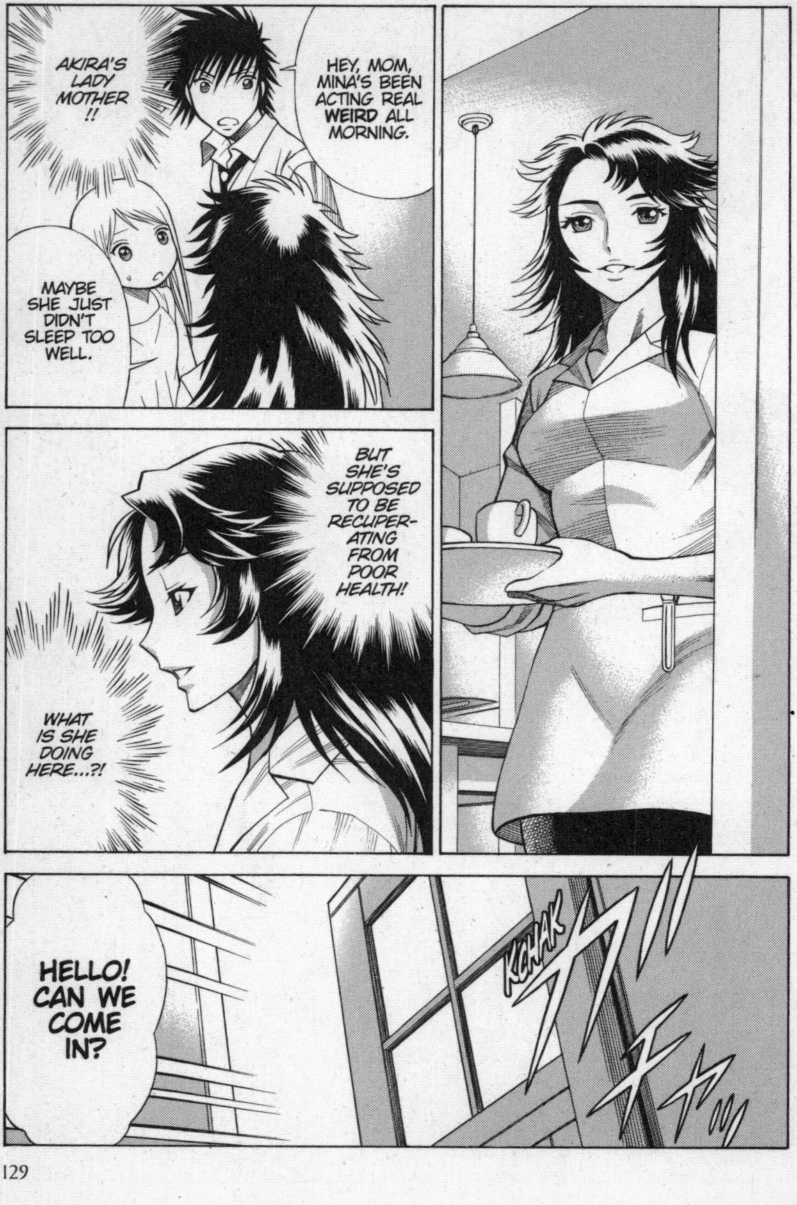
HEY, MOM, MINA'S BEEN ACTING REAL WEIRD ALL MORNING.
AKIRA'S LADY MOTHER !!
MAYBE SHE JUST DIDN'T SLEEP TOO WELL.
BUT SHE'S SUPPOSED TO BE RECUPER-ATING FROM POOR HEALTH!
WHAT IS SHE DOING HERE...?!
KCHAK
HELLO! CAN WE COME IN?

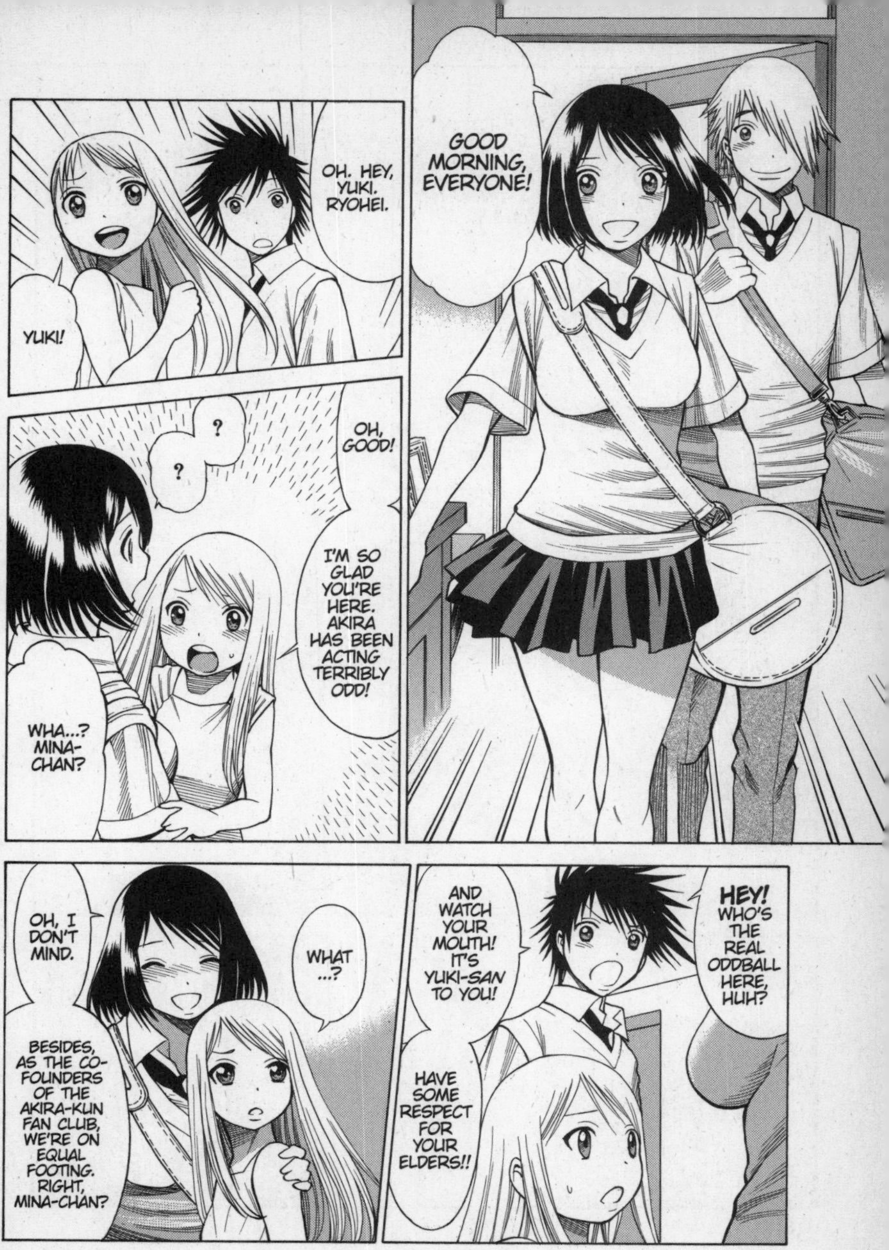
GOOD MORNING, EVERYONE!
OH. HEY, YUKI. RYOHEI.
YUKI!
OH, GOOD!
I'M SO GLAD YOU'RE HERE. AKIRA HAS BEEN ACTING TERRIBLY ODD!
?
?
WHA...? MINA-CHAN?
HEY! WHO'S THE REAL ODDBALL HERE, HUH?
AND WATCH YOUR MOUTH! IT'S YUKI-SAN TO YOU!
HAVE SOME RESPECT FOR YOUR ELDERS!!
WHAT ...?
OH, I DON'T MIND.
BESIDES, AS THE CO-FOUNDERS OF THE AKIRA-KUN FAN CLUB, WE'RE ON EQUAL FOOTING. RIGHT, MINA-CHAN?

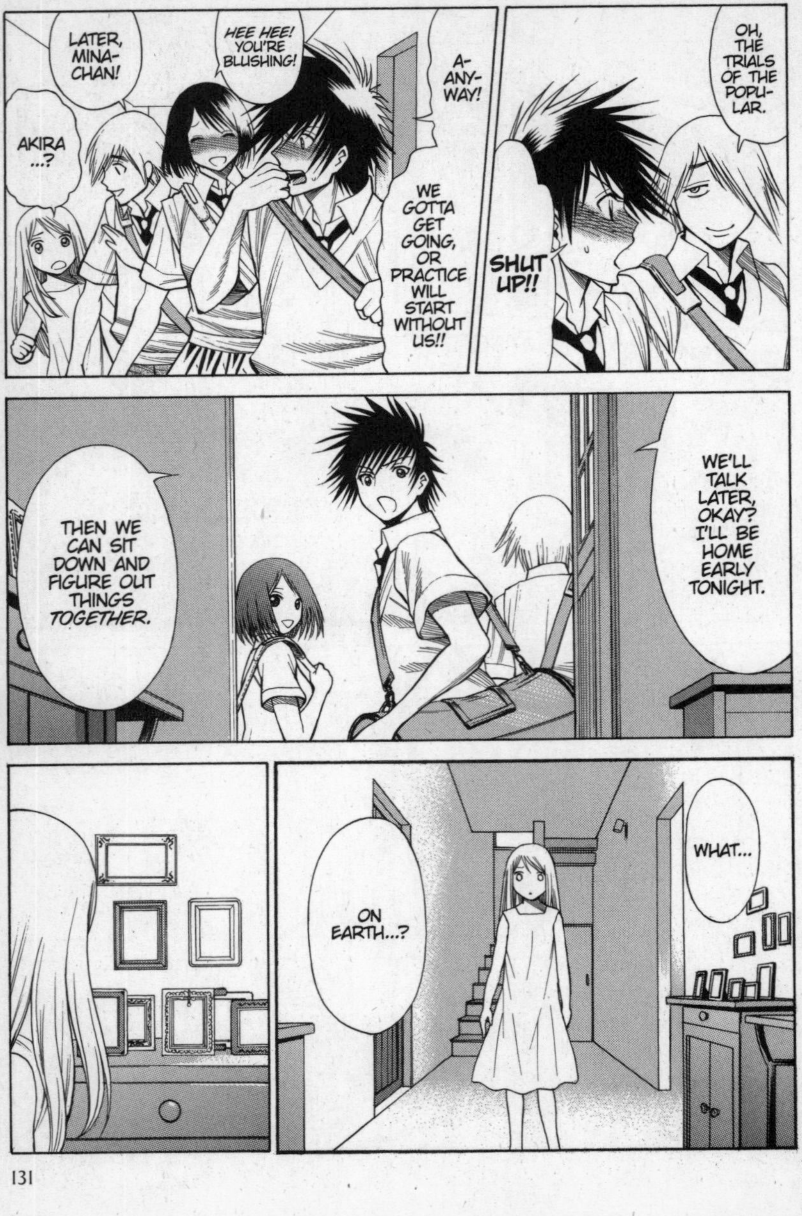
OH, THE TRIALS OF THE POPULAR.
SHUT UP!!
A-ANYWAY!
WE GOTTA GET GOING, OR PRACTICE WILL START WITHOUT US!!
HEE HEE! YOU'RE BLUSHING!
LATER, MINA-CHAN!
AKIRA ...?
WE'LL TALK LATER, OKAY? I'LL BE HOME EARLY TONIGHT.
THEN WE CAN SIT DOWN AND FIGURE OUT THINGS *TOGETHER.*
WHAT...
ON EARTH...?

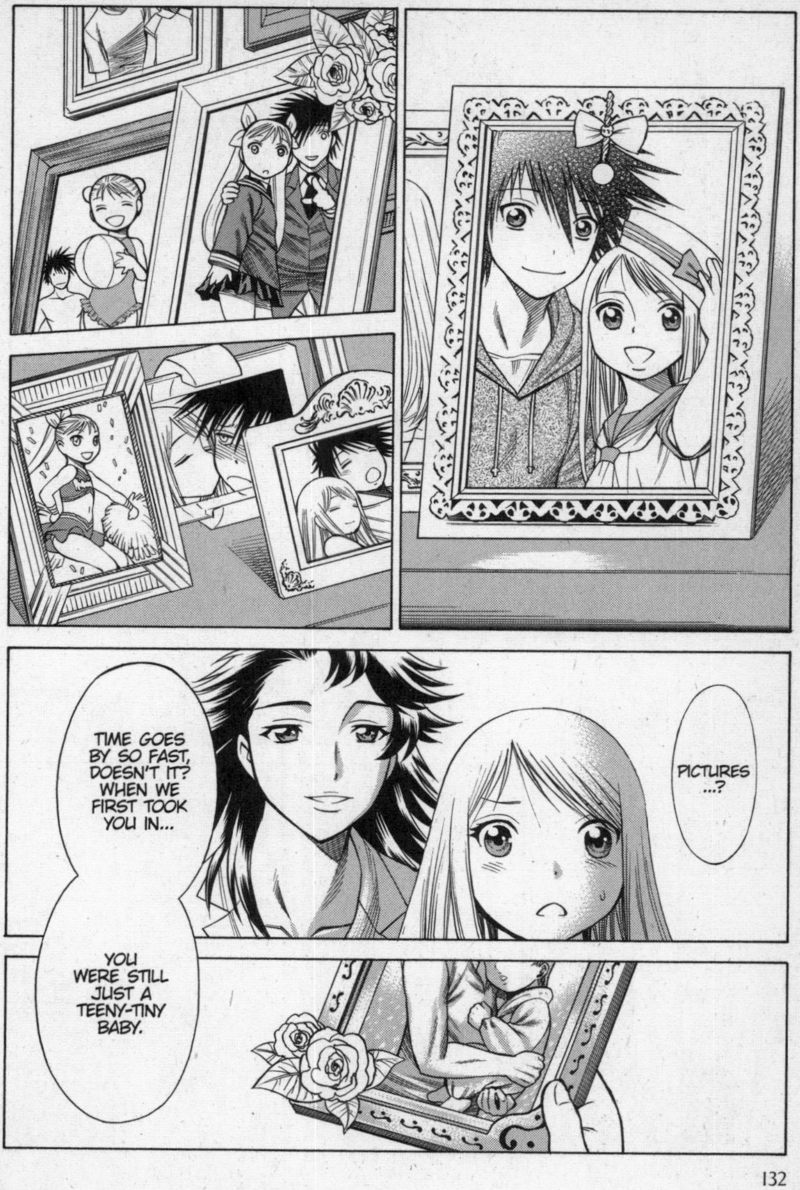
PICTURES ...?
TIME GOES BY SO FAST, DOESN'T IT? WHEN WE FIRST TOOK YOU IN...
YOU WERE STILL JUST A TEENY-TINY BABY.

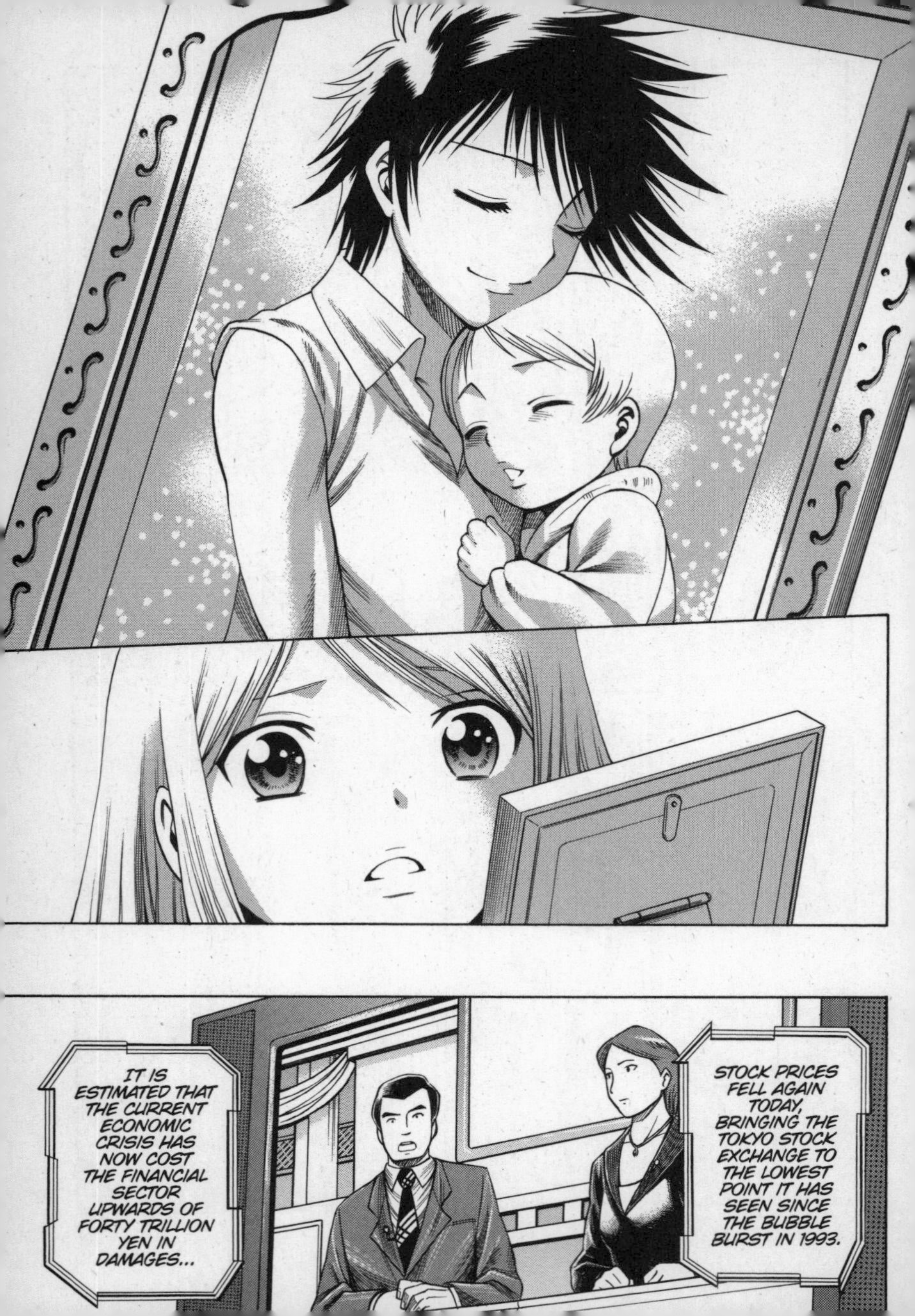
STOCK PRICES FELL AGAIN TODAY, BRINGING THE TOKYO STOCK EXCHANGE TO THE LOWEST POINT IT HAS SEEN SINCE THE BUBBLE BURST IN 1993.
IT IS ESTIMATED THAT THE CURRENT ECONOMIC CRISIS HAS NOW COST THE FINANCIAL SECTOR UPWARDS OF FORTY TRILLION YEN IN DAMAGES...

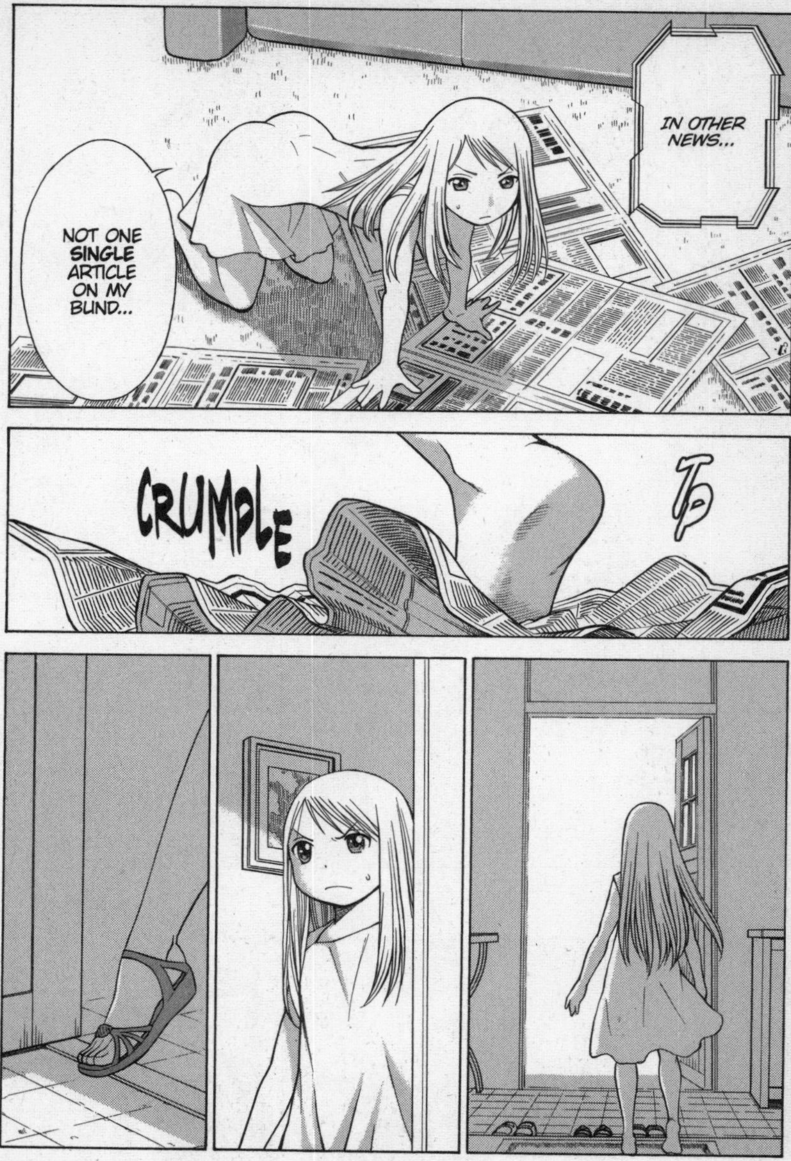
IN OTHER NEWS...
NOT ONE SINGLE ARTICLE ON MY BUND...
Tp
CRUMPLE

HOLD IT RIGHT THERE, YOUNG LADY! YOU CAN'T GO OUTSIDE LIKE THAT!!

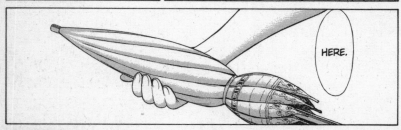

HERE.

STRONG SUNLIGHT IS BAD FOR YOUR SKIN, YOU KNOW.

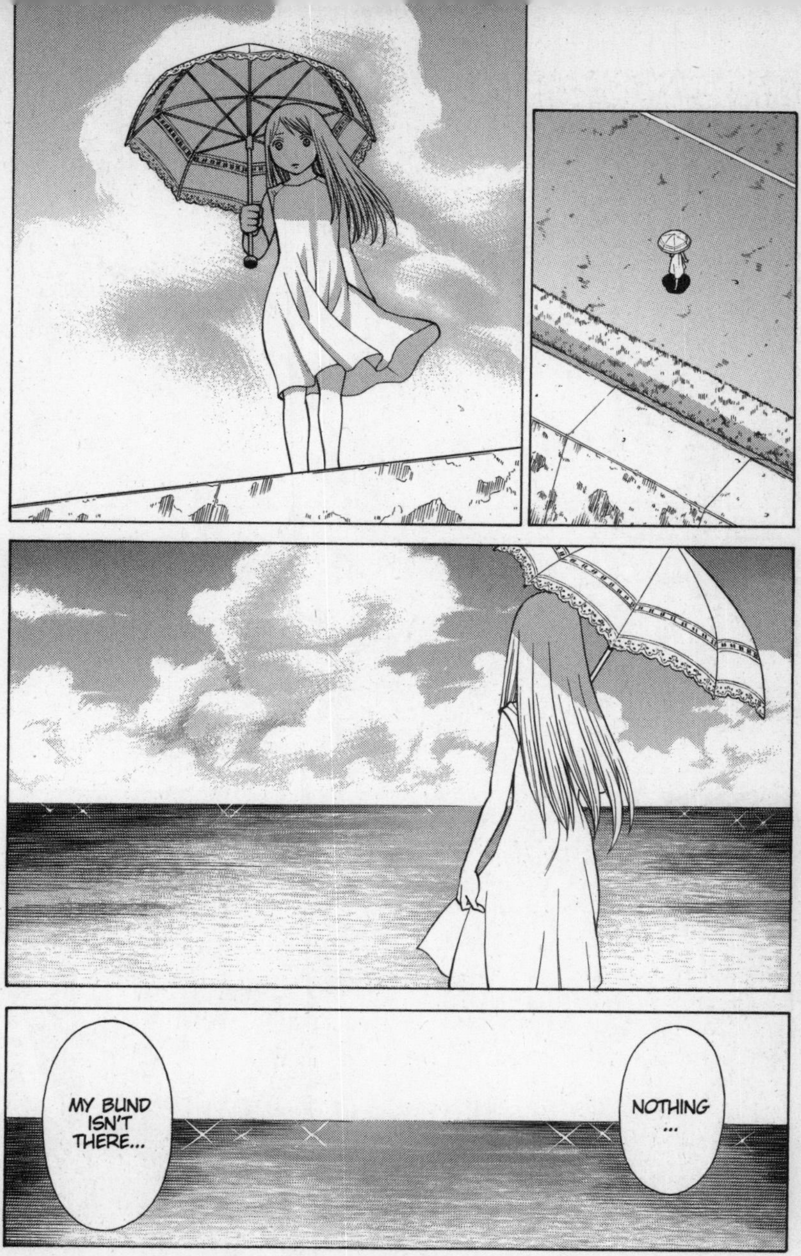
NOTHING ...
MY BLIND ISN'T THERE...

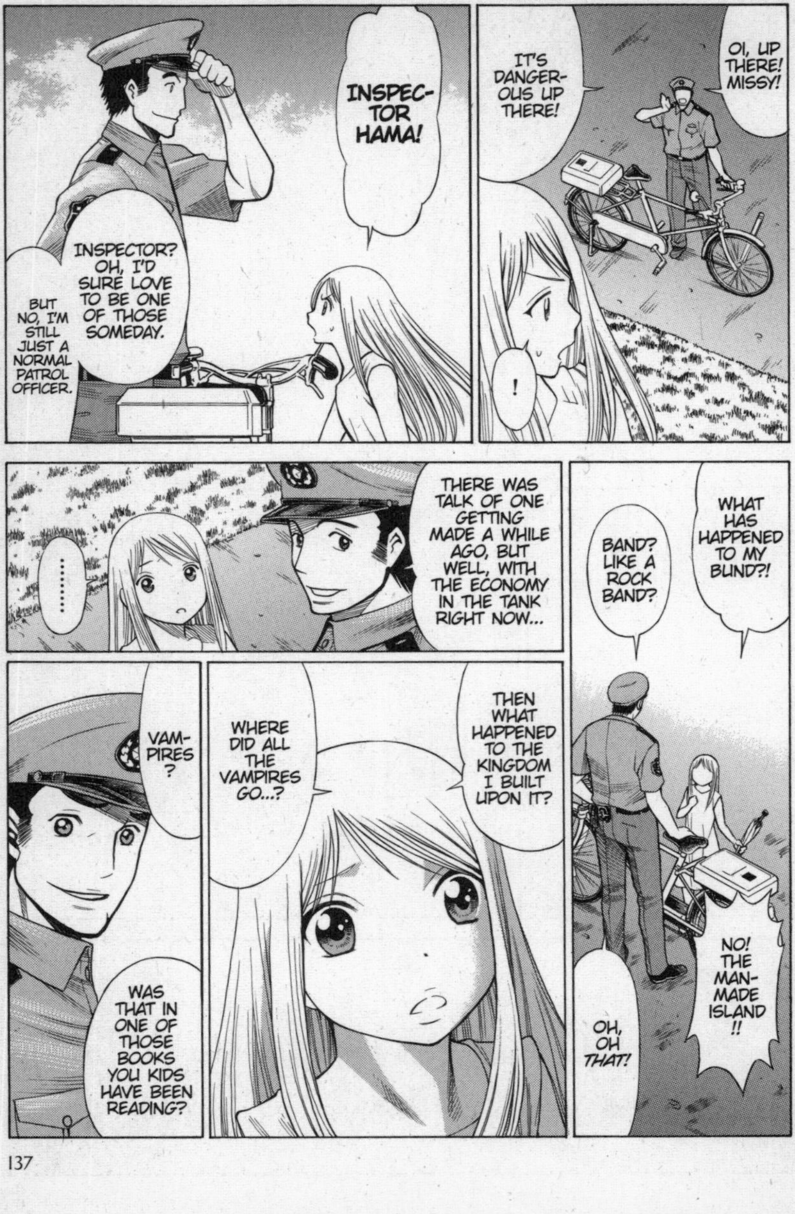
OI, UP THERE! MISSY!
IT'S DANGER-OUS UP THERE!
!
INSPECTOR HAMA!
INSPECTOR? OH, I'D SURE LOVE TO BE ONE OF THOSE SOMEDAY.
BUT NO, I'M STILL JUST A NORMAL PATROL OFFICER.
WHAT HAS HAPPENED TO MY BUND?!
BAND? LIKE A ROCK BAND?
NO! THE MAN-MADE ISLAND !!
OH, OH *THAT!*
THERE WAS TALK OF ONE GETTING MADE A WHILE AGO, BUT WELL, WITH THE ECONOMY IN THE TANK RIGHT NOW...
....
THEN WHAT HAPPENED TO THE KINGDOM I BUILT UPON IT?
WHERE DID ALL THE VAMPIRES GO...?
VAMPIRES?
WAS THAT IN ONE OF THOSE BOOKS YOU KIDS HAVE BEEN READING?

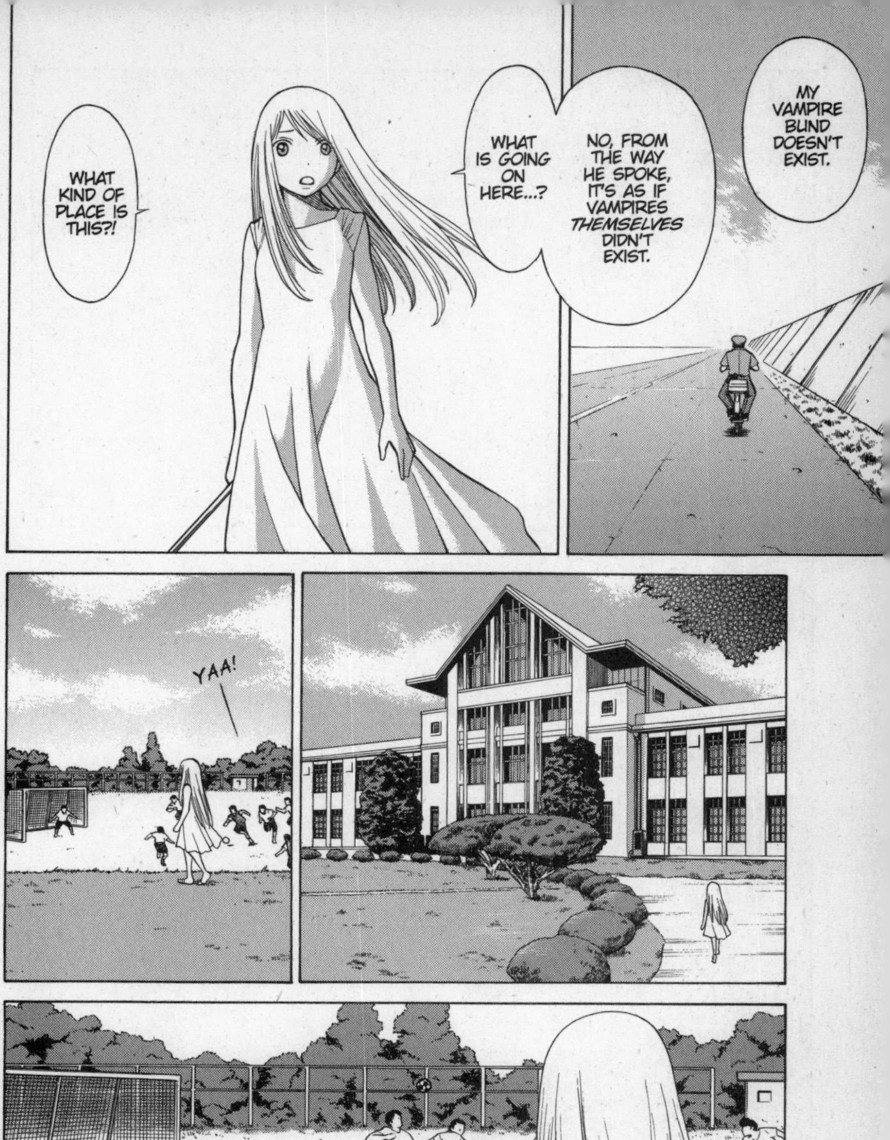
MY VAMPIRE BUND DOESN'T EXIST.
NO, FROM THE WAY HE SPOKE, IT'S AS IF VAMPIRES *THEMSELVES* DIDN'T EXIST.
WHAT IS GOING ON HERE...?
WHAT KIND OF PLACE IS THIS?!
YAA!

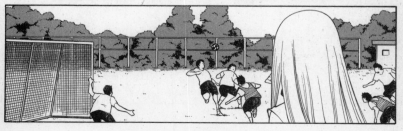

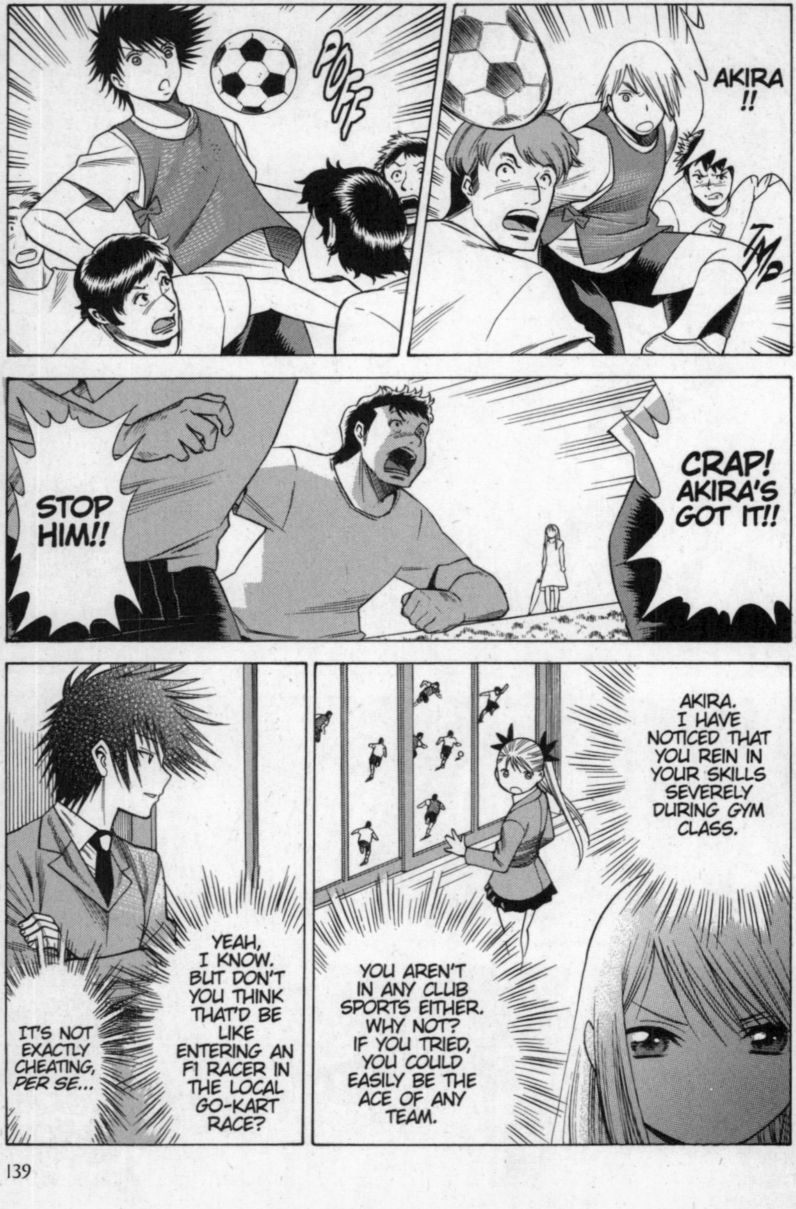
AKIRA !!
TMP
POFF
CRAP! AKIRA'S GOT IT!!
STOP HIM!!
AKIRA. I HAVE NOTICED THAT YOU REIN IN YOUR SKILLS SEVERELY DURING GYM CLASS.
YOU AREN'T IN ANY CLUB SPORTS EITHER. WHY NOT? IF YOU TRIED, YOU COULD EASILY BE THE ACE OF ANY TEAM.
YEAH, I KNOW. BUT DON'T YOU THINK THAT'D BE LIKE ENTERING AN F1 RACER IN THE LOCAL GO-KART RACE?
IT'S NOT EXACTLY CHEATING, PER SE...

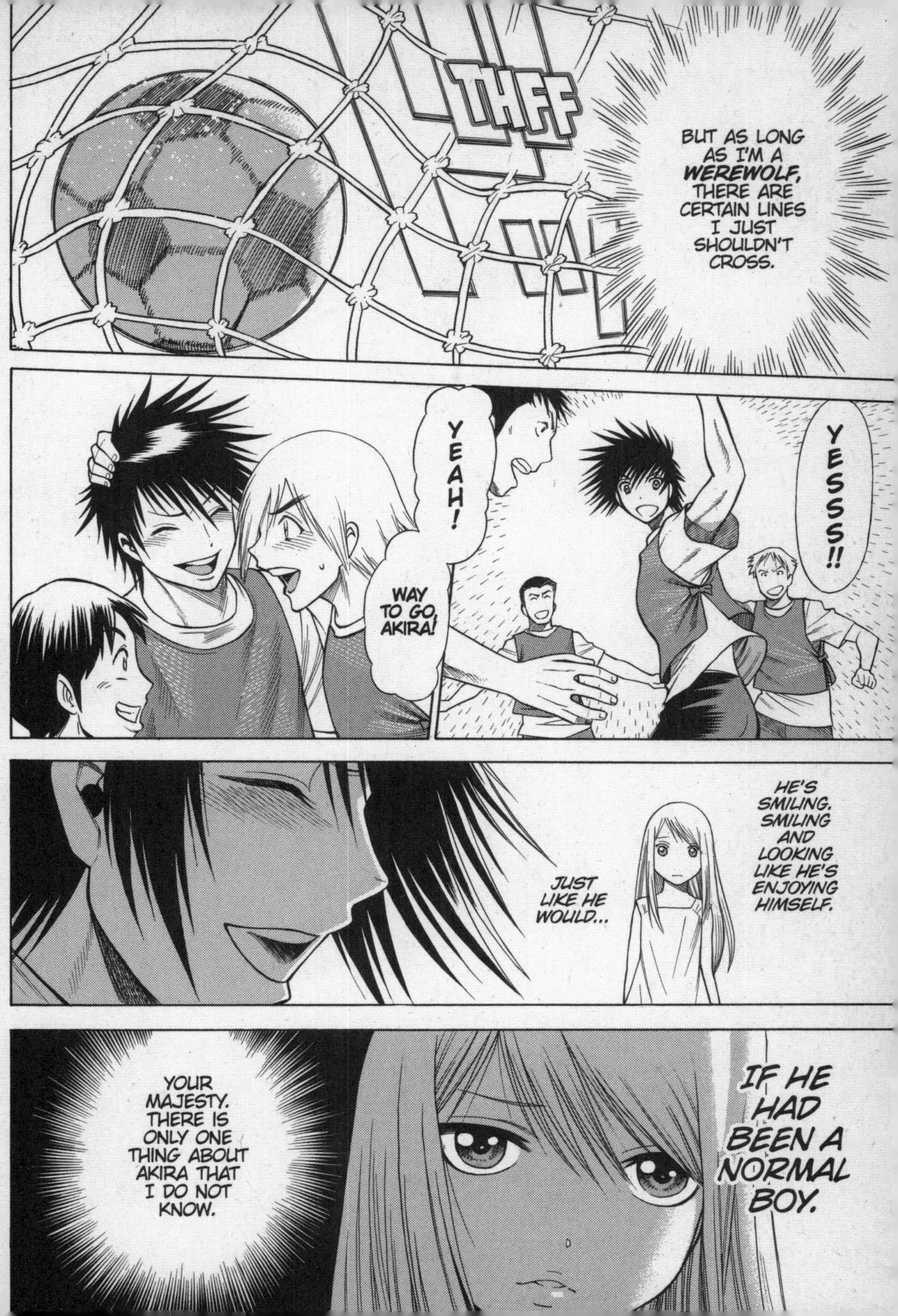
BUT AS LONG AS I'M A **WEREWOLF**, THERE ARE CERTAIN LINES I JUST SHOULDN'T CROSS.
THFF
YESSS!!
YEAH!
WAY TO GO, AKIRA!
HE'S SMILING. SMILING AND LOOKING LIKE HE'S ENJOYING HIMSELF.
JUST LIKE HE WOULD...
IF HE HAD BEEN A NORMAL BOY.
YOUR MAJESTY. THERE IS ONLY ONE THING ABOUT AKIRA THAT I DO NOT KNOW.

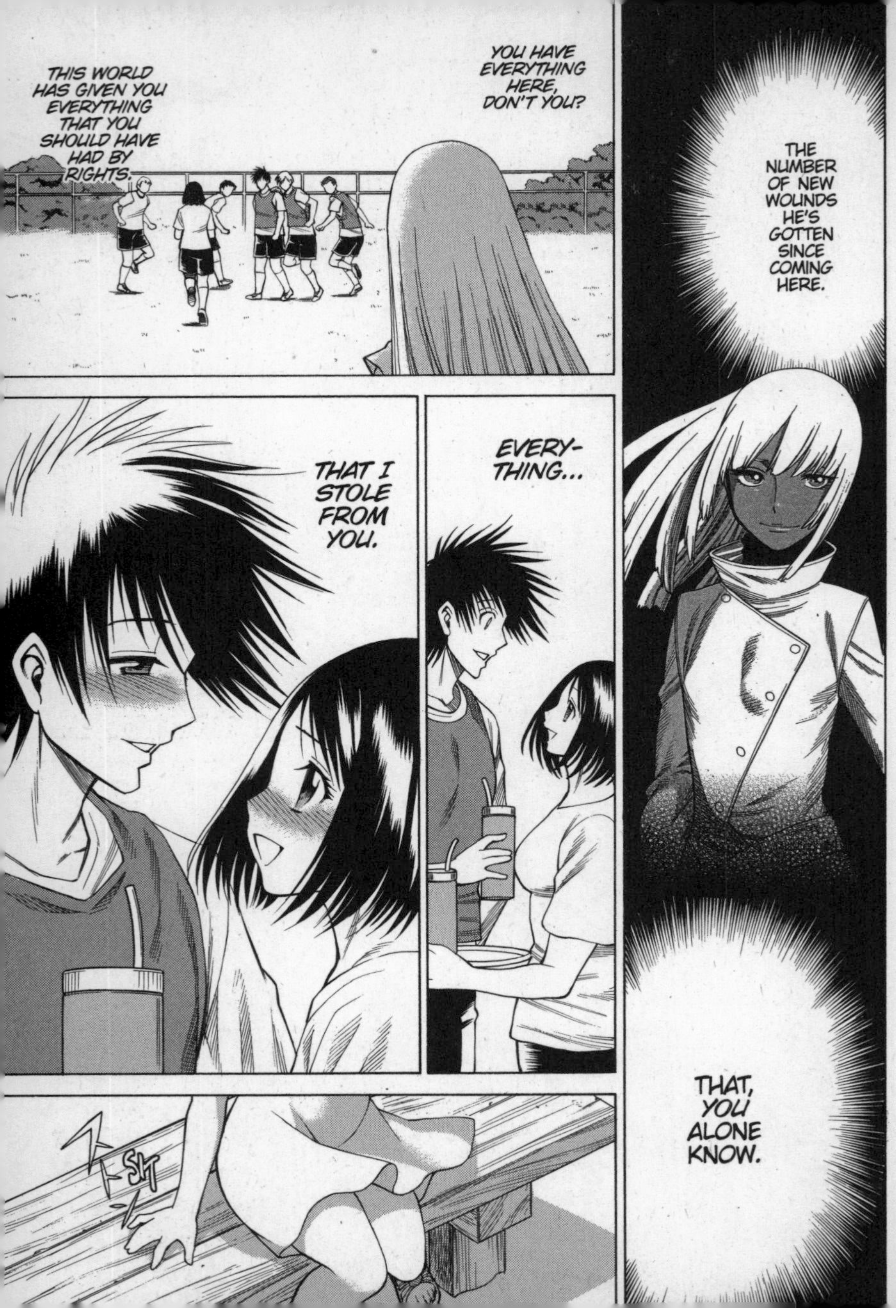
THE NUMBER OF NEW WOUNDS HE'S GOTTEN SINCE COMING HERE.
THAT, YOU ALONE KNOW.
YOU HAVE EVERYTHING HERE, DON'T YOU?
THIS WORLD HAS GIVEN YOU EVERYTHING THAT YOU SHOULD HAVE HAD BY RIGHTS.
EVERY-THING...
THAT I STOLE FROM YOU.
SKT

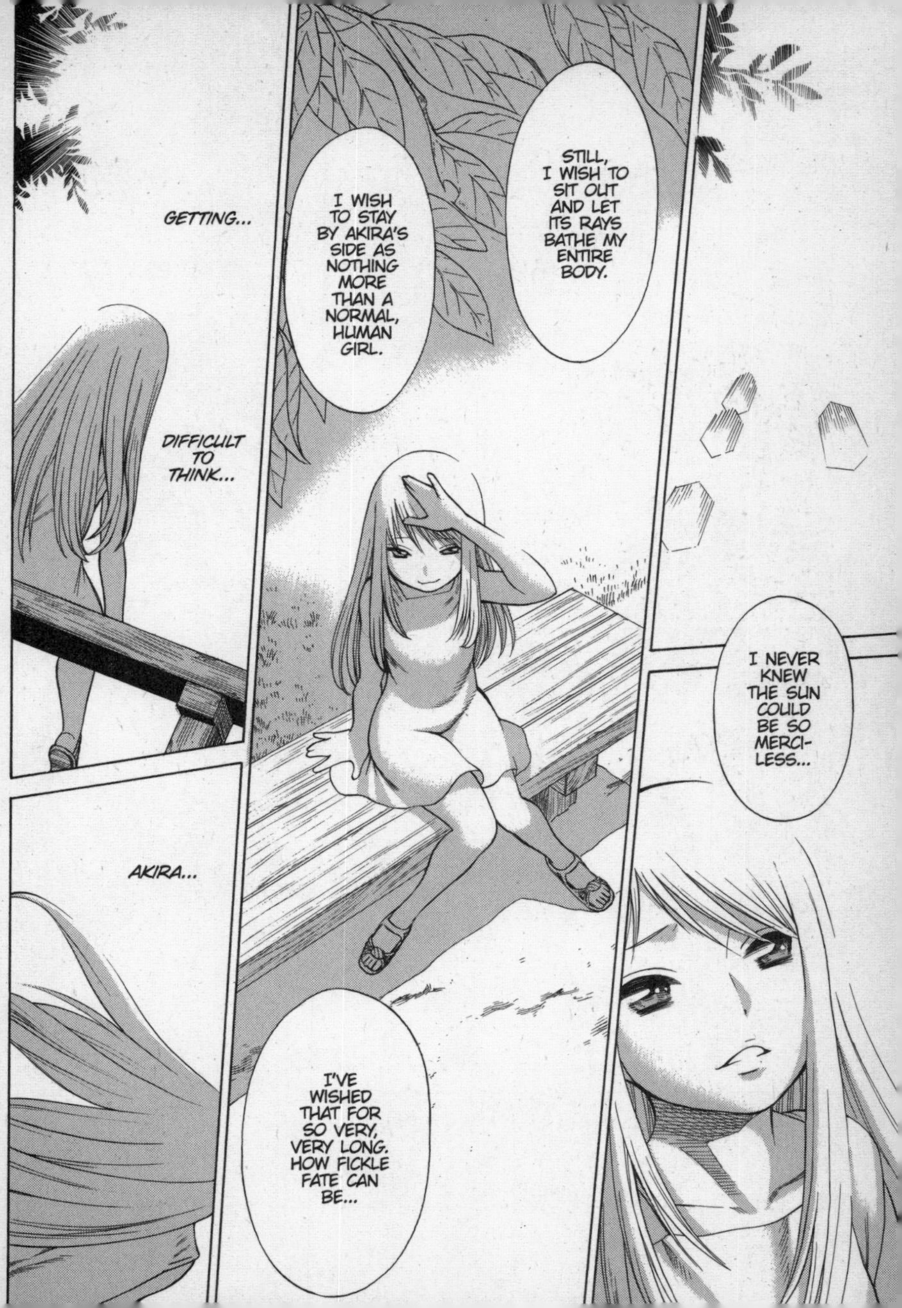
I NEVER KNEW THE SUN COULD BE SO MERCILESS...
STILL, I WISH TO SIT OUT AND LET ITS RAYS BATHE MY ENTIRE BODY.
I WISH TO STAY BY AKIRA'S SIDE AS NOTHING MORE THAN A NORMAL, HUMAN GIRL.
I'VE WISHED THAT FOR SO VERY, VERY LONG. HOW FICKLE FATE CAN BE...
GETTING...
DIFFICULT TO THINK...
AKIRA...

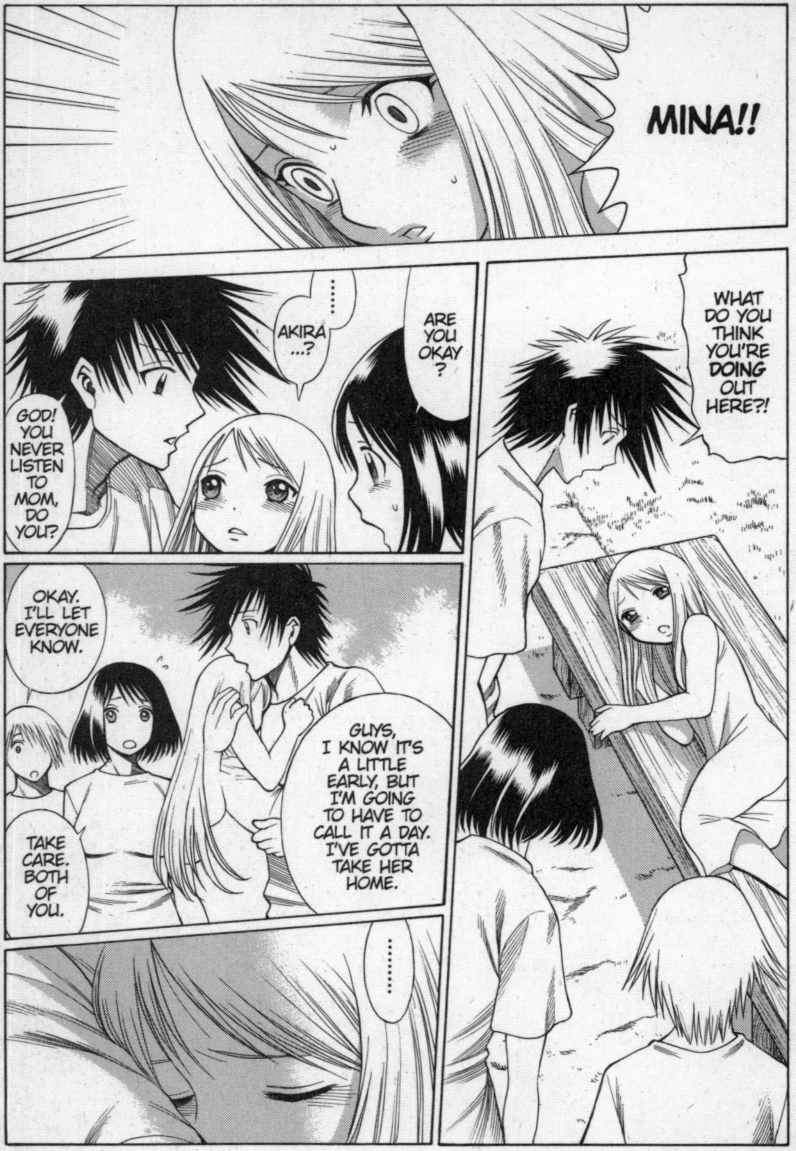

MINA!!
WHAT DO YOU THINK YOU'RE DOING OUT HERE?!
ARE YOU OKAY?
......
AKIRA ...?
GOD! YOU NEVER LISTEN TO MOM, DO YOU?
GUYS, I KNOW IT'S A LITTLE EARLY, BUT I'M GOING TO HAVE TO CALL IT A DAY. I'VE GOTTA TAKE HER HOME.
OKAY. I'LL LET EVERYONE KNOW.
TAKE CARE. BOTH OF YOU.
......

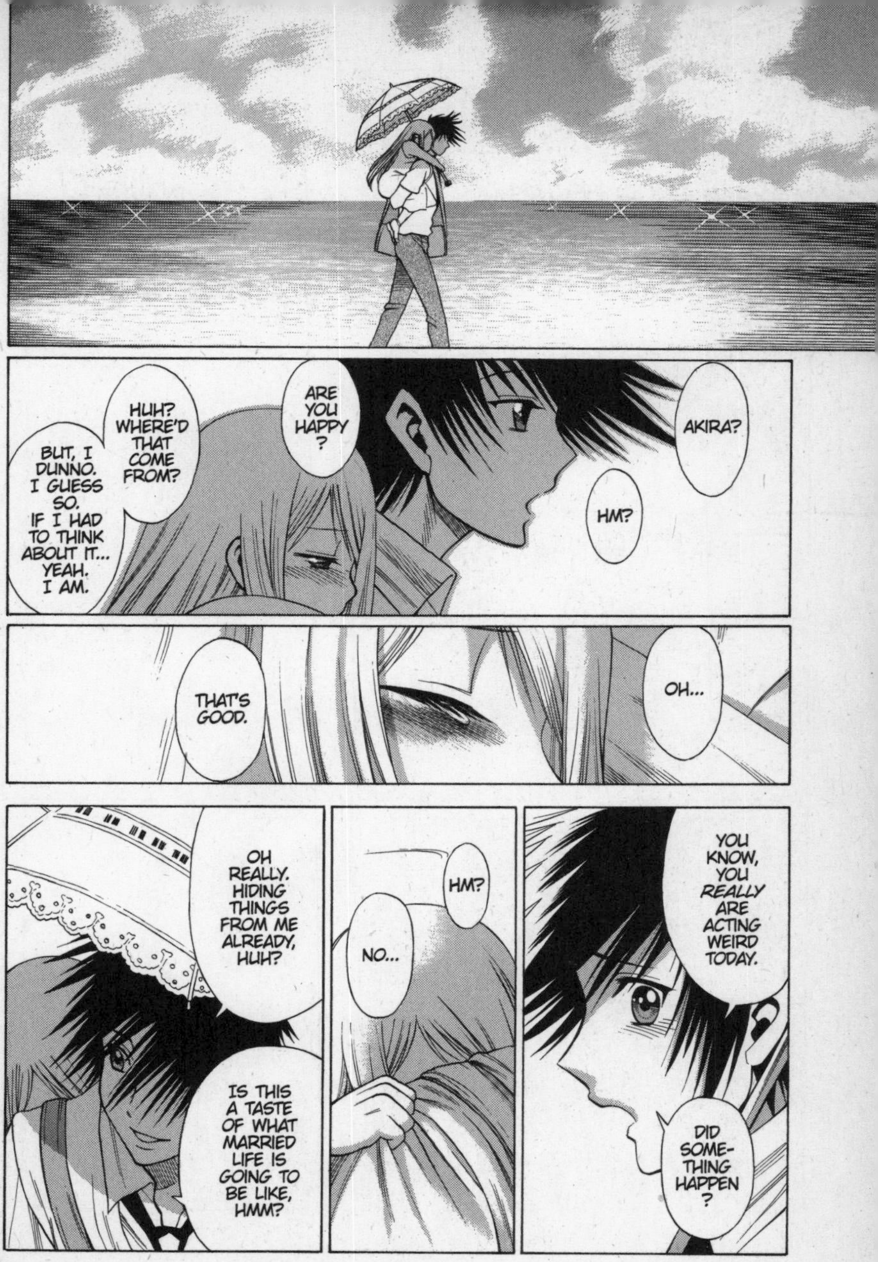
AKIRA?
HM?
ARE YOU HAPPY?
HUH? WHERE'D THAT COME FROM?
BUT, I DUNNO. I GUESS SO. IF I HAD TO THINK ABOUT IT... YEAH. I AM.
OH...
THAT'S GOOD.
YOU KNOW, YOU *REALLY* ARE ACTING WEIRD TODAY.
DID SOMETHING HAPPEN?
HM?
NO...
OH REALLY. HIDING THINGS FROM ME ALREADY, HUH?
IS THIS A TASTE OF WHAT MARRIED LIFE IS GOING TO BE LIKE, HMM?

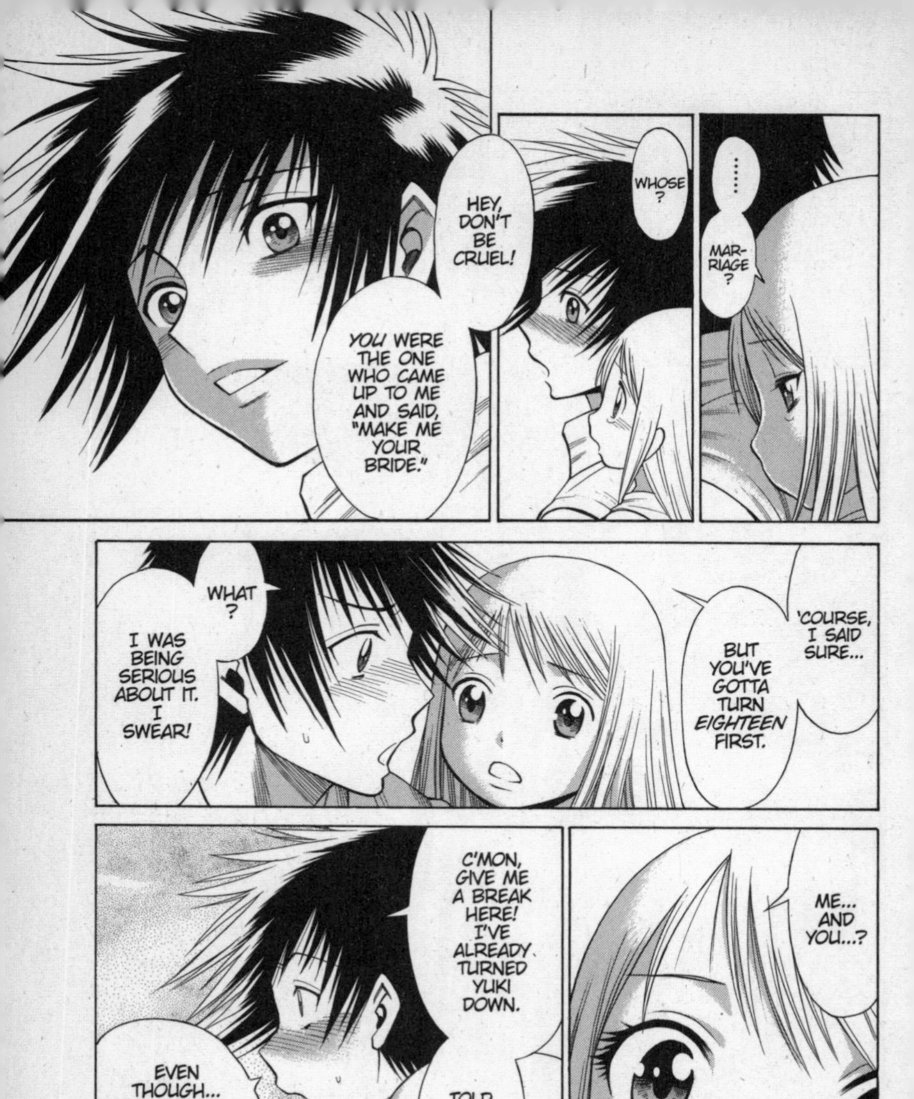
......
MAR-RIAGE?
WHOSE?
HEY, DON'T BE CRUEL!
YOU WERE THE ONE WHO CAME UP TO ME AND SAID, "MAKE ME YOUR BRIDE."
'COURSE, I SAID SURE...
BUT YOU'VE GOTTA TURN *EIGHTEEN* FIRST.
WHAT?
I WAS BEING SERIOUS ABOUT IT. I SWEAR!
ME... AND YOU...?
C'MON, GIVE ME A BREAK HERE! I'VE ALREADY TURNED YUKI DOWN.
TOLD HER THAT I HAD YOU.
EVEN THOUGH... THAT MEANS THE ENTIRE SCHOOL THINKS I'M A CLOSET *LOLICON* NOW!

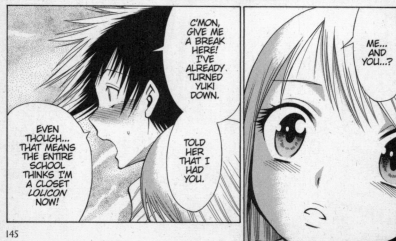

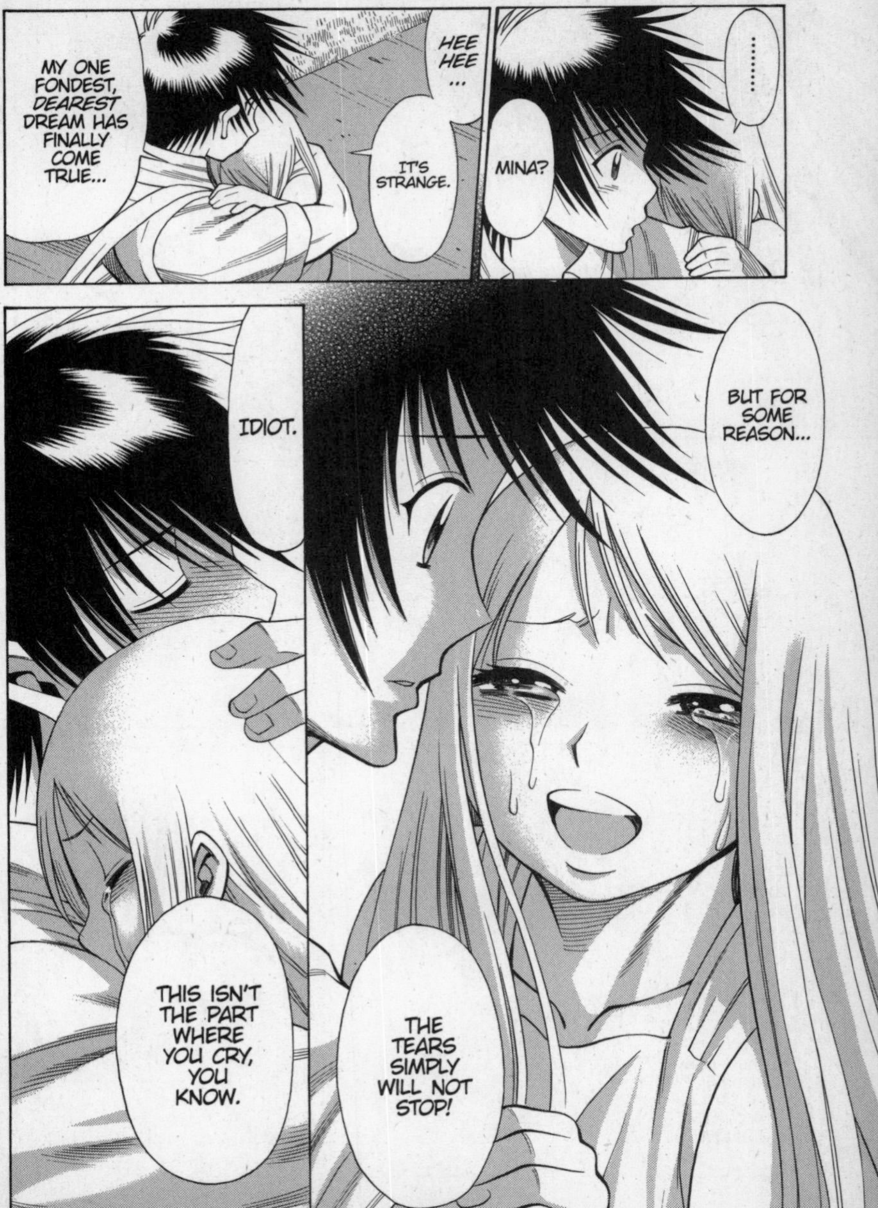
......
MINA?
HEE HEE ...
MY ONE FONDEST, DEAREST DREAM HAS FINALLY COME TRUE...
IT'S STRANGE.
BUT FOR SOME REASON...
THE TEARS SIMPLY WILL NOT STOP!
IDIOT.
THIS ISN'T THE PART WHERE YOU CRY, YOU KNOW.

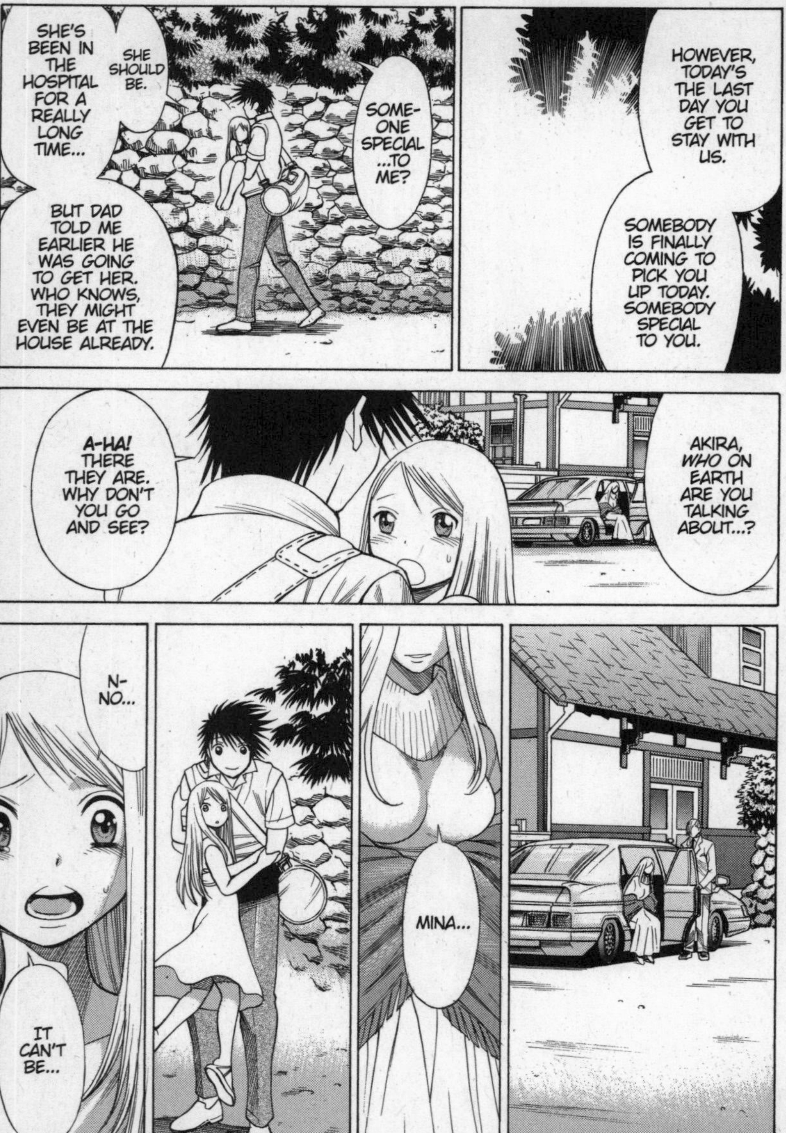
HOWEVER, TODAY'S THE LAST DAY YOU GET TO STAY WITH US.
SOMEBODY IS FINALLY COMING TO PICK YOU UP TODAY. SOMEBODY SPECIAL TO YOU.
SOME-ONE SPECIAL ...TO ME?
SHE SHOULD BE.
SHE'S BEEN IN THE HOSPITAL FOR A REALLY LONG TIME...
BUT DAD TOLD ME EARLIER HE WAS GOING TO GET HER. WHO KNOWS, THEY MIGHT EVEN BE AT THE HOUSE ALREADY.
AKIRA, *WHO ON EARTH* ARE YOU TALKING ABOUT...?
A-HA! THERE THEY ARE. WHY DON'T YOU GO AND SEE?
MINA...
N-NO...
IT CAN'T BE...

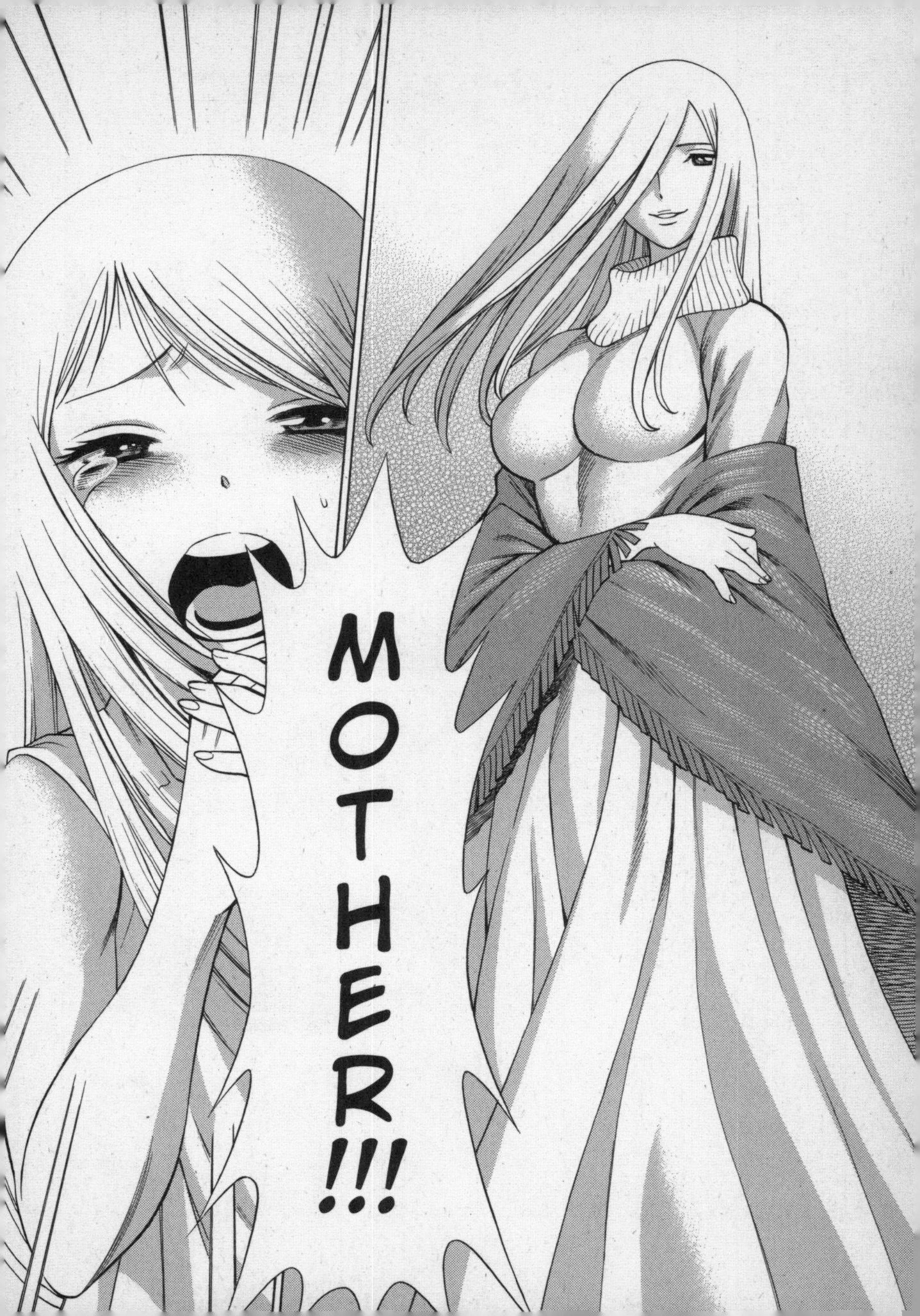
MOTHER!!!

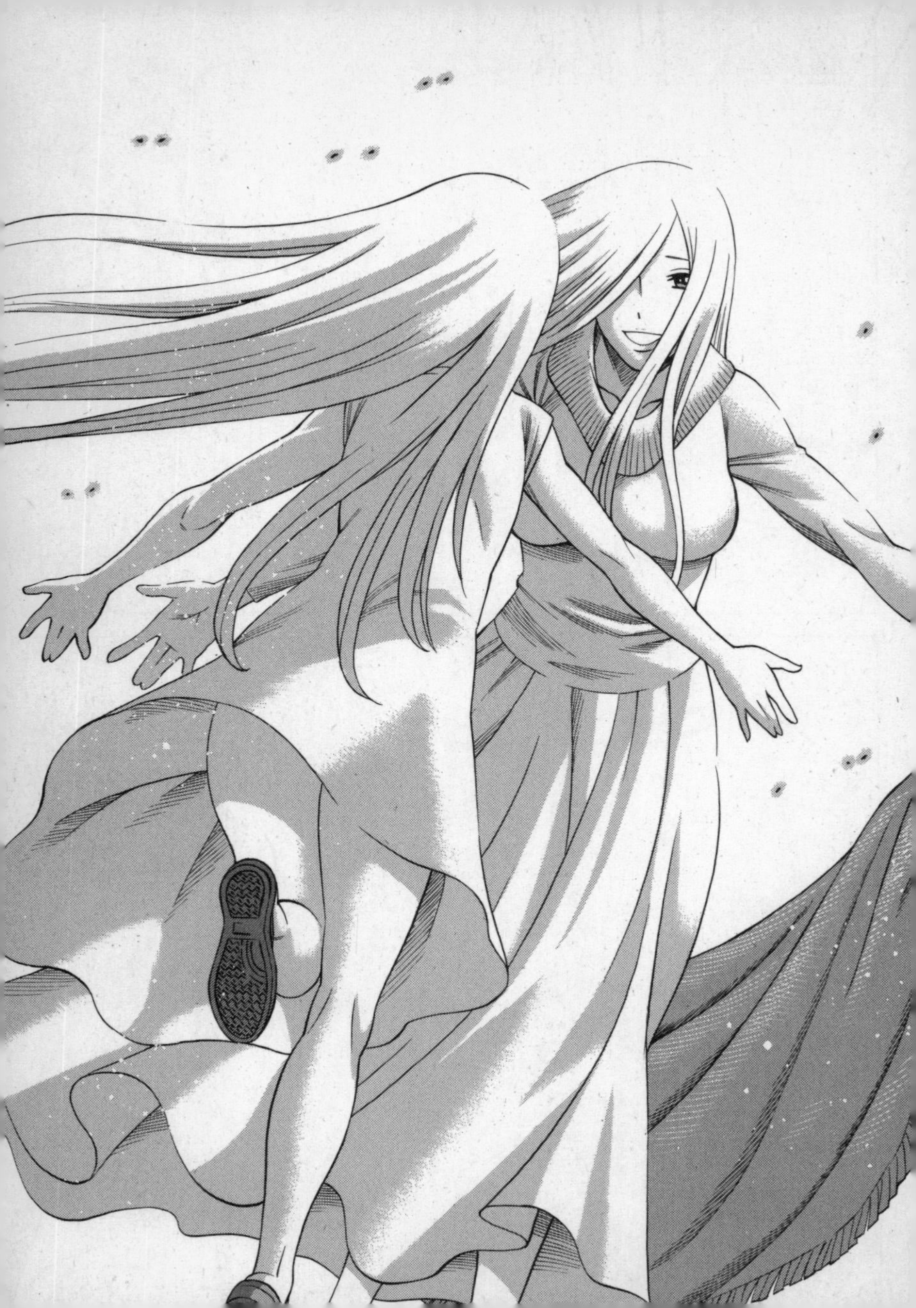

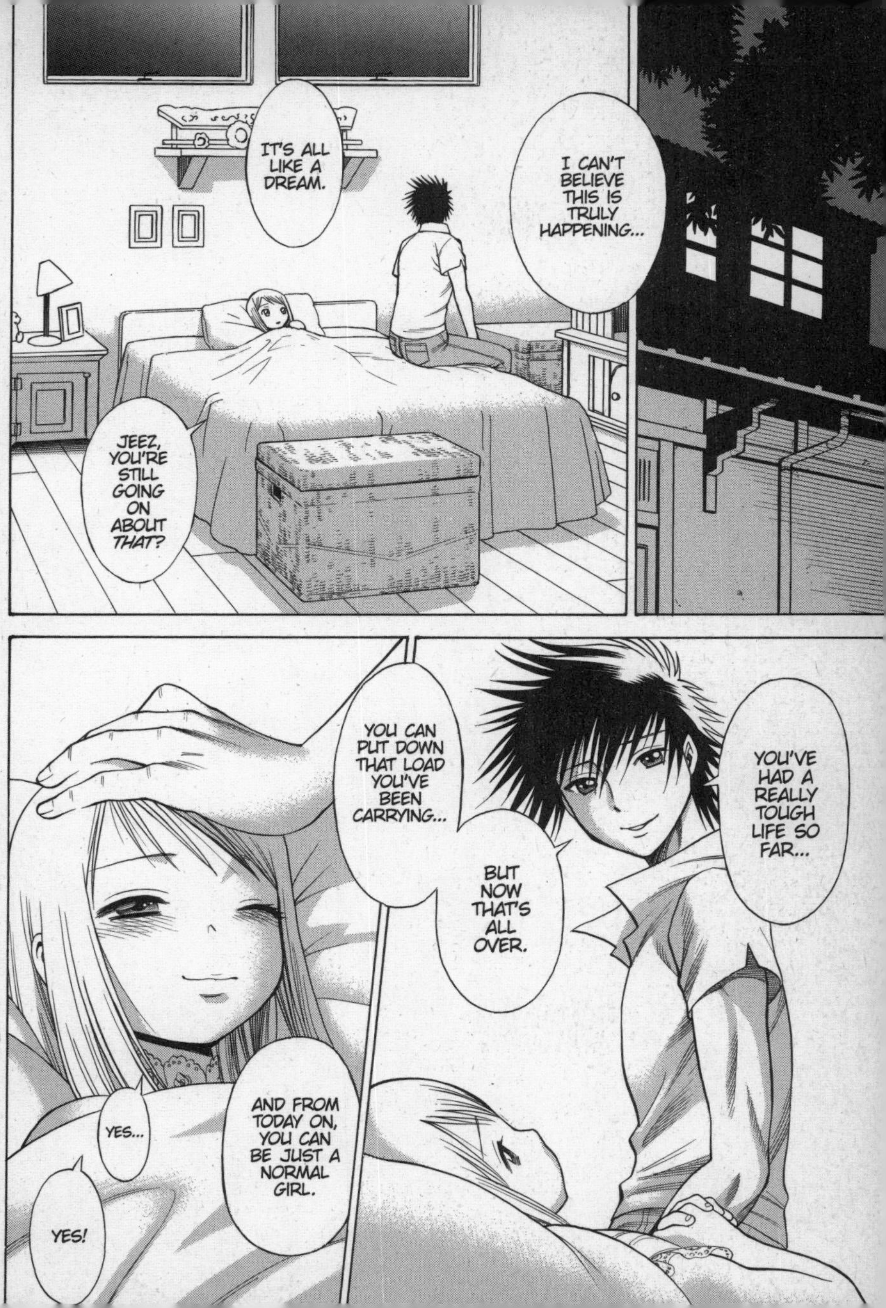
I CAN'T BELIEVE THIS IS TRULY HAPPENING...
IT'S ALL LIKE A DREAM.
JEEZ, YOU'RE STILL GOING ON ABOUT *THAT?*
YOU'VE HAD A REALLY TOUGH LIFE SO FAR...
YOU CAN PUT DOWN THAT LOAD YOU'VE BEEN CARRYING...
BUT NOW THAT'S ALL OVER.
AND FROM TODAY ON, YOU CAN BE JUST A NORMAL GIRL.
YES...
YES!

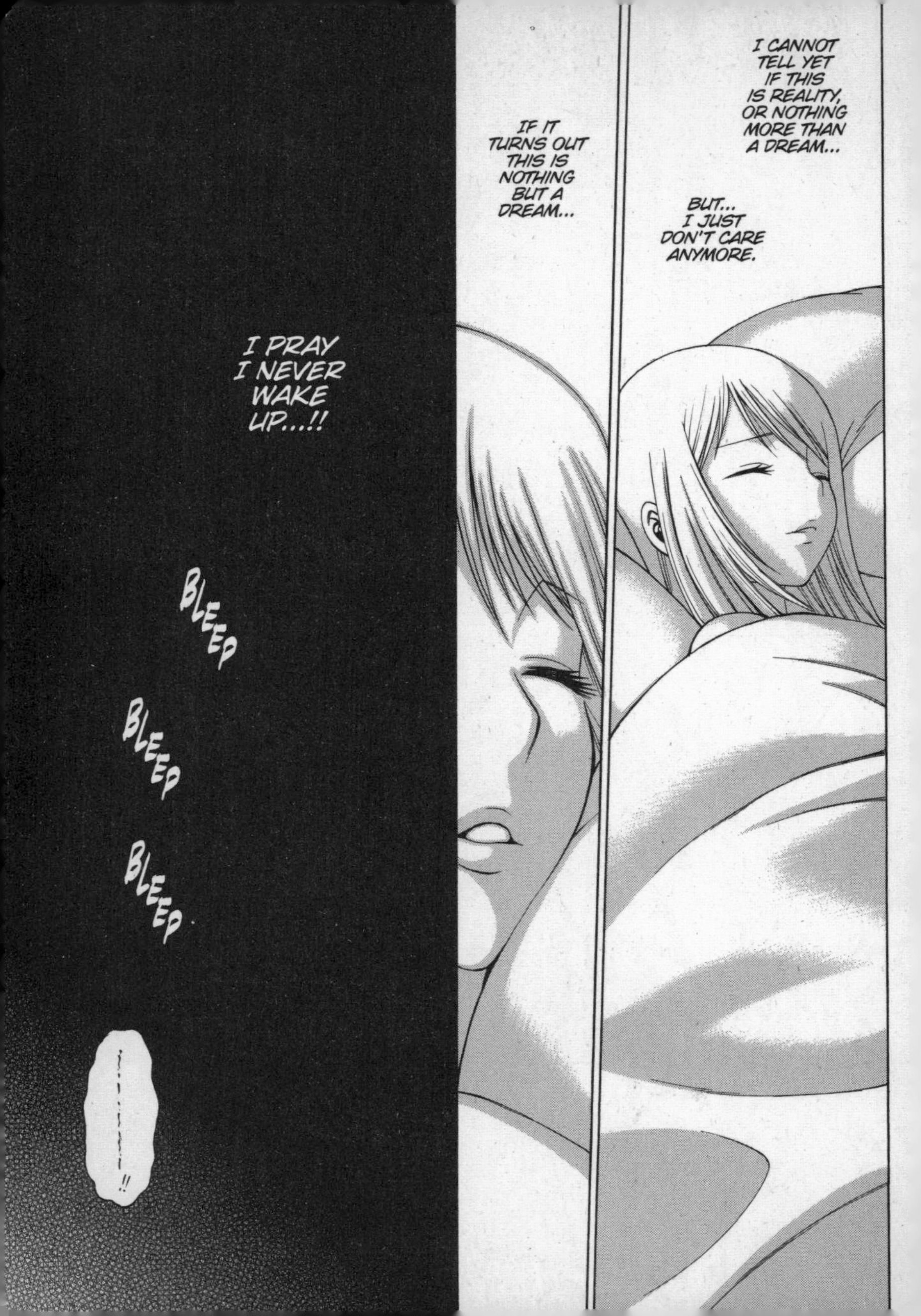
I CANNOT TELL YET IF THIS IS REALITY, OR NOTHING MORE THAN A DREAM...
BUT... I JUST DON'T CARE ANYMORE.
IF IT TURNS OUT THIS IS NOTHING BUT A DREAM...
I PRAY I NEVER WAKE UP...!!
BLEEP
BLEEP
BLEEP
......!!

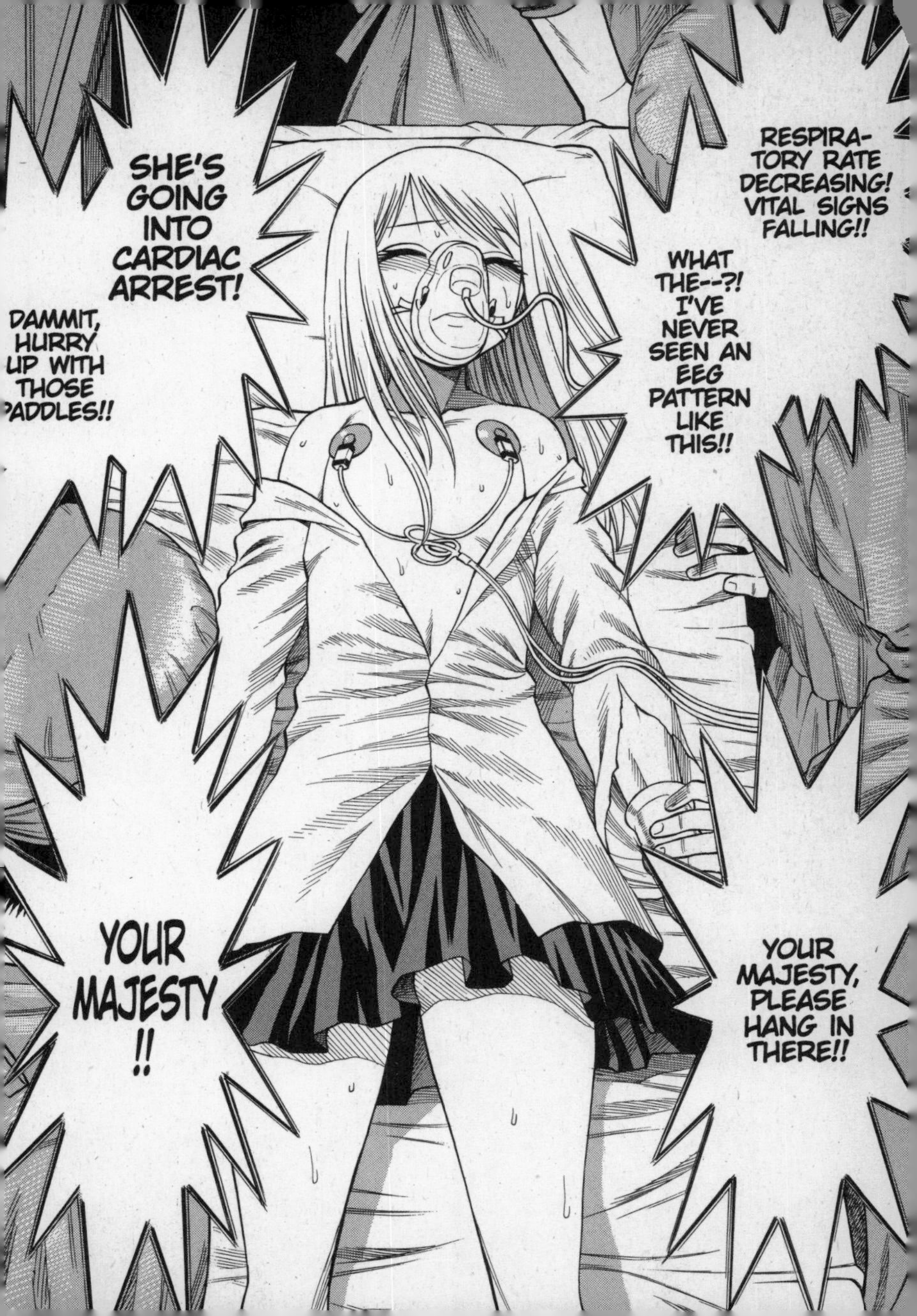
RESPIRATORY RATE DECREASING! VITAL SIGNS FALLING!!
SHE'S GOING INTO CARDIAC ARREST!
WHAT THE--?! I'VE NEVER SEEN AN EEG PATTERN LIKE THIS!!
DAMMIT, HURRY UP WITH THOSE PADDLES!!
YOUR MAJESTY, PLEASE HANG IN THERE!!
YOUR MAJESTY!!

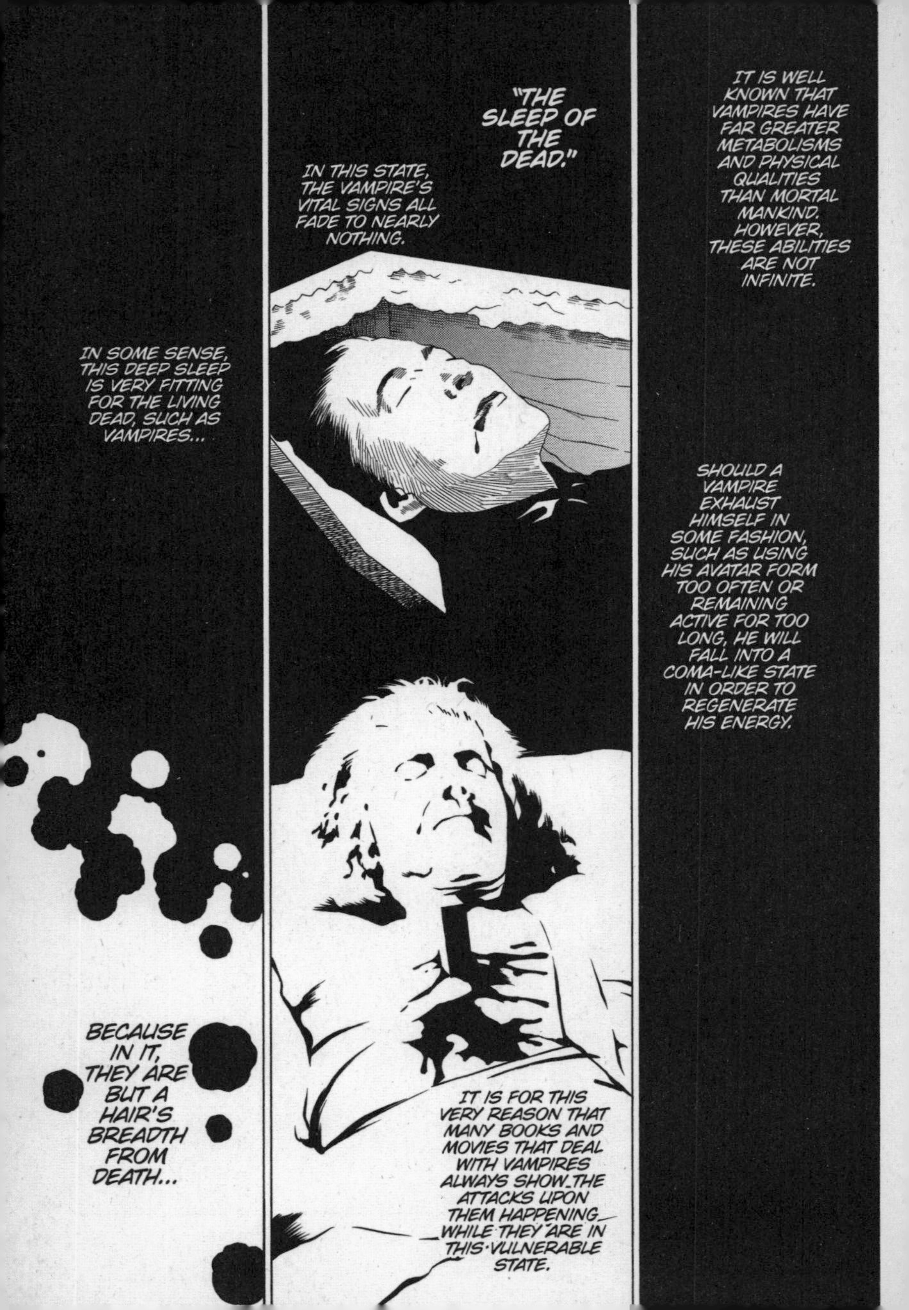
IT IS WELL KNOWN THAT VAMPIRES HAVE FAR GREATER METABOLISMS AND PHYSICAL QUALITIES THAN MORTAL MANKIND. HOWEVER, THESE ABILITIES ARE NOT INFINITE.
SHOULD A VAMPIRE EXHAUST HIMSELF IN SOME FASHION, SUCH AS USING HIS AVATAR FORM TOO OFTEN OR REMAINING ACTIVE FOR TOO LONG, HE WILL FALL INTO A COMA-LIKE STATE IN ORDER TO REGENERATE HIS ENERGY.
"THE SLEEP OF THE DEAD."
IN THIS STATE, THE VAMPIRE'S VITAL SIGNS ALL FADE TO NEARLY NOTHING.
IT IS FOR THIS VERY REASON THAT MANY BOOKS AND MOVIES THAT DEAL WITH VAMPIRES ALWAYS SHOW THE ATTACKS UPON THEM HAPPENING WHILE THEY ARE IN THIS VULNERABLE STATE.
IN SOME SENSE, THIS DEEP SLEEP IS VERY FITTING FOR THE LIVING DEAD, SUCH AS VAMPIRES...
BECAUSE IN IT, THEY ARE BUT A HAIR'S BREADTH FROM DEATH...

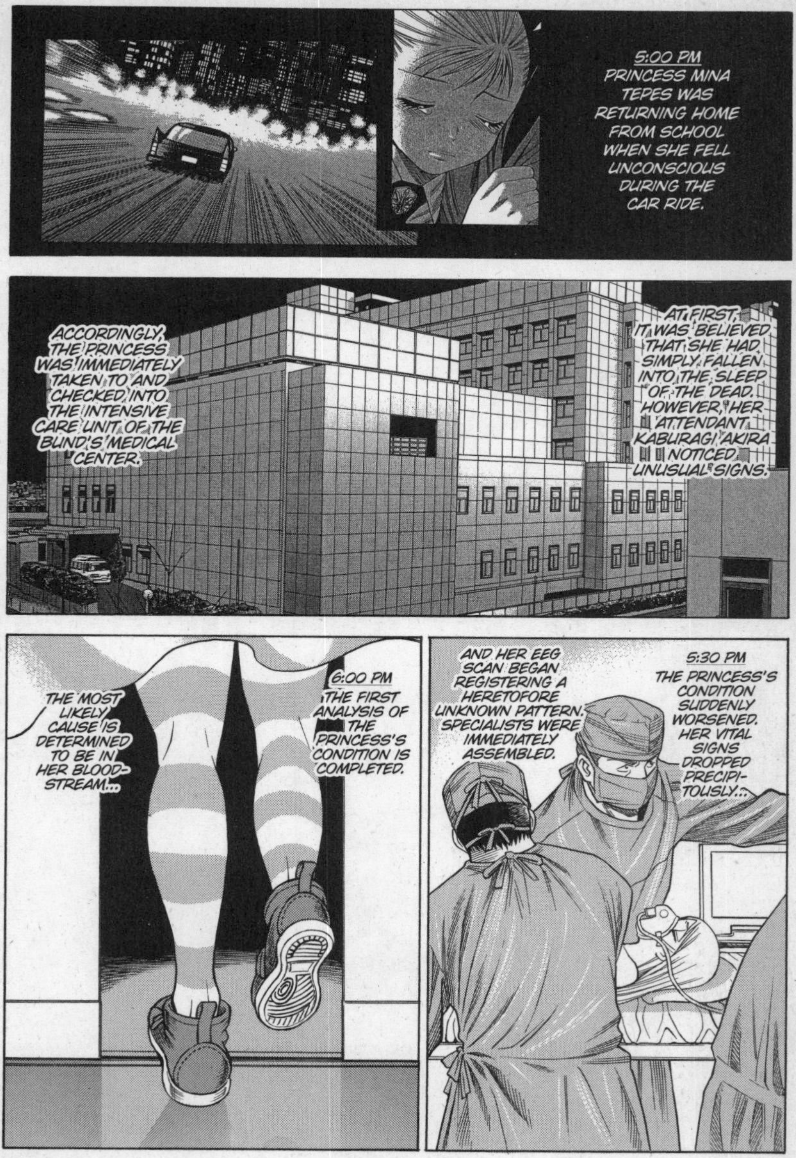
5:00 PM
PRINCESS MINA TEPES WAS RETURNING HOME FROM SCHOOL WHEN SHE FELL UNCONSCIOUS DURING THE CAR RIDE.
AT FIRST, IT WAS BELIEVED THAT SHE HAD SIMPLY FALLEN INTO THE SLEEP OF THE DEAD. HOWEVER, HER ATTENDANT KABURAGI AKIRA NOTICED UNUSUAL SIGNS.
ACCORDINGLY, THE PRINCESS WAS IMMEDIATELY TAKEN TO AND CHECKED INTO THE INTENSIVE CARE UNIT OF THE BUND'S MEDICAL CENTER.
5:30 PM
THE PRINCESS'S CONDITION SUDDENLY WORSENED. HER VITAL SIGNS DROPPED PRECIPI-TOUSLY...
AND HER EEG SCAN BEGAN REGISTERING A HERETOFORE UNKNOWN PATTERN. SPECIALISTS WERE IMMEDIATELY ASSEMBLED.
6:00 PM
THE FIRST ANALYSIS OF THE PRINCESS'S CONDITION IS COMPLETED.
THE MOST LIKELY CAUSE IS DETERMINED TO BE IN HER BLOOD-STREAM...

Chapter 37: What a Wonderful Life!

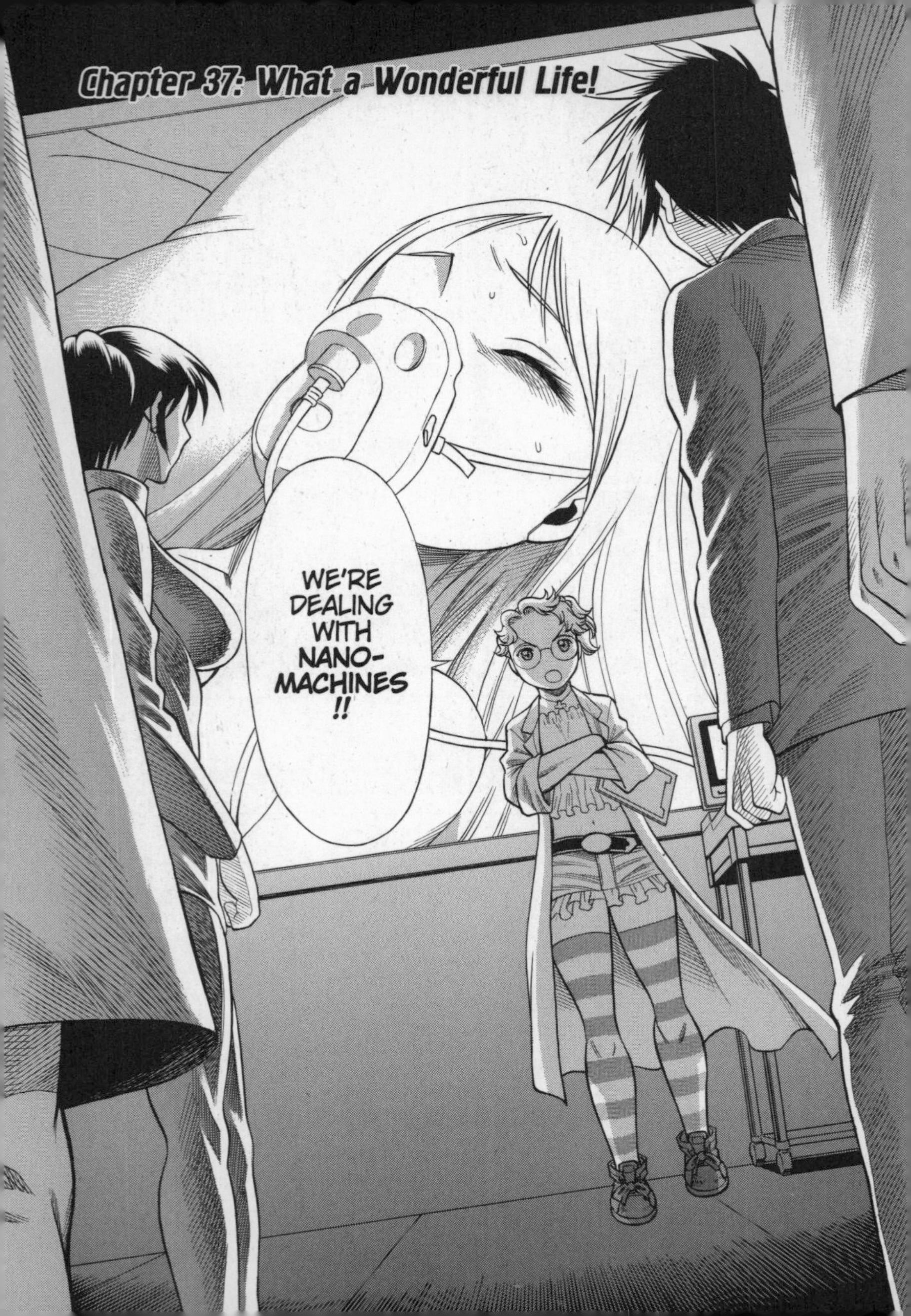
WE'RE DEALING WITH NANO-MACHINES !!

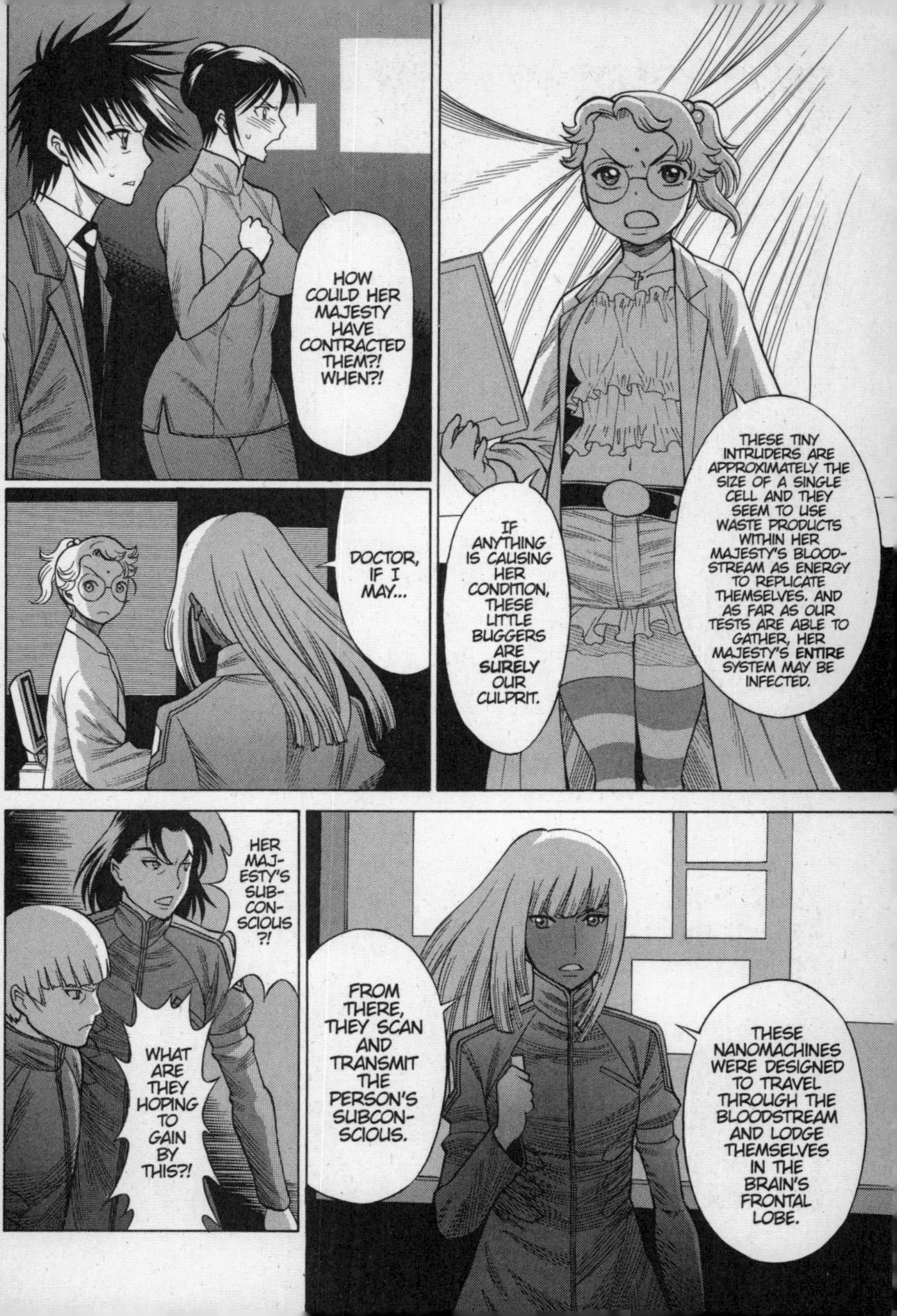
THESE TINY INTRUDERS ARE APPROXIMATELY THE SIZE OF A SINGLE CELL AND THEY SEEM TO USE WASTE PRODUCTS WITHIN HER MAJESTY'S BLOOD-STREAM AS ENERGY TO REPLICATE THEMSELVES. AND AS FAR AS OUR TESTS ARE ABLE TO GATHER, HER MAJESTY'S ENTIRE SYSTEM MAY BE INFECTED.
IF ANYTHING IS CAUSING HER CONDITION, THESE LITTLE BUGGERS ARE SURELY OUR CULPRIT.
HOW COULD HER MAJESTY HAVE CONTRACTED THEM?! WHEN?!
DOCTOR, IF I MAY...
THESE NANOMACHINES WERE DESIGNED TO TRAVEL THROUGH THE BLOODSTREAM AND LODGE THEMSELVES IN THE BRAIN'S FRONTAL LOBE.
FROM THERE, THEY SCAN AND TRANSMIT THE PERSON'S SUBCON-SCIOUS.
HER MAJ-ESTY'S SUB-CON-SCIOUS?!
WHAT ARE THEY HOPING TO GAIN BY THIS?!

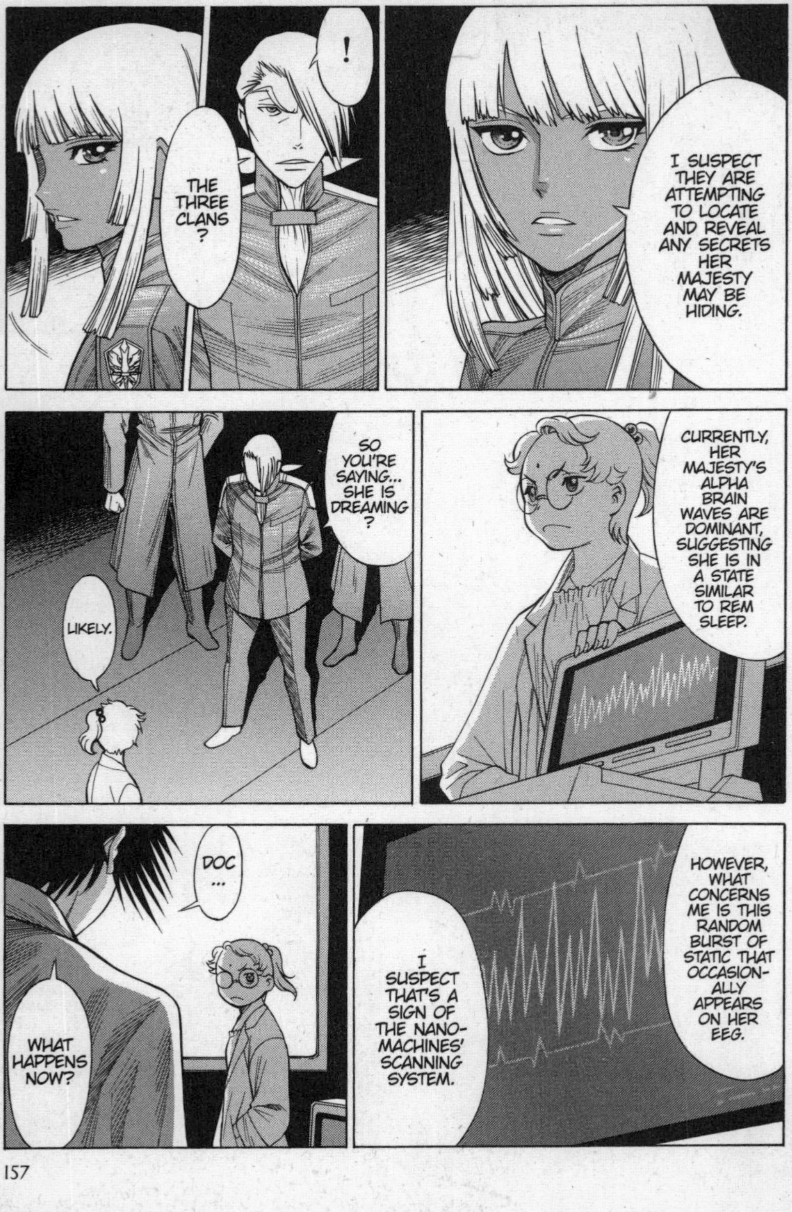
I SUSPECT THEY ARE ATTEMPTING TO LOCATE AND REVEAL ANY SECRETS HER MAJESTY MAY BE HIDING.
!
THE THREE CLANS?
CURRENTLY, HER MAJESTY'S ALPHA BRAIN WAVES ARE DOMINANT, SUGGESTING SHE IS IN A STATE SIMILAR TO REM SLEEP.
SO YOU'RE SAYING... SHE IS DREAMING?
LIKELY.
HOWEVER, WHAT CONCERNS ME IS THIS RANDOM BURST OF STATIC THAT OCCASION-ALLY APPEARS ON HER EEG.
I SUSPECT THAT'S A SIGN OF THE NANO-MACHINES' SCANNING SYSTEM.
DOC...
WHAT HAPPENS NOW?

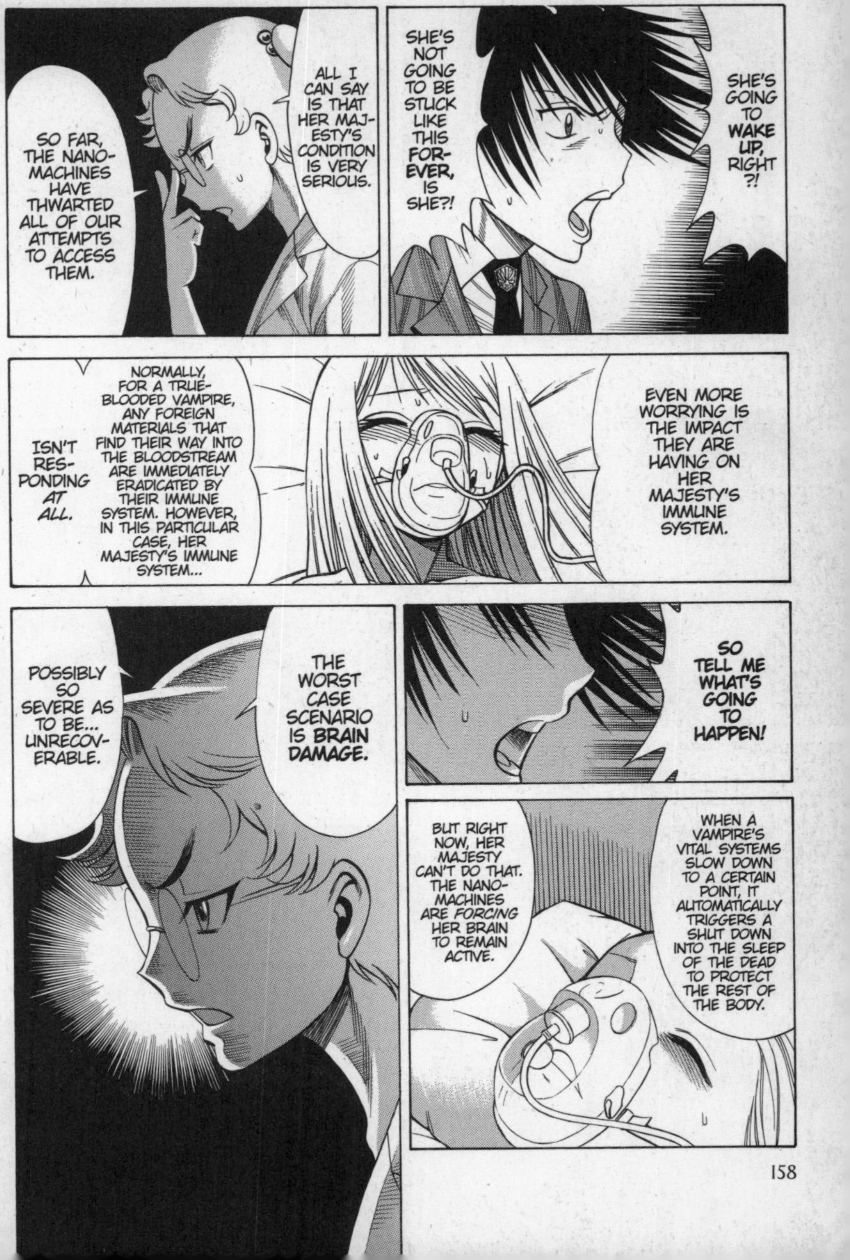
SHE'S GOING TO WAKE UP, RIGHT?!
SHE'S NOT GOING TO BE STUCK LIKE THIS FOREVER, IS SHE?!
ALL I CAN SAY IS THAT HER MAJESTY'S CONDITION IS VERY SERIOUS.
SO FAR, THE NANO-MACHINES HAVE THWARTED ALL OF OUR ATTEMPTS TO ACCESS THEM.
EVEN MORE WORRYING IS THE IMPACT THEY ARE HAVING ON HER MAJESTY'S IMMUNE SYSTEM.
NORMALLY, FOR A TRUE-BLOODED VAMPIRE, ANY FOREIGN MATERIALS THAT FIND THEIR WAY INTO THE BLOODSTREAM ARE IMMEDIATELY ERADICATED BY THEIR IMMUNE SYSTEM. HOWEVER, IN THIS PARTICULAR CASE, HER MAJESTY'S IMMUNE SYSTEM...
ISN'T RESPONDING AT ALL.
SO TELL ME WHAT'S GOING TO HAPPEN!
WHEN A VAMPIRE'S VITAL SYSTEMS SLOW DOWN TO A CERTAIN POINT, IT AUTOMATICALLY TRIGGERS A SHUT DOWN INTO THE SLEEP OF THE DEAD TO PROTECT THE REST OF THE BODY.
BUT RIGHT NOW, HER MAJESTY CAN'T DO THAT. THE NANO-MACHINES ARE FORCING HER BRAIN TO REMAIN ACTIVE.
THE WORST CASE SCENARIO IS BRAIN DAMAGE.
POSSIBLY SO SEVERE AS TO BE... UNRECOVERABLE.

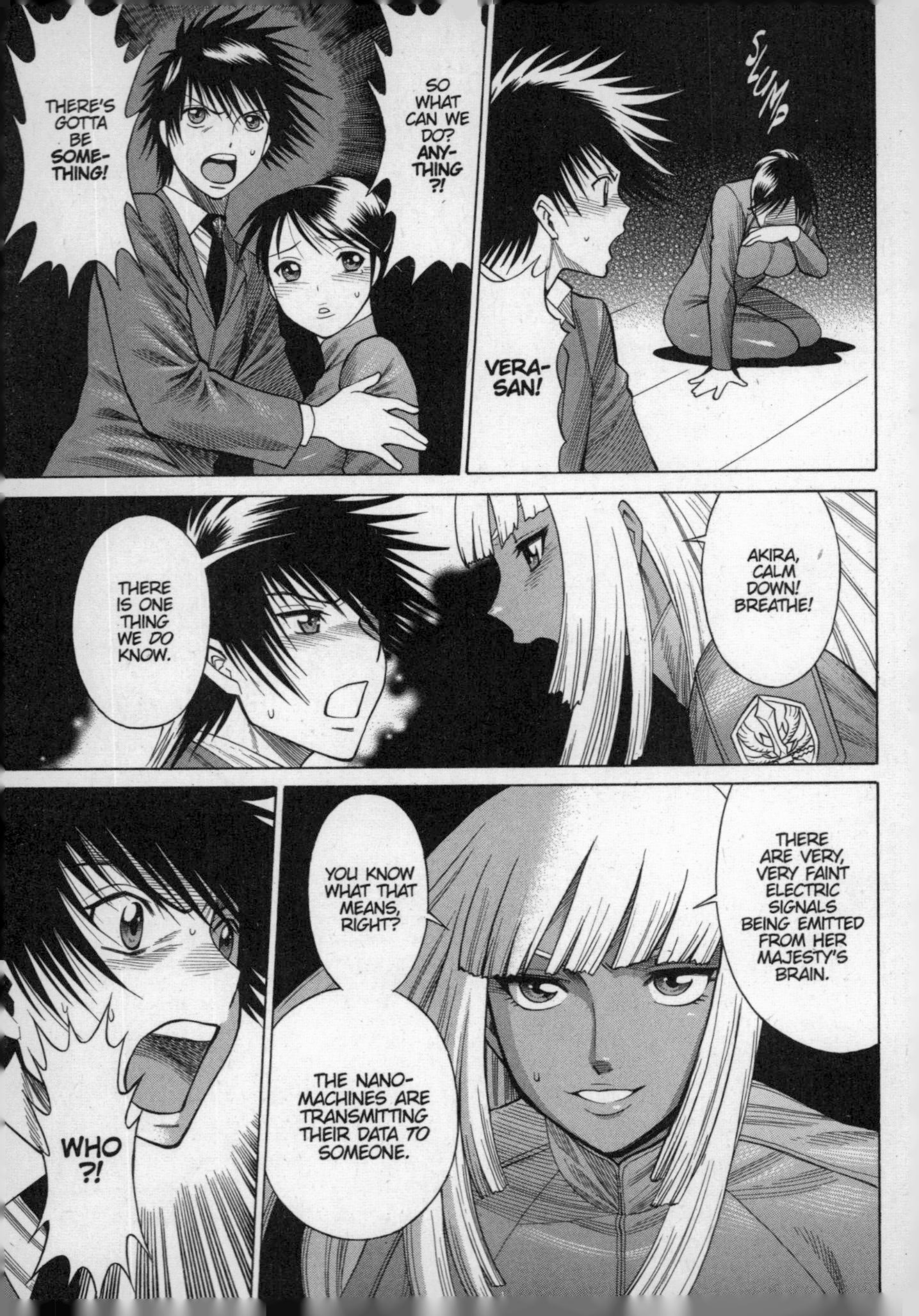
SLUMP
VERA-SAN!
SO WHAT CAN WE DO? ANYTHING?!
THERE'S GOTTA BE SOMETHING!
AKIRA, CALM DOWN! BREATHE!
THERE IS ONE THING WE *DO* KNOW.
THERE ARE VERY, VERY FAINT ELECTRIC SIGNALS BEING EMITTED FROM HER MAJESTY'S BRAIN.
YOU KNOW WHAT THAT MEANS, RIGHT?
THE NANO-MACHINES ARE TRANSMITTING THEIR DATA TO SOMEONE.
WHO?!

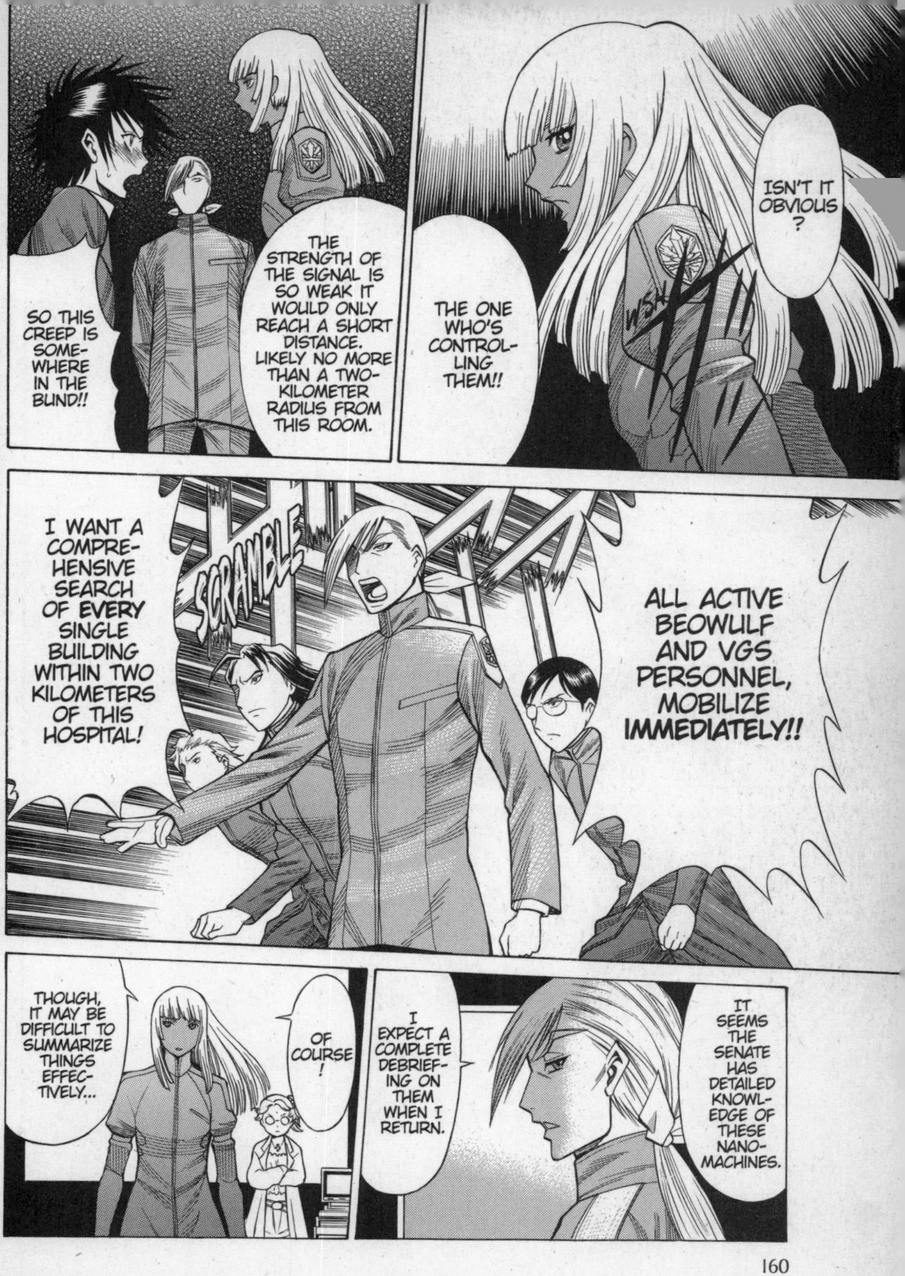

ISN'T IT OBVIOUS ?
WSH
THE ONE WHO'S CONTROL-LING THEM!!
THE STRENGTH OF THE SIGNAL IS SO WEAK IT WOULD ONLY REACH A SHORT DISTANCE. LIKELY NO MORE THAN A TWO-KILOMETER RADIUS FROM THIS ROOM.
SO THIS CREEP IS SOME-WHERE IN THE BUND!!
ALL ACTIVE BEOWULF AND VGS PERSONNEL, MOBILIZE IMMEDIATELY!!
SCRAMBLE
I WANT A COMPRE-HENSIVE SEARCH OF EVERY SINGLE BUILDING WITHIN TWO KILOMETERS OF THIS HOSPITAL!
IT SEEMS THE SENATE HAS DETAILED KNOWL-EDGE OF THESE NANO-MACHINES.
I EXPECT A COMPLETE DEBRIEF-ING ON THEM WHEN I RETURN.
OF COURSE !
THOUGH, IT MAY BE DIFFICULT TO SUMMARIZE THINGS EFFEC-TIVELY...

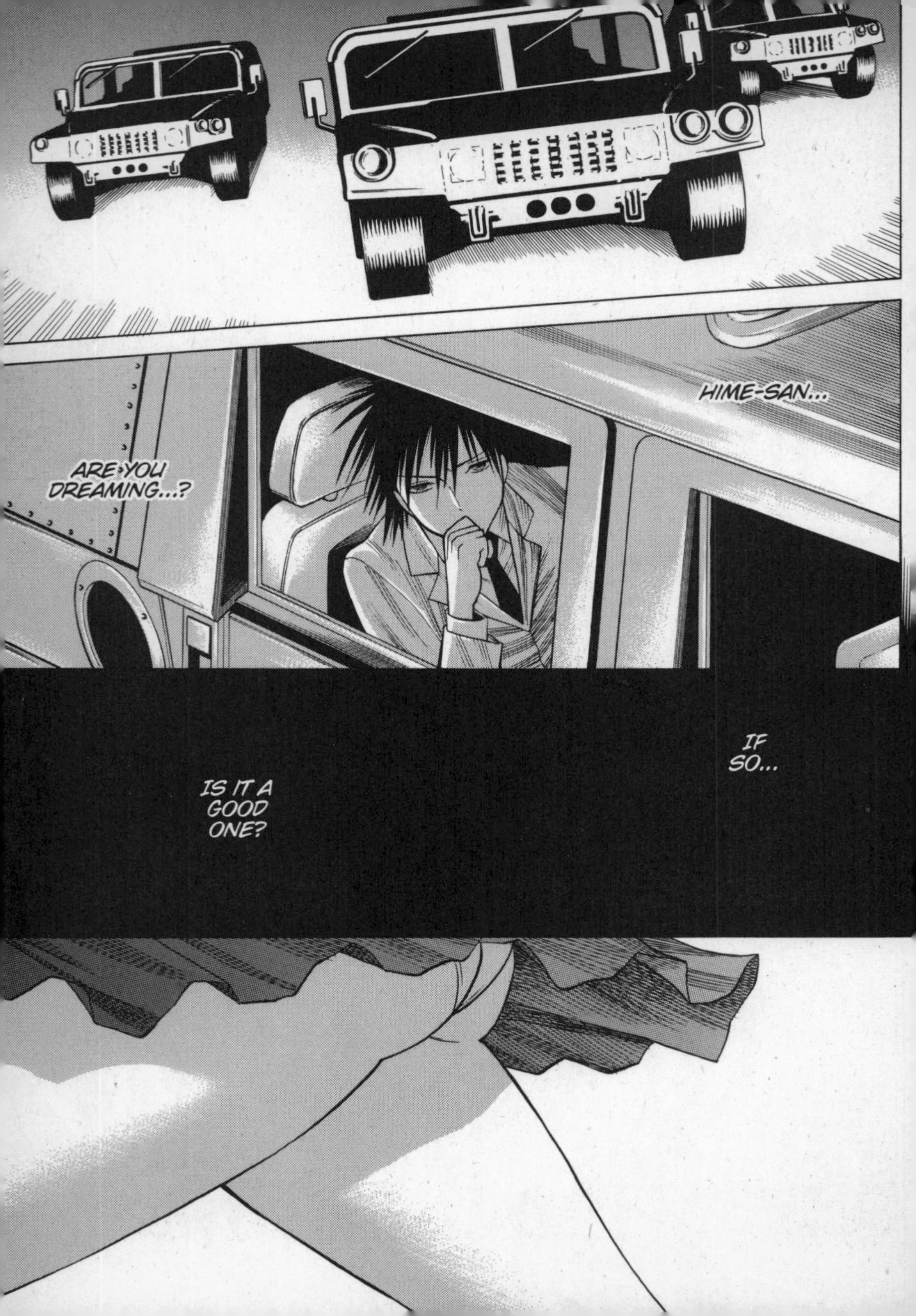
HIME-SAN...
ARE YOU DREAMING...?
IF SO...
IS IT A GOOD ONE?

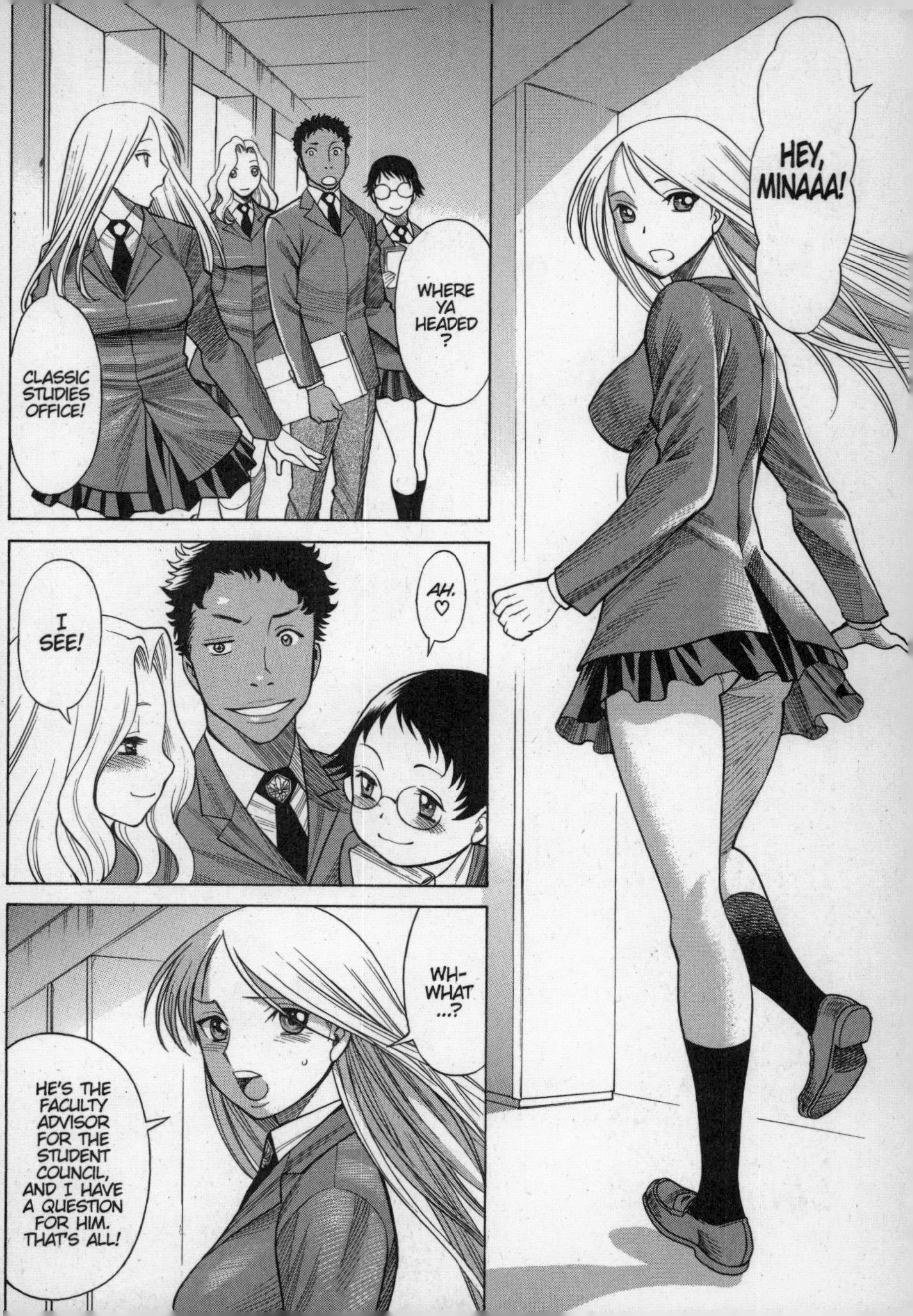
HEY, MINAAA!
WHERE YA HEADED ?
CLASSIC STUDIES OFFICE!
AH. ♡
I SEE!
WH- WHAT ...?
HE'S THE FACULTY ADVISOR FOR THE STUDENT COUNCIL, AND I HAVE A QUESTION FOR HIM. THAT'S ALL!

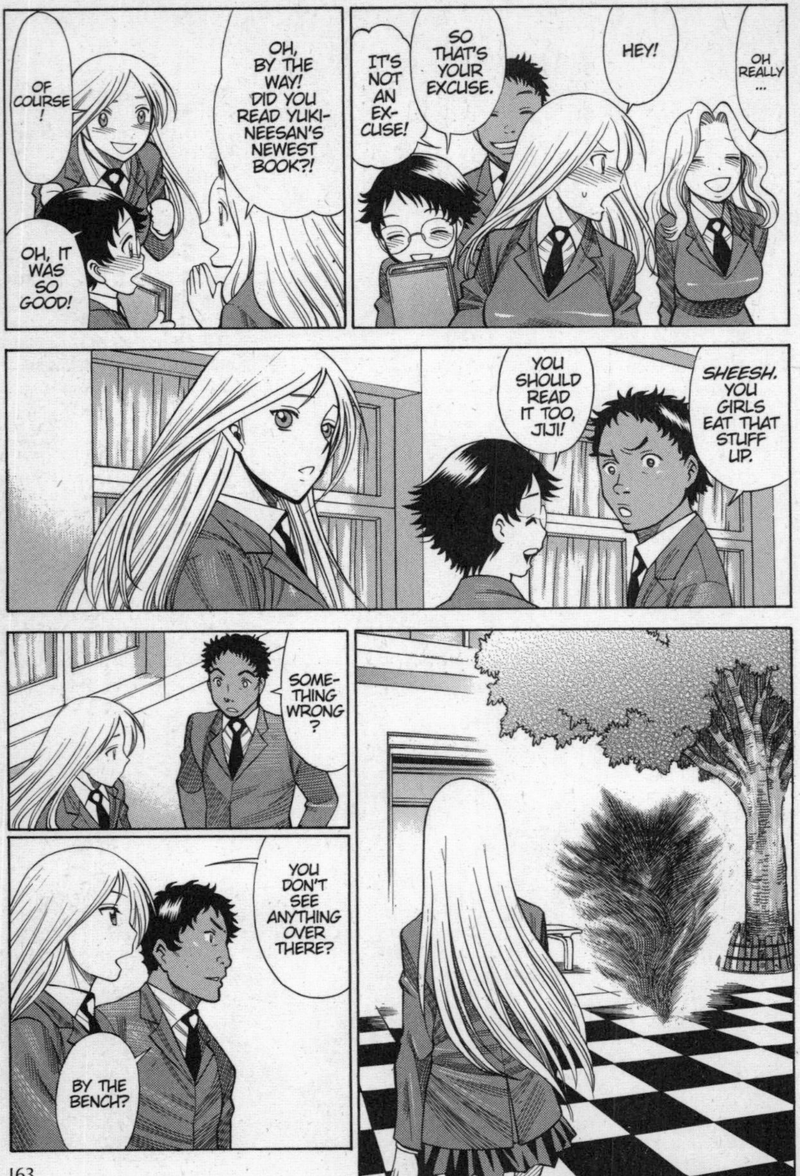
OH REALLY ...
HEY!
SO THAT'S YOUR EXCUSE.
IT'S NOT AN EX-CUSE!
OH, BY THE WAY! DID YOU READ YUKI-NEESAN'S NEWEST BOOK?!
OF COURSE!
OH, IT WAS SO GOOD!
SHEESH. YOU GIRLS EAT THAT STUFF UP.
YOU SHOULD READ IT TOO, JIJI!
SOME-THING WRONG?
YOU DON'T SEE ANYTHING OVER THERE?
BY THE BENCH?

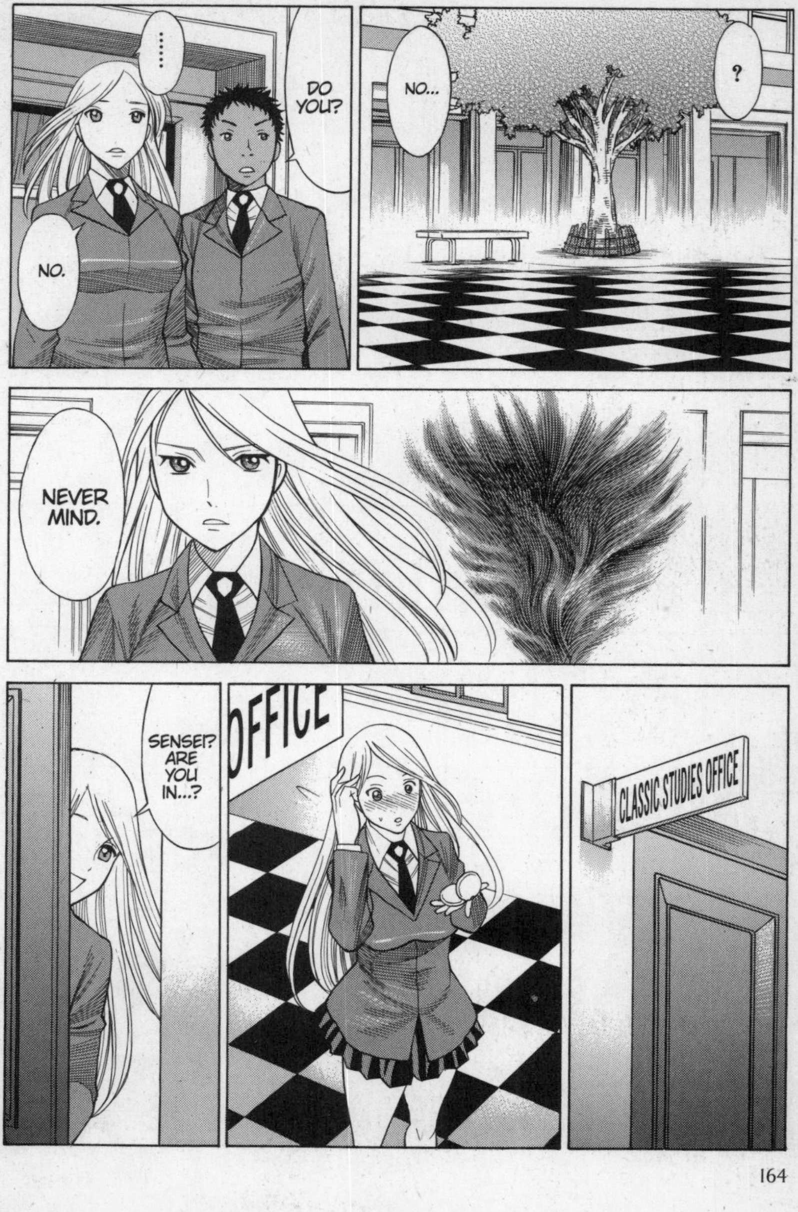
?
NO...
DO YOU?
......
NO.
NEVER MIND.
CLASSIC STUDIES OFFICE
OFFICE
SENSEI? ARE YOU IN...?

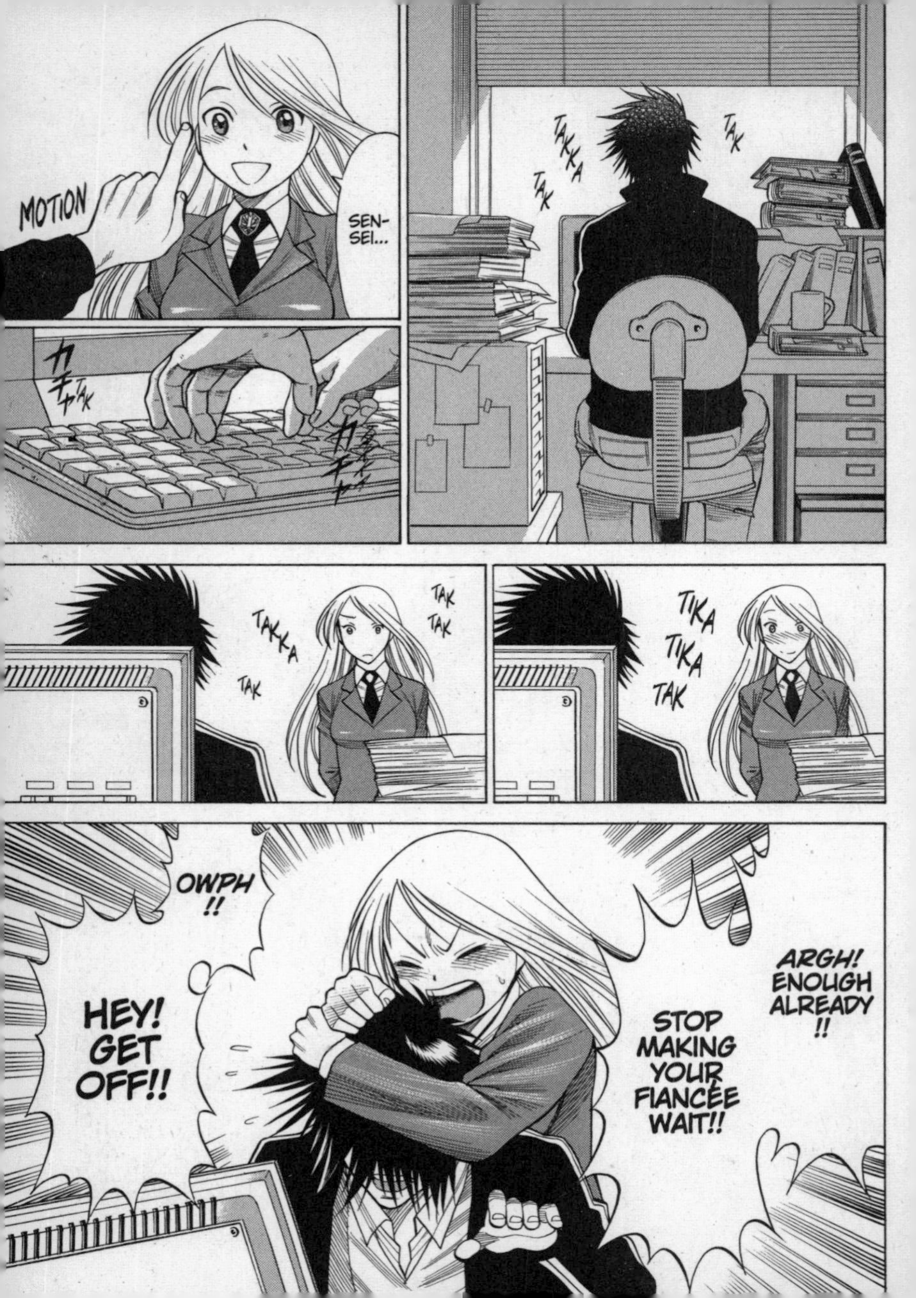

TAKKA
TAK
TAK
MOTION
SEN-SEI...
カチャ
TAK
カチャ
TIKA
TIKA
TAK
TAK
TAK
TAKKA
TAK
ARGH! ENOUGH ALREADY!!
STOP MAKING YOUR FIANCÉE WAIT!!
OWPH!!
HEY! GET OFF!!

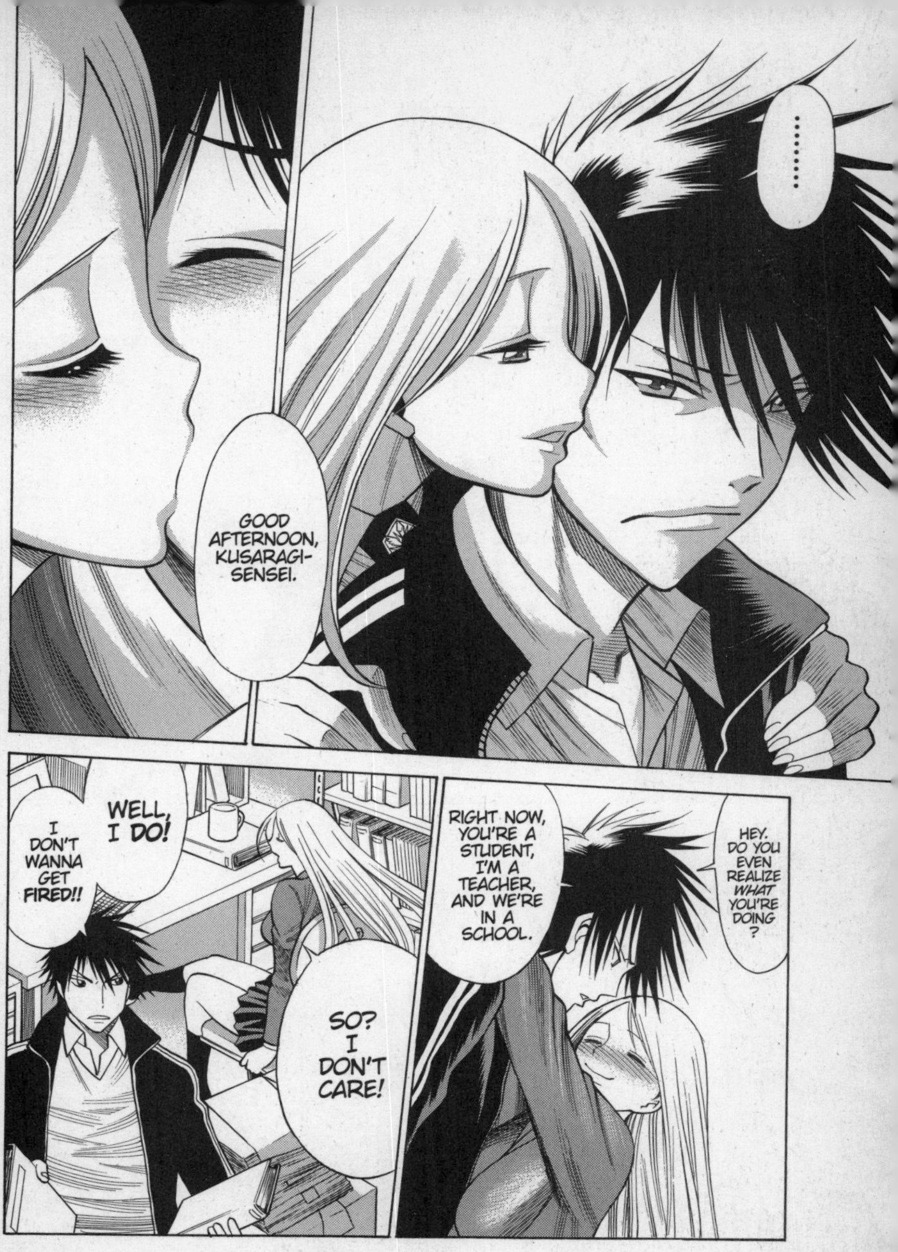
......
GOOD AFTERNOON, KUSARAGI-SENSEI.
HEY. DO YOU EVEN REALIZE *WHAT* YOU'RE DOING?
RIGHT NOW, YOU'RE A STUDENT, I'M A TEACHER, AND WE'RE IN A SCHOOL.
SO? I DON'T CARE!
WELL, I DO!
I DON'T WANNA GET FIRED!!

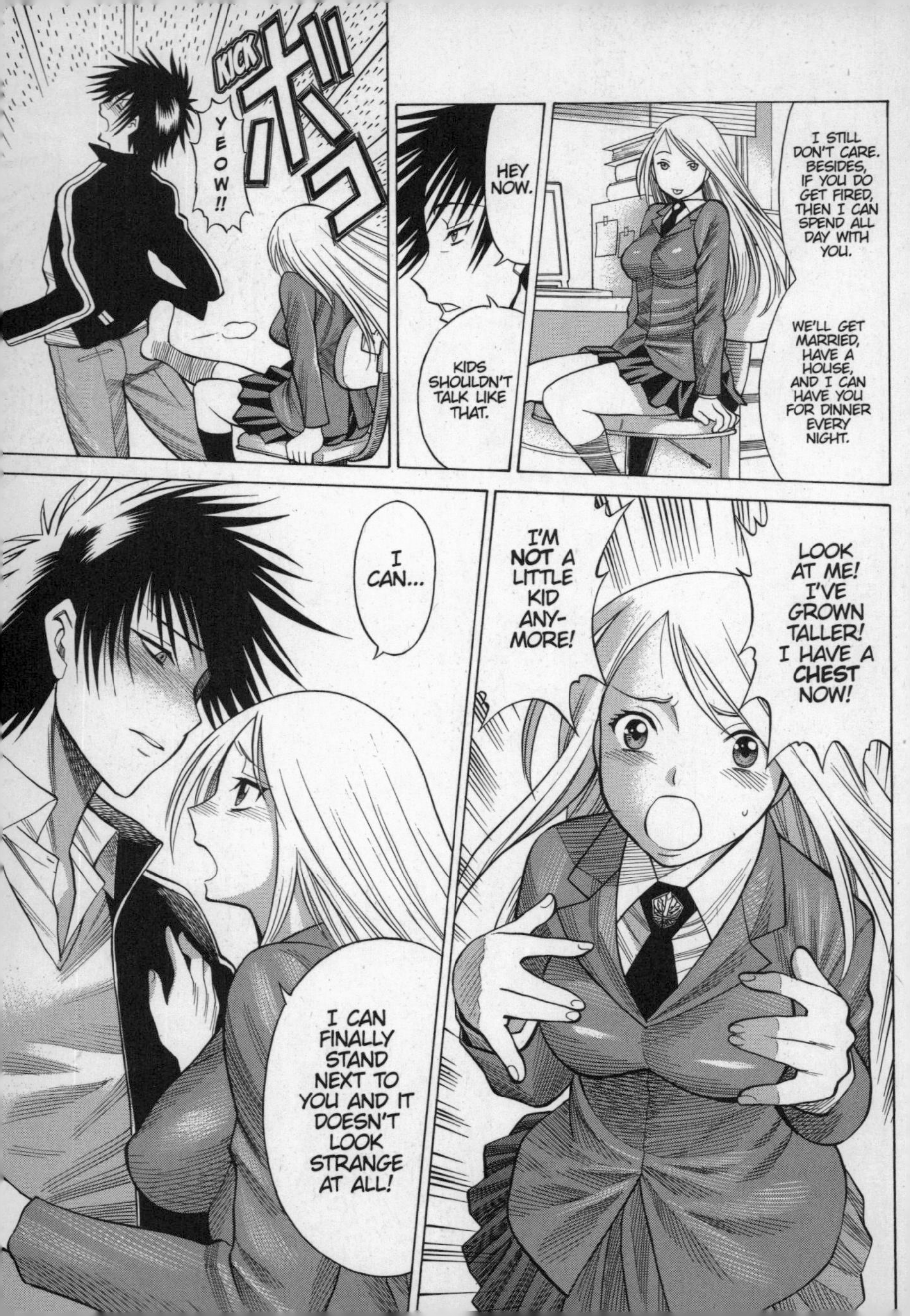

I STILL DON'T CARE. BESIDES, IF YOU DO GET FIRED, THEN I CAN SPEND ALL DAY WITH YOU.
WE'LL GET MARRIED, HAVE A HOUSE, AND I CAN HAVE YOU FOR DINNER EVERY NIGHT.
HEY NOW.
KIDS SHOULDN'T TALK LIKE THAT.
KICK
ボコ
YEOW!!
LOOK AT ME! I'VE GROWN TALLER! I HAVE A CHEST NOW!
I'M NOT A LITTLE KID ANYMORE!
I CAN...
I CAN FINALLY STAND NEXT TO YOU AND IT DOESN'T LOOK STRANGE AT ALL!

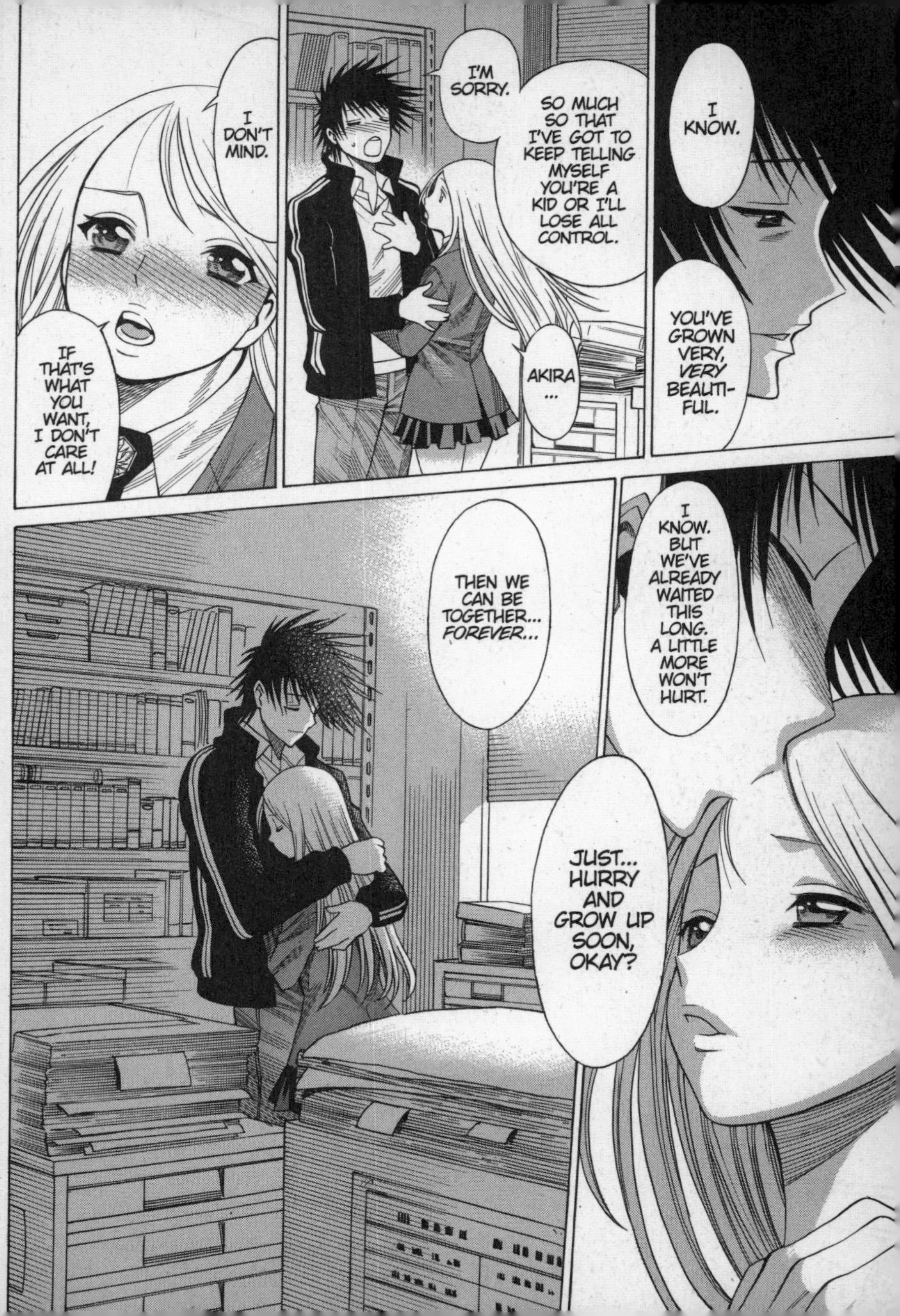
I KNOW.
YOU'VE GROWN VERY, *VERY* BEAUTIFUL.
I'M SORRY.
SO MUCH SO THAT I'VE GOT TO KEEP TELLING MYSELF YOU'RE A KID OR I'LL LOSE ALL CONTROL.
AKIRA...
I DON'T MIND.
IF THAT'S WHAT YOU WANT, I DON'T CARE AT ALL!
I KNOW. BUT WE'VE ALREADY WAITED THIS LONG. A LITTLE MORE WON'T HURT.
JUST... HURRY AND GROW UP SOON, OKAY?
THEN WE CAN BE TOGETHER... *FOREVER*...

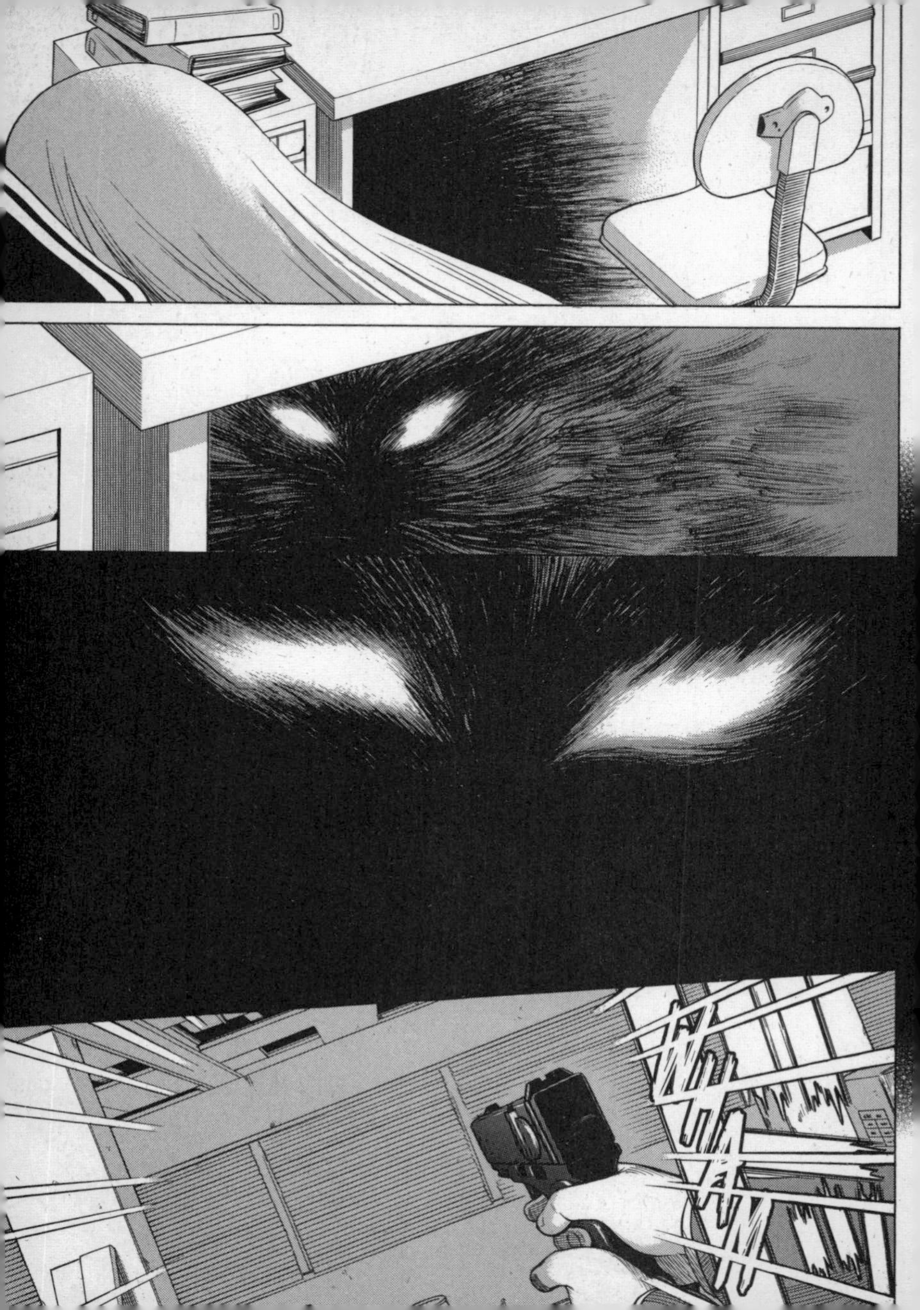
WHAM

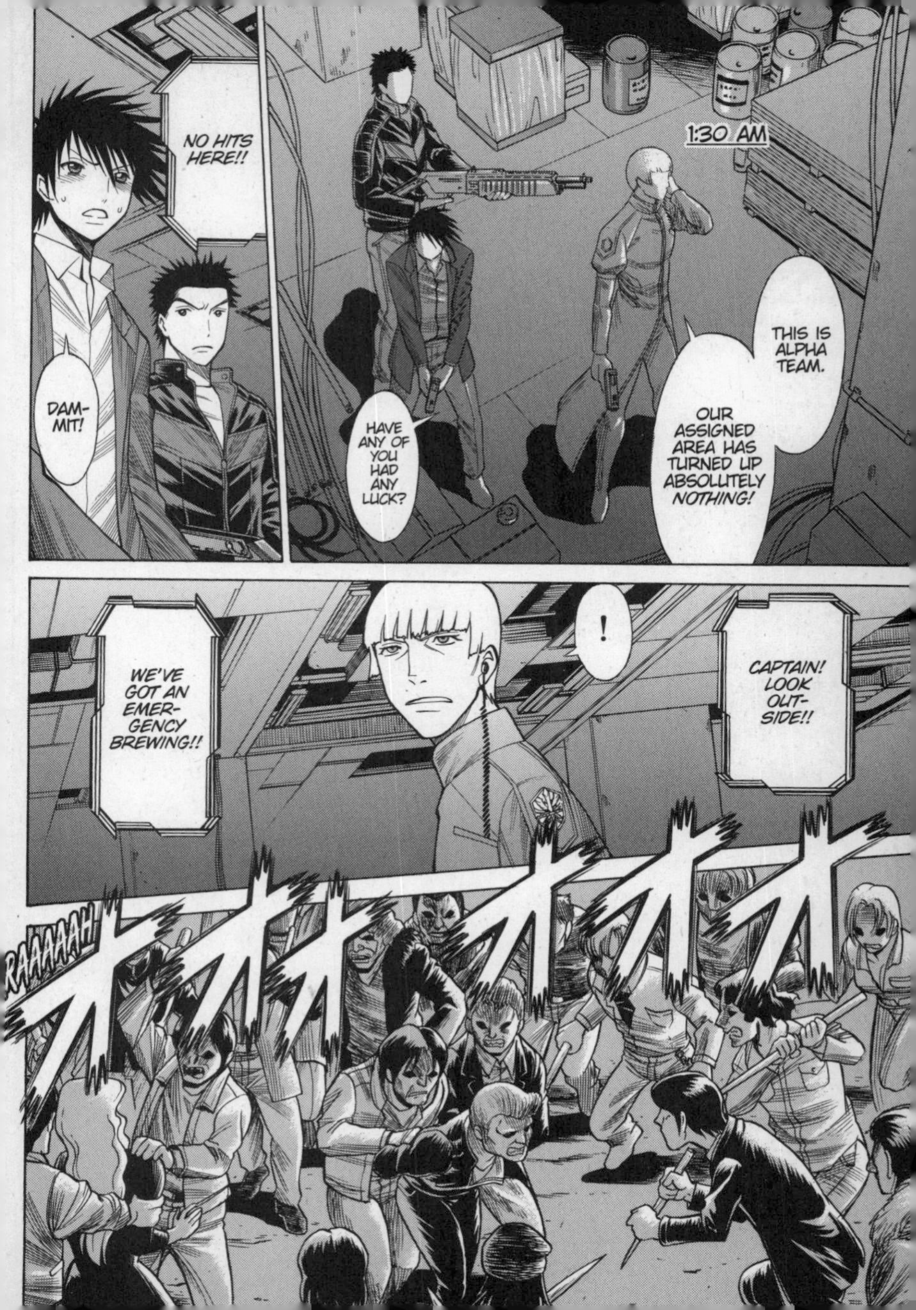
1:30 AM
THIS IS ALPHA TEAM.
OUR ASSIGNED AREA HAS TURNED UP ABSOLUTELY *NOTHING!*
HAVE ANY OF YOU HAD ANY LUCK?
NO HITS HERE!!
DAM-MIT!
CAPTAIN! LOOK OUT-SIDE!!
!
WE'VE GOT AN EMER-GENCY BREWING!!
RAAAAAH

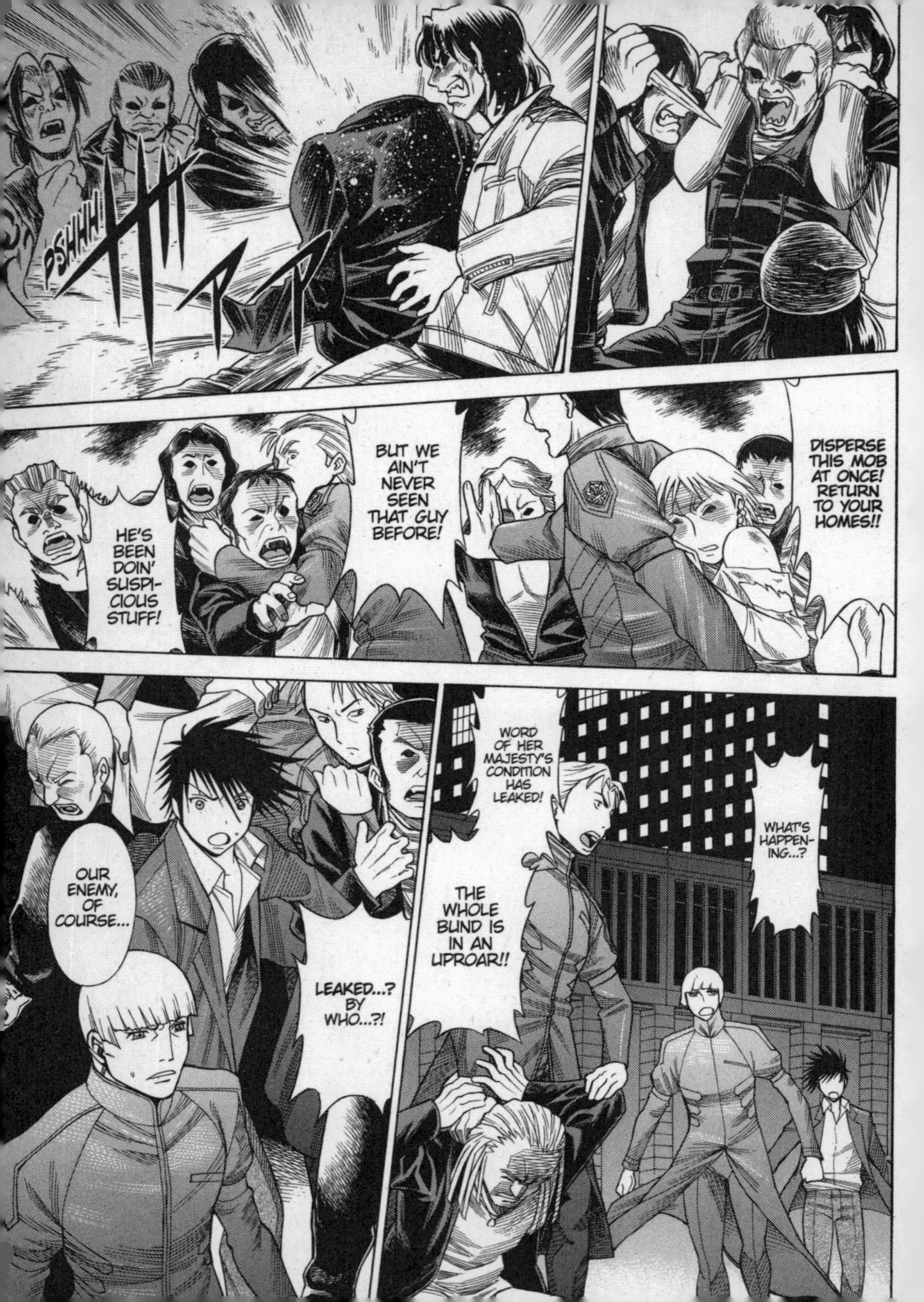
PSHHH
DISPERSE THIS MOB AT ONCE! RETURN TO YOUR HOMES!!
BUT WE AIN'T NEVER SEEN THAT GUY BEFORE!
HE'S BEEN DOIN' SUSPICIOUS STUFF!
WHAT'S HAPPENING...?
WORD OF HER MAJESTY'S CONDITION HAS LEAKED!
THE WHOLE BUND IS IN AN UPROAR!!
LEAKED...? BY WHO...?!
OUR ENEMY, OF COURSE...

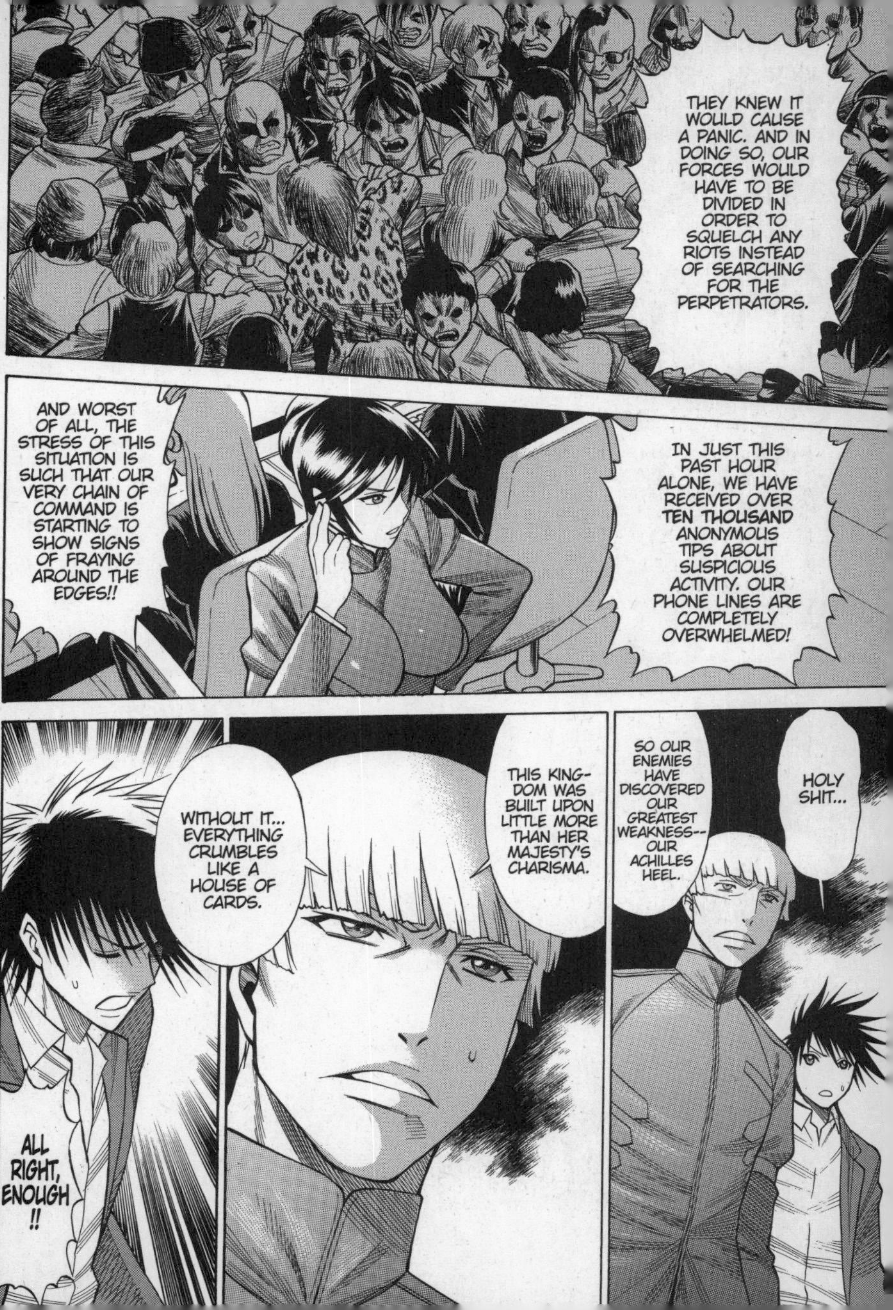
THEY KNEW IT WOULD CAUSE A PANIC. AND IN DOING SO, OUR FORCES WOULD HAVE TO BE DIVIDED IN ORDER TO SQUELCH ANY RIOTS INSTEAD OF SEARCHING FOR THE PERPETRATORS.
IN JUST THIS PAST HOUR ALONE, WE HAVE RECEIVED OVER **TEN THOUSAND** ANONYMOUS TIPS ABOUT SUSPICIOUS ACTIVITY. OUR PHONE LINES ARE COMPLETELY OVERWHELMED!
AND WORST OF ALL, THE STRESS OF THIS SITUATION IS SUCH THAT OUR VERY CHAIN OF COMMAND IS STARTING TO SHOW SIGNS OF FRAYING AROUND THE EDGES!!
HOLY SHIT...
SO OUR ENEMIES HAVE DISCOVERED OUR GREATEST WEAKNESS-- OUR ACHILLES HEEL.
THIS KING-DOM WAS BUILT UPON LITTLE MORE THAN HER MAJESTY'S CHARISMA.
WITHOUT IT... EVERYTHING CRUMBLES LIKE A HOUSE OF CARDS.
ALL RIGHT, ENOUGH !!

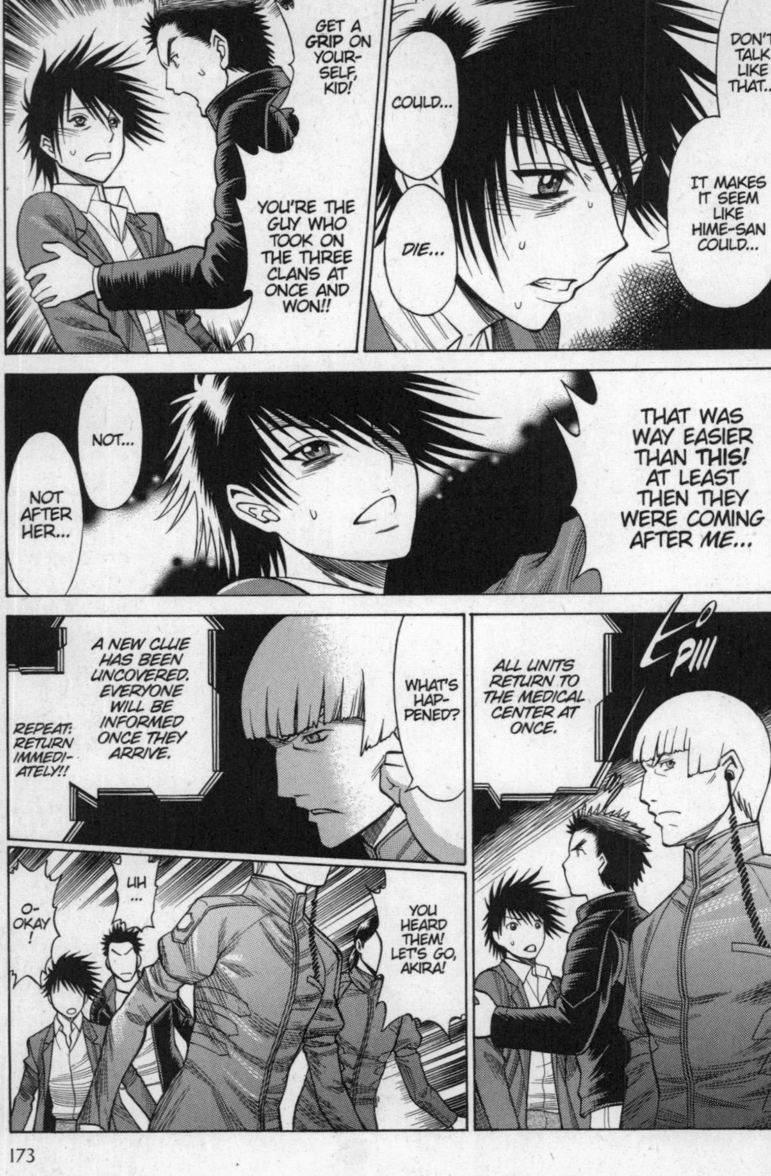
DON'T TALK LIKE THAT...
IT MAKES IT SEEM LIKE HIME-SAN COULD...
COULD...
DIE...
GET A GRIP ON YOUR-SELF, KID!
YOU'RE THE GUY WHO TOOK ON THE THREE CLANS AT ONCE AND WON!!
THAT WAS WAY EASIER THAN THIS! AT LEAST THEN THEY WERE COMING AFTER ME...
NOT...
NOT AFTER HER...
PIII
ALL UNITS RETURN TO THE MEDICAL CENTER AT ONCE.
WHAT'S HAP-PENED?
A NEW CLUE HAS BEEN UNCOVERED. EVERYONE WILL BE INFORMED ONCE THEY ARRIVE.
REPEAT: RETURN IMMEDI-ATELY!!
YOU HEARD THEM! LET'S GO, AKIRA!
UH ...
O-OKAY!

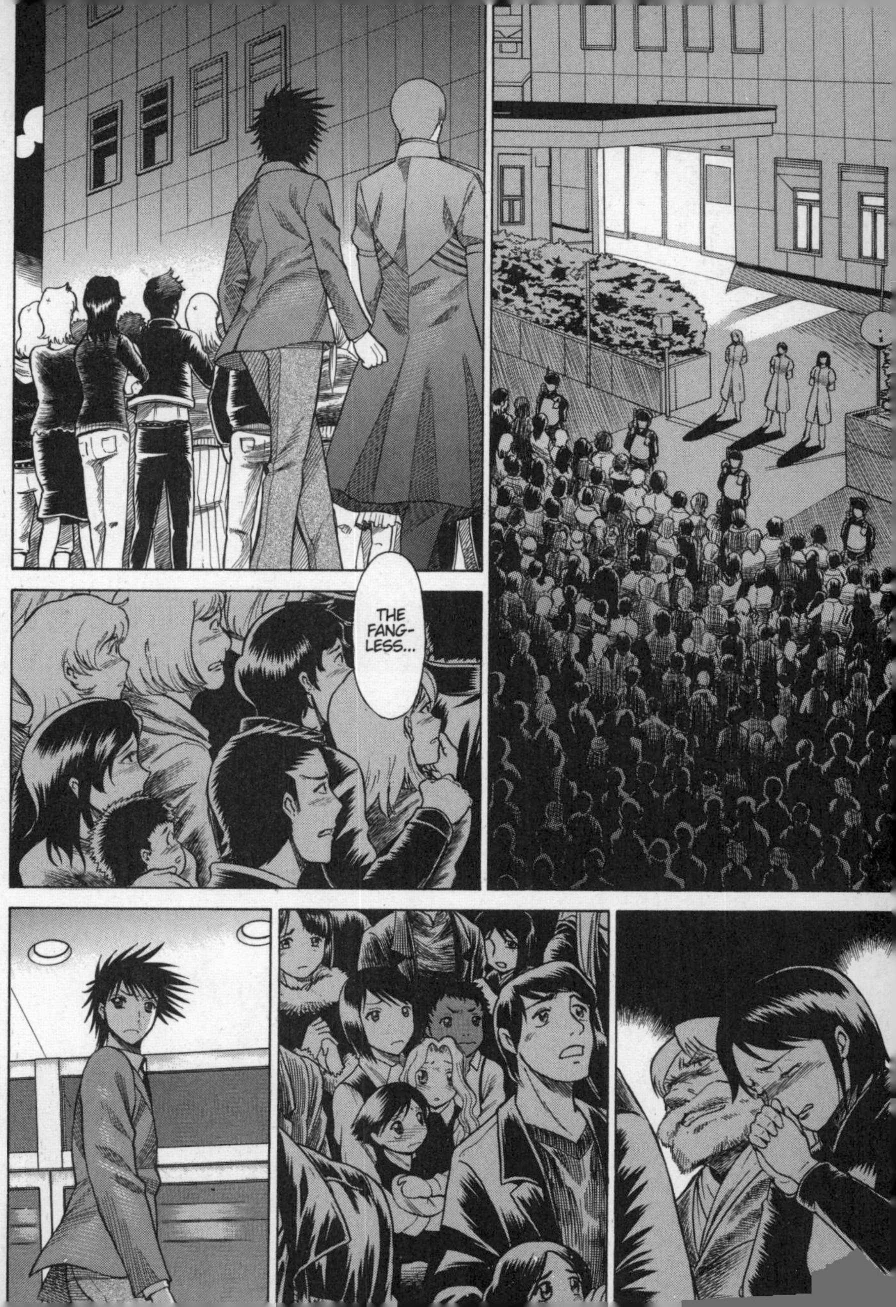
THE FANG-LESS...

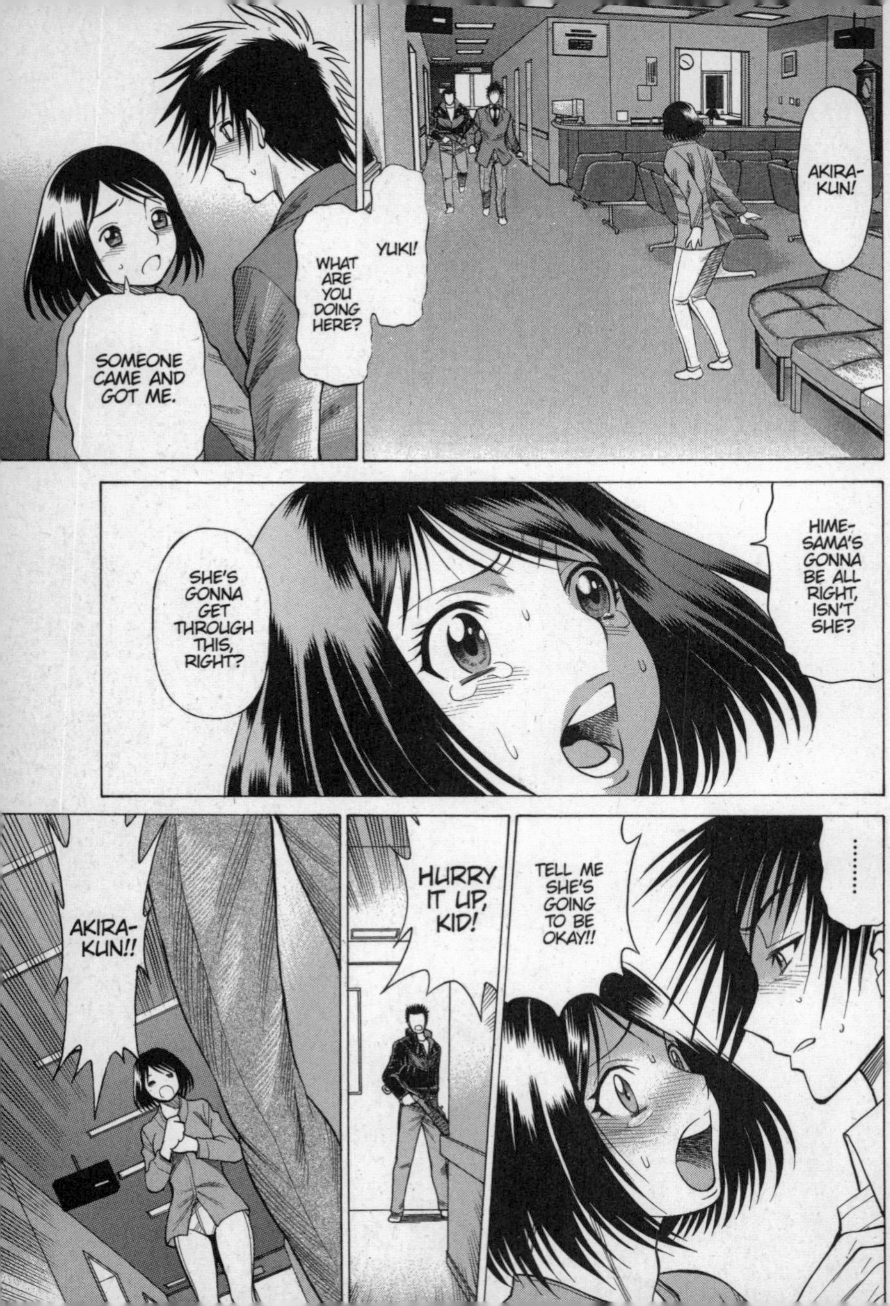
AKIRA-KUN!
YUKI!
WHAT ARE YOU DOING HERE?
SOMEONE CAME AND GOT ME.
HIME-SAMA'S GONNA BE ALL RIGHT, ISN'T SHE?
SHE'S GONNA GET THROUGH THIS, RIGHT?
......
TELL ME SHE'S GOING TO BE OKAY!!
HURRY IT UP, KID!
AKIRA-KUN!!

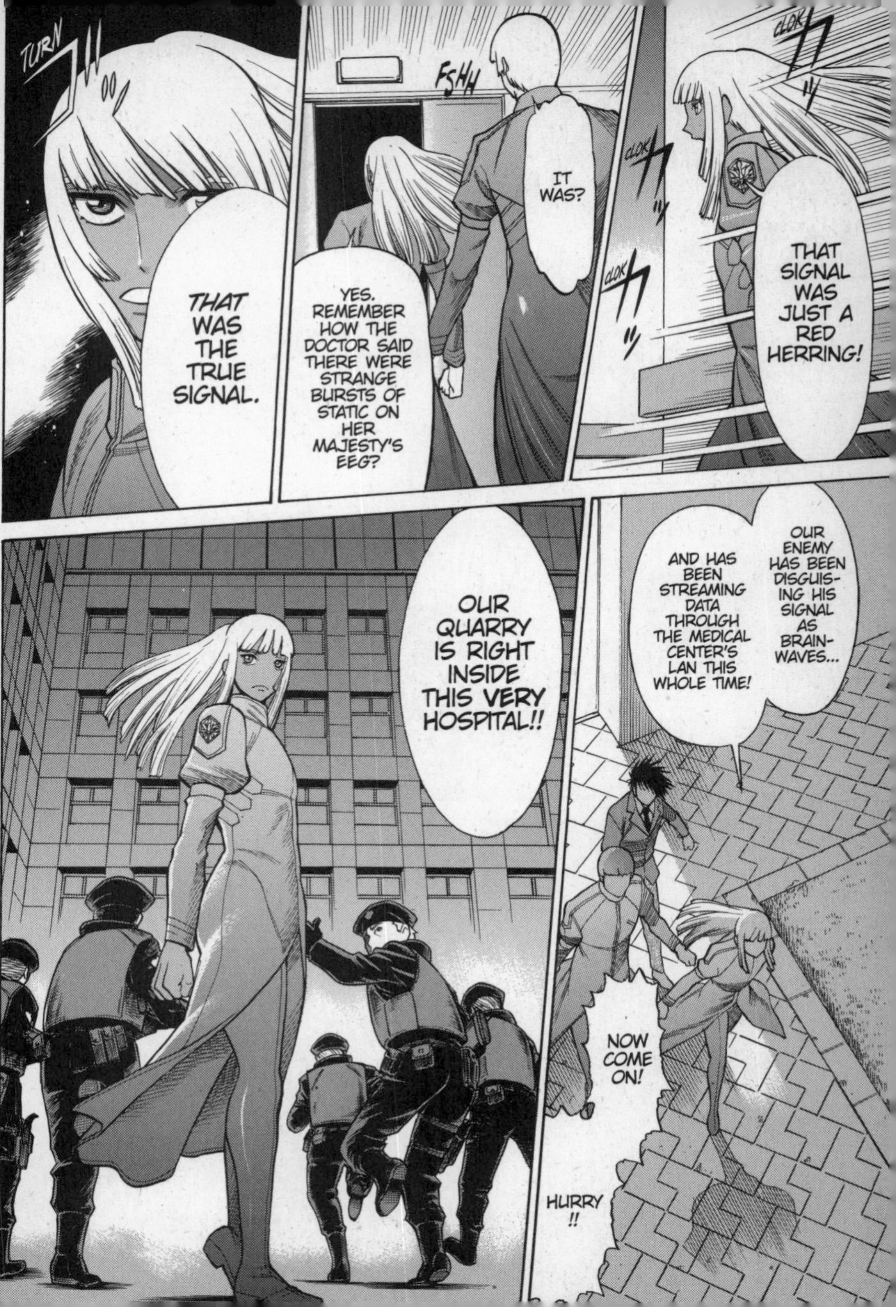
CLOK
CLOK
CLOK
THAT SIGNAL WAS JUST A RED HERRING!
FSHH
IT WAS?
YES. REMEMBER HOW THE DOCTOR SAID THERE WERE STRANGE BURSTS OF STATIC ON HER MAJESTY'S EEG?
TURN
THAT WAS THE TRUE SIGNAL.
OUR ENEMY HAS BEEN DISGUIS-ING HIS SIGNAL AS BRAIN-WAVES...
AND HAS BEEN STREAMING DATA THROUGH THE MEDICAL CENTER'S LAN THIS WHOLE TIME!
NOW COME ON!
HURRY!!
OUR QUARRY IS RIGHT INSIDE THIS VERY HOSPITAL!!

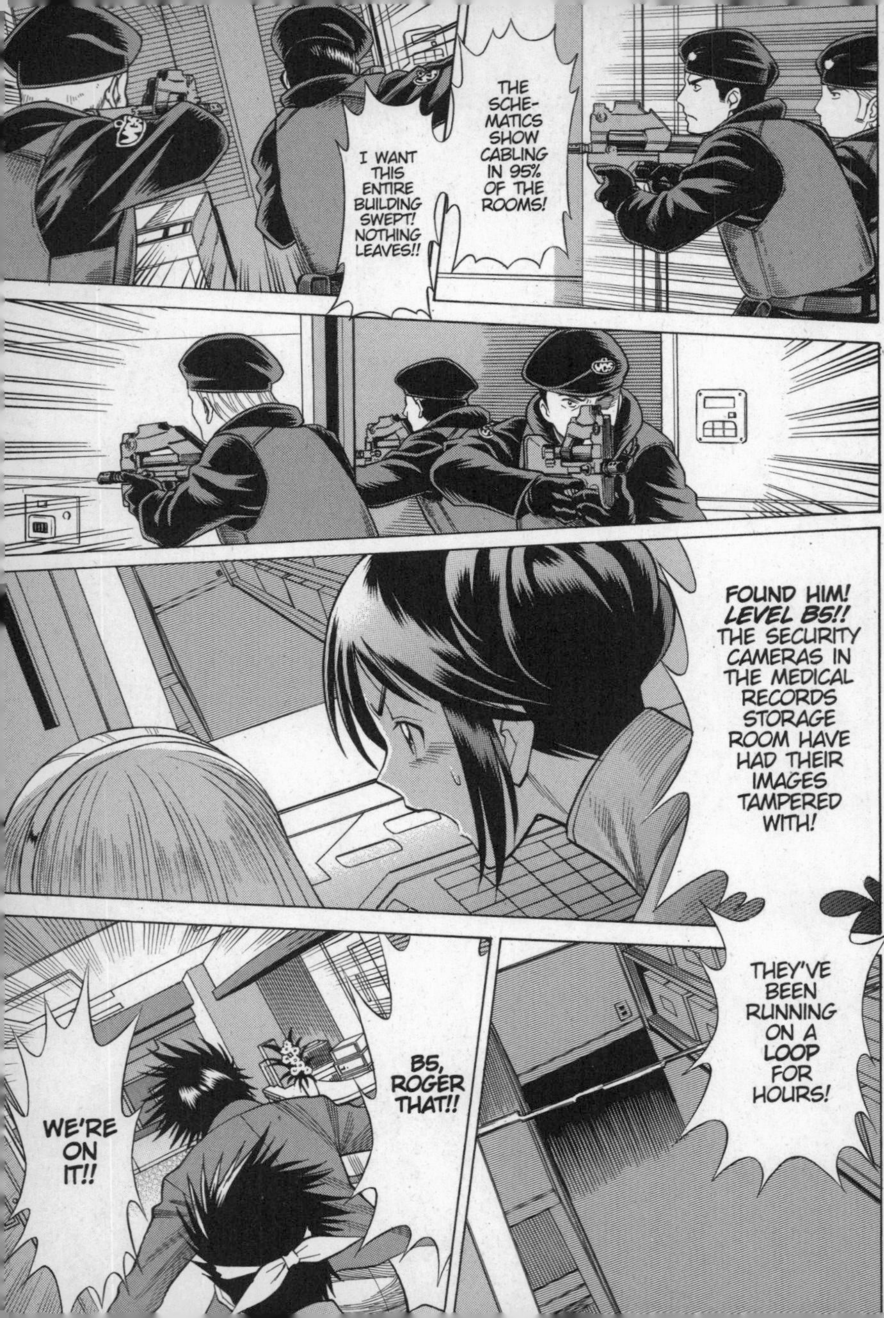
THE SCHEMATICS SHOW CABLING IN 95% OF THE ROOMS!
I WANT THIS ENTIRE BUILDING SWEPT! NOTHING LEAVES!!
FOUND HIM! LEVEL B5!! THE SECURITY CAMERAS IN THE MEDICAL RECORDS STORAGE ROOM HAVE HAD THEIR IMAGES TAMPERED WITH!
THEY'VE BEEN RUNNING ON A LOOP FOR HOURS!
B5, ROGER THAT!!
WE'RE ON IT!!

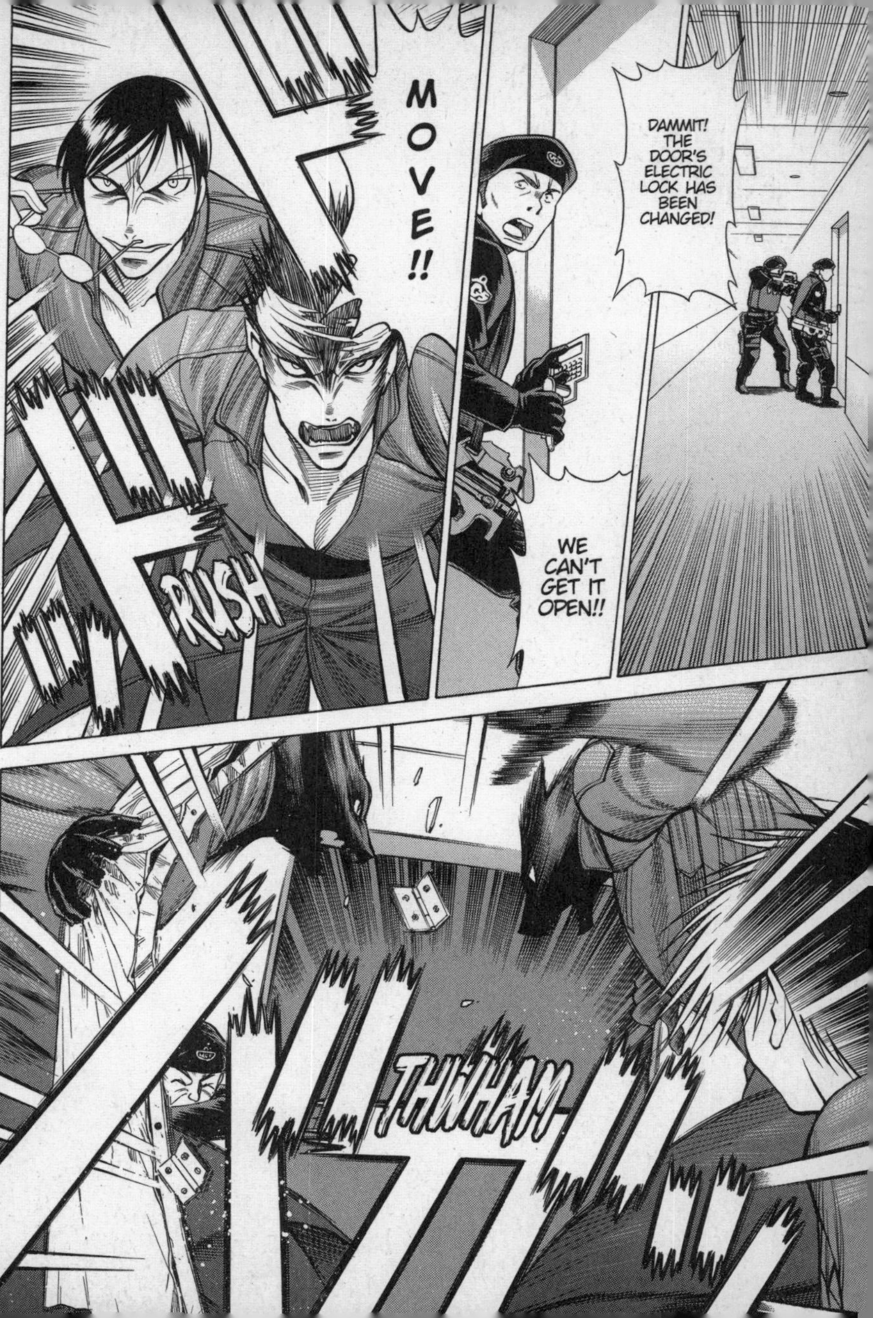
DAMMIT! THE DOOR'S ELECTRIC LOCK HAS BEEN CHANGED!
WE CAN'T GET IT OPEN!!
MOVE!!
RUSH
THWHAM

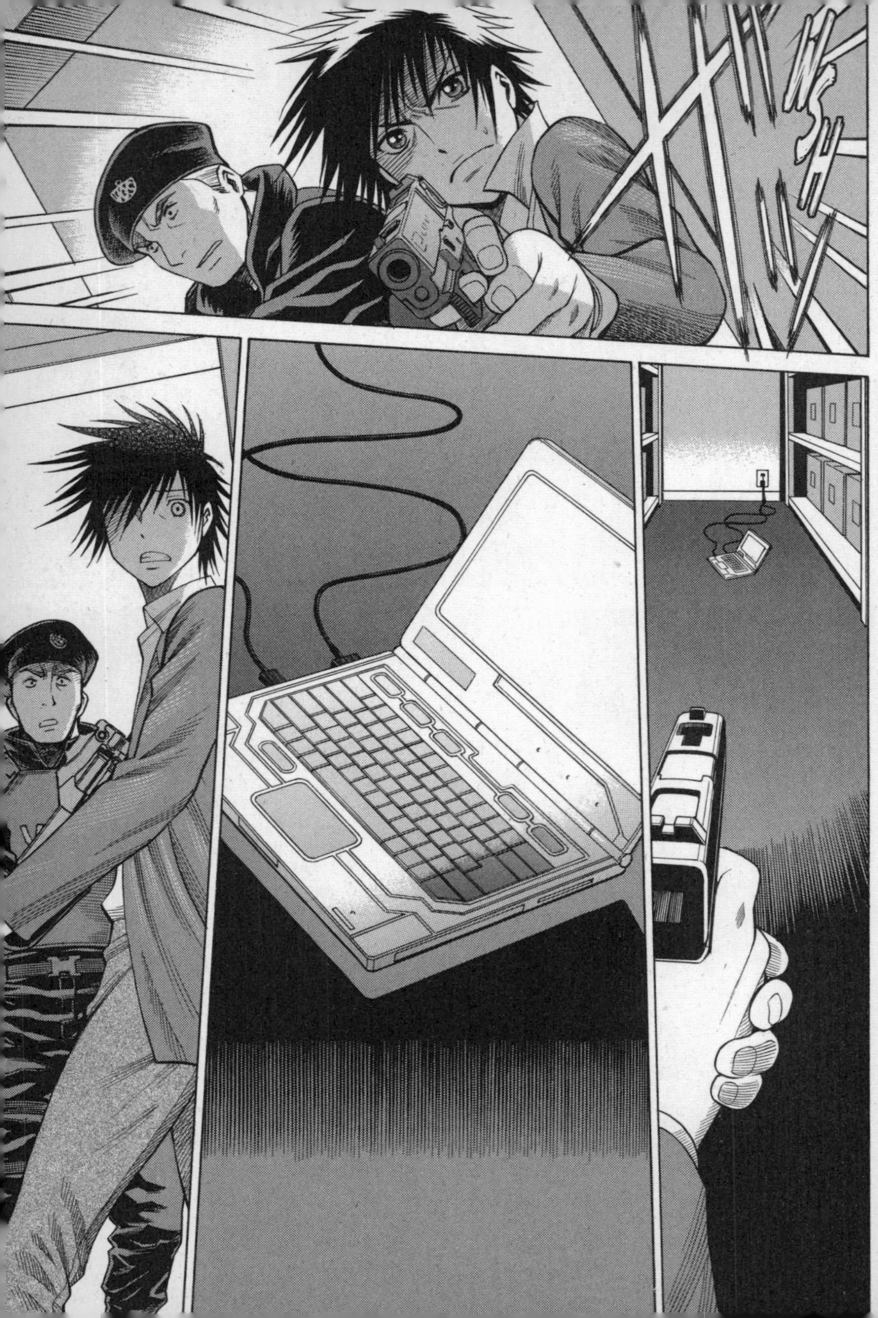

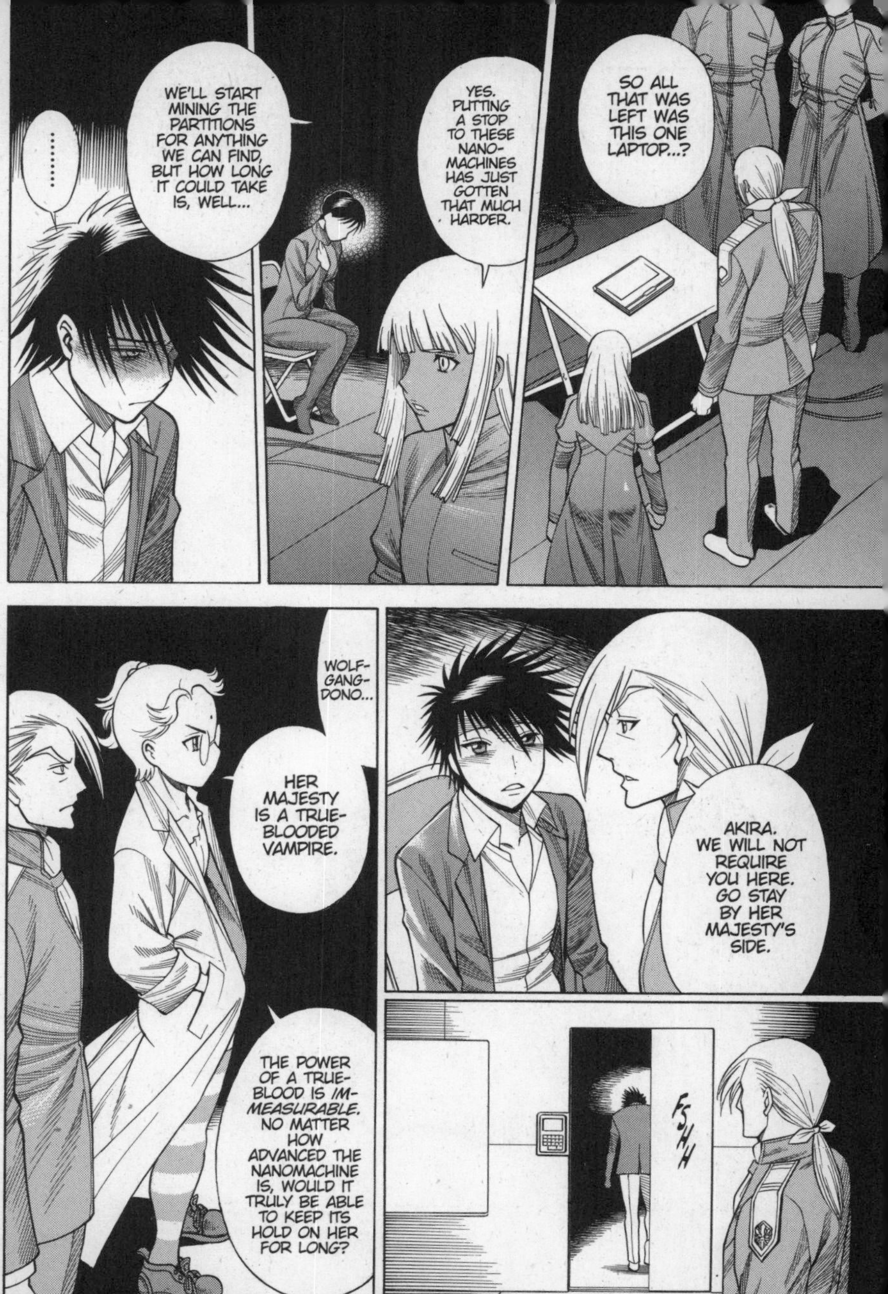
SO ALL THAT WAS LEFT WAS THIS ONE LAPTOP...?
YES. PUTTING A STOP TO THESE NANO-MACHINES HAS JUST GOTTEN THAT MUCH HARDER.
WE'LL START MINING THE PARTITIONS FOR ANYTHING WE CAN FIND, BUT HOW LONG IT COULD TAKE IS, WELL...
......
AKIRA. WE WILL NOT REQUIRE YOU HERE. GO STAY BY HER MAJESTY'S SIDE.
FSHH
WOLF-GANG-DONO...
HER MAJESTY IS A TRUE-BLOODED VAMPIRE.
THE POWER OF A TRUE-BLOOD IS *IM-MEASURABLE*. NO MATTER HOW ADVANCED THE NANOMACHINE IS, WOULD IT TRULY BE ABLE TO KEEP ITS HOLD ON HER FOR LONG?

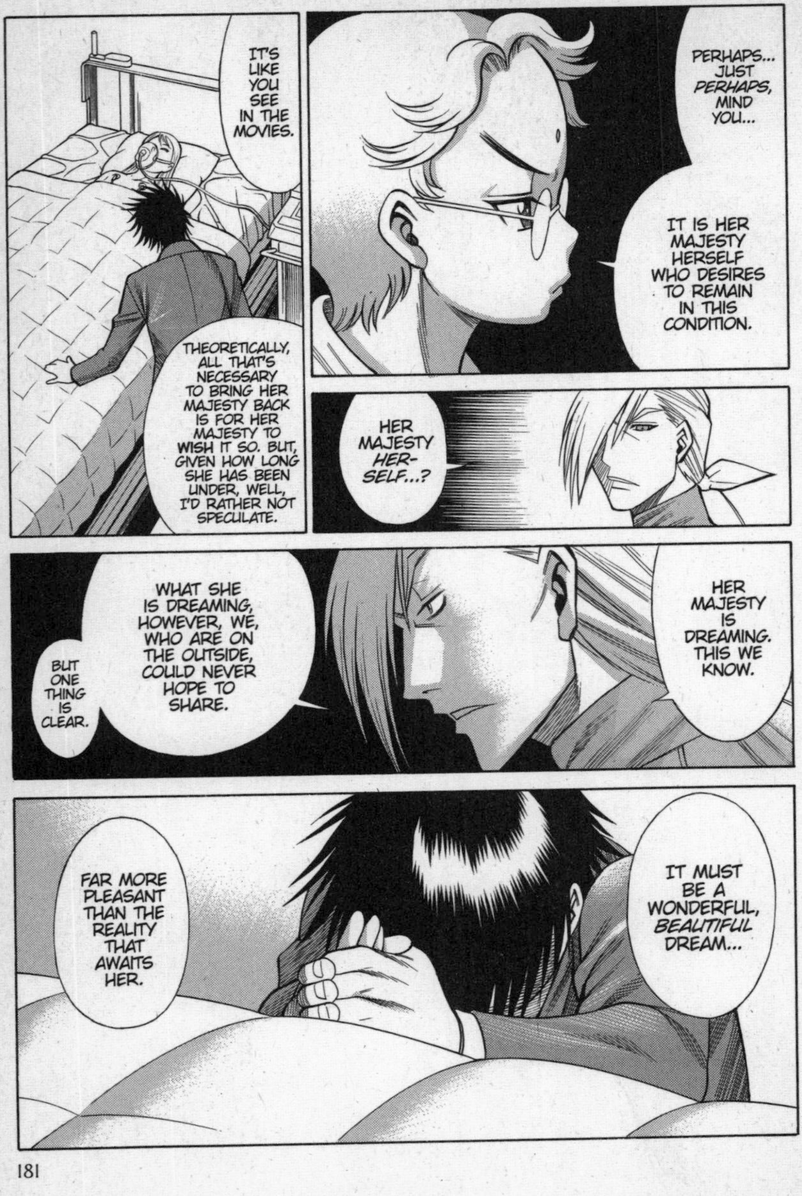
PERHAPS... JUST *PERHAPS*, MIND YOU...
IT IS HER MAJESTY HERSELF WHO DESIRES TO REMAIN IN THIS CONDITION.
HER MAJESTY *HER-SELF*...?
IT'S LIKE YOU SEE IN THE MOVIES.
THEORETICALLY, ALL THAT'S NECESSARY TO BRING HER MAJESTY BACK IS FOR HER MAJESTY TO WISH IT SO. BUT, GIVEN HOW LONG SHE HAS BEEN UNDER, WELL, I'D RATHER NOT SPECULATE.
HER MAJESTY IS DREAMING. THIS WE KNOW.
WHAT SHE IS DREAMING, HOWEVER, WE, WHO ARE ON THE OUTSIDE, COULD NEVER HOPE TO SHARE.
BUT ONE THING IS CLEAR.
IT MUST BE A WONDERFUL, *BEAUTIFUL* DREAM...
FAR MORE PLEASANT THAN THE REALITY THAT AWAITS HER.

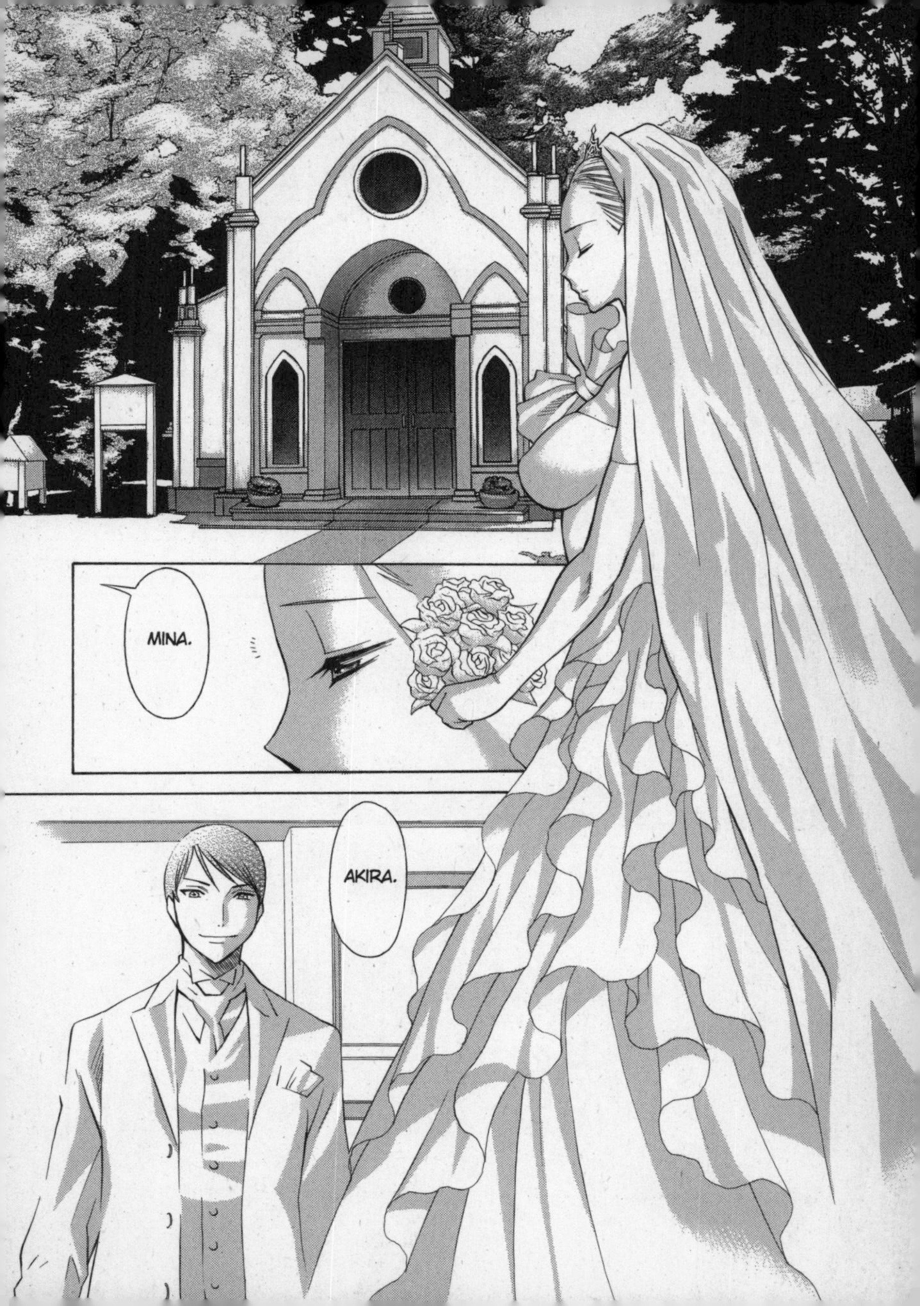
MINA.
AKIRA.

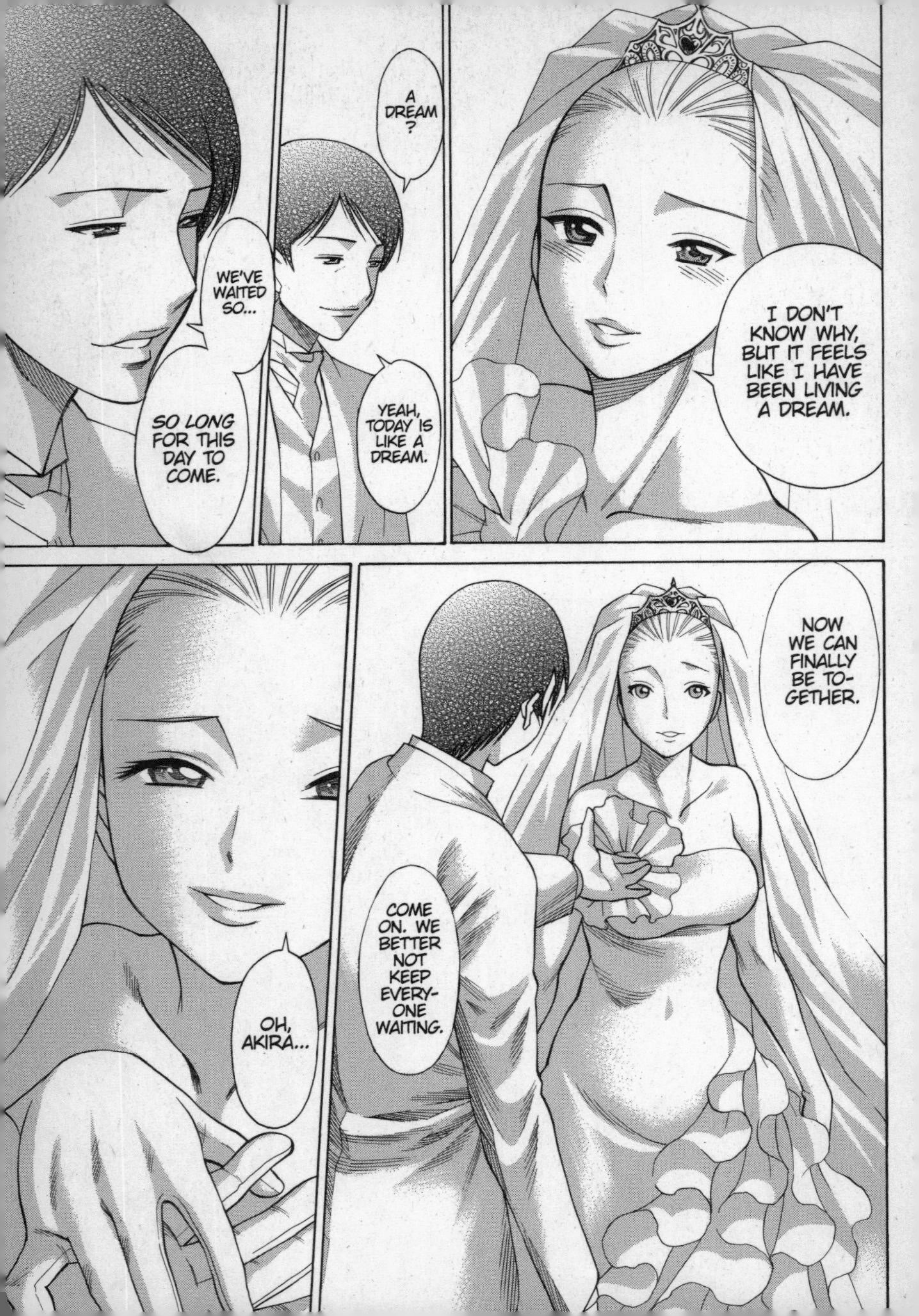
I DON'T KNOW WHY, BUT IT FEELS LIKE I HAVE BEEN LIVING A DREAM.
A DREAM ?
YEAH, TODAY IS LIKE A DREAM.
WE'VE WAITED SO...
SO LONG FOR THIS DAY TO COME.
NOW WE CAN FINALLY BE TO-GETHER.
COME ON. WE BETTER NOT KEEP EVERY-ONE WAITING.
OH, AKIRA...

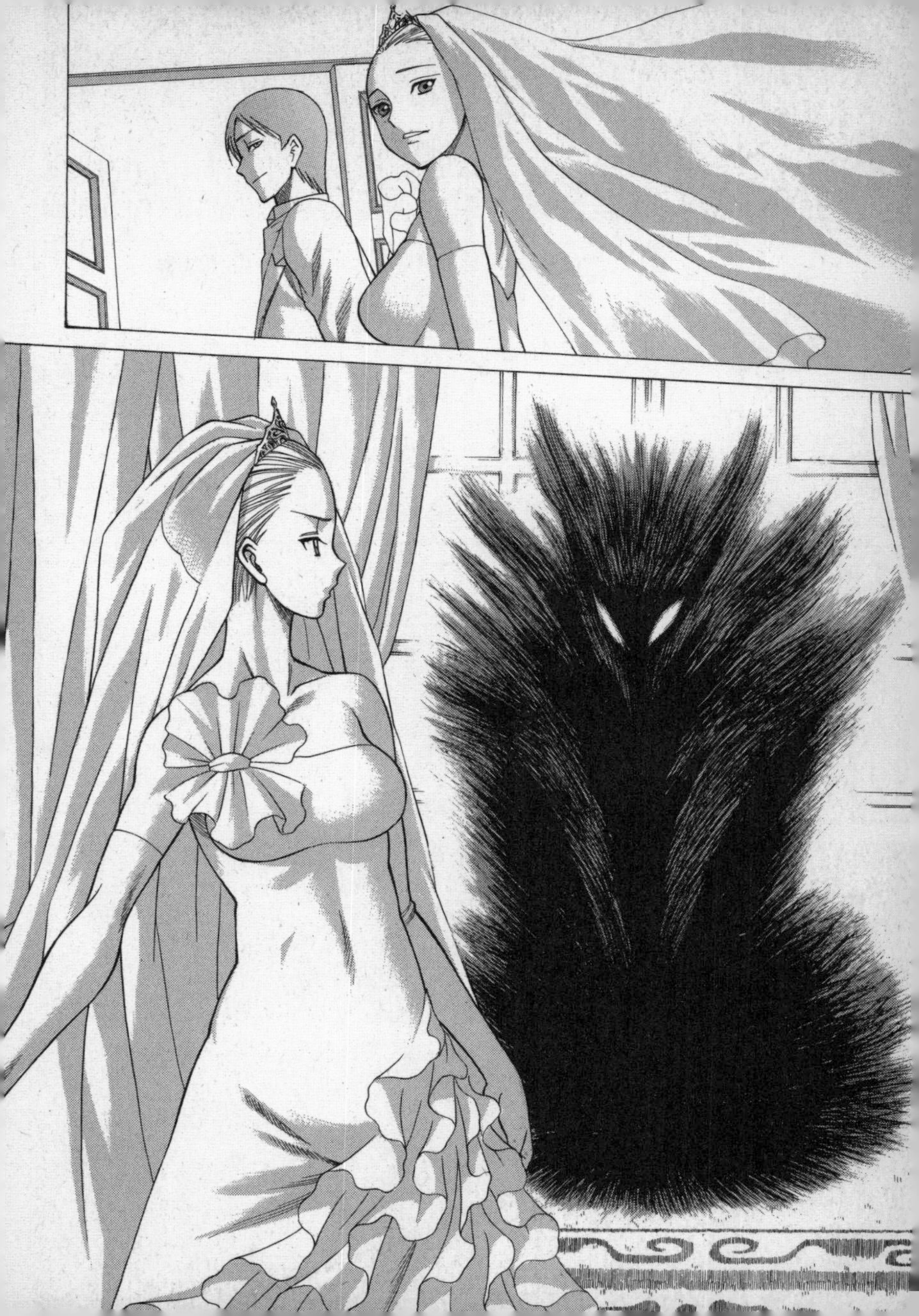

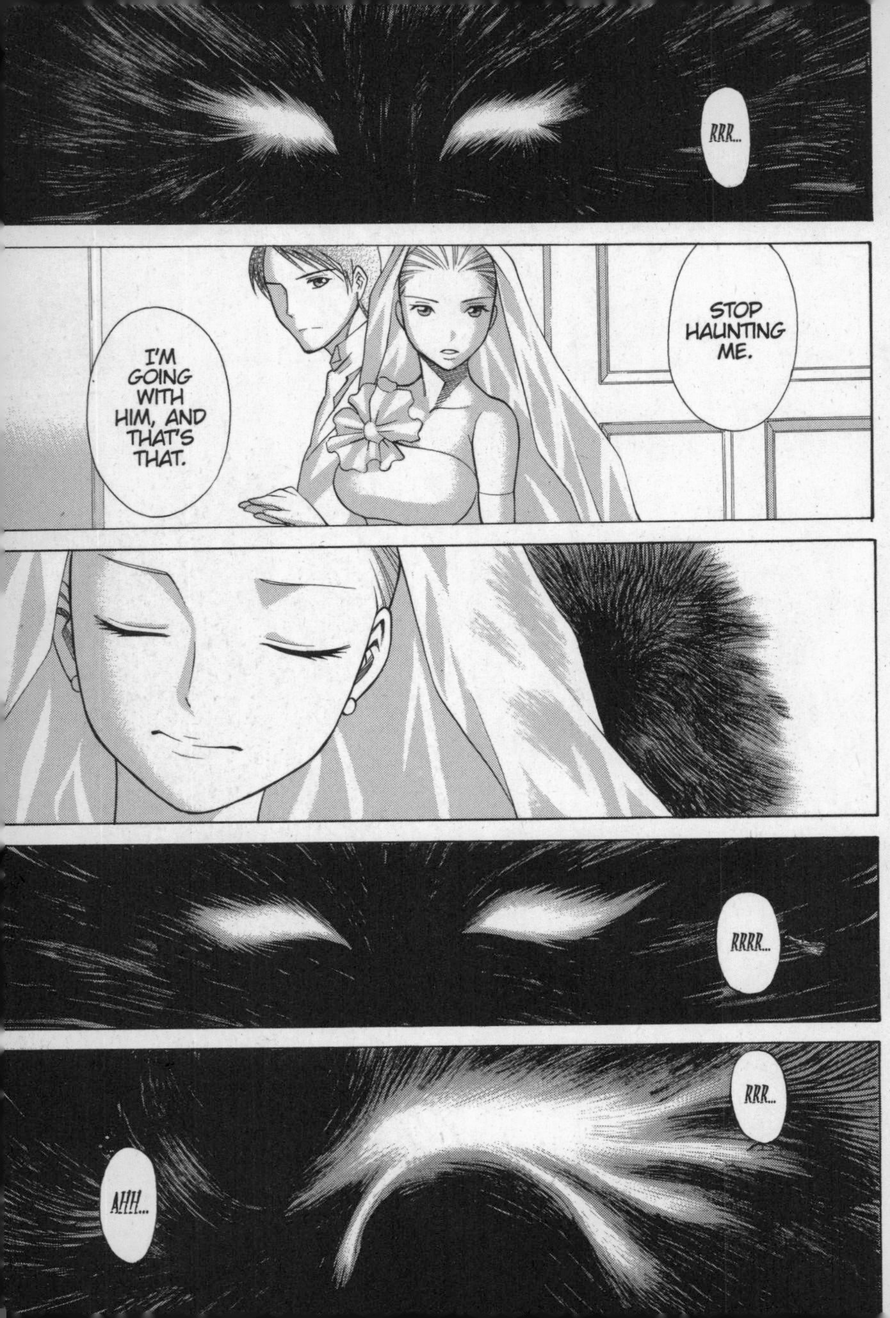
RRR...
STOP HAUNTING ME.
I'M GOING WITH HIM, AND THAT'S THAT.
RRRR...
RRR...
AHH...

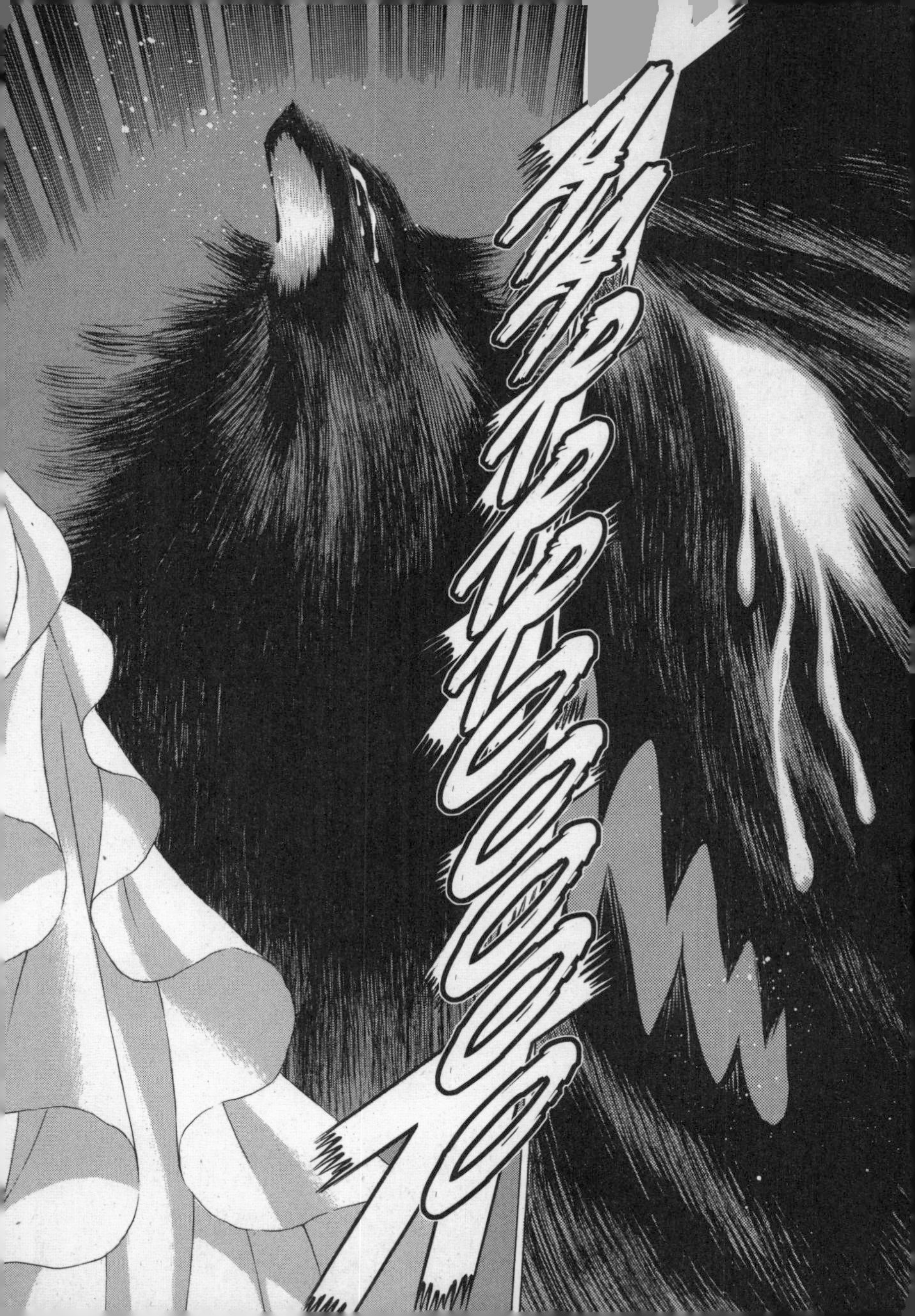

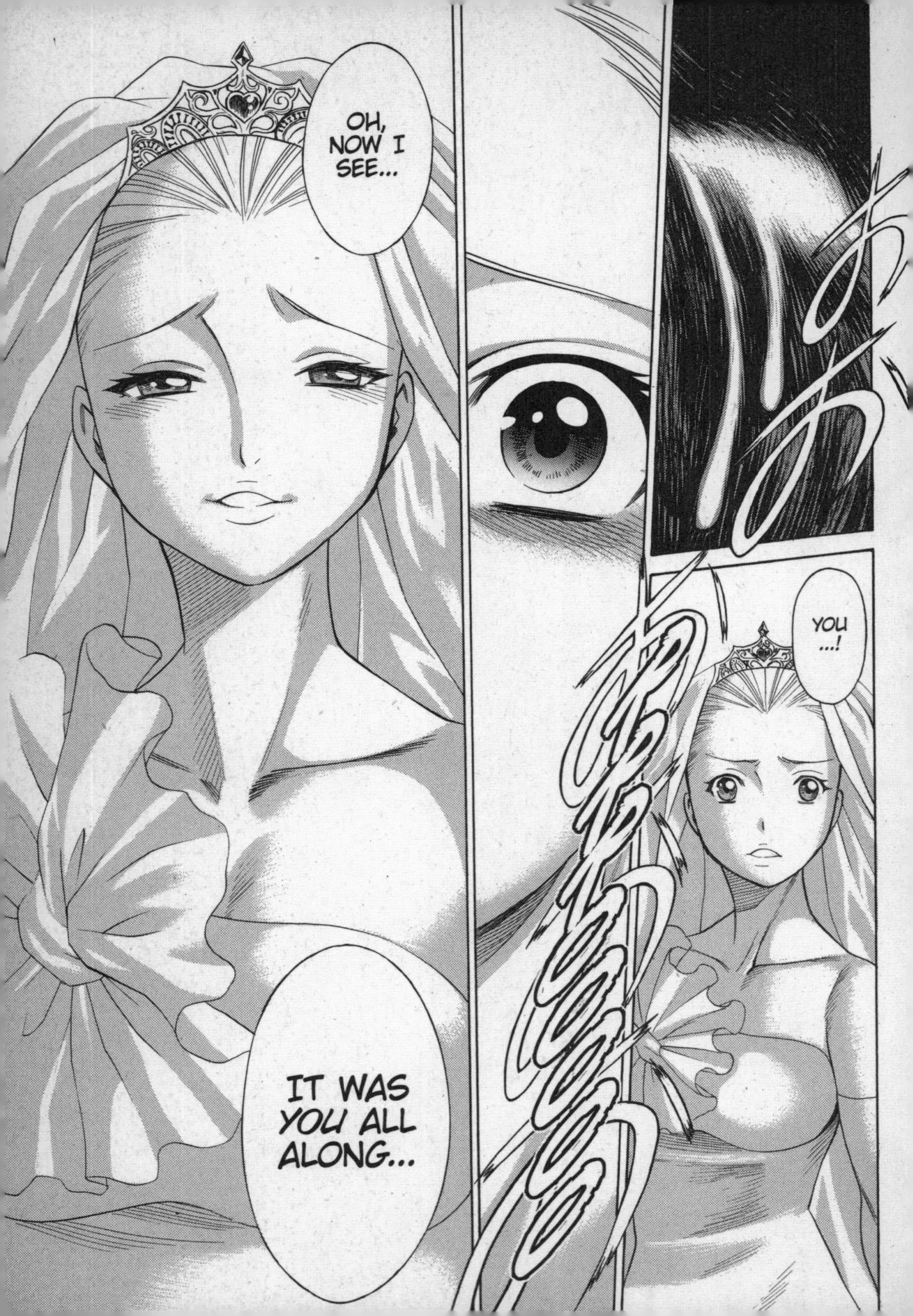
YOU ...!
OH, NOW I SEE...
IT WAS YOU ALL ALONG...

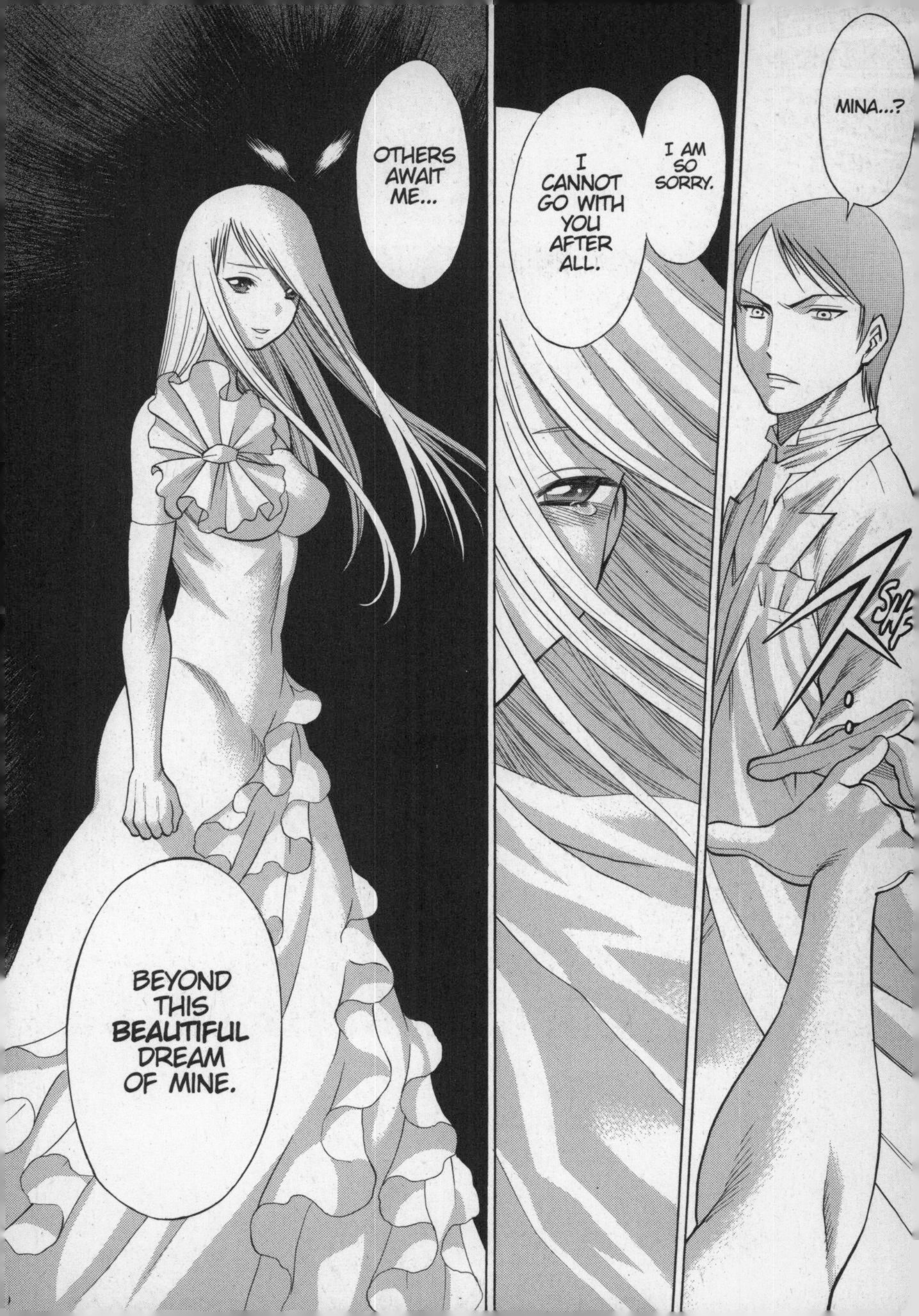
MINA...?
I AM SO SORRY.
I CANNOT GO WITH YOU AFTER ALL.
OTHERS AWAIT ME...
BEYOND THIS BEAUTIFUL DREAM OF MINE.

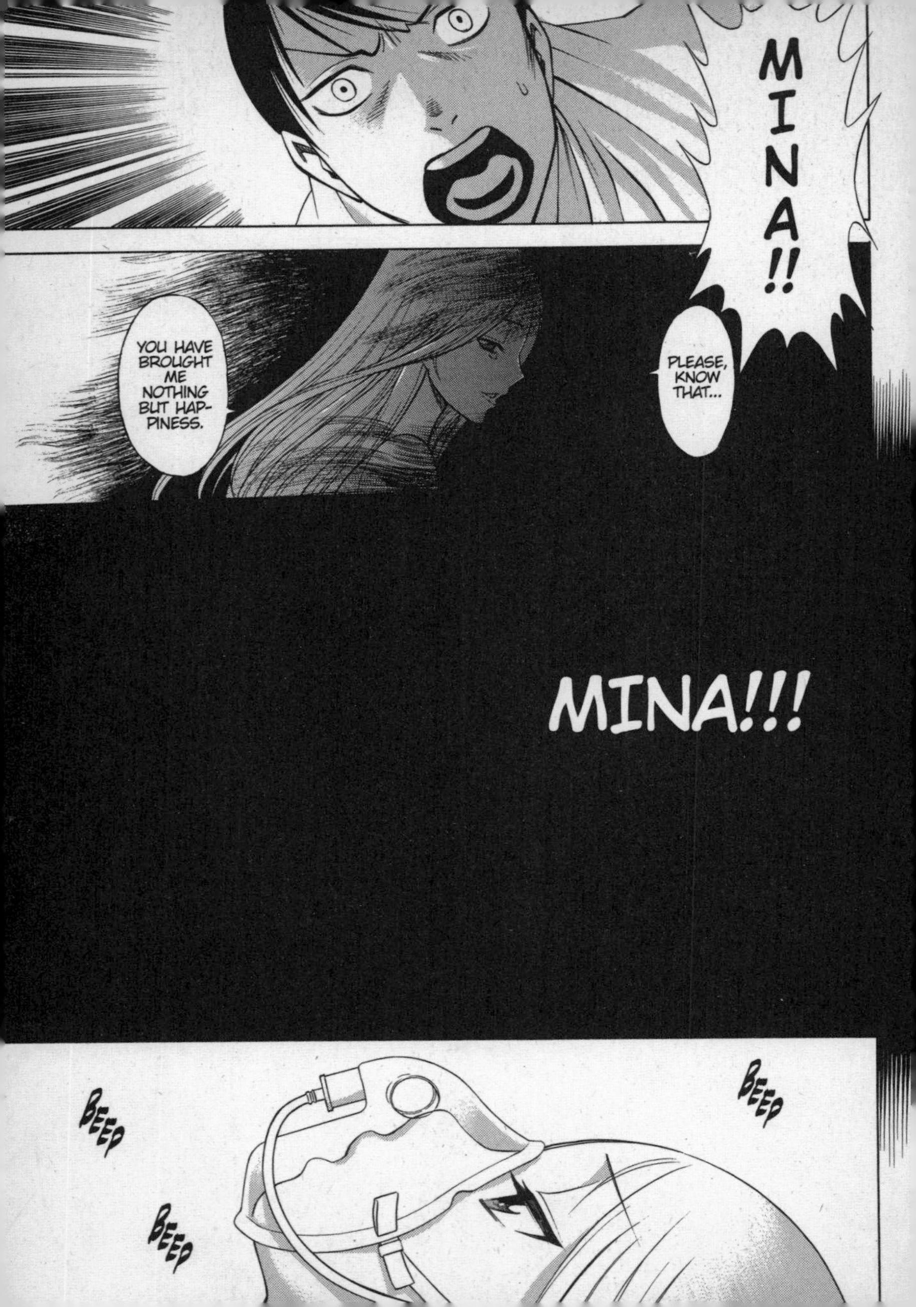
MINA!!
PLEASE, KNOW THAT...
YOU HAVE BROUGHT ME NOTHING BUT HAP-PINESS.
MINA!!!
BEEP
BEEP
BEEP

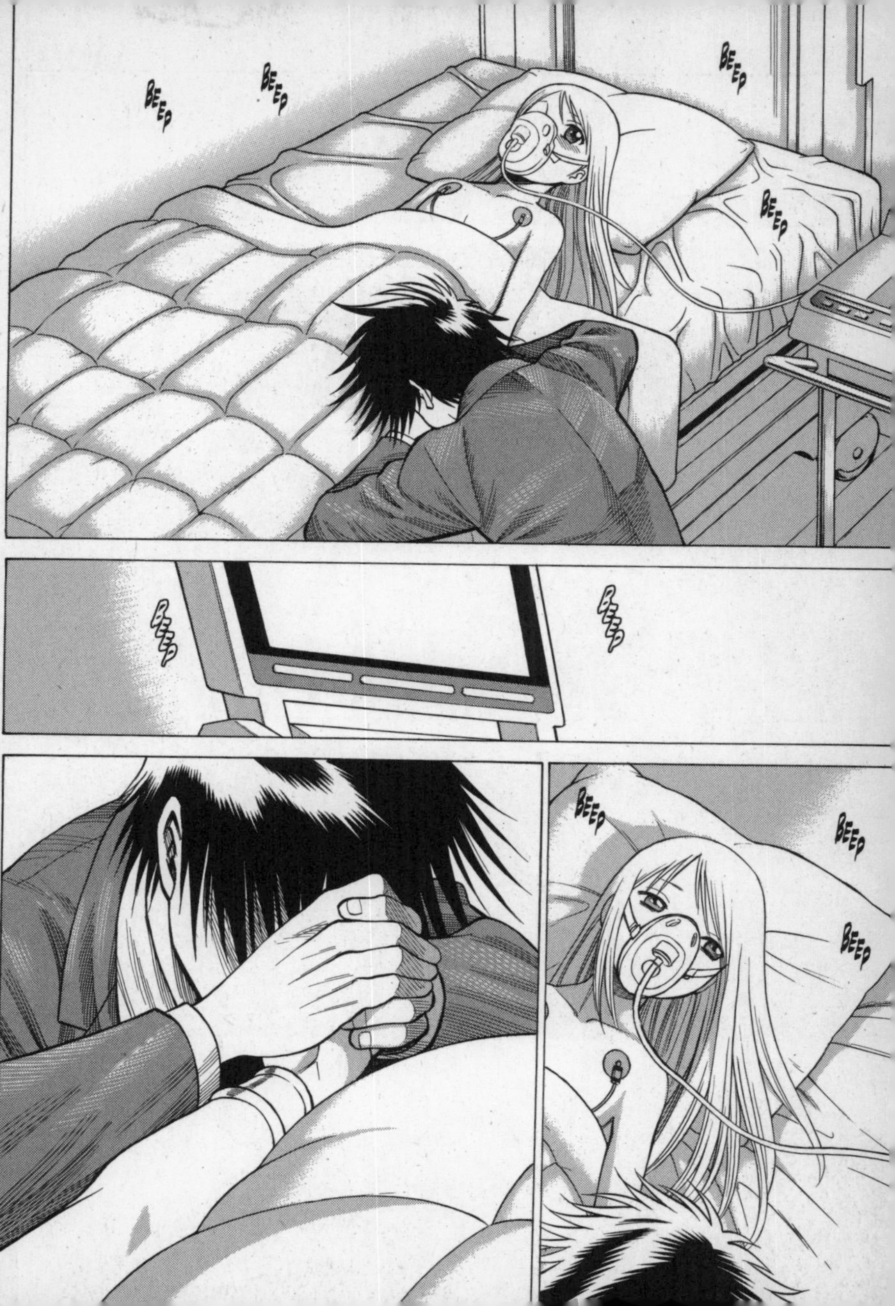
BEEP
BEEP
BEEP
BEEP
BEEP
BEEP
BEEP
BEEP
BEEP

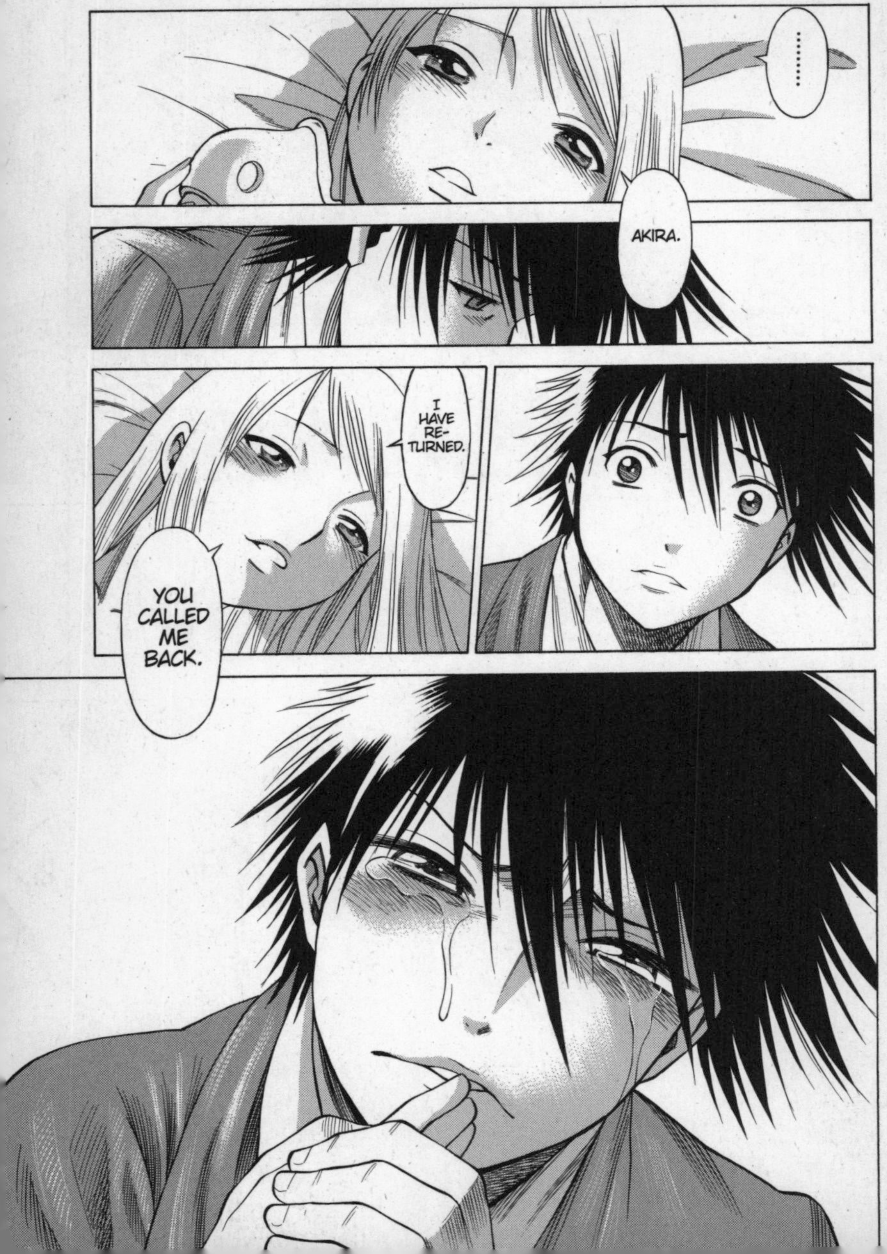
......
AKIRA.
I HAVE RE- TURNED.
YOU CALLED ME BACK.

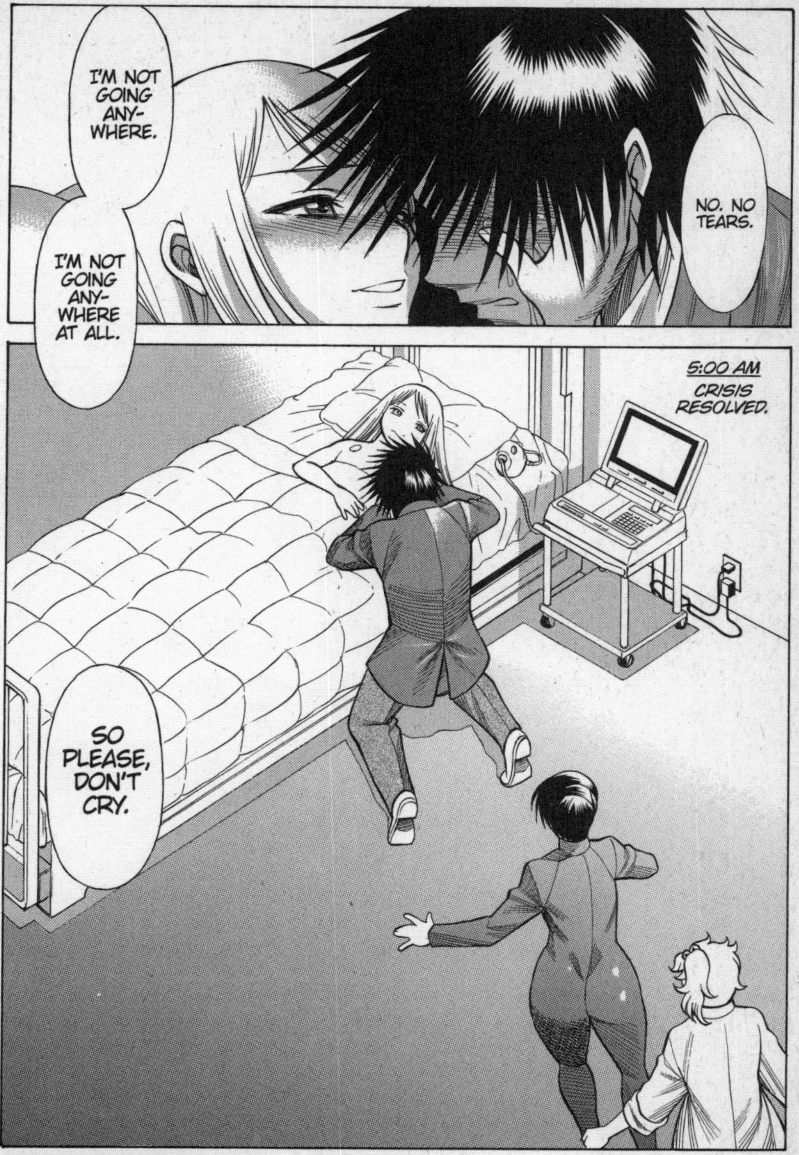
NO. NO TEARS.
I'M NOT GOING ANY-WHERE.
I'M NOT GOING ANY-WHERE AT ALL.
5:00 AM
CRISIS RESOLVED.
SO PLEASE, DON'T CRY.

TO BE CONTINUED

STAFF

JUGGERNAUT

TAKASHI KOMATSU

KENICHI NAKAMONO

RYUSUKE TAKIGUCHI

SPECIAL THANKS

HIROSHI YAGUMO

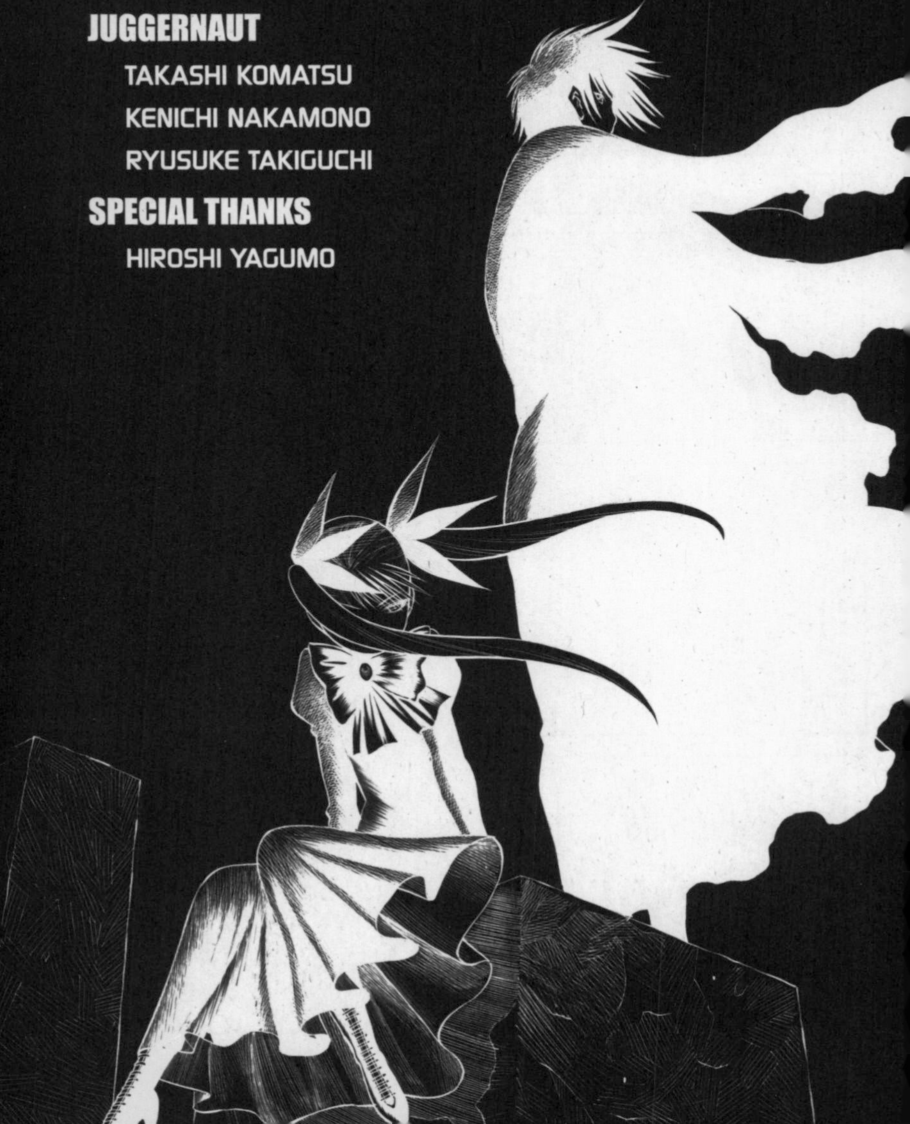

DANCE with the VAMPIRE MAID

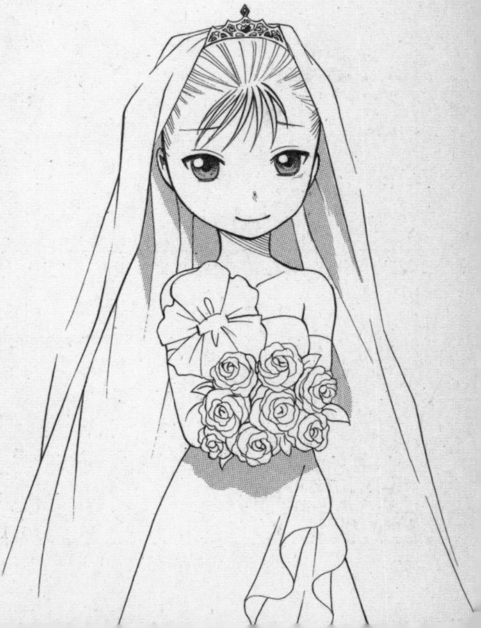

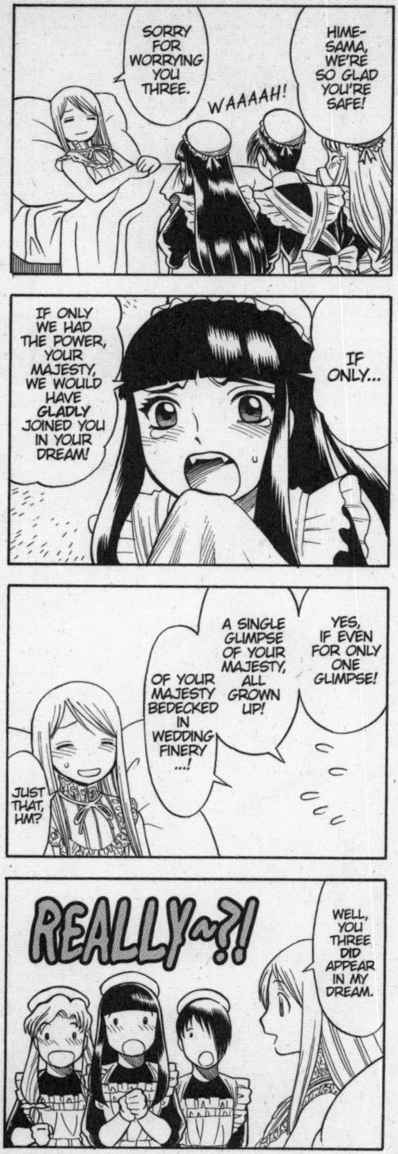
HIME-SAMA, WE'RE SO GLAD YOU'RE SAFE!
WAAAAH!
SORRY FOR WORRYING YOU THREE.
IF ONLY...
IF ONLY WE HAD THE POWER, YOUR MAJESTY, WE WOULD HAVE GLADLY JOINED YOU IN YOUR DREAM!
YES, IF EVEN FOR ONLY ONE GLIMPSE!
A SINGLE GLIMPSE OF YOUR MAJESTY, ALL GROWN UP!
OF YOUR MAJESTY BEDECKED IN WEDDING FINERY ...!
JUST THAT, HM?
WELL, YOU THREE DID APPEAR IN MY DREAM.
REALLY~?!

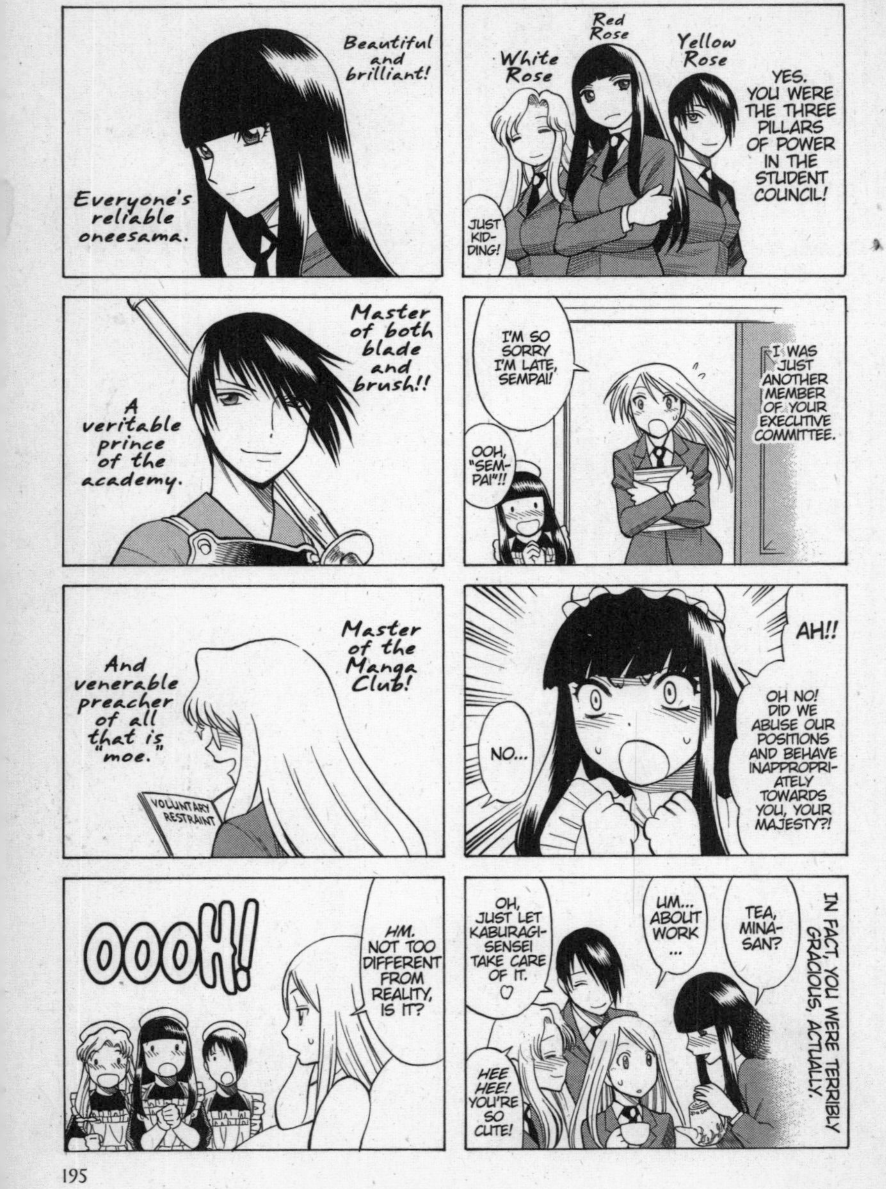
Red Rose
Yellow Rose
White Rose
YES. YOU WERE THE THREE PILLARS OF POWER IN THE STUDENT COUNCIL!
JUST KID-DING!
I WAS JUST ANOTHER MEMBER OF YOUR EXECUTIVE COMMITTEE.
I'M SO SORRY I'M LATE, SEMPAI!
OOH, "SEM-PAI"!!
AH!!
OH NO! DID WE ABUSE OUR POSITIONS AND BEHAVE INAPPROPRI-ATELY TOWARDS YOU, YOUR MAJESTY?!
NO...
IN FACT, YOU WERE TERRIBLY GRACIOUS, ACTUALLY.
TEA, MINA-SAN?
UM... ABOUT WORK ...
OH, JUST LET KABURAGI-SENSEI TAKE CARE OF IT. ♡
HEE HEE! YOU'RE SO CUTE!
Beautiful and brilliant!
Everyone's reliable oneesama.
Master of both blade and brush!!
A veritable prince of the academy.
Master of the Manga Club!
And venerable preacher of all that is "moe."
VOLUNTARY RESTRAINT
HM. NOT TOO DIFFERENT FROM REALITY, IS IT?
OOOH!

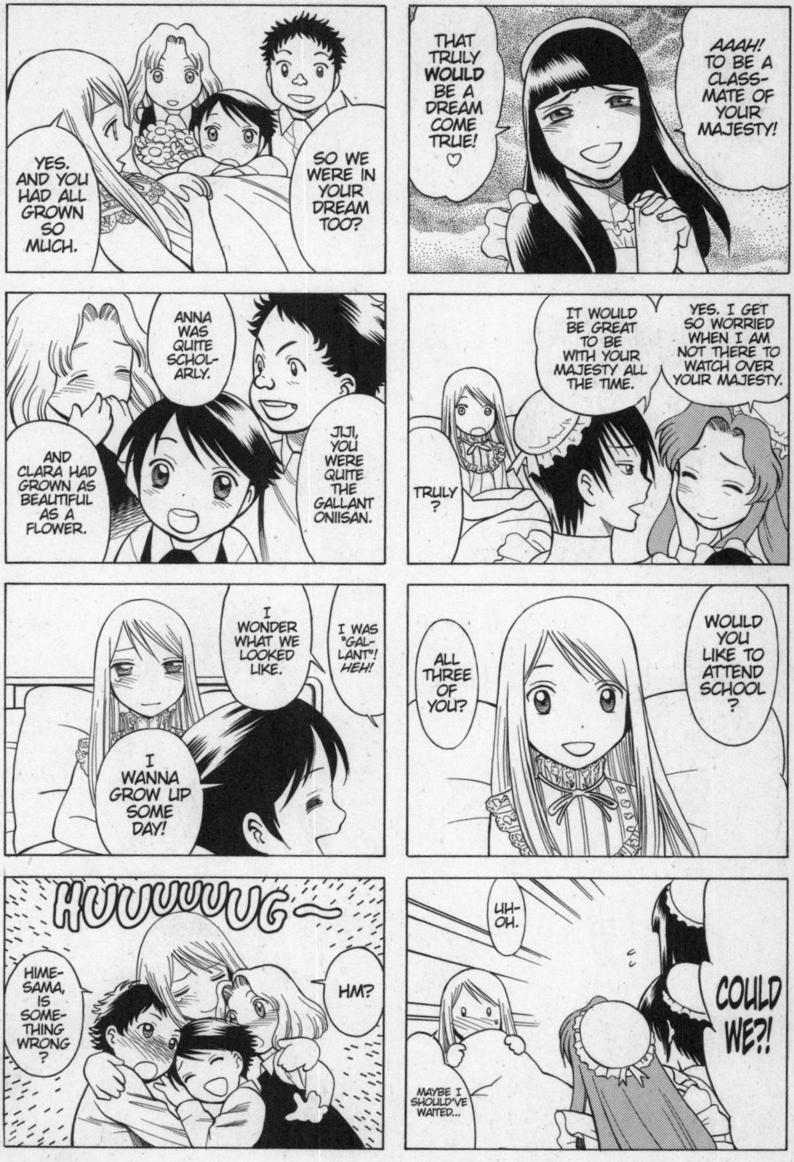
AAAH! TO BE A CLASSMATE OF YOUR MAJESTY!
THAT TRULY WOULD BE A DREAM COME TRUE! ♡
SO WE WERE IN YOUR DREAM TOO?
YES. AND YOU HAD ALL GROWN SO MUCH.
YES. I GET SO WORRIED WHEN I AM NOT THERE TO WATCH OVER YOUR MAJESTY.
IT WOULD BE GREAT TO BE WITH YOUR MAJESTY ALL THE TIME.
TRULY?
ANNA WAS QUITE SCHOLARLY.
JIJI, YOU WERE QUITE THE GALLANT ONIISAN.
AND CLARA HAD GROWN AS BEAUTIFUL AS A FLOWER.
WOULD YOU LIKE TO ATTEND SCHOOL?
ALL THREE OF YOU?
I WAS "GALLANT"! HEH!
I WONDER WHAT WE LOOKED LIKE.
I WANNA GROW UP SOME DAY!
COULD WE?!
UH-OH.
MAYBE I SHOULD'VE WAITED...
HUUUUUUG~
HM?
HIME-SAMA, IS SOMETHING WRONG?